Lucifer

✠

The Wolf Beneath the Tree

Mike Carey
Writer

Peter Gross, Ryan Kelly
P. Craig Russell, Ted Naifeh
Artists

Daniel Vozzo, Lovern Kindzierski
Colorists

Jared K. Fletcher, Ken Lopez
Letterers

Christopher Moeller
Michael Wm. Kaluta
Tara McPherson
Original Series Covers

Based on characters created by
Neil Gaiman, Sam Kieth and Mike Dringenberg

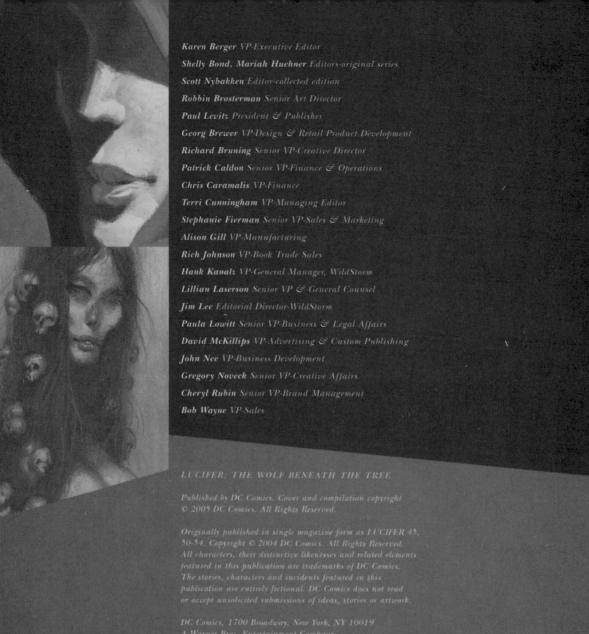

Karen Berger *VP-Executive Editor*

Shelly Bond, Mariah Huehner *Editors-original series*

Scott Nybakken *Editor-collected edition*

Robbin Brosterman *Senior Art Director*

Paul Levitz *President & Publisher*

Georg Brewer *VP-Design & Retail Product Development*

Richard Bruning *Senior VP-Creative Director*

Patrick Caldon *Senior VP-Finance & Operations*

Chris Caramalis *VP-Finance*

Terri Cunningham *VP-Managing Editor*

Stephanie Fierman *Senior VP-Sales & Marketing*

Alison Gill *VP-Manufacturing*

Rich Johnson *VP-Book Trade Sales*

Hank Kanalz *VP-General Manager, WildStorm*

Lillian Laserson *Senior VP & General Counsel*

Jim Lee *Editorial Director-WildStorm*

Paula Lowitt *Senior VP-Business & Legal Affairs*

David McKillips *VP-Advertising & Custom Publishing*

John Nee *VP-Business Development*

Gregory Noveck *Senior VP-Creative Affairs*

Cheryl Rubin *Senior VP-Brand Management*

Bob Wayne *VP-Sales*

LUCIFER: THE WOLF BENEATH THE TREE

*Published by DC Comics. Cover and compilation copyright
© 2005 DC Comics. All Rights Reserved.*

*Originally published in single magazine form as LUCIFER 45,
50-54. Copyright © 2004 DC Comics. All Rights Reserved.
All characters, their distinctive likenesses and related elements
featured in this publication are trademarks of DC Comics.
The stories, characters and incidents featured in this
publication are entirely fictional. DC Comics does not read
or accept unsolicited submissions of ideas, stories or artwork.*

*DC Comics, 1700 Broadway, New York, NY 10019
A Warner Bros. Entertainment Company
Printed in Canada. Second Printing.
ISBN: 1-4012-0502-X
ISBN 13: 978-1-4012-0502-7
Cover illustrations by Christopher Moeller.
Logo design by Alex Jay.*

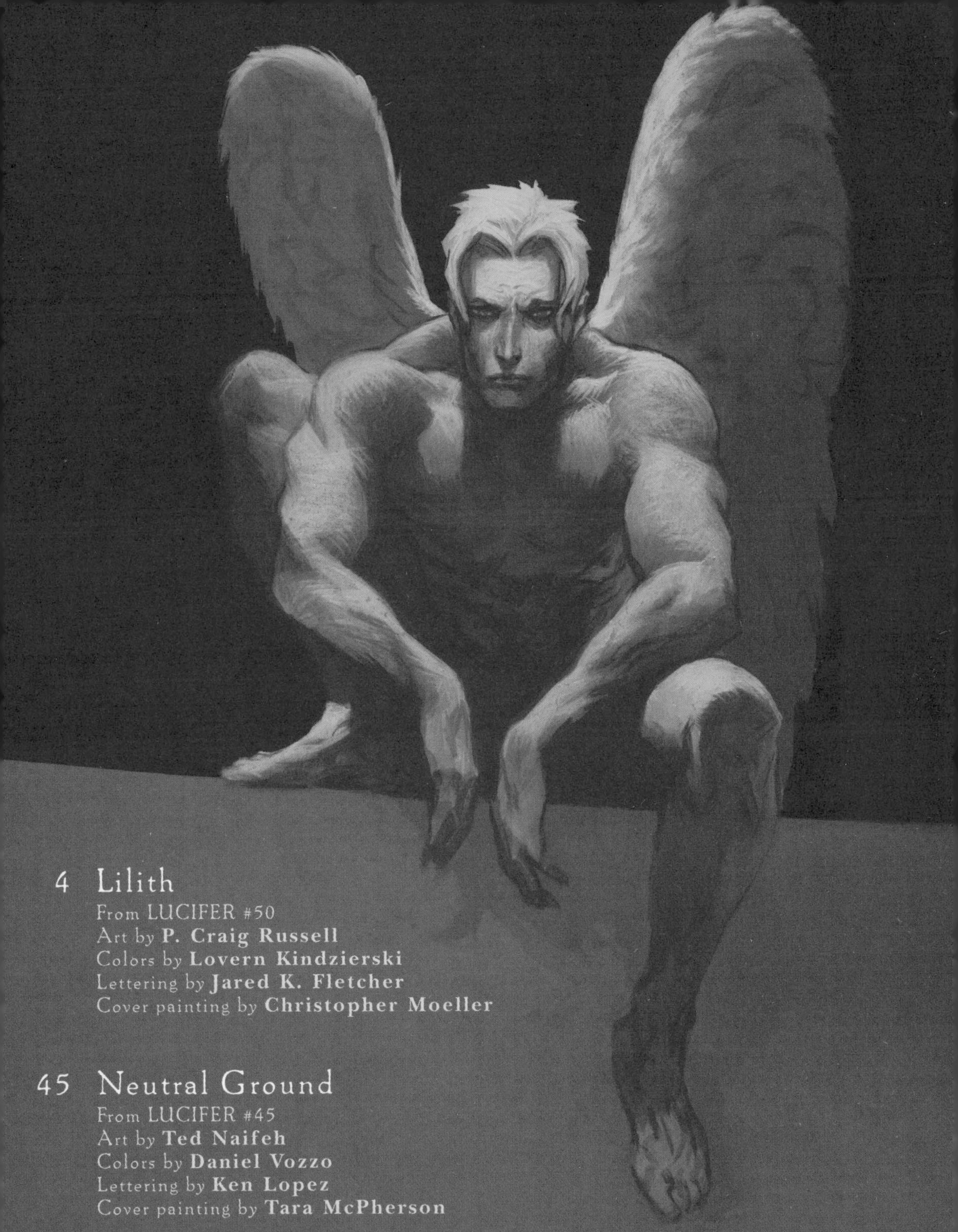

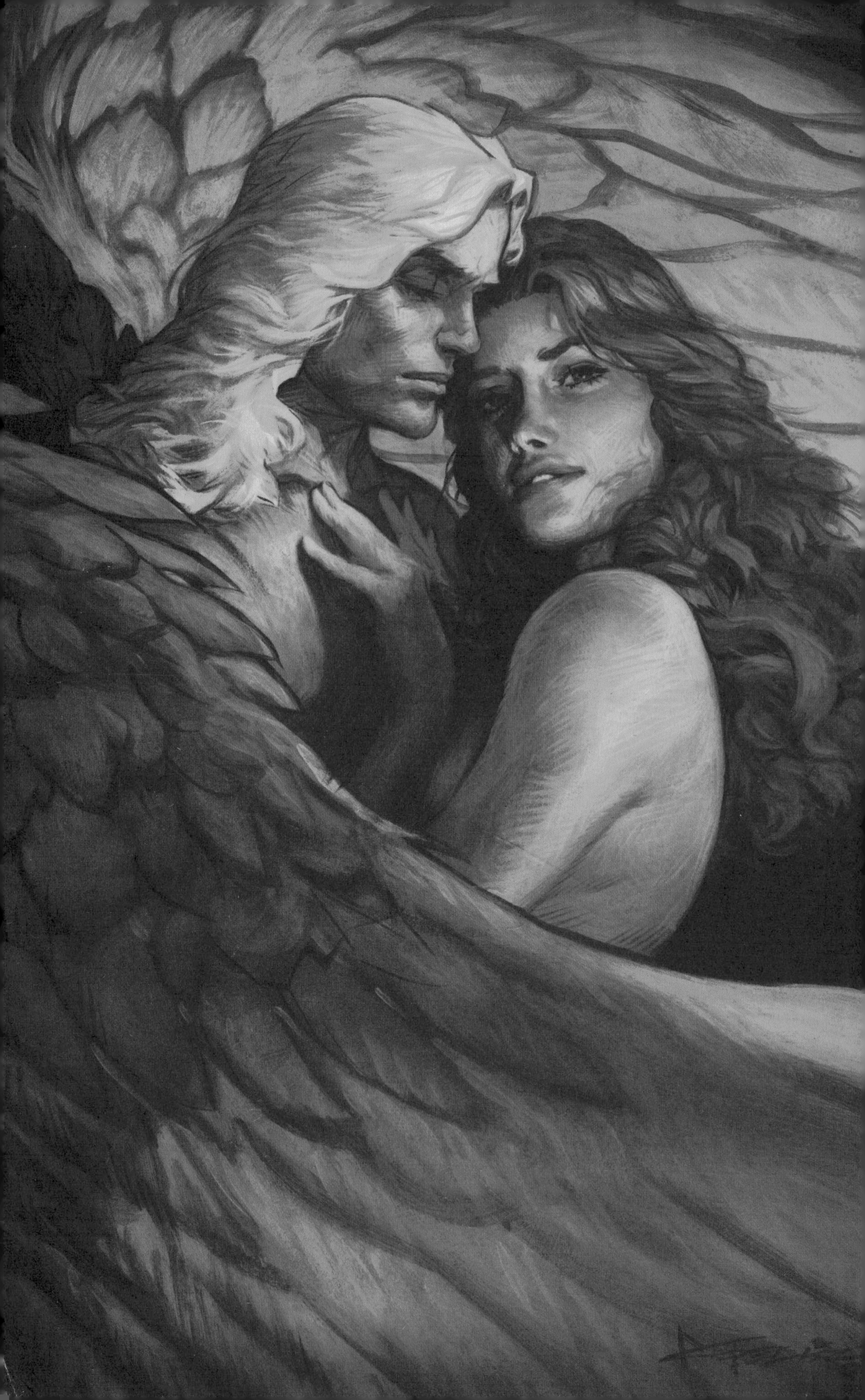

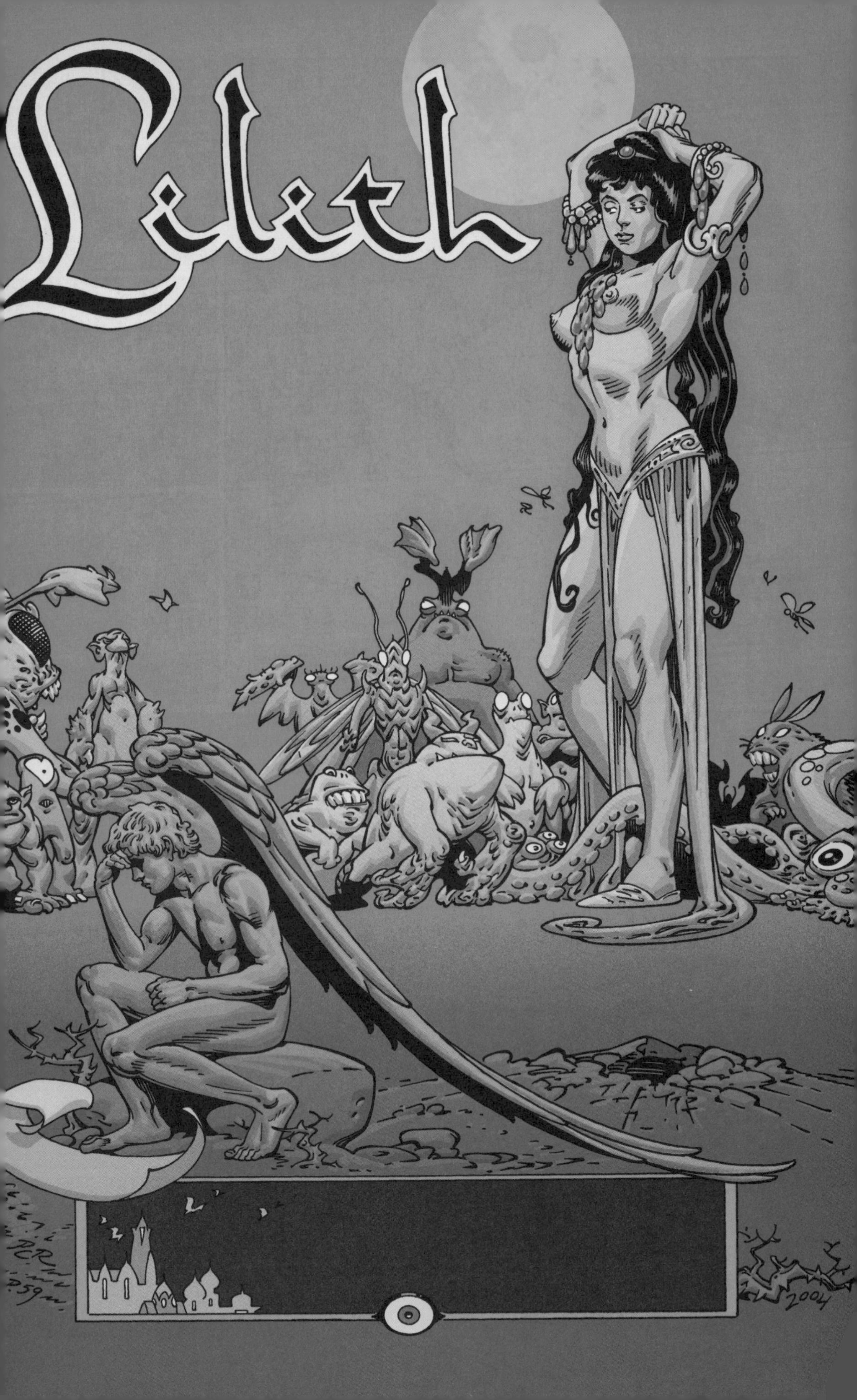
Lilith
2004

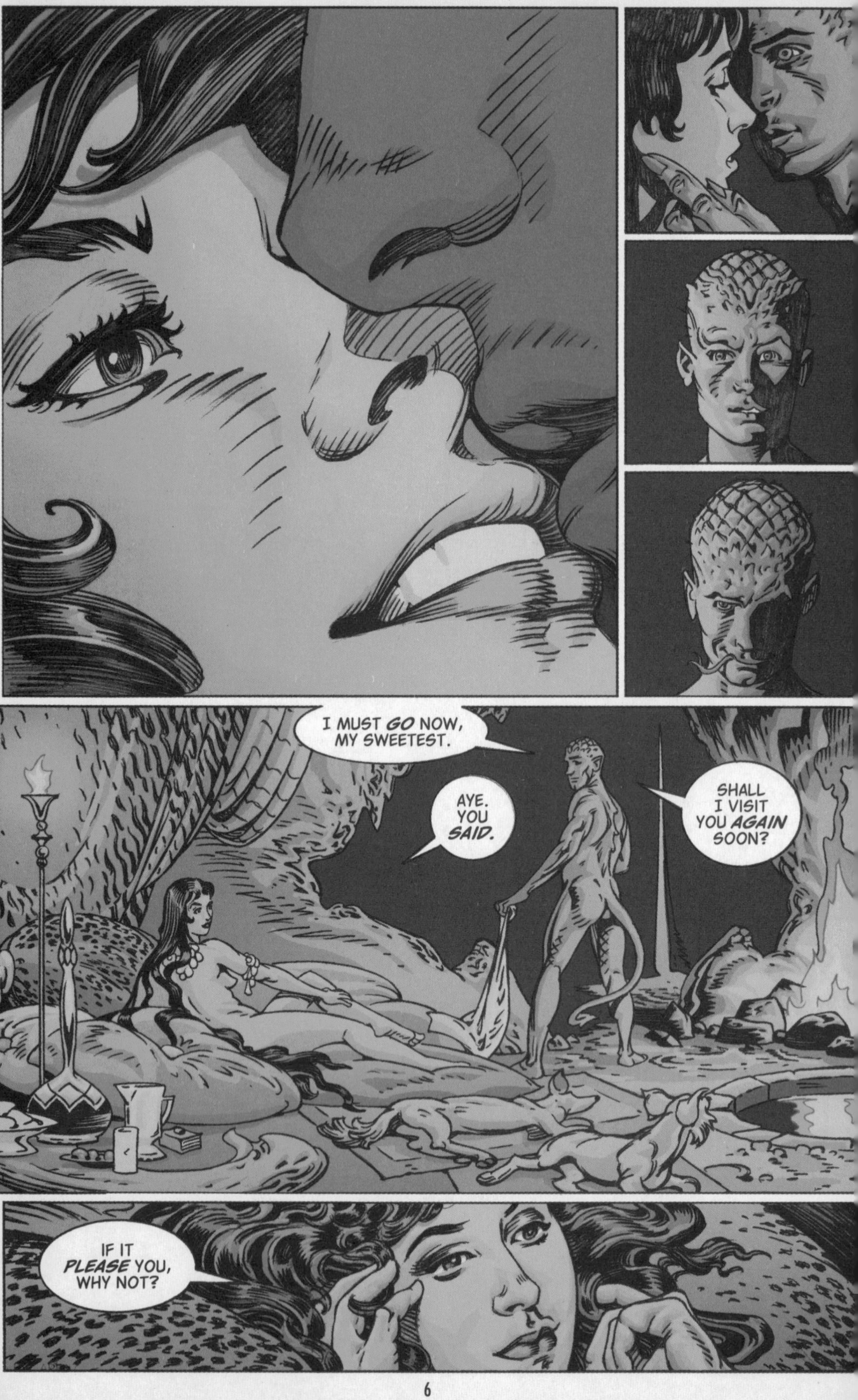
I MUST GO NOW, MY SWEETEST.
AYE. YOU SAID.
SHALL I VISIT YOU AGAIN SOON?
IF IT PLEASE YOU, WHY NOT?

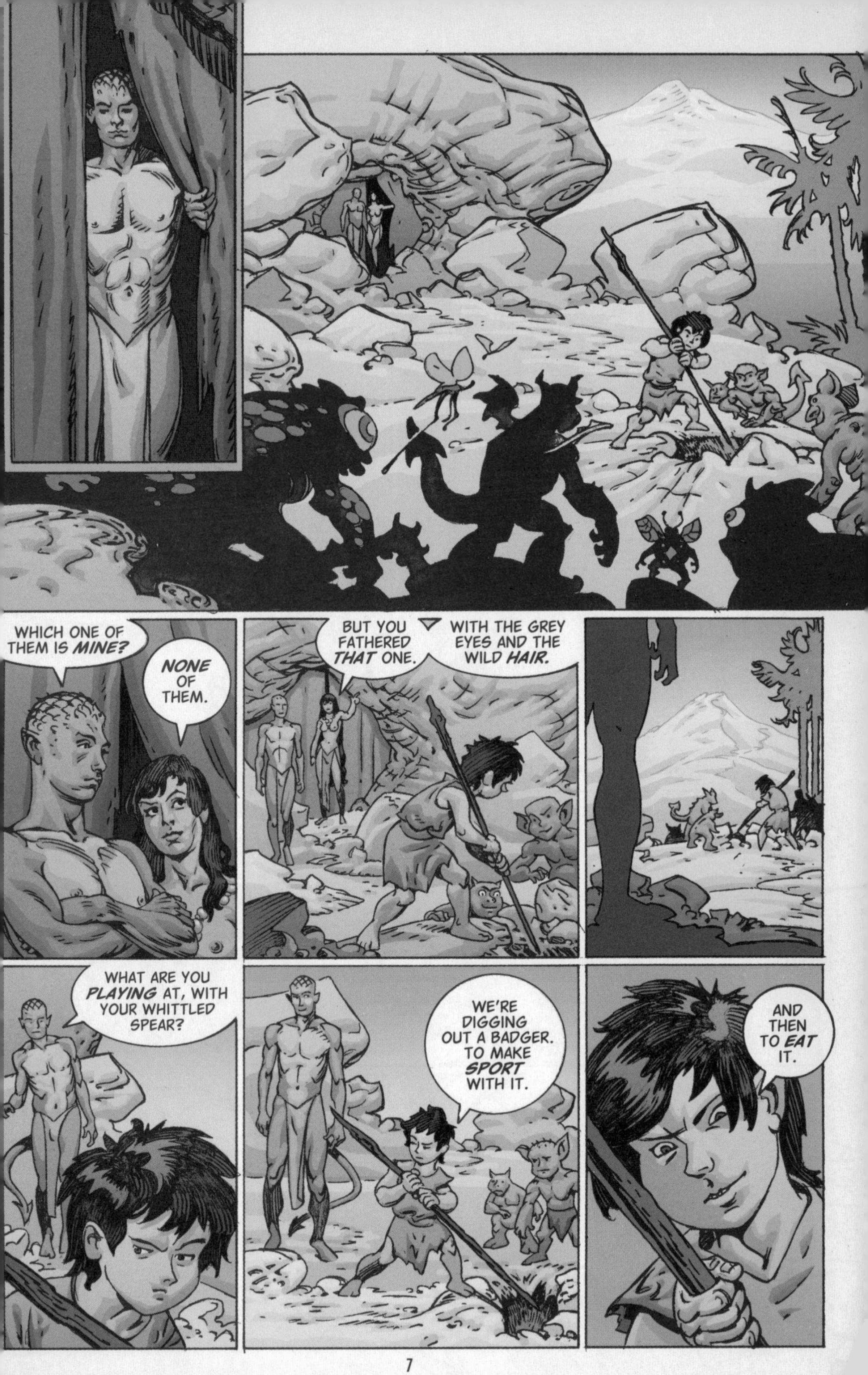
WHICH ONE OF THEM IS *MINE?*
NONE OF THEM.
BUT YOU FATHERED *THAT* ONE.
WITH THE GREY EYES AND THE WILD *HAIR.*
WHAT ARE YOU *PLAYING* AT, WITH YOUR WHITTLED SPEAR?
WE'RE DIGGING OUT A BADGER. TO MAKE *SPORT* WITH IT.
AND THEN TO *EAT* IT.

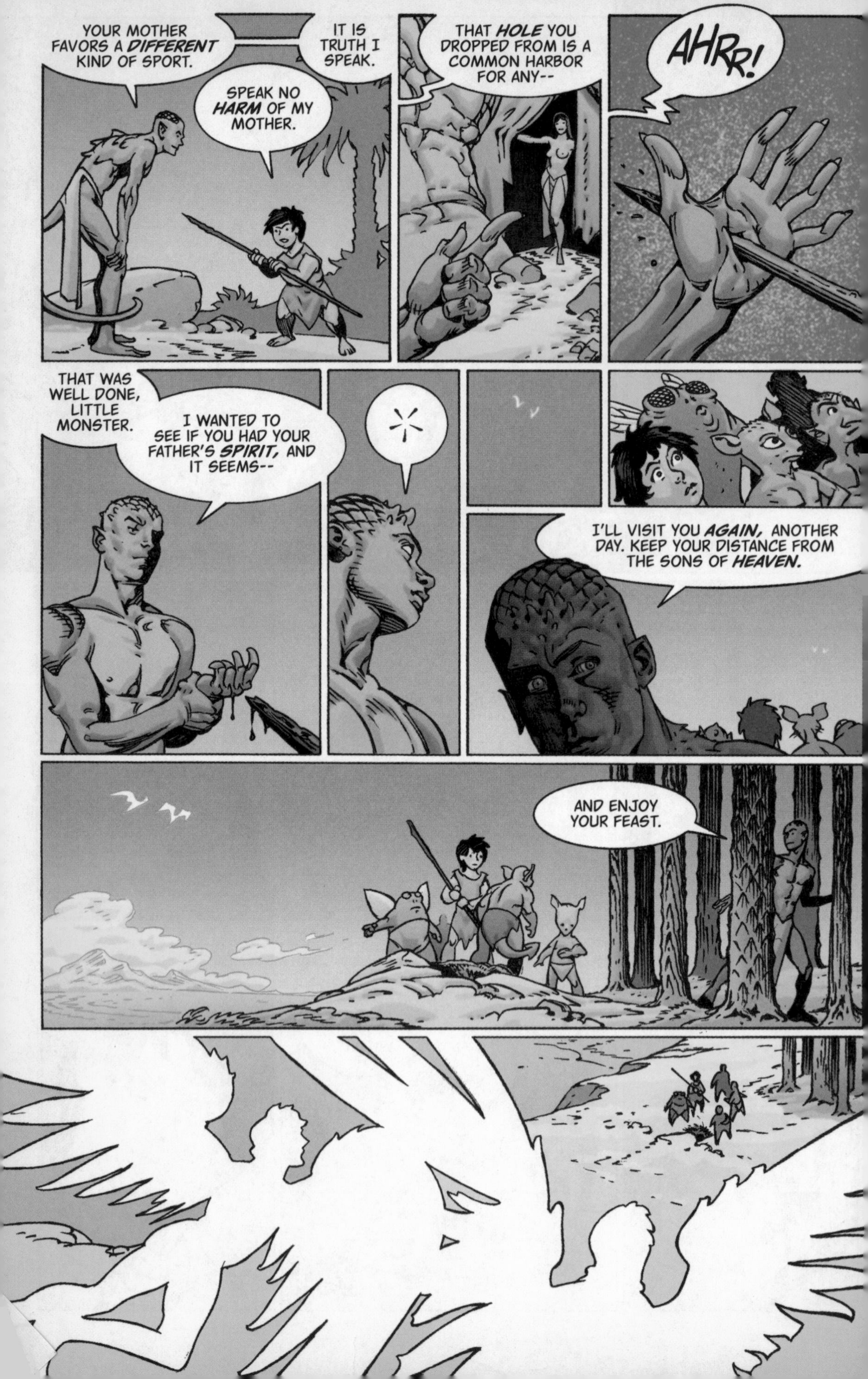

YOUR MOTHER FAVORS A DIFFERENT KIND OF SPORT.
SPEAK NO HARM OF MY MOTHER.
IT IS TRUTH I SPEAK.
THAT HOLE YOU DROPPED FROM IS A COMMON HARBOR FOR ANY--
AHRR!
THAT WAS WELL DONE, LITTLE MONSTER.
I WANTED TO SEE IF YOU HAD YOUR FATHER'S SPIRIT, AND IT SEEMS--
I'LL VISIT YOU AGAIN, ANOTHER DAY. KEEP YOUR DISTANCE FROM THE SONS OF HEAVEN.
AND ENJOY YOUR FEAST.

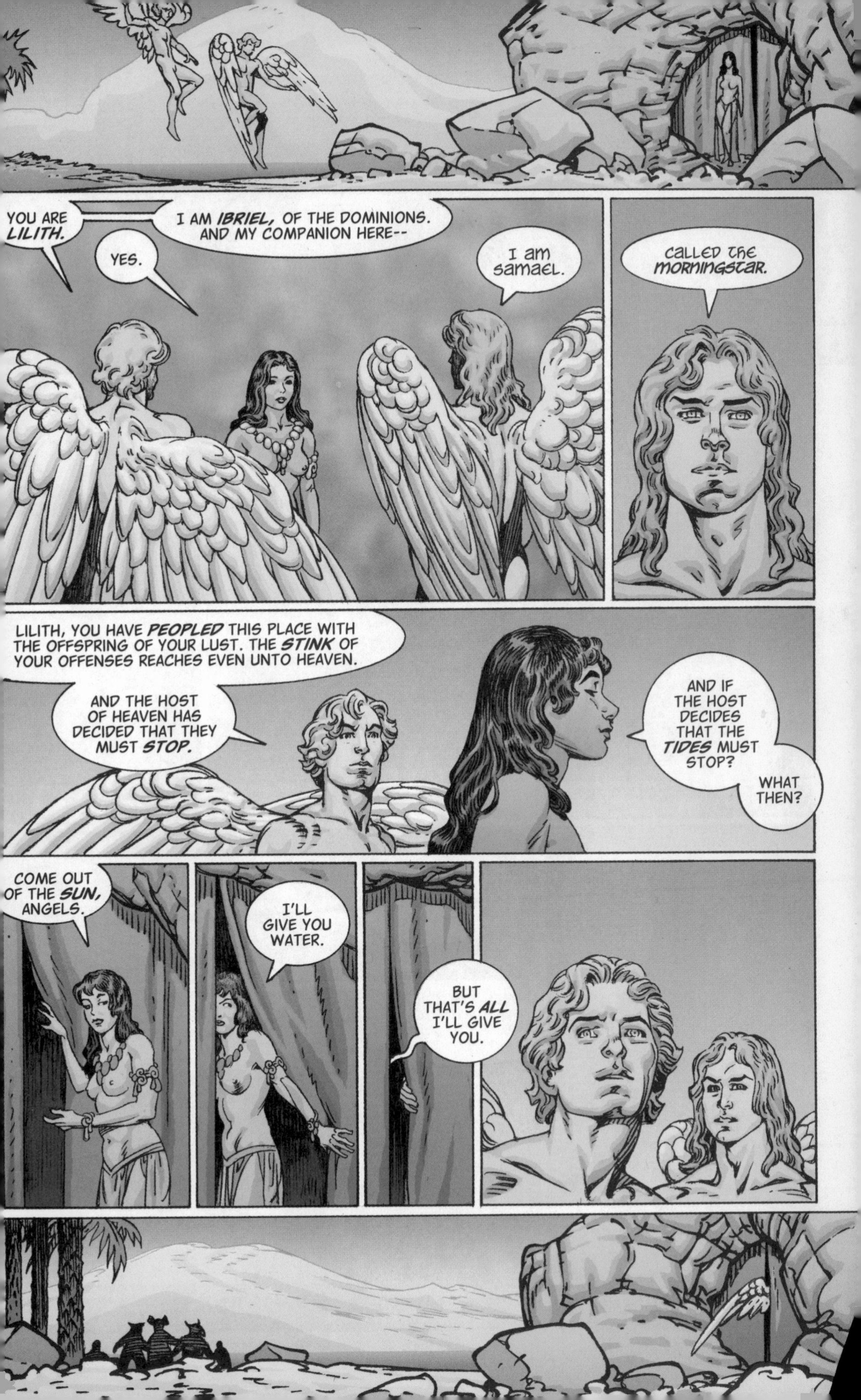

YOU ARE LILITH.
YES.
I AM IBRIEL, OF THE DOMINIONS. AND MY COMPANION HERE--
I am Samael.
Called the Morningstar.
LILITH, YOU HAVE PEOPLED THIS PLACE WITH THE OFFSPRING OF YOUR LUST. THE STINK OF YOUR OFFENSES REACHES EVEN UNTO HEAVEN.
AND THE HOST OF HEAVEN HAS DECIDED THAT THEY MUST STOP.
AND IF THE HOST DECIDES THAT THE TIDES MUST STOP?
WHAT THEN?
COME OUT OF THE SUN, ANGELS.
I'LL GIVE YOU WATER.
BUT THAT'S ALL I'LL GIVE YOU.

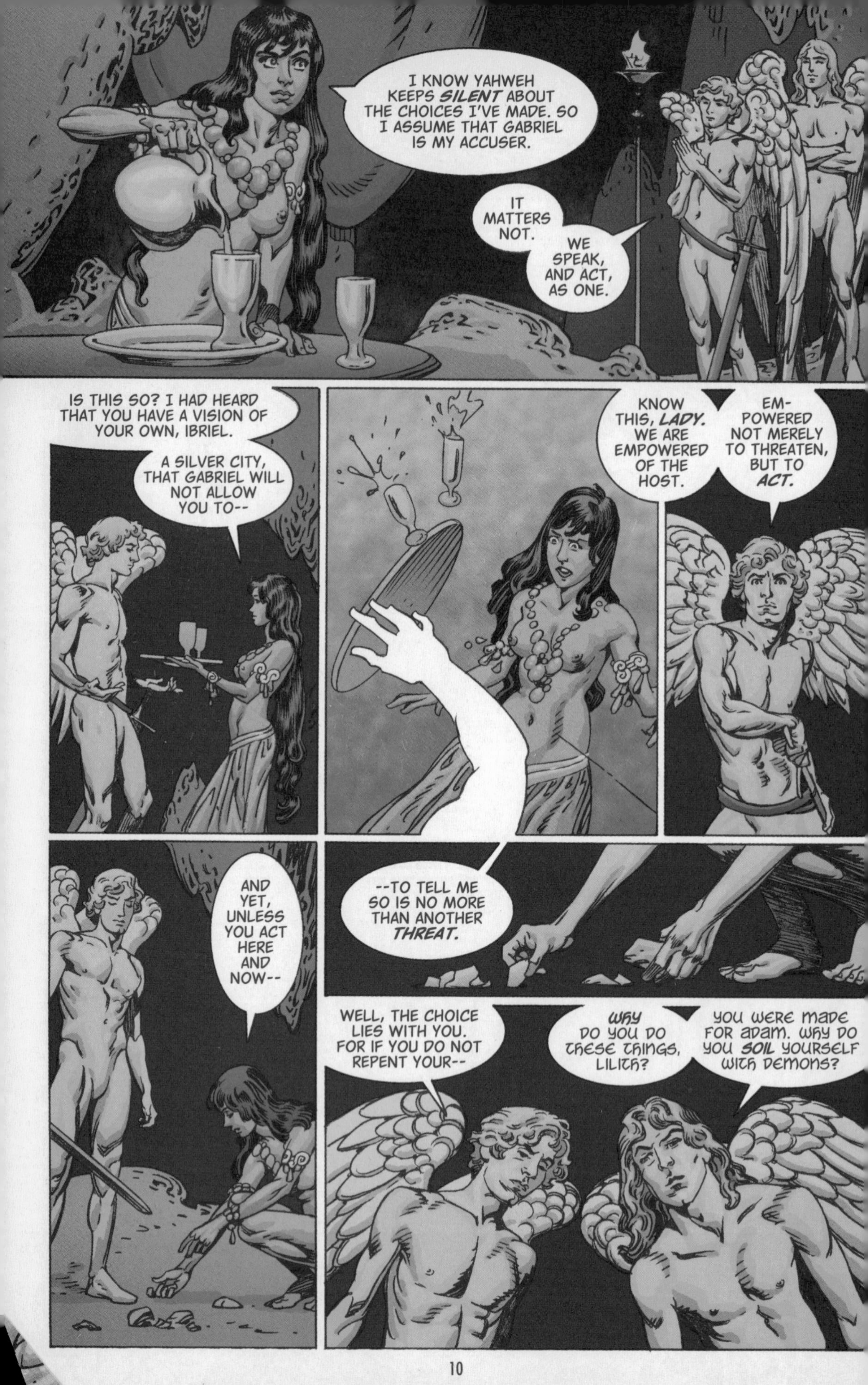
I KNOW YAHWEH KEEPS *SILENT* ABOUT THE CHOICES I'VE MADE. SO I ASSUME THAT GABRIEL IS MY ACCUSER.
IT MATTERS NOT.
WE SPEAK, AND ACT, AS ONE.
IS THIS SO? I HAD HEARD THAT YOU HAVE A VISION OF YOUR OWN, IBRIEL.
A SILVER CITY, THAT GABRIEL WILL NOT ALLOW YOU TO--
KNOW THIS, *LADY.* WE ARE EMPOWERED OF THE HOST.
EM-POWERED NOT MERELY TO THREATEN, BUT TO *ACT.*
AND YET, UNLESS YOU ACT HERE AND NOW--
--TO TELL ME SO IS NO MORE THAN ANOTHER *THREAT.*
WELL, THE CHOICE LIES WITH YOU. FOR IF YOU DO NOT REPENT YOUR--
WHY DO YOU DO THESE THINGS, LILITH?
YOU WERE MADE FOR ADAM. WHY DO YOU *SOIL* YOURSELF WITH DEMONS?

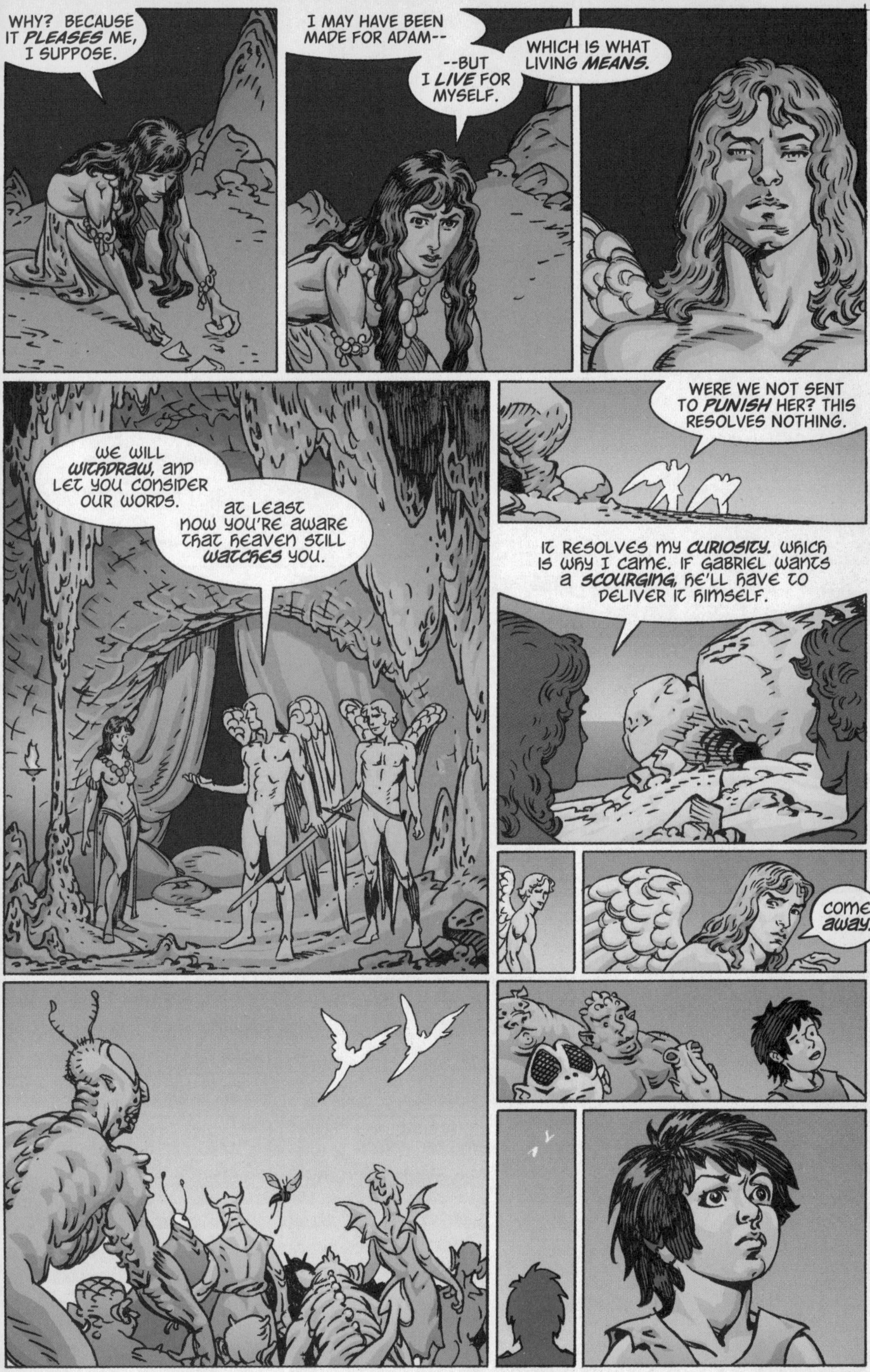

WHY? BECAUSE IT PLEASES ME, I SUPPOSE.
I MAY HAVE BEEN MADE FOR ADAM--
--BUT I LIVE FOR MYSELF.
WHICH IS WHAT LIVING MEANS.
WE WILL WITHDRAW, AND LET YOU CONSIDER OUR WORDS.
AT LEAST NOW YOU'RE AWARE THAT HEAVEN STILL WATCHES YOU.
WERE WE NOT SENT TO PUNISH HER? THIS RESOLVES NOTHING.
IT RESOLVES MY CURIOSITY. WHICH IS WHY I CAME. IF GABRIEL WANTS A SCOURGING, HE'LL HAVE TO DELIVER IT HIMSELF.
COME AWAY.

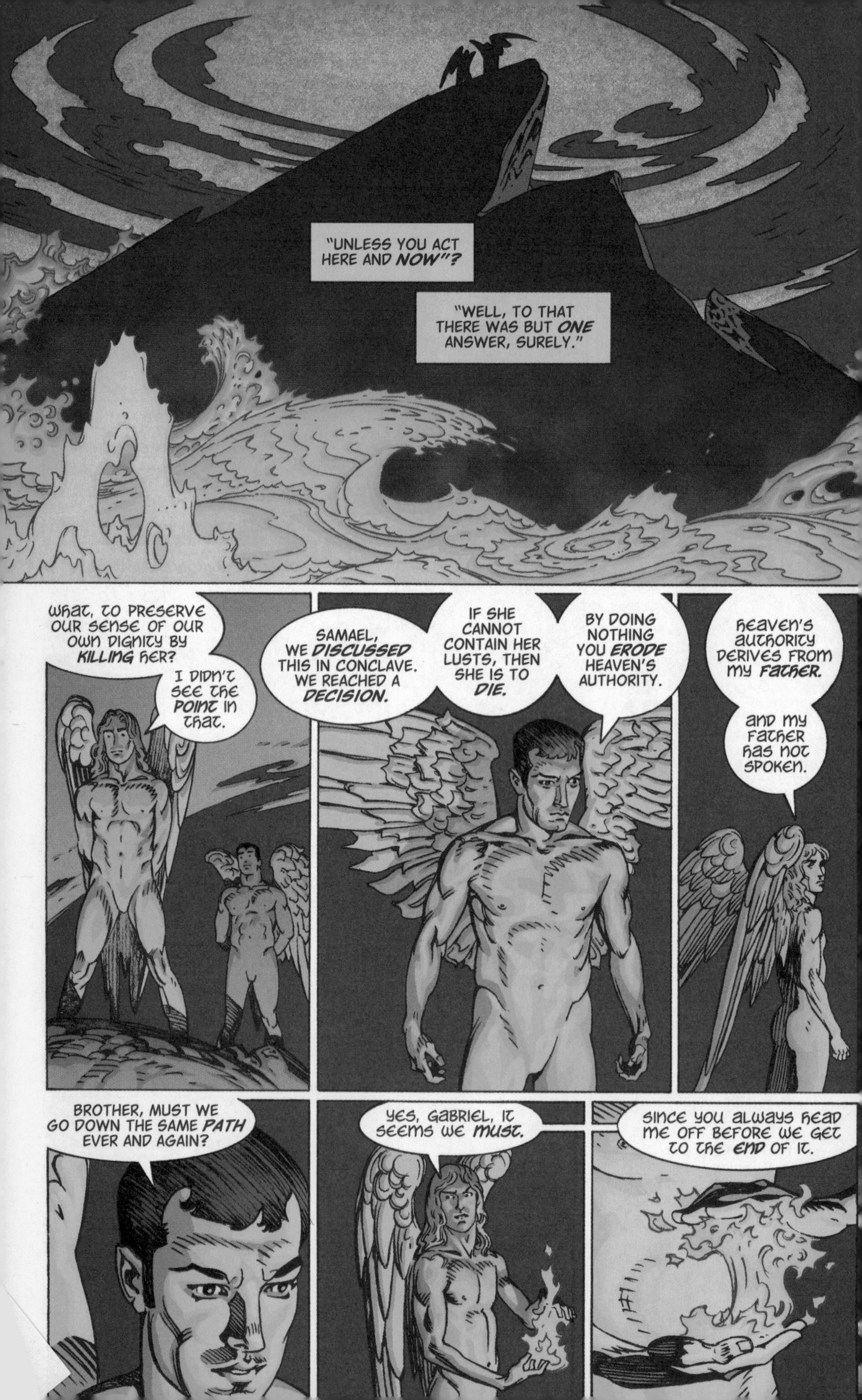
"UNLESS YOU ACT HERE AND NOW"?
"WELL, TO THAT THERE WAS BUT ONE ANSWER, SURELY."
WHAT, TO PRESERVE OUR SENSE OF OUR OWN DIGNITY BY KILLING HER?
I DIDN'T SEE THE POINT IN THAT.
SAMAEL, WE DISCUSSED THIS IN CONCLAVE. WE REACHED A DECISION.
IF SHE CANNOT CONTAIN HER LUSTS, THEN SHE IS TO DIE.
BY DOING NOTHING YOU ERODE HEAVEN'S AUTHORITY.
HEAVEN'S AUTHORITY DERIVES FROM MY FATHER.
AND MY FATHER HAS NOT SPOKEN.
BROTHER, MUST WE GO DOWN THE SAME PATH EVER AND AGAIN?
YES, GABRIEL, IT SEEMS WE MUST.
SINCE YOU ALWAYS HEAD ME OFF BEFORE WE GET TO THE END OF IT.

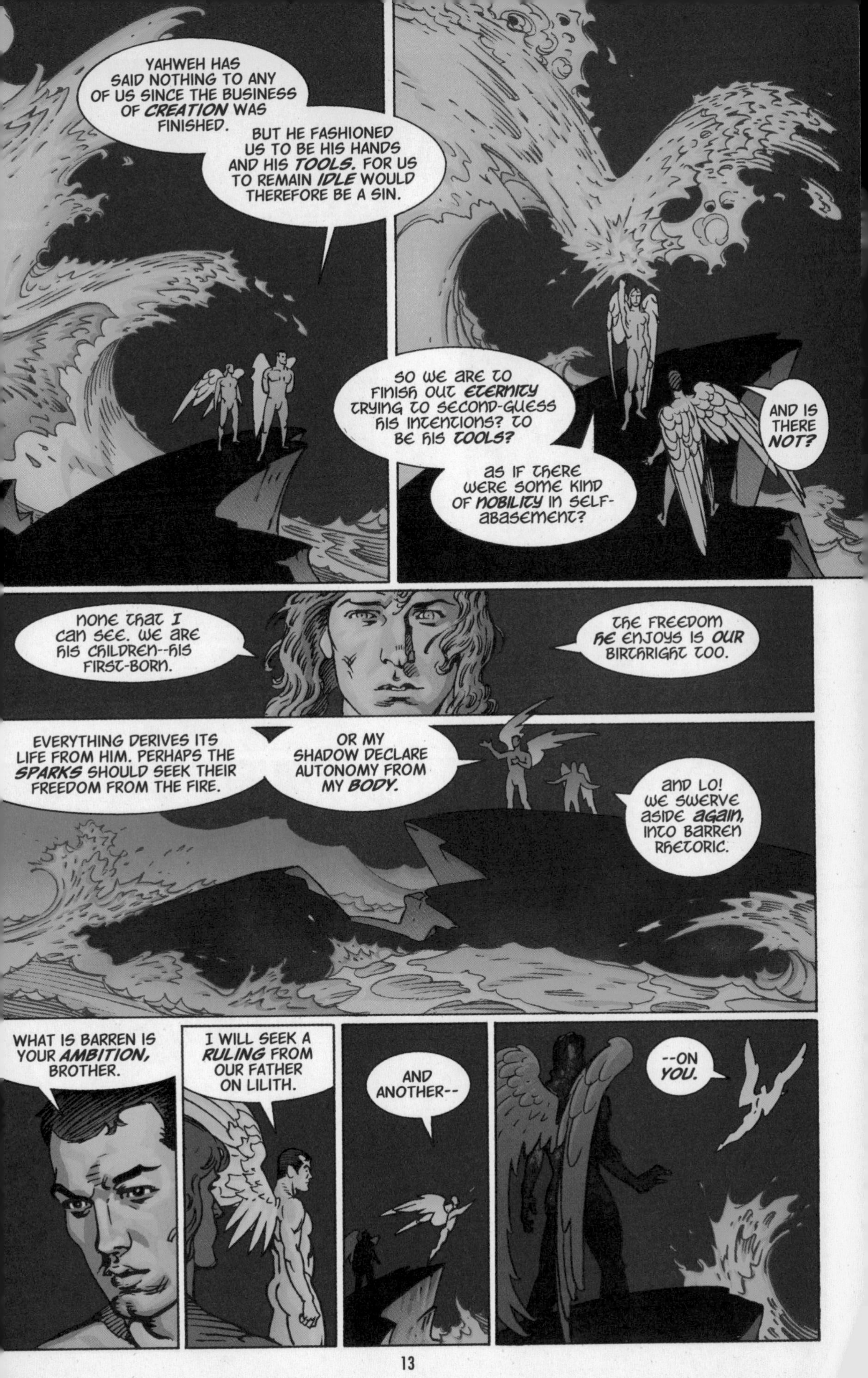
YAHWEH HAS SAID NOTHING TO ANY OF US SINCE THE BUSINESS OF CREATION WAS FINISHED.
BUT HE FASHIONED US TO BE HIS HANDS AND HIS TOOLS. FOR US TO REMAIN IDLE WOULD THEREFORE BE A SIN.
SO WE ARE TO FINISH OUT ETERNITY TRYING TO SECOND-GUESS HIS INTENTIONS? TO BE HIS TOOLS?
AS IF THERE WERE SOME KIND OF NOBILITY IN SELF-ABASEMENT?
AND IS THERE NOT?
NONE THAT I CAN SEE. WE ARE HIS CHILDREN--HIS FIRST-BORN.
THE FREEDOM HE ENJOYS IS OUR BIRTHRIGHT TOO.
EVERYTHING DERIVES ITS LIFE FROM HIM. PERHAPS THE SPARKS SHOULD SEEK THEIR FREEDOM FROM THE FIRE.
OR MY SHADOW DECLARE AUTONOMY FROM MY BODY.
AND LO! WE SWERVE ASIDE AGAIN, INTO BARREN RHETORIC.
WHAT IS BARREN IS YOUR AMBITION, BROTHER.
I WILL SEEK A RULING FROM OUR FATHER ON LILITH.
AND ANOTHER--
--ON YOU.

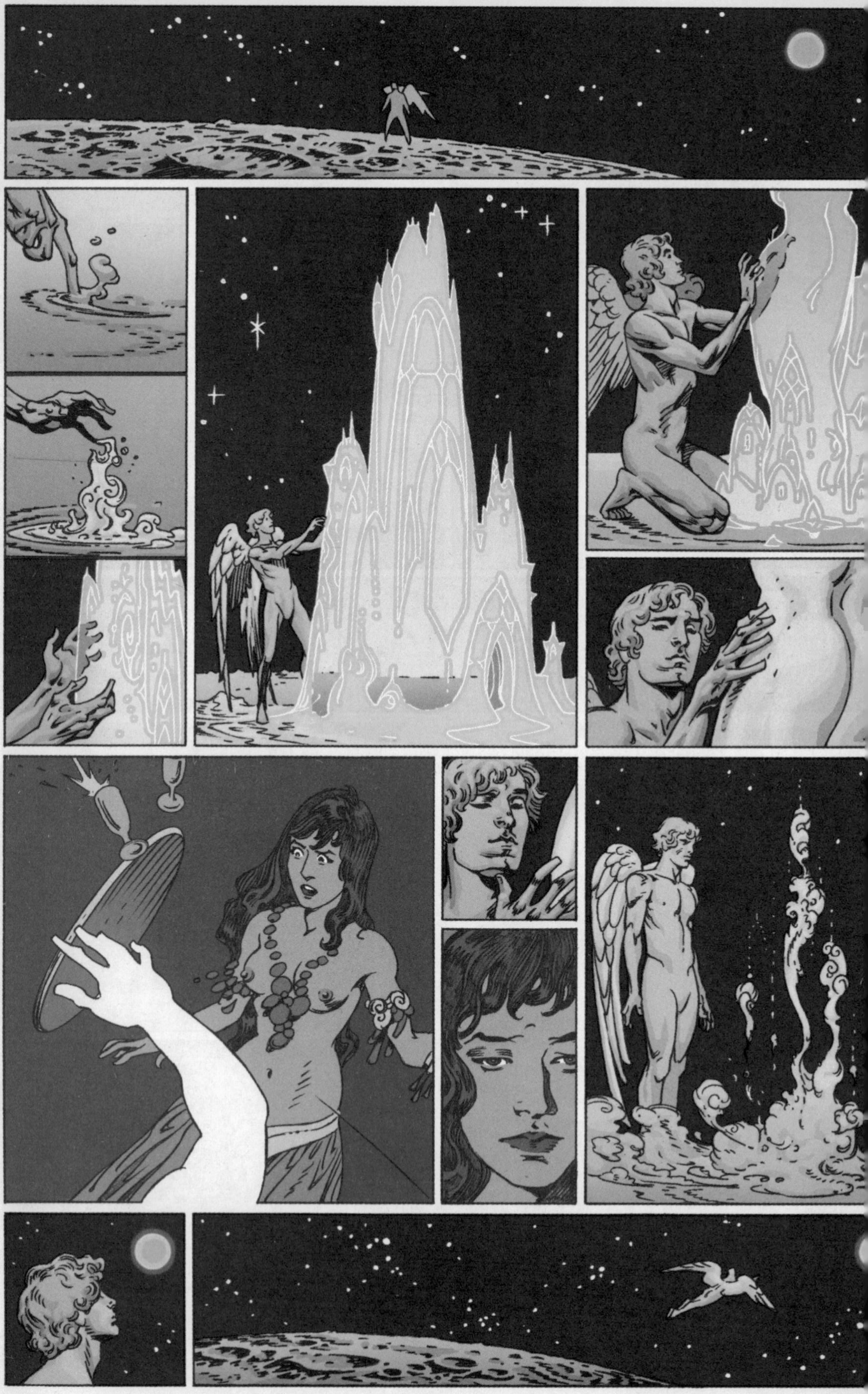

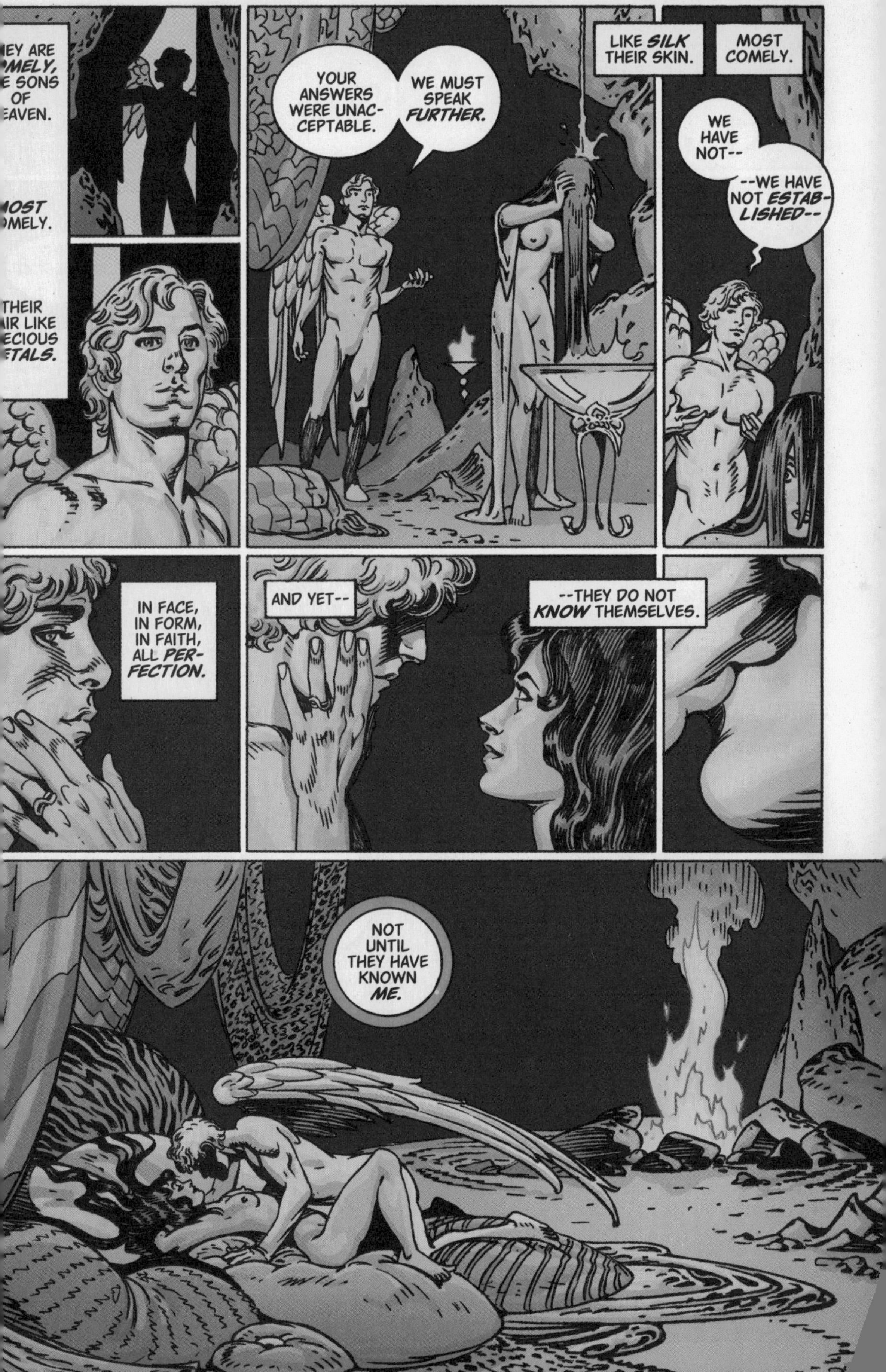

EY ARE
MELY,
E SONS
OF
EAVEN.
MOST
MELY.
THEIR
IR LIKE
ECIOUS
ETALS.
YOUR ANSWERS WERE UNACCEPTABLE.
WE MUST SPEAK FURTHER.
LIKE SILK THEIR SKIN.
MOST COMELY.
WE HAVE NOT--
--WE HAVE NOT ESTABLISHED--
IN FACE, IN FORM, IN FAITH, ALL PERFECTION.
AND YET--
--THEY DO NOT KNOW THEMSELVES.
NOT UNTIL THEY HAVE KNOWN ME.

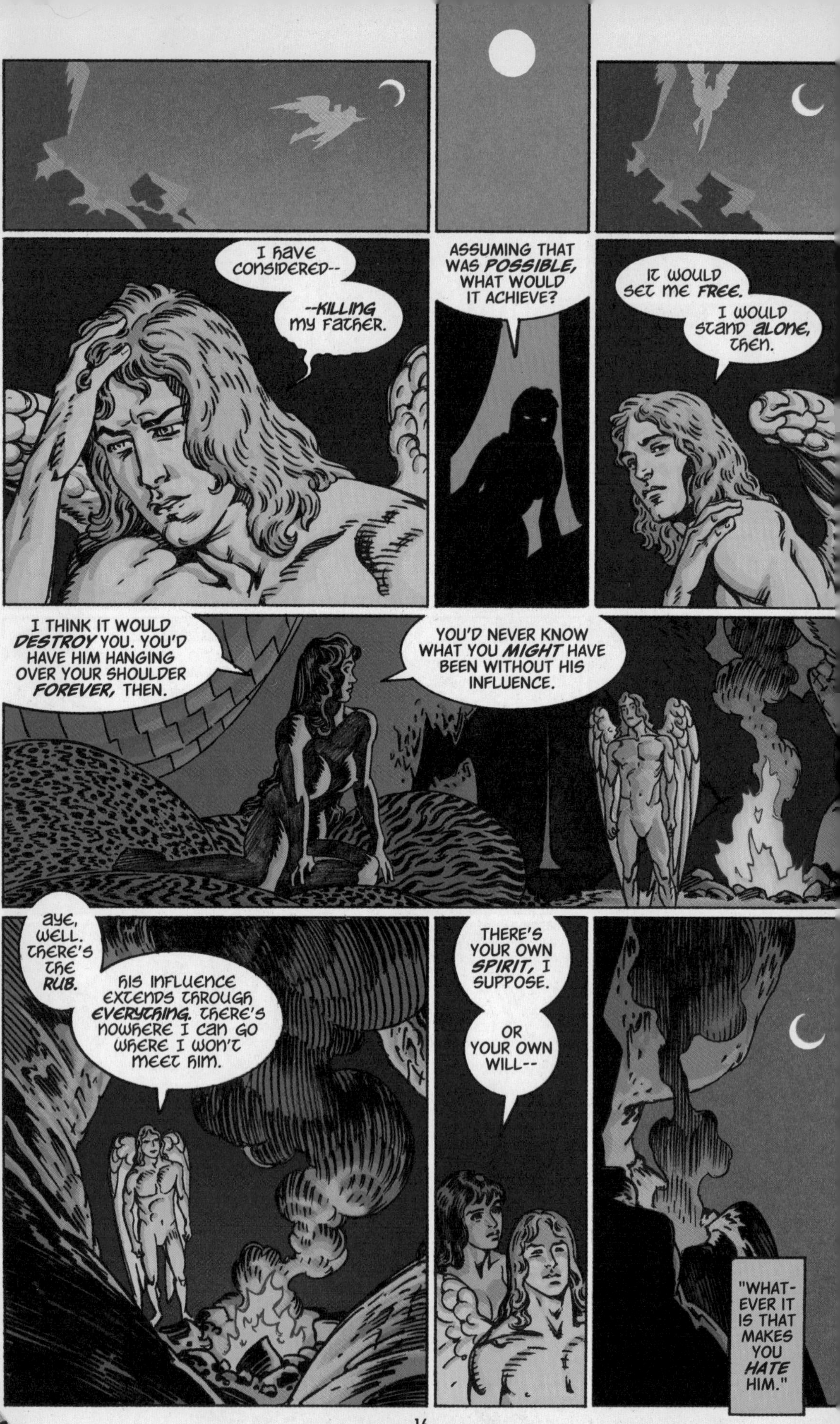

I HAVE CONSIDERED--
--KILLING MY FATHER.
ASSUMING THAT WAS POSSIBLE, WHAT WOULD IT ACHIEVE?
IT WOULD SET ME FREE.
I WOULD STAND ALONE, THEN.
I THINK IT WOULD DESTROY YOU. YOU'D HAVE HIM HANGING OVER YOUR SHOULDER FOREVER, THEN.
YOU'D NEVER KNOW WHAT YOU MIGHT HAVE BEEN WITHOUT HIS INFLUENCE.
AYE, WELL. THERE'S THE RUB.
HIS INFLUENCE EXTENDS THROUGH EVERYTHING. THERE'S NOWHERE I CAN GO WHERE I WON'T MEET HIM.
THERE'S YOUR OWN SPIRIT, I SUPPOSE.
OR YOUR OWN WILL--
"WHATEVER IT IS THAT MAKES YOU HATE HIM."

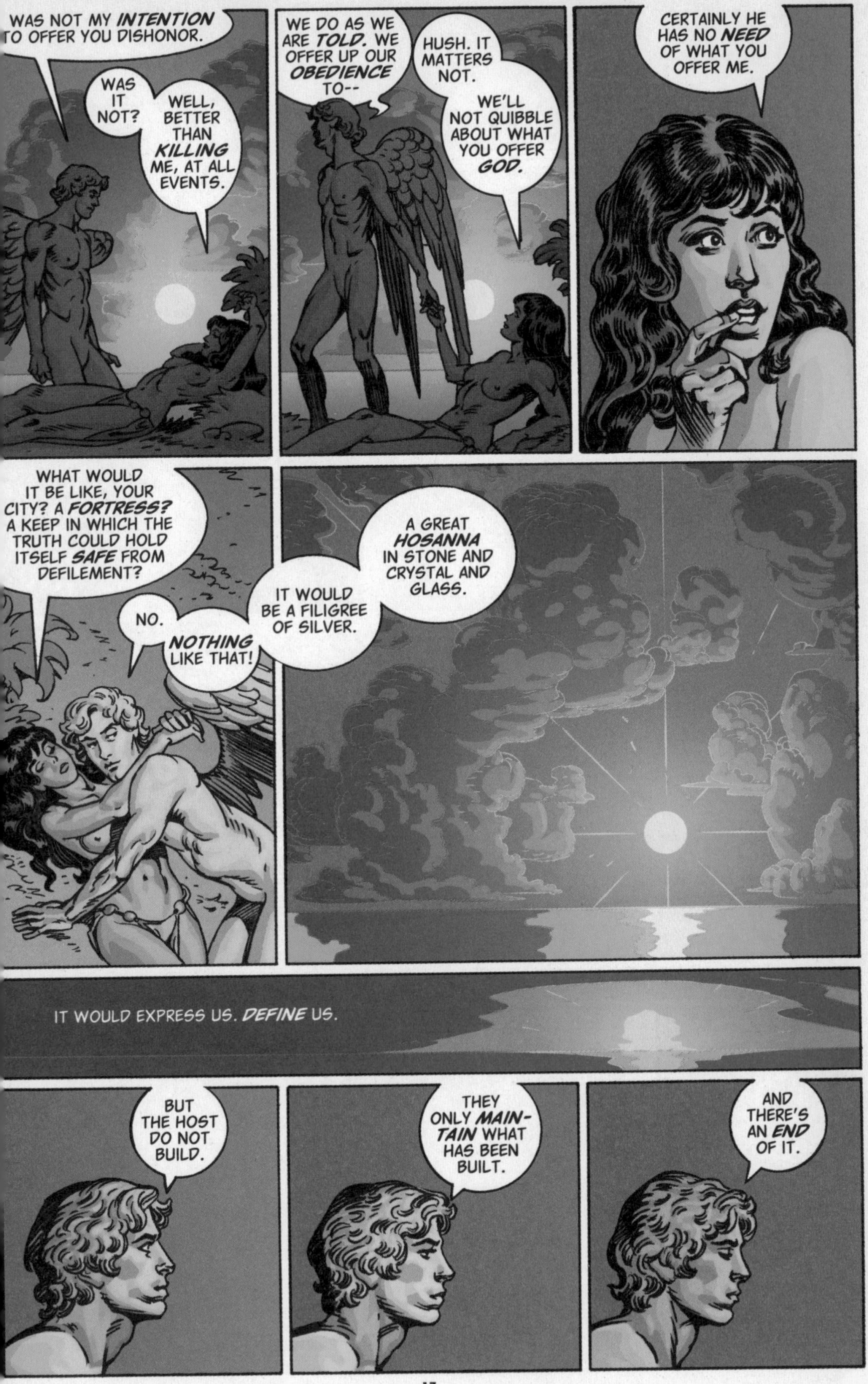

WAS NOT MY INTENTION TO OFFER YOU DISHONOR.
WAS IT NOT?
WELL, BETTER THAN KILLING ME, AT ALL EVENTS.
WE DO AS WE ARE TOLD. WE OFFER UP OUR OBEDIENCE TO--
HUSH. IT MATTERS NOT.
WE'LL NOT QUIBBLE ABOUT WHAT YOU OFFER GOD.
CERTAINLY HE HAS NO NEED OF WHAT YOU OFFER ME.
WHAT WOULD IT BE LIKE, YOUR CITY? A FORTRESS? A KEEP IN WHICH THE TRUTH COULD HOLD ITSELF SAFE FROM DEFILEMENT?
NO.
NOTHING LIKE THAT!
IT WOULD BE A FILIGREE OF SILVER.
A GREAT HOSANNA IN STONE AND CRYSTAL AND GLASS.
IT WOULD EXPRESS US. DEFINE US.
BUT THE HOST DO NOT BUILD.
THEY ONLY MAIN-TAIN WHAT HAS BEEN BUILT.
AND THERE'S AN END OF IT.

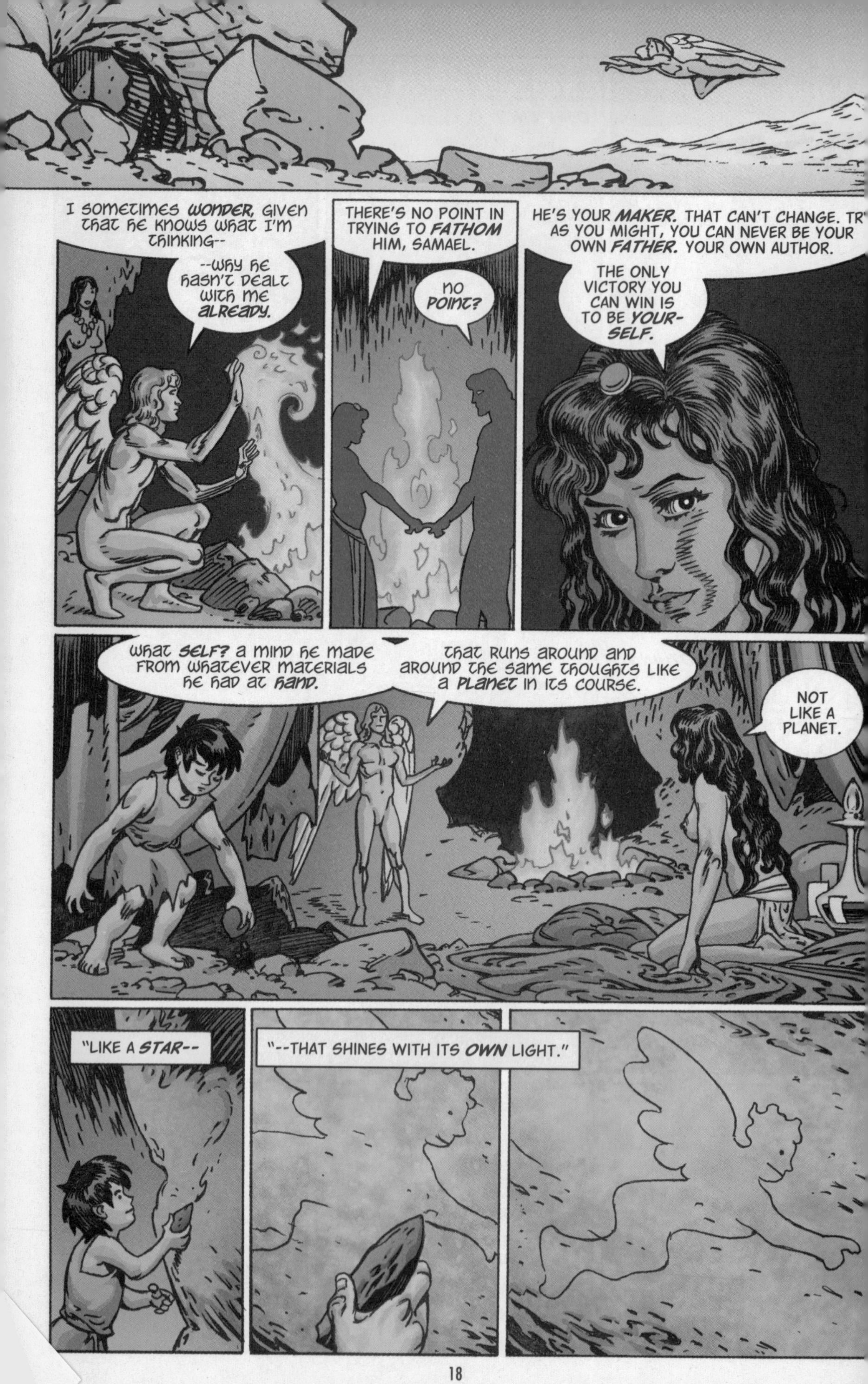

I SOMETIMES WONDER, GIVEN THAT HE KNOWS WHAT I'M THINKING--
--WHY HE HASN'T DEALT WITH ME ALREADY.
THERE'S NO POINT IN TRYING TO FATHOM HIM, SAMAEL.
NO POINT?
HE'S YOUR MAKER. THAT CAN'T CHANGE. TRY AS YOU MIGHT, YOU CAN NEVER BE YOUR OWN FATHER. YOUR OWN AUTHOR.
THE ONLY VICTORY YOU CAN WIN IS TO BE YOURSELF.
WHAT SELF? A MIND HE MADE FROM WHATEVER MATERIALS HE HAD AT HAND.
THAT RUNS AROUND AND AROUND THE SAME THOUGHTS LIKE A PLANET IN ITS COURSE.
NOT LIKE A PLANET.
"LIKE A STAR--
"--THAT SHINES WITH ITS OWN LIGHT."

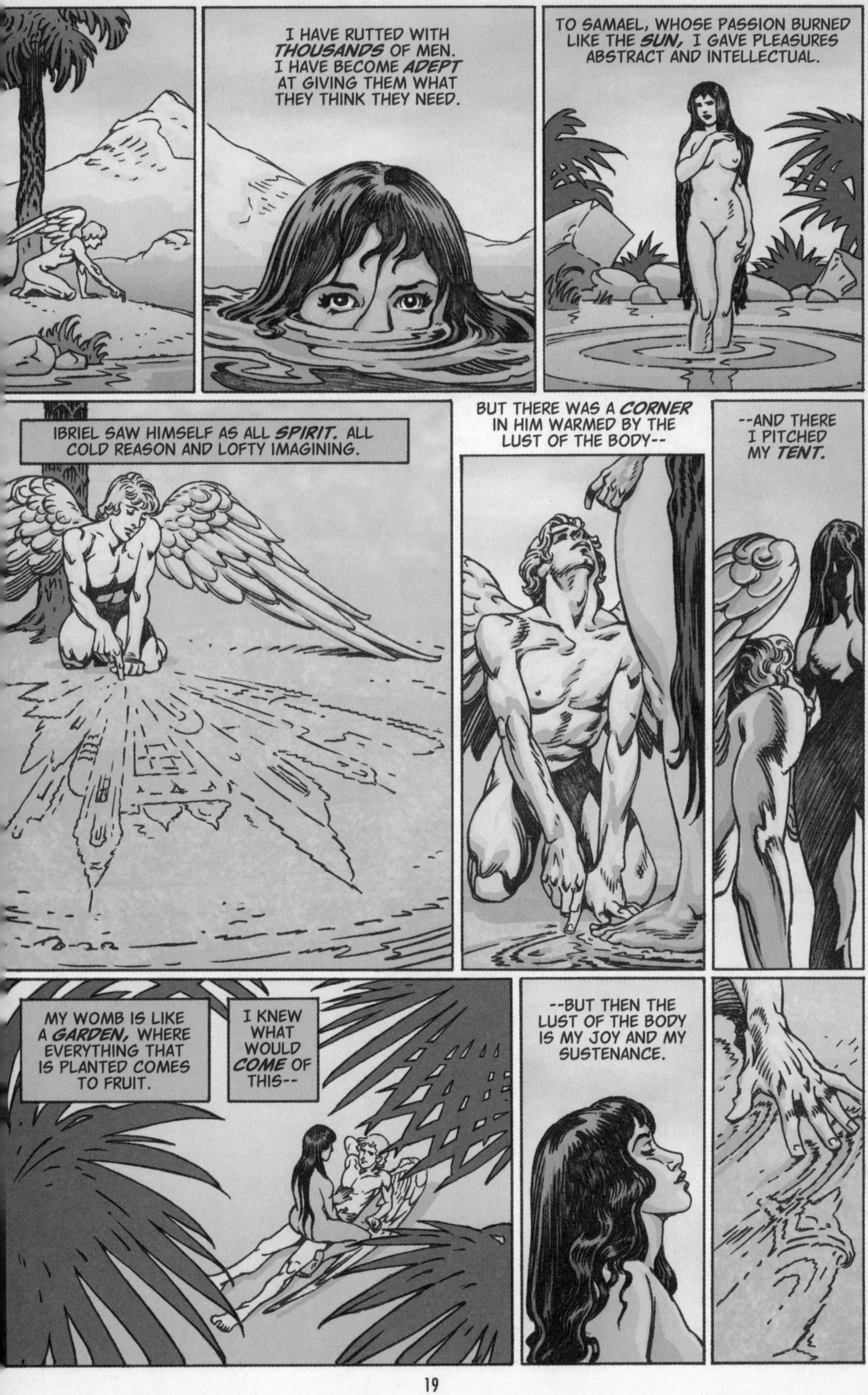

I HAVE RUTTED WITH THOUSANDS OF MEN. I HAVE BECOME ADEPT AT GIVING THEM WHAT THEY THINK THEY NEED.
TO SAMAEL, WHOSE PASSION BURNED LIKE THE SUN, I GAVE PLEASURES ABSTRACT AND INTELLECTUAL.
IBRIEL SAW HIMSELF AS ALL SPIRIT. ALL COLD REASON AND LOFTY IMAGINING.
BUT THERE WAS A CORNER IN HIM WARMED BY THE LUST OF THE BODY--
--AND THERE I PITCHED MY TENT.
MY WOMB IS LIKE A GARDEN, WHERE EVERYTHING THAT IS PLANTED COMES TO FRUIT.
I KNEW WHAT WOULD COME OF THIS--
--BUT THEN THE LUST OF THE BODY IS MY JOY AND MY SUSTENANCE.

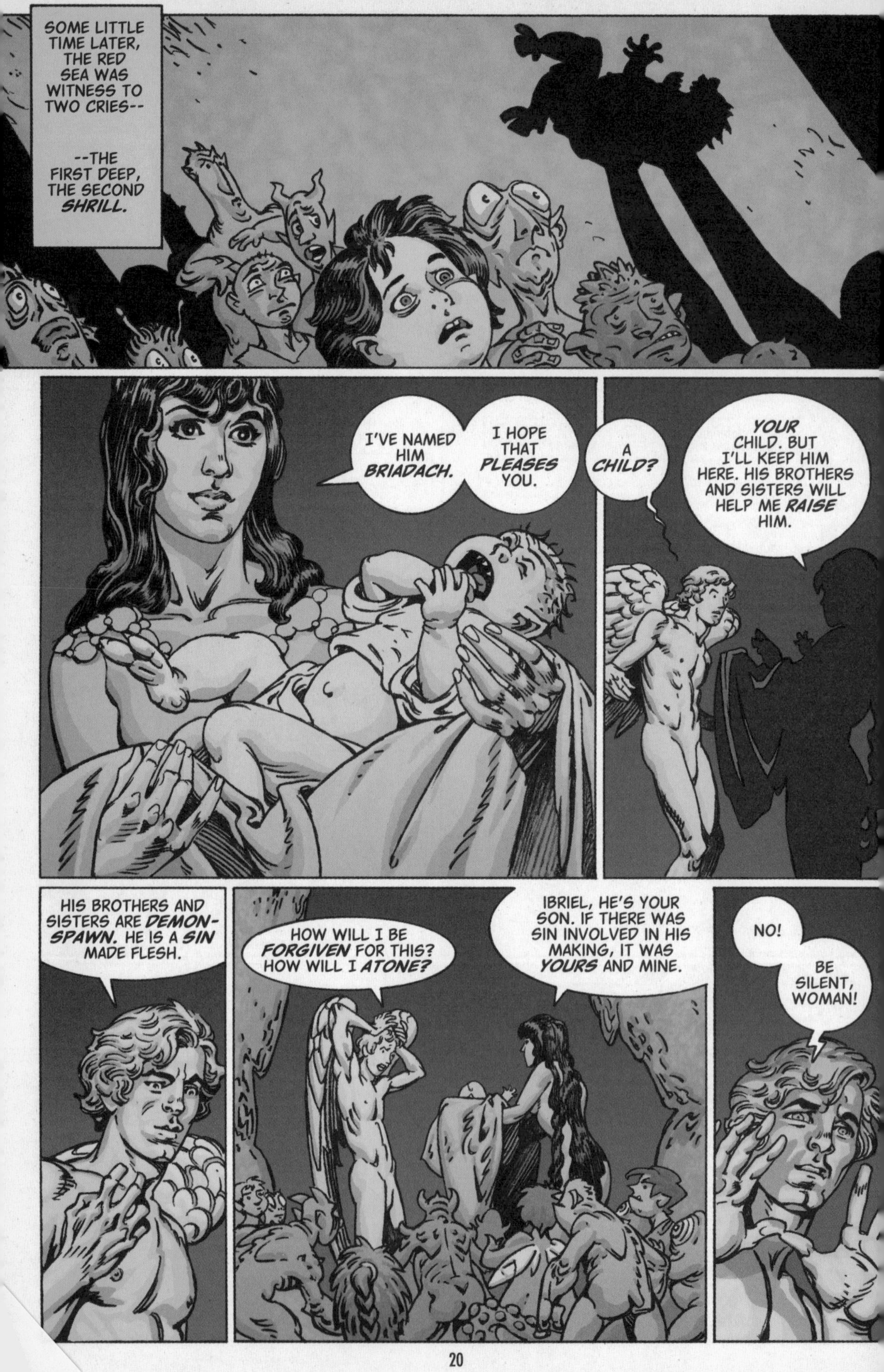
SOME LITTLE TIME LATER, THE RED SEA WAS WITNESS TO TWO CRIES--
--THE FIRST DEEP, THE SECOND SHRILL.
I'VE NAMED HIM BRIADACH.
I HOPE THAT PLEASES YOU.
A CHILD?
YOUR CHILD. BUT I'LL KEEP HIM HERE. HIS BROTHERS AND SISTERS WILL HELP ME RAISE HIM.
HIS BROTHERS AND SISTERS ARE DEMON-SPAWN. HE IS A SIN MADE FLESH.
HOW WILL I BE FORGIVEN FOR THIS? HOW WILL I ATONE?
IBRIEL, HE'S YOUR SON. IF THERE WAS SIN INVOLVED IN HIS MAKING, IT WAS YOURS AND MINE.
NO!
BE SILENT, WOMAN!

YOU! YOU HAVE ENTRAPPED ME! SEDUCED ME! I NEVER WANTED THIS--

--AND I WILL NOT LET YOU--

*

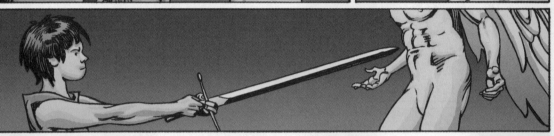

I MUST *THINK* ABOUT THIS. I MUST DECIDE WHAT CAN BE *DONE*.

IBRIEL!

I'LL SEE YOU. OR-- OR SEND *WORD* TO YOU.

MOST COMELY--

--AND MOST *CRUEL*.

21

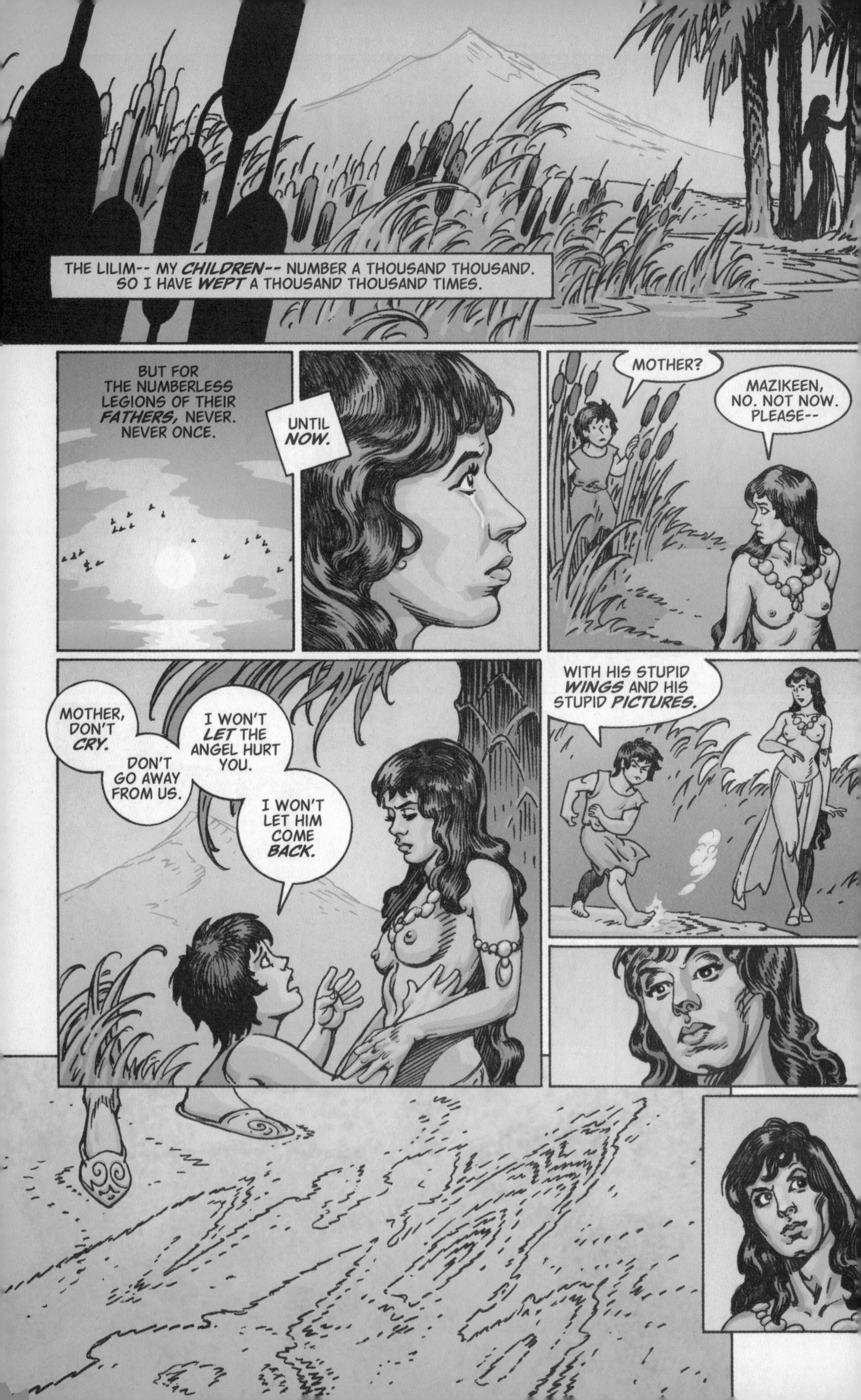
THE LILIM-- MY CHILDREN-- NUMBER A THOUSAND THOUSAND. SO I HAVE WEPT A THOUSAND THOUSAND TIMES.
BUT FOR THE NUMBERLESS LEGIONS OF THEIR FATHERS, NEVER. NEVER ONCE.
UNTIL NOW.
MOTHER?
MAZIKEEN, NO. NOT NOW. PLEASE--
MOTHER, DON'T CRY.
DON'T GO AWAY FROM US.
I WON'T LET THE ANGEL HURT YOU.
I WON'T LET HIM COME BACK.
WITH HIS STUPID WINGS AND HIS STUPID PICTURES.

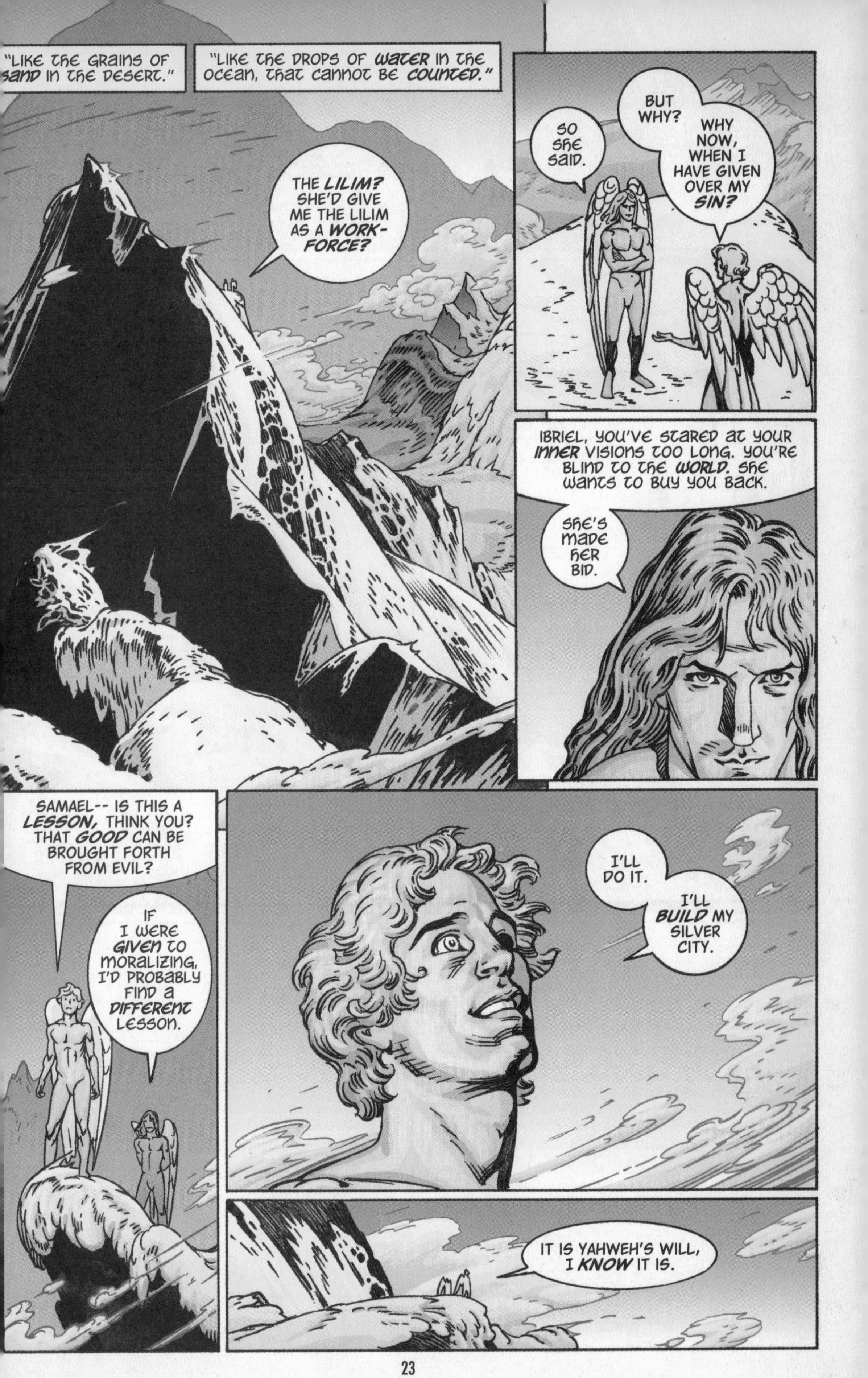
"LIKE THE GRAINS OF SAND IN THE DESERT."
"LIKE THE DROPS OF WATER IN THE OCEAN, THAT CANNOT BE COUNTED."
THE LILIM? SHE'D GIVE ME THE LILIM AS A WORK-FORCE?
SO SHE SAID.
BUT WHY?
WHY NOW, WHEN I HAVE GIVEN OVER MY SIN?
IBRIEL, YOU'VE STARED AT YOUR INNER VISIONS TOO LONG. YOU'RE BLIND TO THE WORLD. SHE WANTS TO BUY YOU BACK.
SHE'S MADE HER BID.
SAMAEL-- IS THIS A LESSON, THINK YOU? THAT GOOD CAN BE BROUGHT FORTH FROM EVIL?
IF I WERE GIVEN TO MORALIZING, I'D PROBABLY FIND A DIFFERENT LESSON.
I'LL DO IT.
I'LL BUILD MY SILVER CITY.
IT IS YAHWEH'S WILL, I KNOW IT IS.

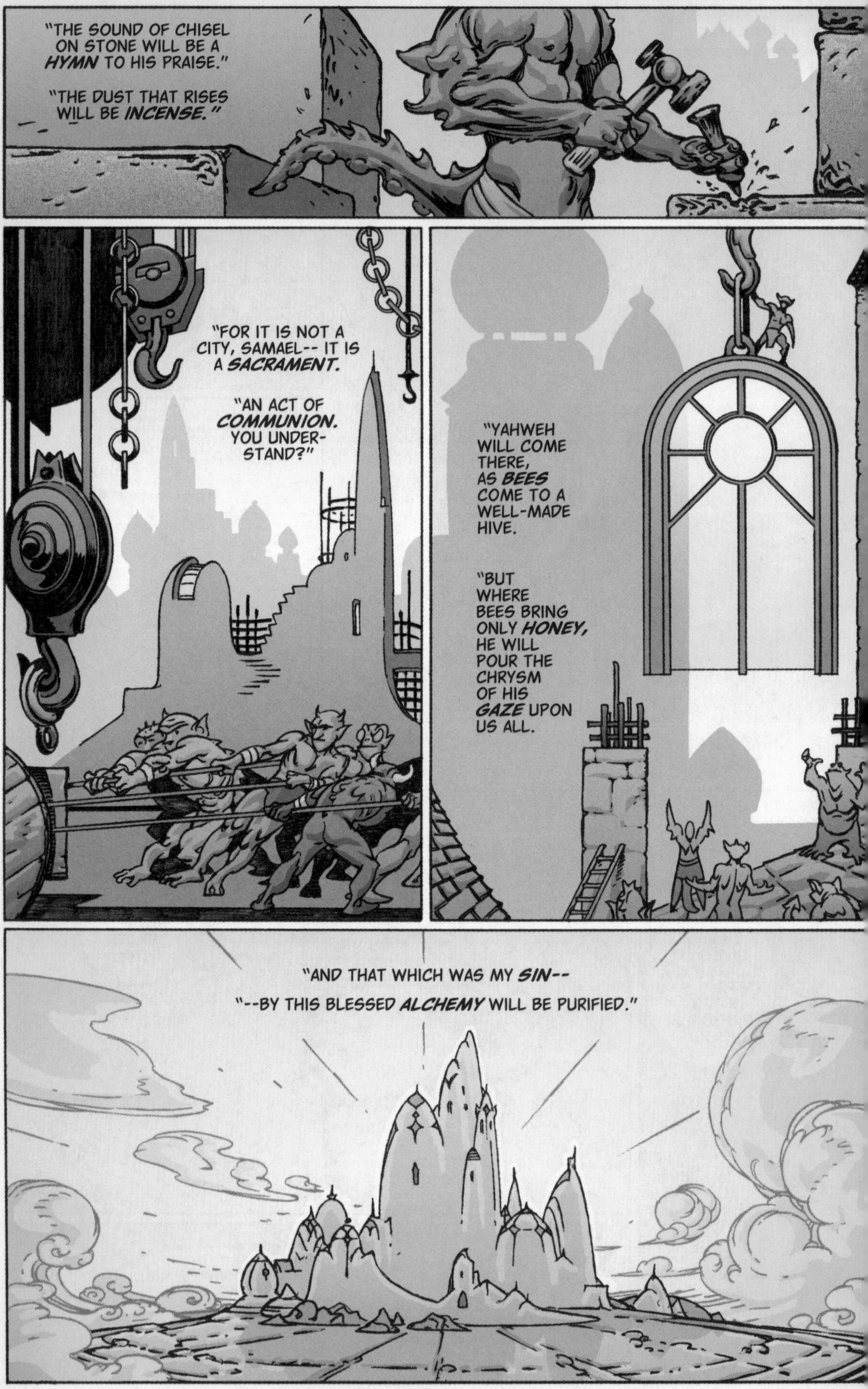
"THE SOUND OF CHISEL ON STONE WILL BE A HYMN TO HIS PRAISE."
"THE DUST THAT RISES WILL BE INCENSE."
"FOR IT IS NOT A CITY, SAMAEL-- IT IS A SACRAMENT.
"AN ACT OF COMMUNION. YOU UNDERSTAND?"
"YAHWEH WILL COME THERE, AS BEES COME TO A WELL-MADE HIVE.
"BUT WHERE BEES BRING ONLY HONEY, HE WILL POUR THE CHRYSM OF HIS GAZE UPON US ALL.
"AND THAT WHICH WAS MY SIN--
"--BY THIS BLESSED ALCHEMY WILL BE PURIFIED."

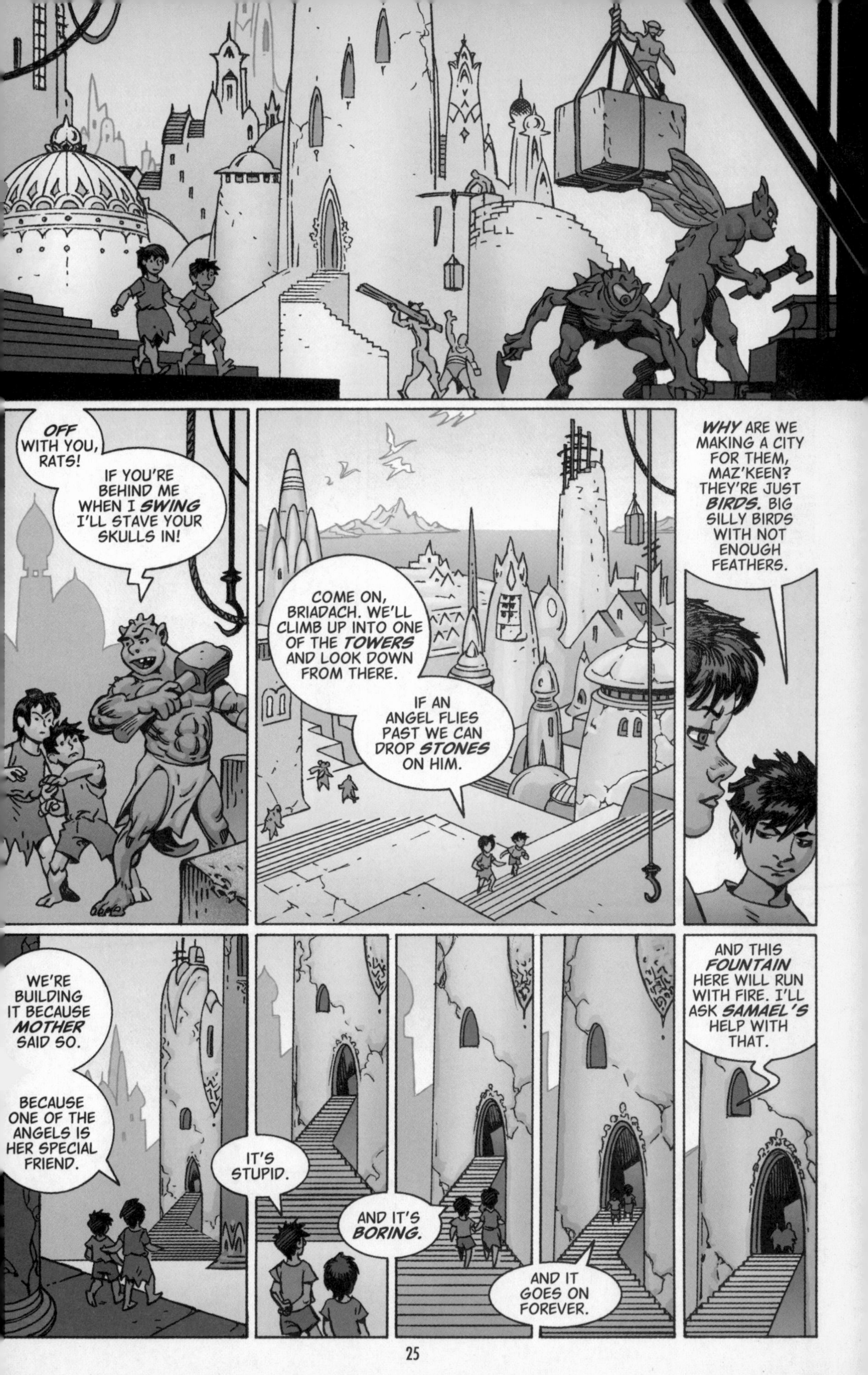
OFF WITH YOU, RATS!
IF YOU'RE BEHIND ME WHEN I SWING I'LL STAVE YOUR SKULLS IN!
COME ON, BRIADACH. WE'LL CLIMB UP INTO ONE OF THE TOWERS AND LOOK DOWN FROM THERE.
IF AN ANGEL FLIES PAST WE CAN DROP STONES ON HIM.
WHY ARE WE MAKING A CITY FOR THEM, MAZ'KEEN? THEY'RE JUST BIRDS. BIG SILLY BIRDS WITH NOT ENOUGH FEATHERS.
WE'RE BUILDING IT BECAUSE MOTHER SAID SO.
BECAUSE ONE OF THE ANGELS IS HER SPECIAL FRIEND.
IT'S STUPID.
AND IT'S BORING.
AND IT GOES ON FOREVER.
AND THIS FOUNTAIN HERE WILL RUN WITH FIRE. I'LL ASK SAMAEL'S HELP WITH THAT.

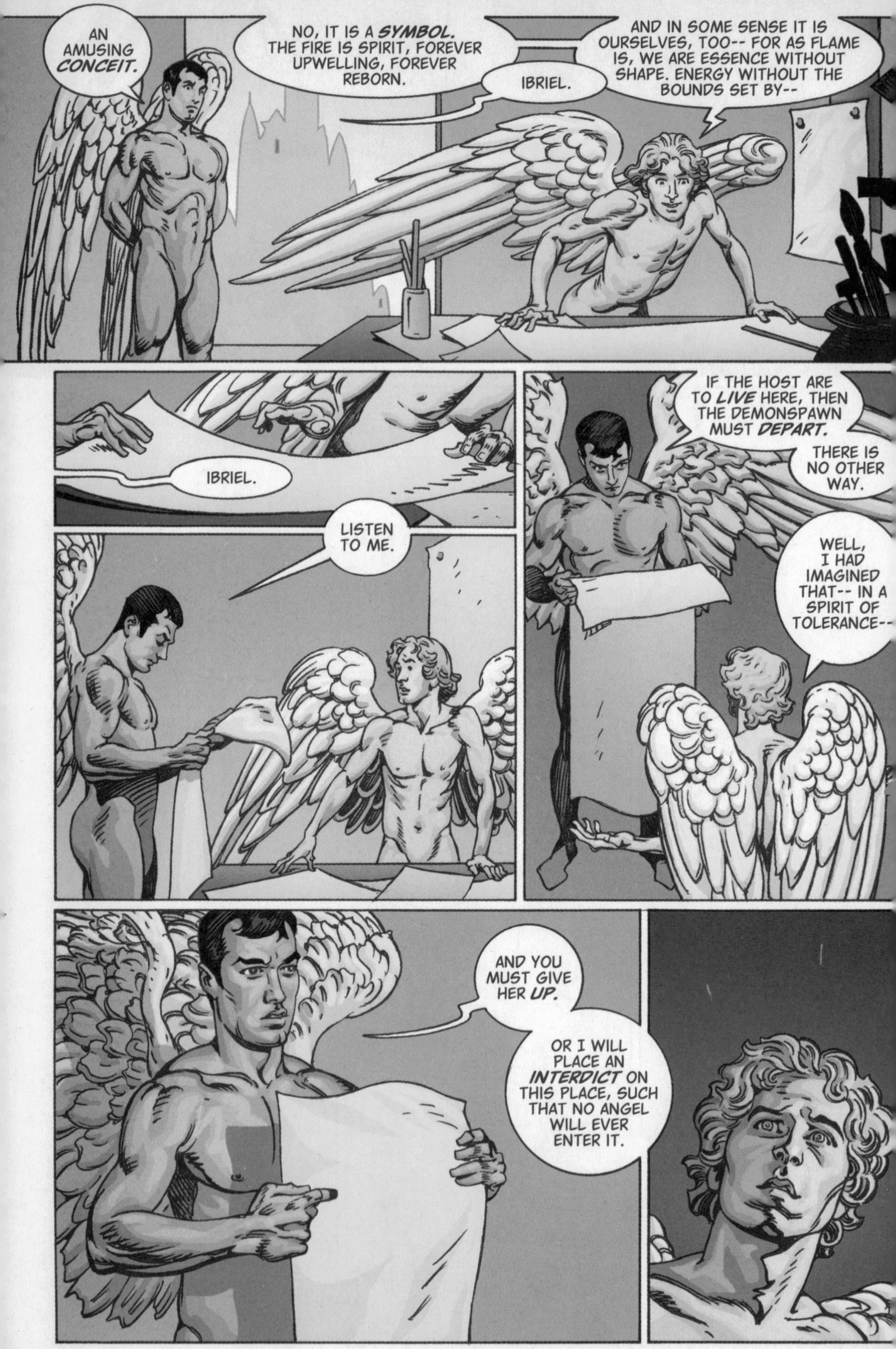
AN AMUSING CONCEIT.
NO, IT IS A SYMBOL. THE FIRE IS SPIRIT, FOREVER UPWELLING, FOREVER REBORN.
AND IN SOME SENSE IT IS OURSELVES, TOO-- FOR AS FLAME IS, WE ARE ESSENCE WITHOUT SHAPE. ENERGY WITHOUT THE BOUNDS SET BY--
IBRIEL.
IBRIEL.
LISTEN TO ME.
IF THE HOST ARE TO LIVE HERE, THEN THE DEMONSPAWN MUST DEPART.
THERE IS NO OTHER WAY.
WELL, I HAD IMAGINED THAT-- IN A SPIRIT OF TOLERANCE--
AND YOU MUST GIVE HER UP.
OR I WILL PLACE AN INTERDICT ON THIS PLACE, SUCH THAT NO ANGEL WILL EVER ENTER IT.

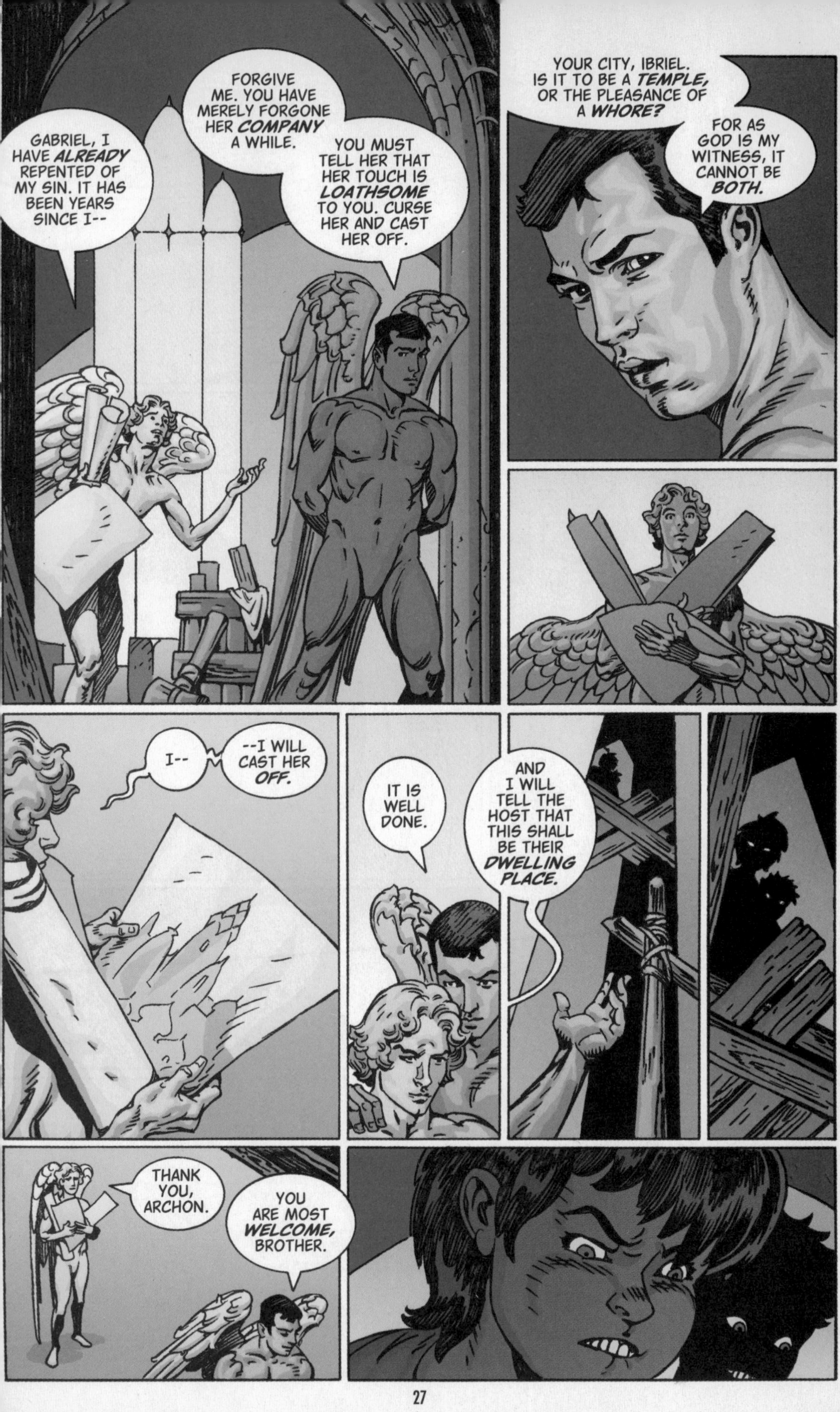
GABRIEL, I HAVE ALREADY REPENTED OF MY SIN. IT HAS BEEN YEARS SINCE I--
FORGIVE ME. YOU HAVE MERELY FORGONE HER COMPANY A WHILE.
YOU MUST TELL HER THAT HER TOUCH IS LOATHSOME TO YOU. CURSE HER AND CAST HER OFF.
YOUR CITY, IBRIEL. IS IT TO BE A TEMPLE, OR THE PLEASANCE OF A WHORE?
FOR AS GOD IS MY WITNESS, IT CANNOT BE BOTH.
I--
--I WILL CAST HER OFF.
IT IS WELL DONE.
AND I WILL TELL THE HOST THAT THIS SHALL BE THEIR DWELLING PLACE.
THANK YOU, ARCHON.
YOU ARE MOST WELCOME, BROTHER.

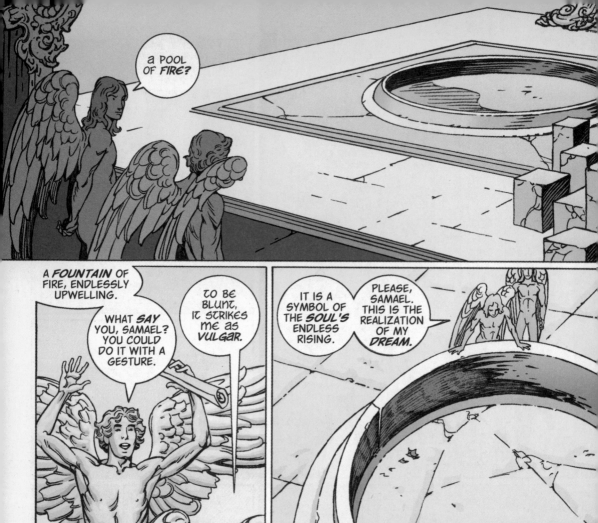

A POOL OF *FIRE?*

A *FOUNTAIN* OF FIRE, ENDLESSLY UPWELLING.

WHAT *SAY* YOU, SAMAEL? YOU COULD DO IT WITH A GESTURE.

TO BE *BLUNT,* IT STRIKES ME AS *VULGAR.*

IT IS A SYMBOL OF THE *SOUL'S* ENDLESS RISING.

PLEASE, SAMAEL. THIS IS THE REALIZATION OF MY *DREAM.*

IF THIS WERE *YOUR* DREAM, I'D EXPECT *HER* TO BE IN IT.

BUT I SUPPOSE YOU KNOW YOUR *OWN* MIND BEST.

SAMAEL, IT WOULD MEAN A GREAT *DEAL* TO ME.

WELL, I'LL *THINK* ABOUT IT.

AND I'LL LET YOU *KNOW.*

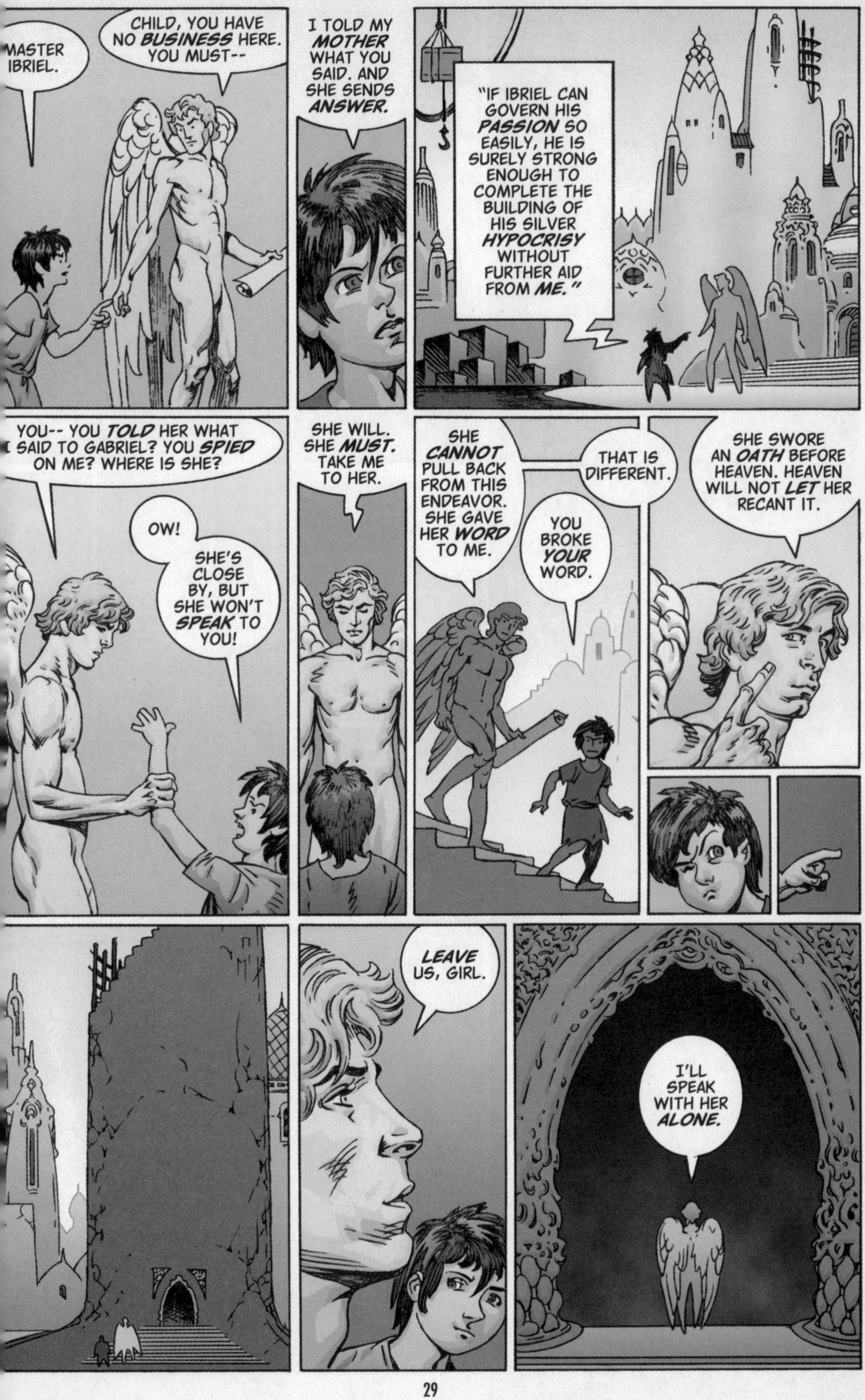
MASTER IBRIEL.
CHILD, YOU HAVE NO BUSINESS HERE. YOU MUST--
I TOLD MY MOTHER WHAT YOU SAID. AND SHE SENDS ANSWER.
"IF IBRIEL CAN GOVERN HIS PASSION SO EASILY, HE IS SURELY STRONG ENOUGH TO COMPLETE THE BUILDING OF HIS SILVER HYPOCRISY WITHOUT FURTHER AID FROM ME."
YOU-- YOU TOLD HER WHAT I SAID TO GABRIEL? YOU SPIED ON ME? WHERE IS SHE?
OW!
SHE'S CLOSE BY, BUT SHE WON'T SPEAK TO YOU!
SHE WILL. SHE MUST. TAKE ME TO HER.
SHE CANNOT PULL BACK FROM THIS ENDEAVOR. SHE GAVE HER WORD TO ME.
THAT IS DIFFERENT.
YOU BROKE YOUR WORD.
SHE SWORE AN OATH BEFORE HEAVEN. HEAVEN WILL NOT LET HER RECANT IT.
LEAVE US, GIRL.
I'LL SPEAK WITH HER ALONE.

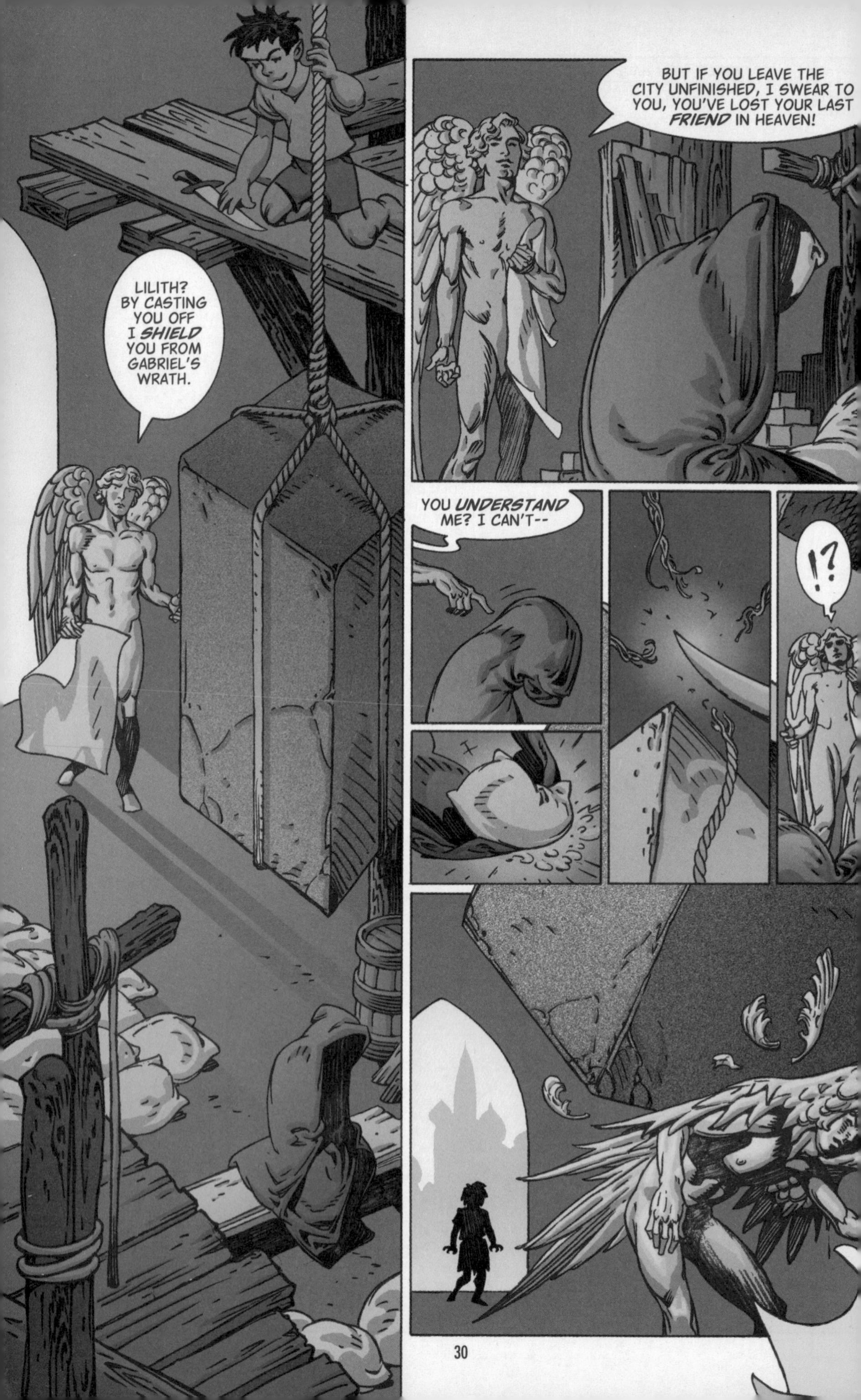
LILITH? BY CASTING YOU OFF I SHIELD YOU FROM GABRIEL'S WRATH.
BUT IF YOU LEAVE THE CITY UNFINISHED, I SWEAR TO YOU, YOU'VE LOST YOUR LAST FRIEND IN HEAVEN!
YOU UNDERSTAND ME? I CAN'T--
!?

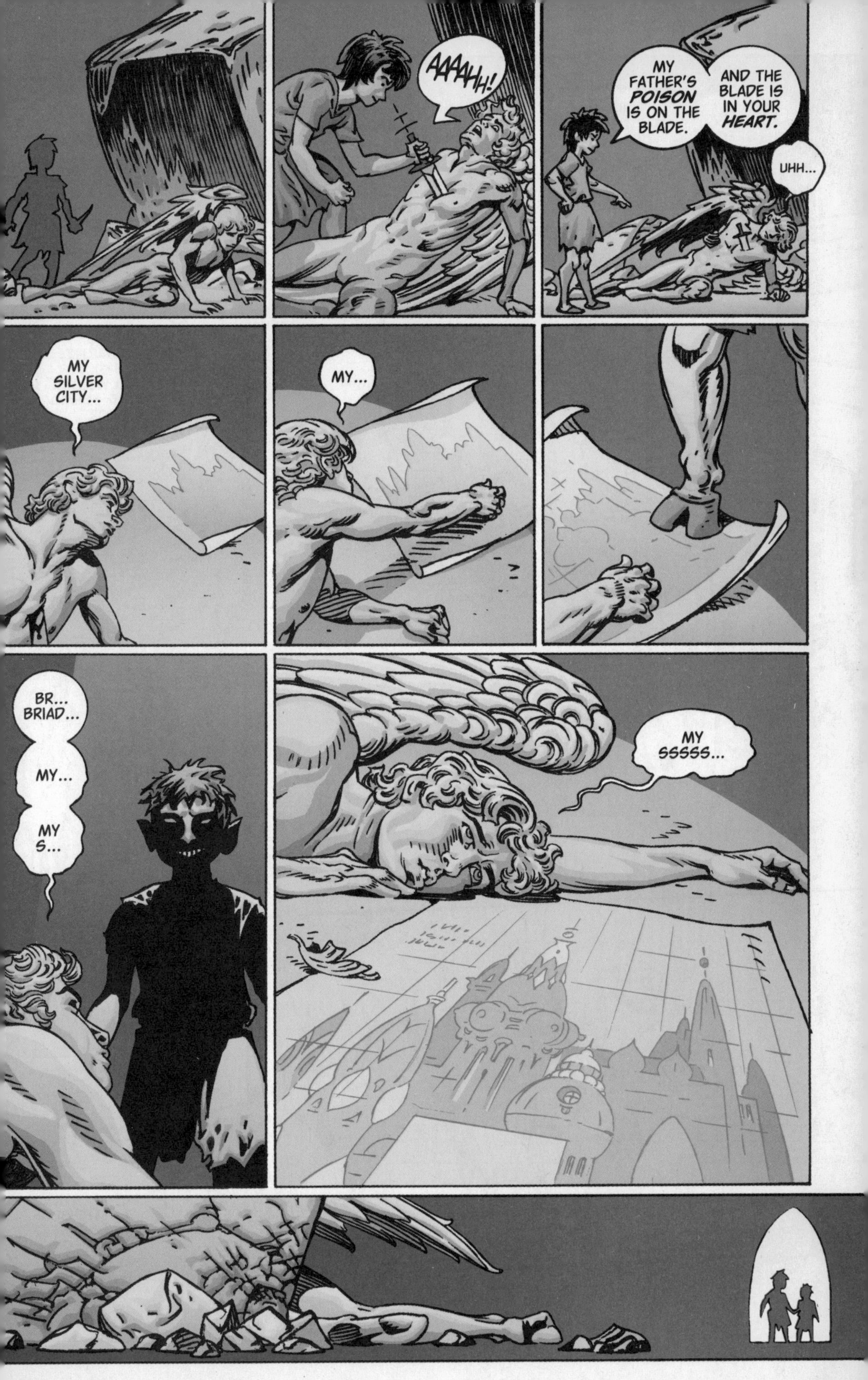
AAAAHH!
MY FATHER'S POISON IS ON THE BLADE.
AND THE BLADE IS IN YOUR HEART.
UHH...
MY SILVER CITY...
MY...
BR... BRIAD...
MY...
MY S...
MY SSSSS...

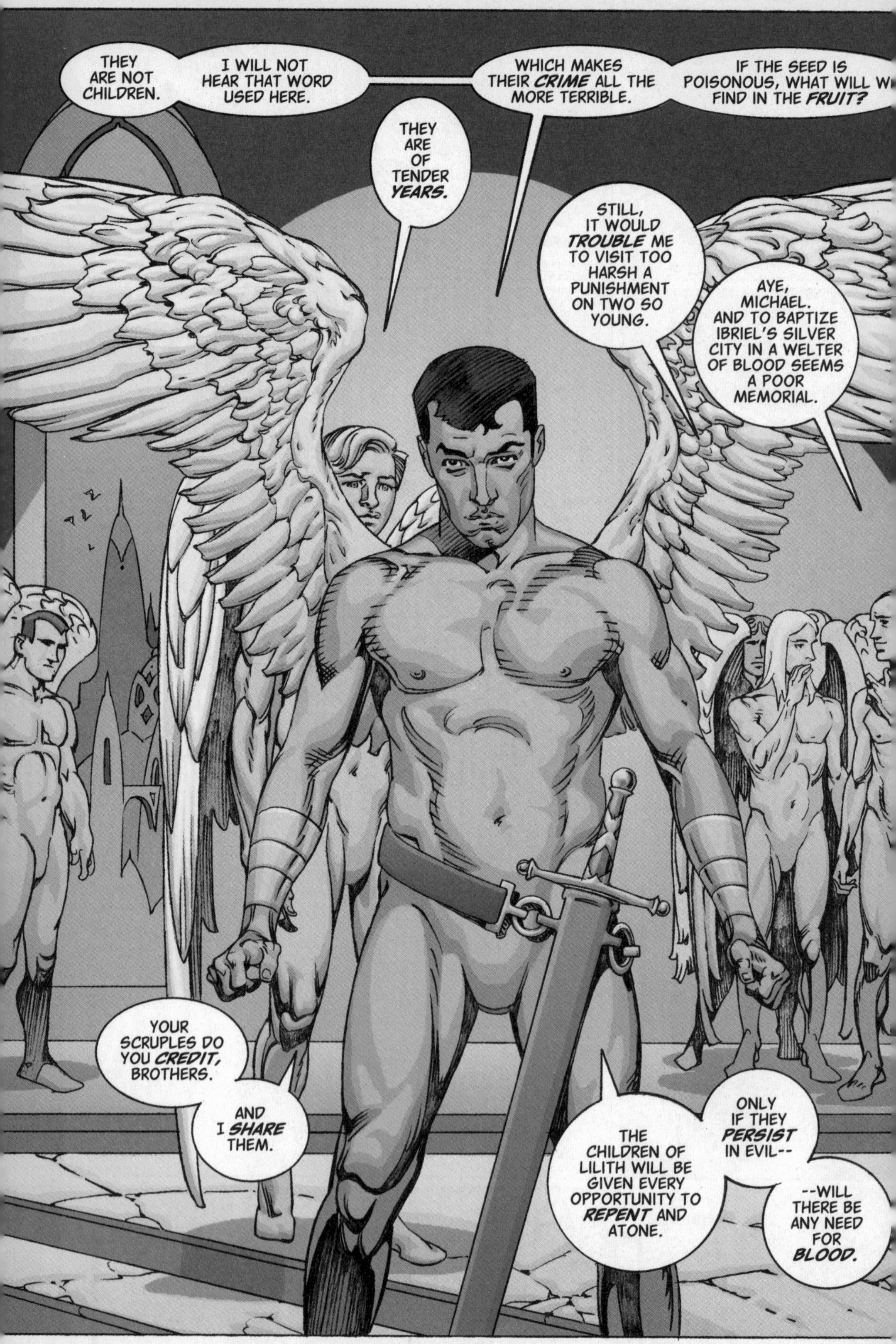
THEY ARE NOT CHILDREN.
I WILL NOT HEAR THAT WORD USED HERE.
THEY ARE OF TENDER YEARS.
WHICH MAKES THEIR CRIME ALL THE MORE TERRIBLE.
IF THE SEED IS POISONOUS, WHAT WILL W FIND IN THE FRUIT?
STILL, IT WOULD TROUBLE ME TO VISIT TOO HARSH A PUNISHMENT ON TWO SO YOUNG.
AYE, MICHAEL. AND TO BAPTIZE IBRIEL'S SILVER CITY IN A WELTER OF BLOOD SEEMS A POOR MEMORIAL.
YOUR SCRUPLES DO YOU CREDIT, BROTHERS.
AND I SHARE THEM.
THE CHILDREN OF LILITH WILL BE GIVEN EVERY OPPORTUNITY TO REPENT AND ATONE.
ONLY IF THEY PERSIST IN EVIL--
--WILL THERE BE ANY NEED FOR BLOOD.

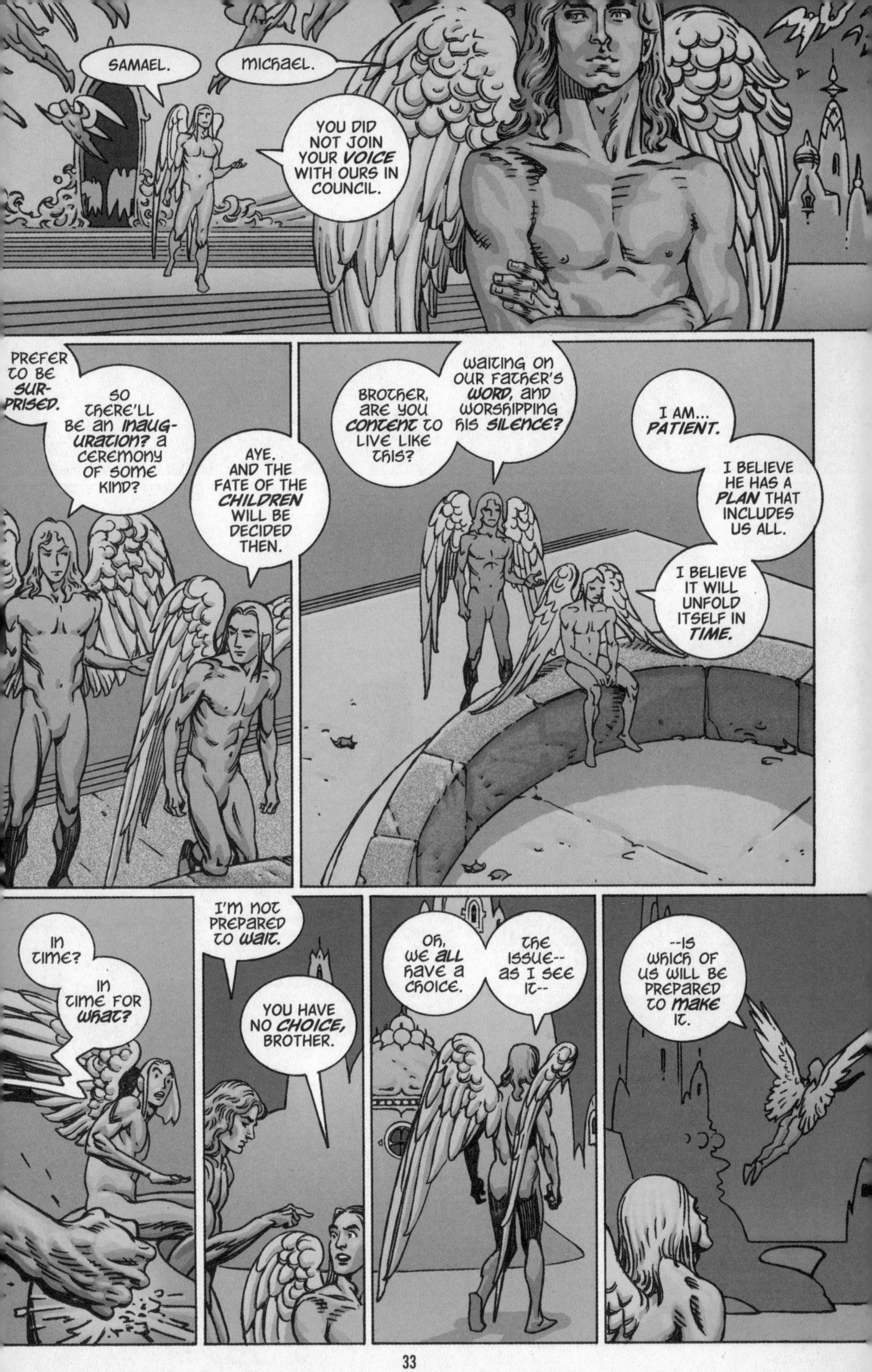
SAMAEL.
MICHAEL.
YOU DID NOT JOIN YOUR VOICE WITH OURS IN COUNCIL.
PREFER TO BE SURPRISED.
SO THERE'LL BE AN INAUGURATION? A CEREMONY OF SOME KIND?
AYE. AND THE FATE OF THE CHILDREN WILL BE DECIDED THEN.
BROTHER, ARE YOU CONTENT TO LIVE LIKE THIS?
WAITING ON OUR FATHER'S WORD, AND WORSHIPPING HIS SILENCE?
I AM... PATIENT.
I BELIEVE HE HAS A PLAN THAT INCLUDES US ALL.
I BELIEVE IT WILL UNFOLD ITSELF IN TIME.
IN TIME?
IN TIME FOR WHAT?
I'M NOT PREPARED TO WAIT.
YOU HAVE NO CHOICE, BROTHER.
OH, WE ALL HAVE A CHOICE.
THE ISSUE-- AS I SEE IT--
--IS WHICH OF US WILL BE PREPARED TO MAKE IT.

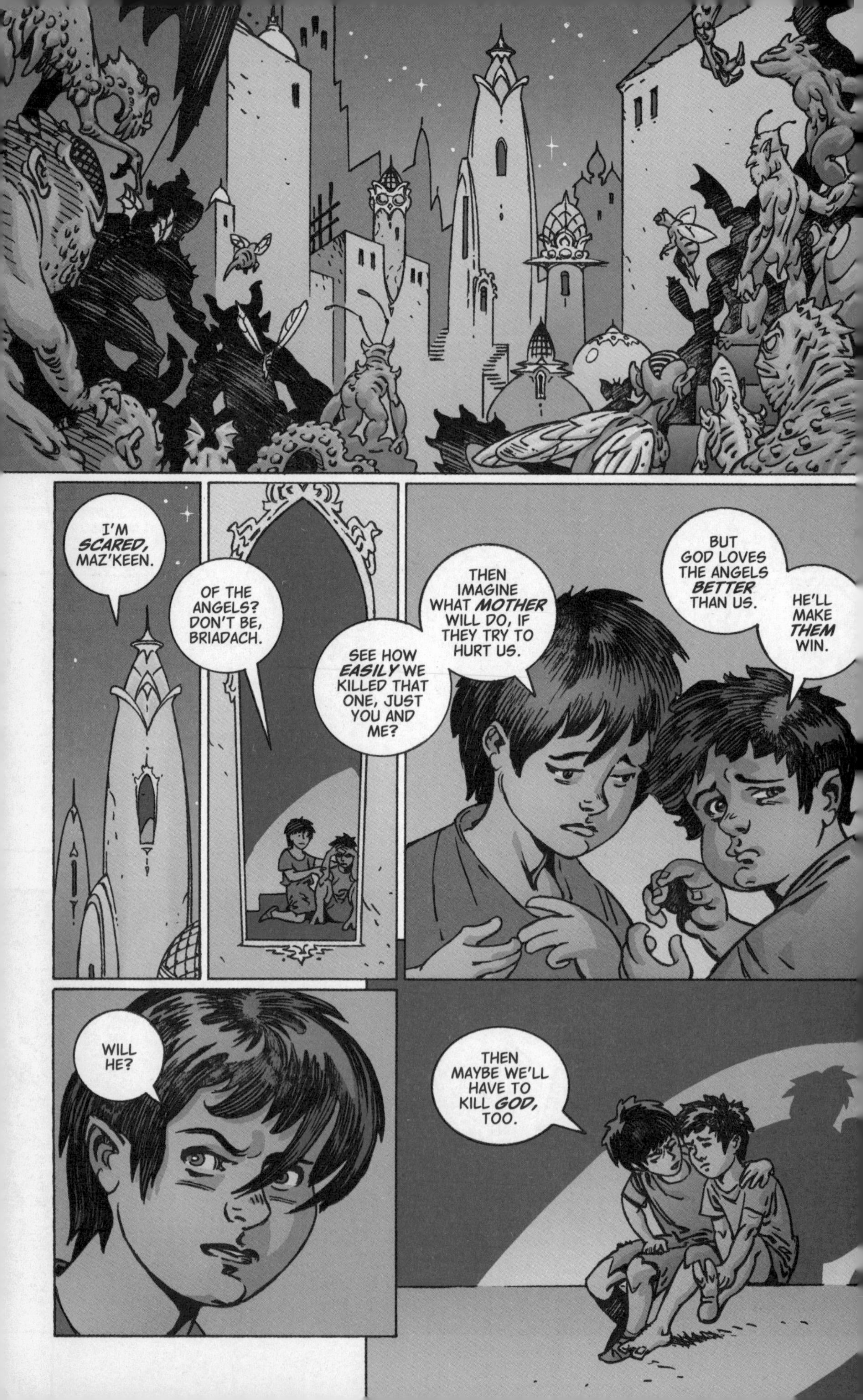
I'M SCARED, MAZ'KEEN.
OF THE ANGELS? DON'T BE, BRIADACH.
SEE HOW EASILY WE KILLED THAT ONE, JUST YOU AND ME?
THEN IMAGINE WHAT MOTHER WILL DO, IF THEY TRY TO HURT US.
BUT GOD LOVES THE ANGELS BETTER THAN US.
HE'LL MAKE THEM WIN.
WILL HE?
THEN MAYBE WE'LL HAVE TO KILL GOD, TOO.

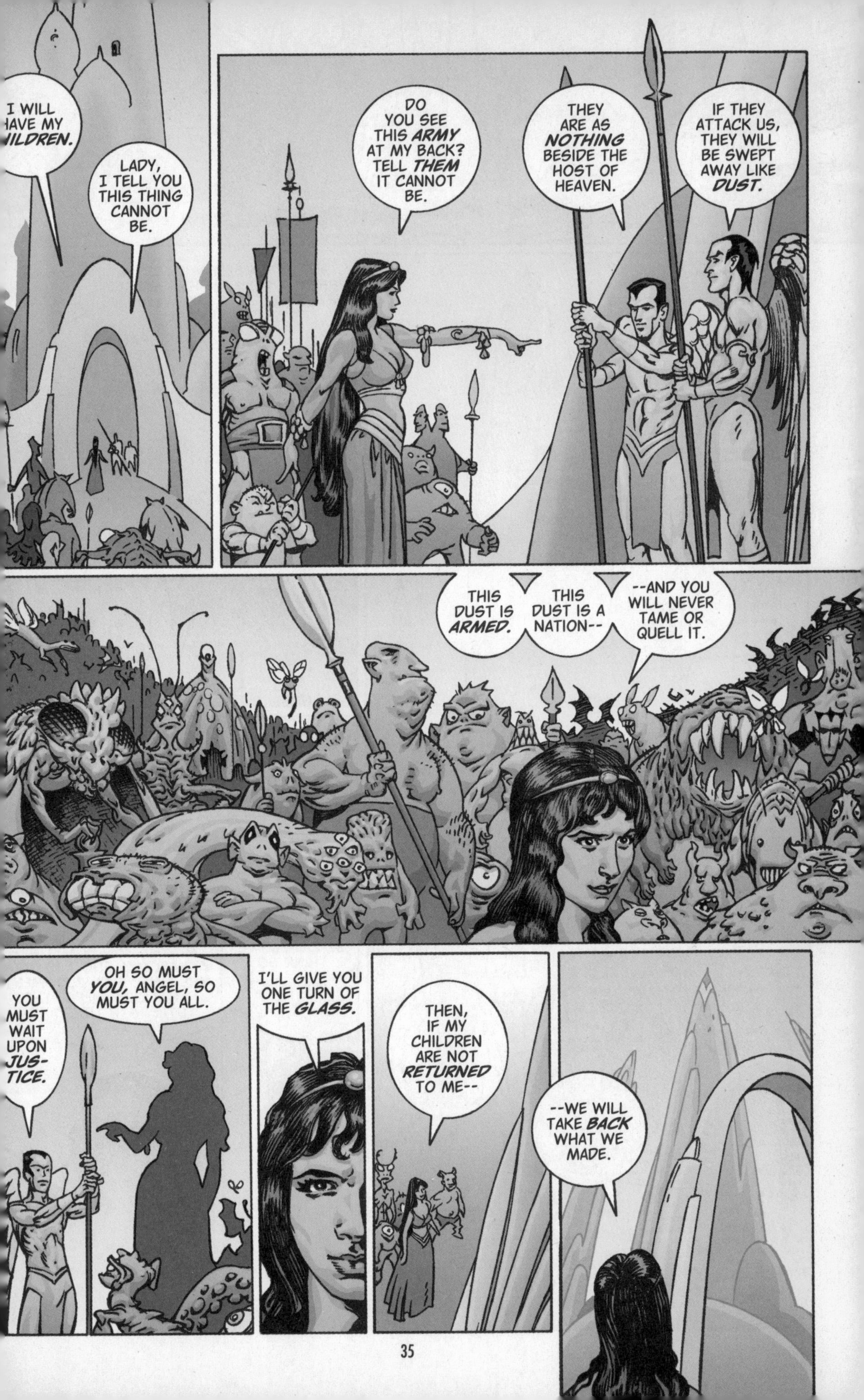

I WILL HAVE MY ILDREN.
LADY, I TELL YOU THIS THING CANNOT BE.
DO YOU SEE THIS ARMY AT MY BACK? TELL THEM IT CANNOT BE.
THEY ARE AS NOTHING BESIDE THE HOST OF HEAVEN.
IF THEY ATTACK US, THEY WILL BE SWEPT AWAY LIKE DUST.
THIS DUST IS ARMED.
THIS DUST IS A NATION--
--AND YOU WILL NEVER TAME OR QUELL IT.
YOU MUST WAIT UPON JUS-TICE.
OH SO MUST YOU, ANGEL, SO MUST YOU ALL.
I'LL GIVE YOU ONE TURN OF THE GLASS.
THEN, IF MY CHILDREN ARE NOT RETURNED TO ME--
--WE WILL TAKE BACK WHAT WE MADE.

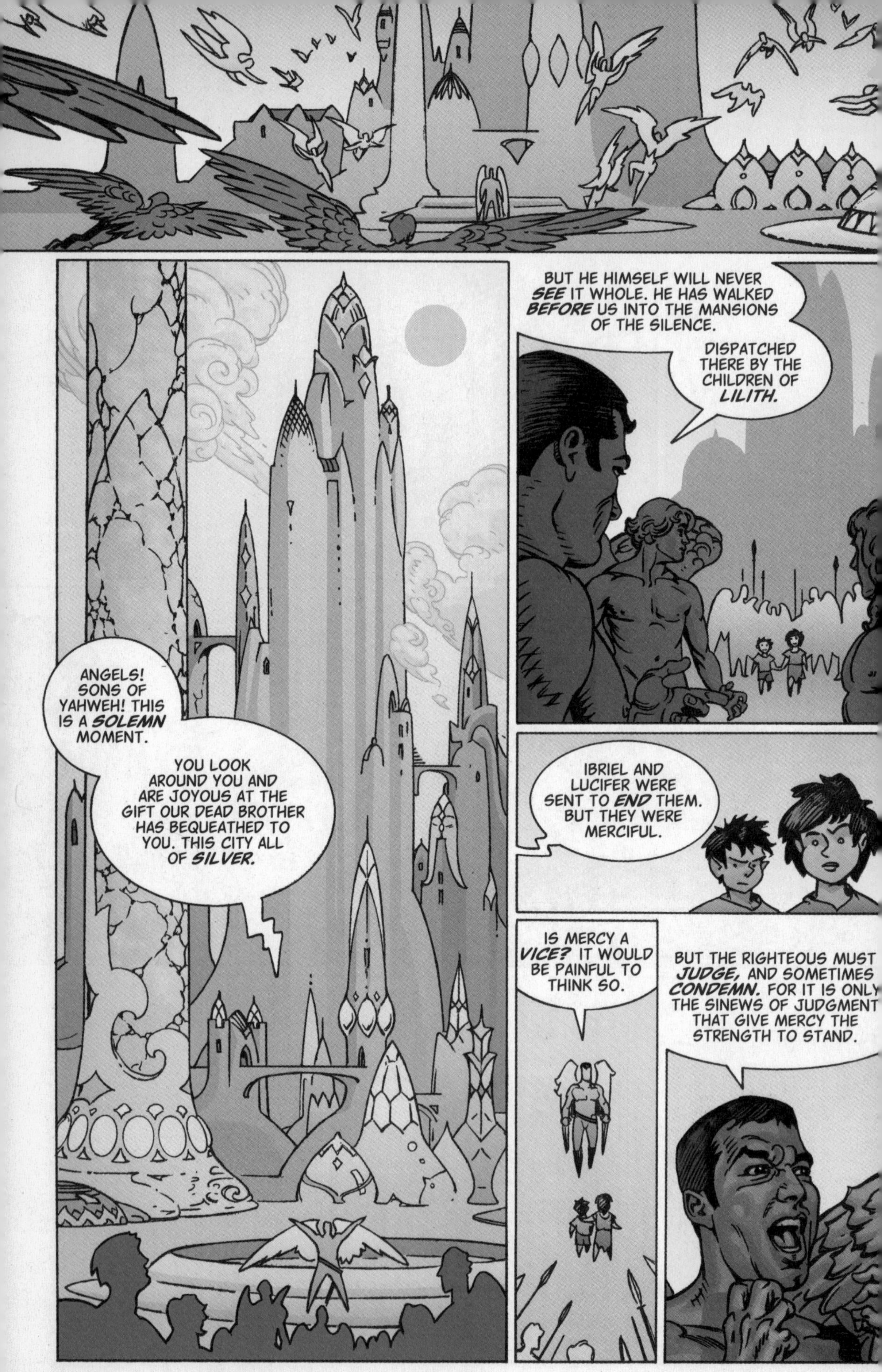
ANGELS! SONS OF YAHWEH! THIS IS A SOLEMN MOMENT.
YOU LOOK AROUND YOU AND ARE JOYOUS AT THE GIFT OUR DEAD BROTHER HAS BEQUEATHED TO YOU. THIS CITY ALL OF SILVER.
BUT HE HIMSELF WILL NEVER SEE IT WHOLE. HE HAS WALKED BEFORE US INTO THE MANSIONS OF THE SILENCE.
DISPATCHED THERE BY THE CHILDREN OF LILITH.
IBRIEL AND LUCIFER WERE SENT TO END THEM. BUT THEY WERE MERCIFUL.
IS MERCY A VICE? IT WOULD BE PAINFUL TO THINK SO.
BUT THE RIGHTEOUS MUST JUDGE, AND SOMETIMES CONDEMN. FOR IT IS ONLY THE SINEWS OF JUDGMENT THAT GIVE MERCY THE STRENGTH TO STAND.

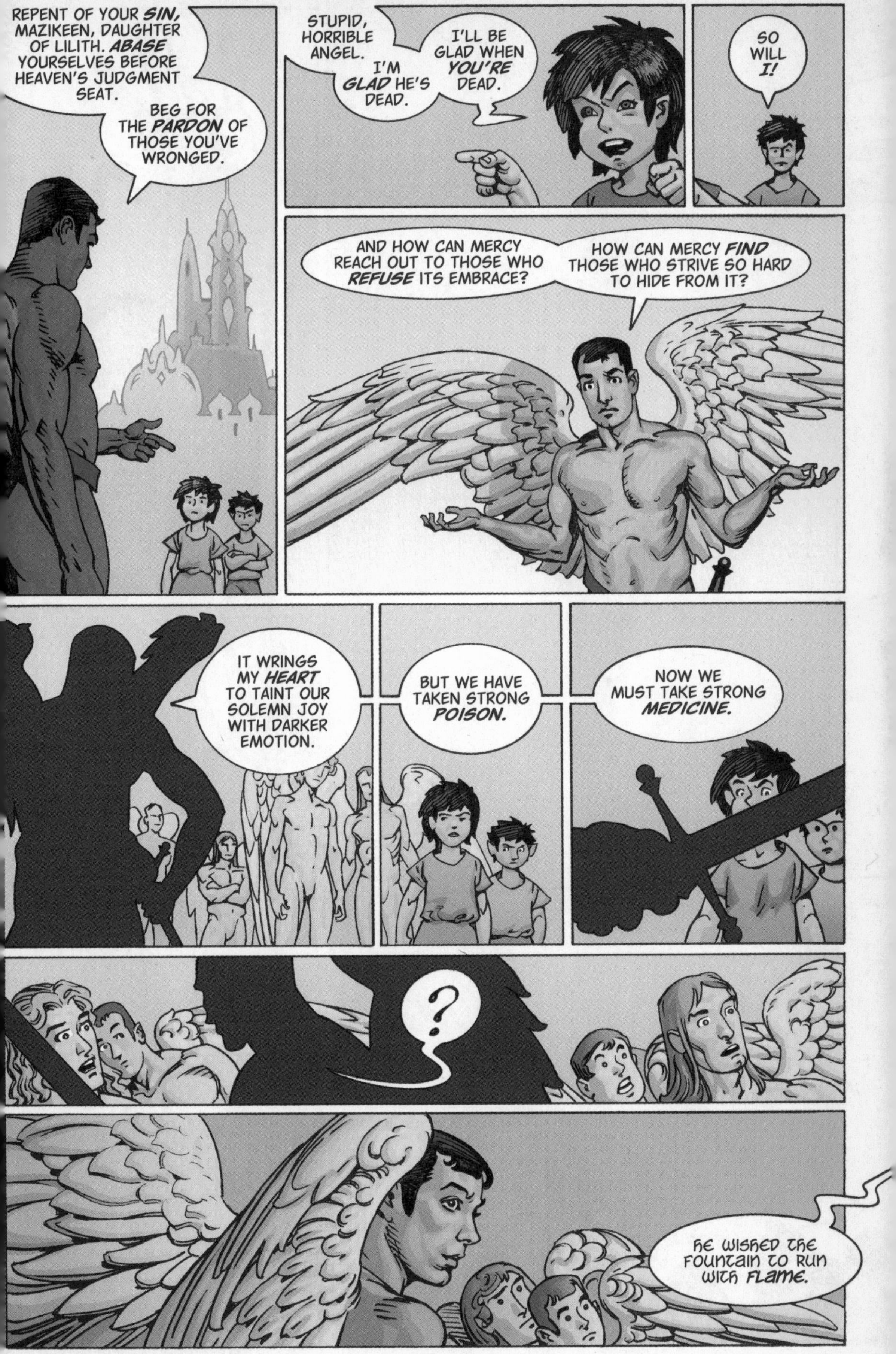
REPENT OF YOUR SIN, MAZIKEEN, DAUGHTER OF LILITH. ABASE YOURSELVES BEFORE HEAVEN'S JUDGMENT SEAT.
BEG FOR THE PARDON OF THOSE YOU'VE WRONGED.
STUPID, HORRIBLE ANGEL.
I'M GLAD HE'S DEAD.
I'LL BE GLAD WHEN YOU'RE DEAD.
SO WILL I!
AND HOW CAN MERCY REACH OUT TO THOSE WHO REFUSE ITS EMBRACE?
HOW CAN MERCY FIND THOSE WHO STRIVE SO HARD TO HIDE FROM IT?
IT WRINGS MY HEART TO TAINT OUR SOLEMN JOY WITH DARKER EMOTION.
BUT WE HAVE TAKEN STRONG POISON.
NOW WE MUST TAKE STRONG MEDICINE.
?
HE WISHED THE FOUNTAIN TO RUN WITH FLAME.

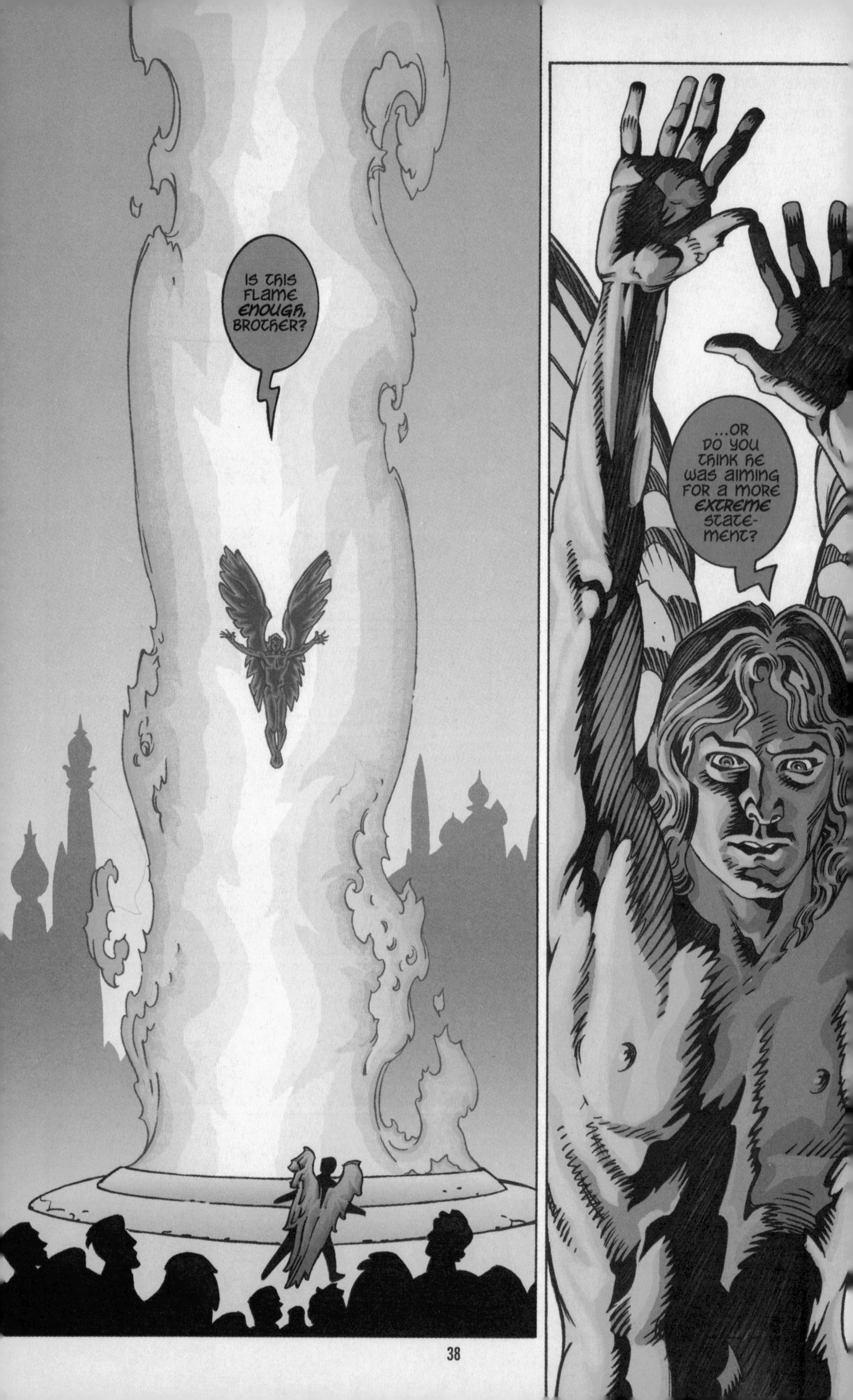
IS THIS FLAME ENOUGH, BROTHER?
...OR DO YOU THINK HE WAS AIMING FOR A MORE EXTREME STATE-MENT?

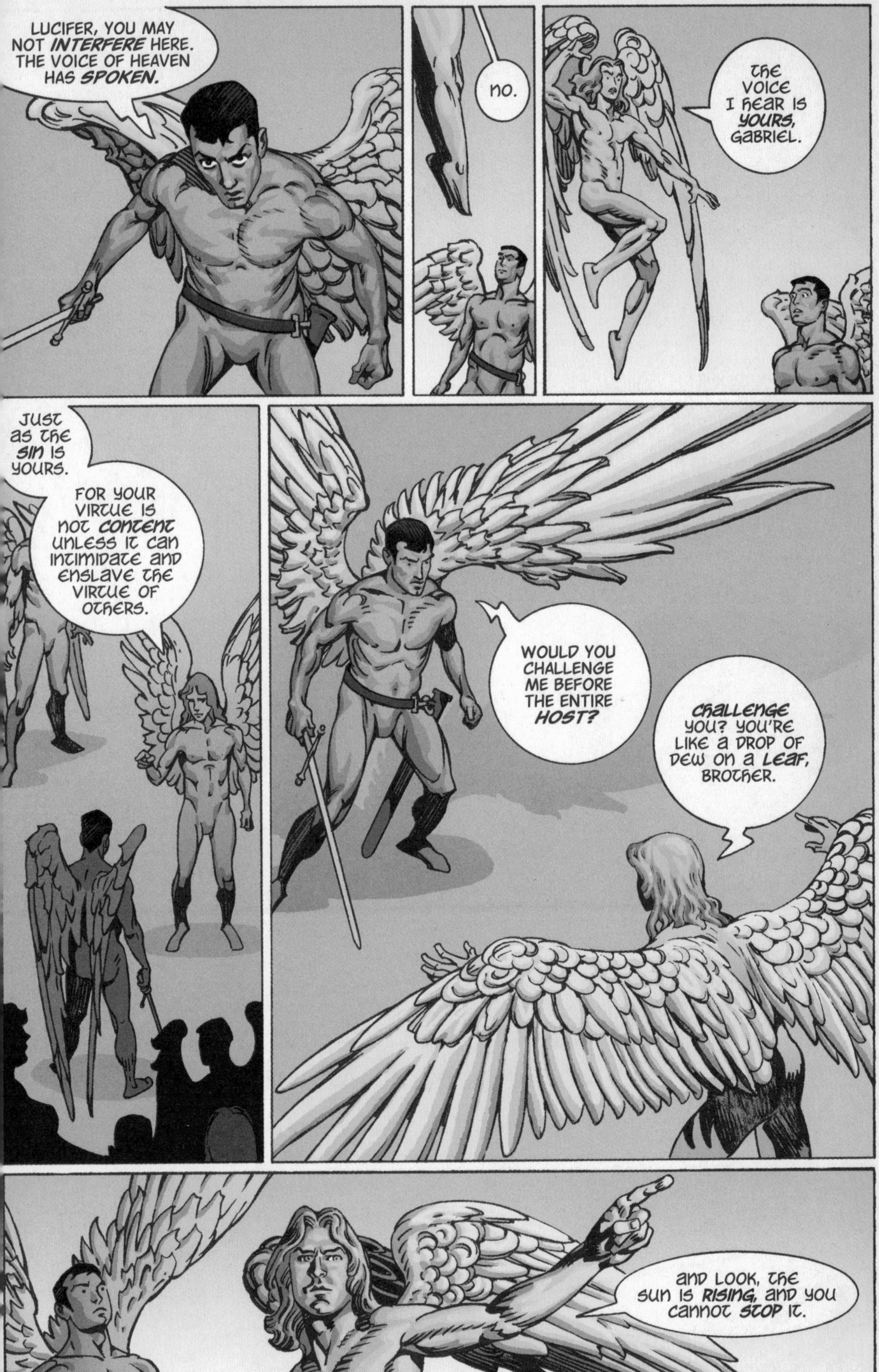
LUCIFER, YOU MAY NOT INTERFERE HERE. THE VOICE OF HEAVEN HAS SPOKEN.
NO.
THE VOICE I HEAR IS YOURS, GABRIEL.
JUST AS THE SIN IS YOURS.
FOR YOUR VIRTUE IS NOT CONTENT UNLESS IT CAN INTIMIDATE AND ENSLAVE THE VIRTUE OF OTHERS.
WOULD YOU CHALLENGE ME BEFORE THE ENTIRE HOST?
CHALLENGE YOU? YOU'RE LIKE A DROP OF DEW ON A LEAF, BROTHER.
AND LOOK, THE SUN IS RISING, AND YOU CANNOT STOP IT.

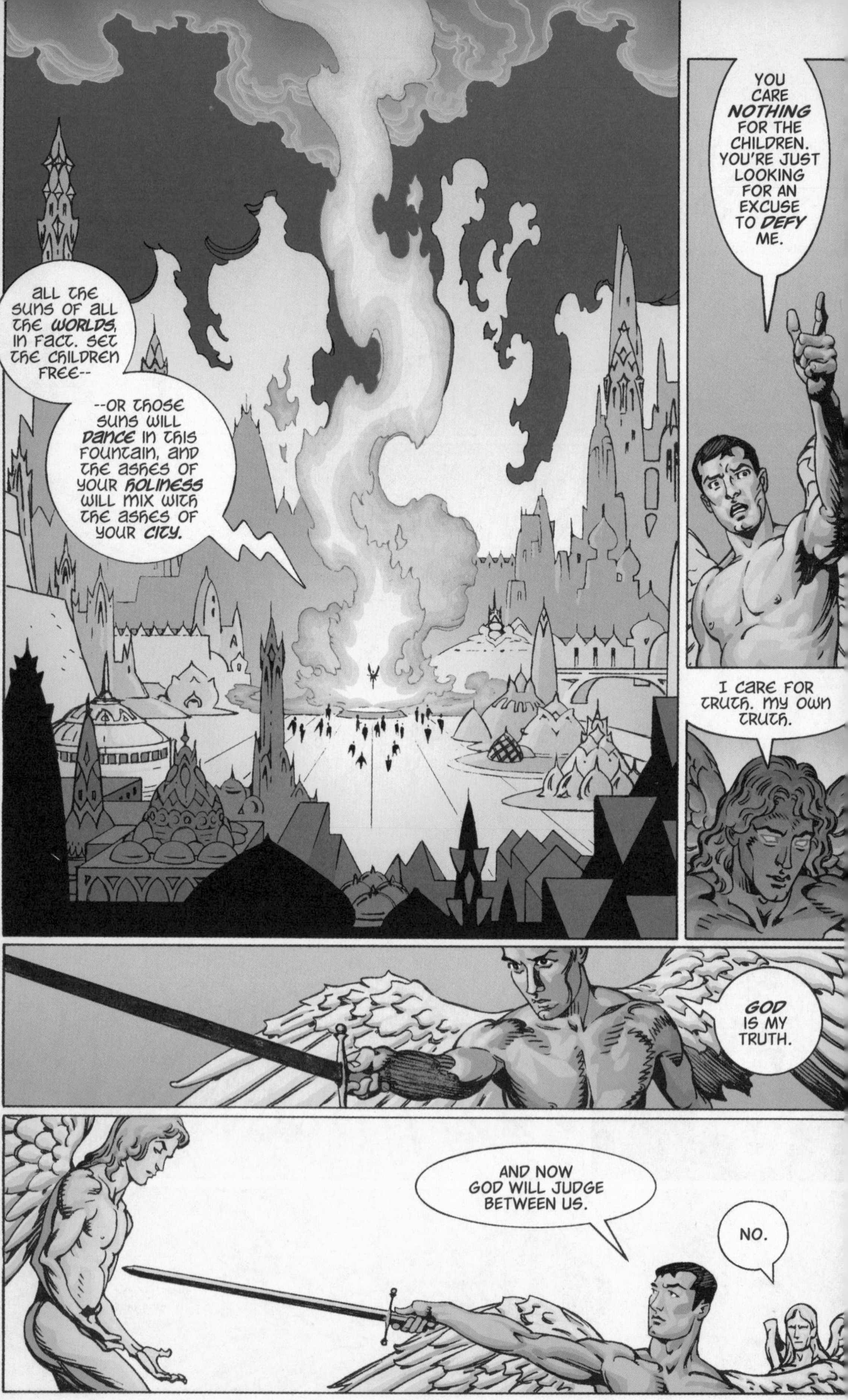
ALL THE SUNS OF ALL THE WORLDS, IN FACT. SET THE CHILDREN FREE--
--OR THOSE SUNS WILL DANCE IN THIS FOUNTAIN, AND THE ASHES OF YOUR HOLINESS WILL MIX WITH THE ASHES OF YOUR CITY.
YOU CARE NOTHING FOR THE CHILDREN. YOU'RE JUST LOOKING FOR AN EXCUSE TO DEFY ME.
I CARE FOR TRUTH. MY OWN TRUTH.
GOD IS MY TRUTH.
AND NOW GOD WILL JUDGE BETWEEN US.
NO.

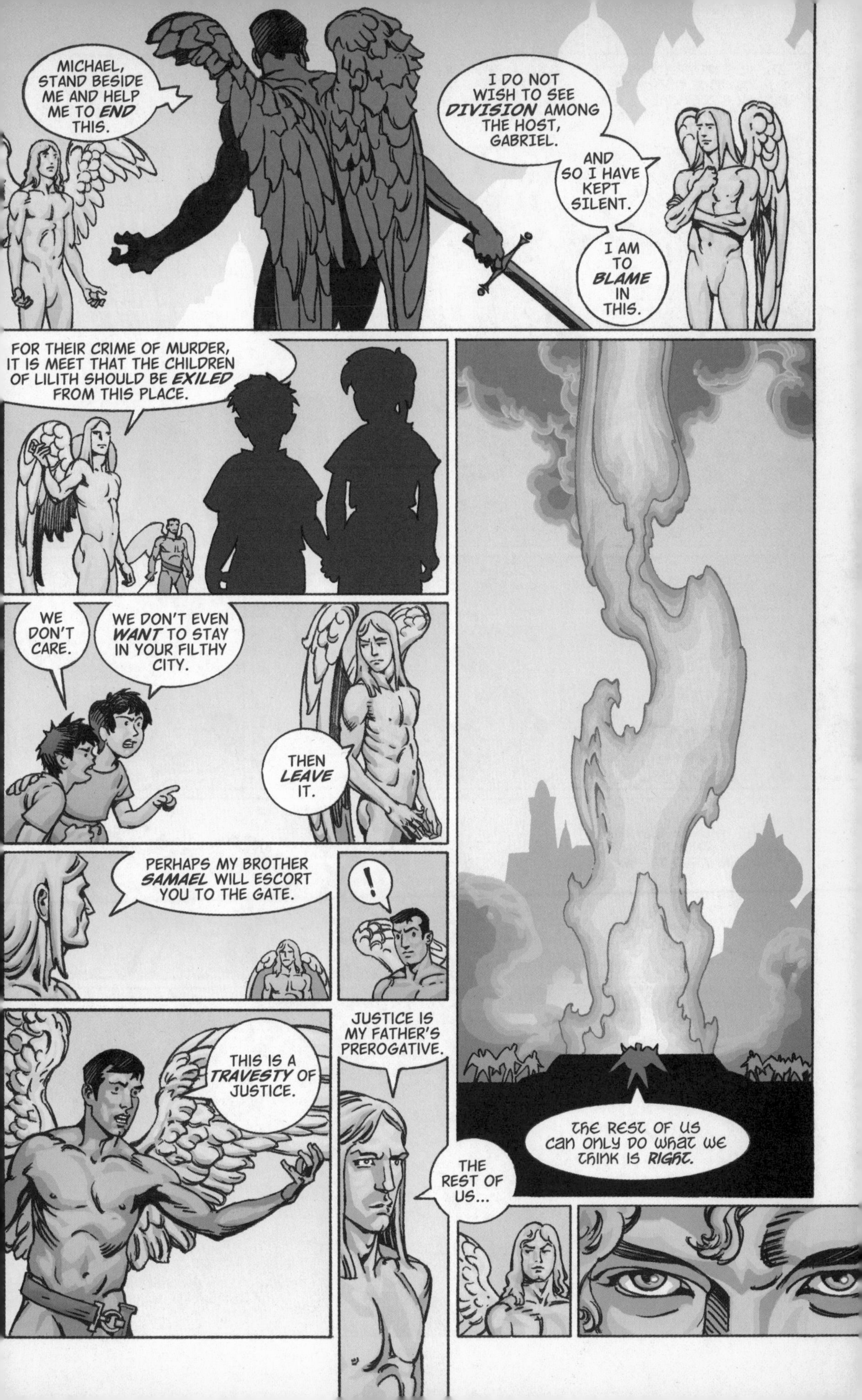
MICHAEL, STAND BESIDE ME AND HELP ME TO END THIS.
I DO NOT WISH TO SEE DIVISION AMONG THE HOST, GABRIEL.
AND SO I HAVE KEPT SILENT.
I AM TO BLAME IN THIS.
FOR THEIR CRIME OF MURDER, IT IS MEET THAT THE CHILDREN OF LILITH SHOULD BE EXILED FROM THIS PLACE.
WE DON'T CARE.
WE DON'T EVEN WANT TO STAY IN YOUR FILTHY CITY.
THEN LEAVE IT.
PERHAPS MY BROTHER SAMAEL WILL ESCORT YOU TO THE GATE.
!
THIS IS A TRAVESTY OF JUSTICE.
JUSTICE IS MY FATHER'S PREROGATIVE.
THE REST OF US...
THE REST OF US CAN ONLY DO WHAT WE THINK IS RIGHT.

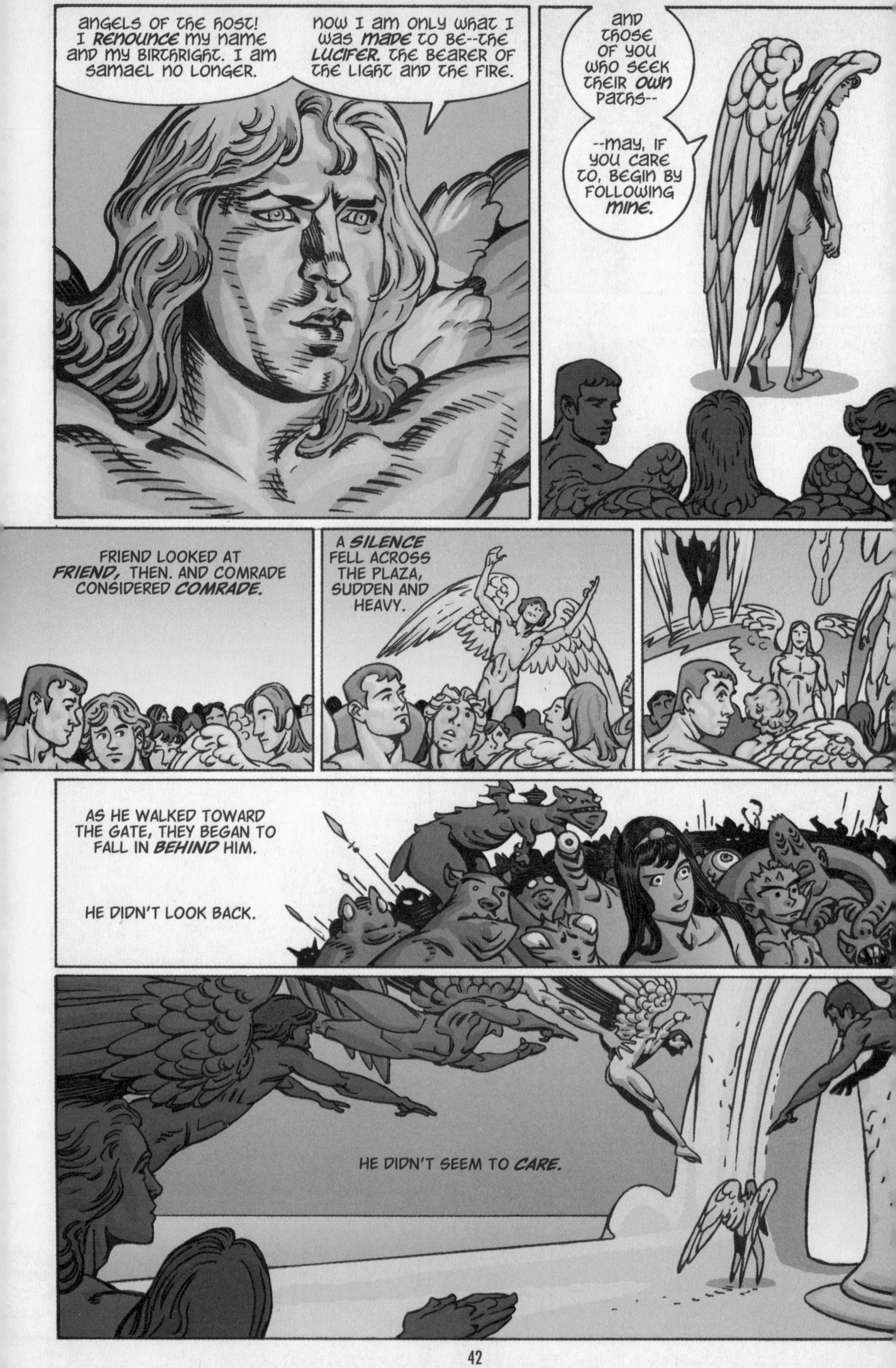
ANGELS OF THE HOST! I RENOUNCE MY NAME AND MY BIRTHRIGHT. I AM SAMAEL NO LONGER.
NOW I AM ONLY WHAT I WAS MADE TO BE--THE LUCIFER. THE BEARER OF THE LIGHT AND THE FIRE.
AND THOSE OF YOU WHO SEEK THEIR OWN PATHS--
--MAY, IF YOU CARE TO, BEGIN BY FOLLOWING MINE.
FRIEND LOOKED AT FRIEND, THEN. AND COMRADE CONSIDERED COMRADE.
A SILENCE FELL ACROSS THE PLAZA, SUDDEN AND HEAVY.
AS HE WALKED TOWARD THE GATE, THEY BEGAN TO FALL IN BEHIND HIM.
HE DIDN'T LOOK BACK.
HE DIDN'T SEEM TO CARE.

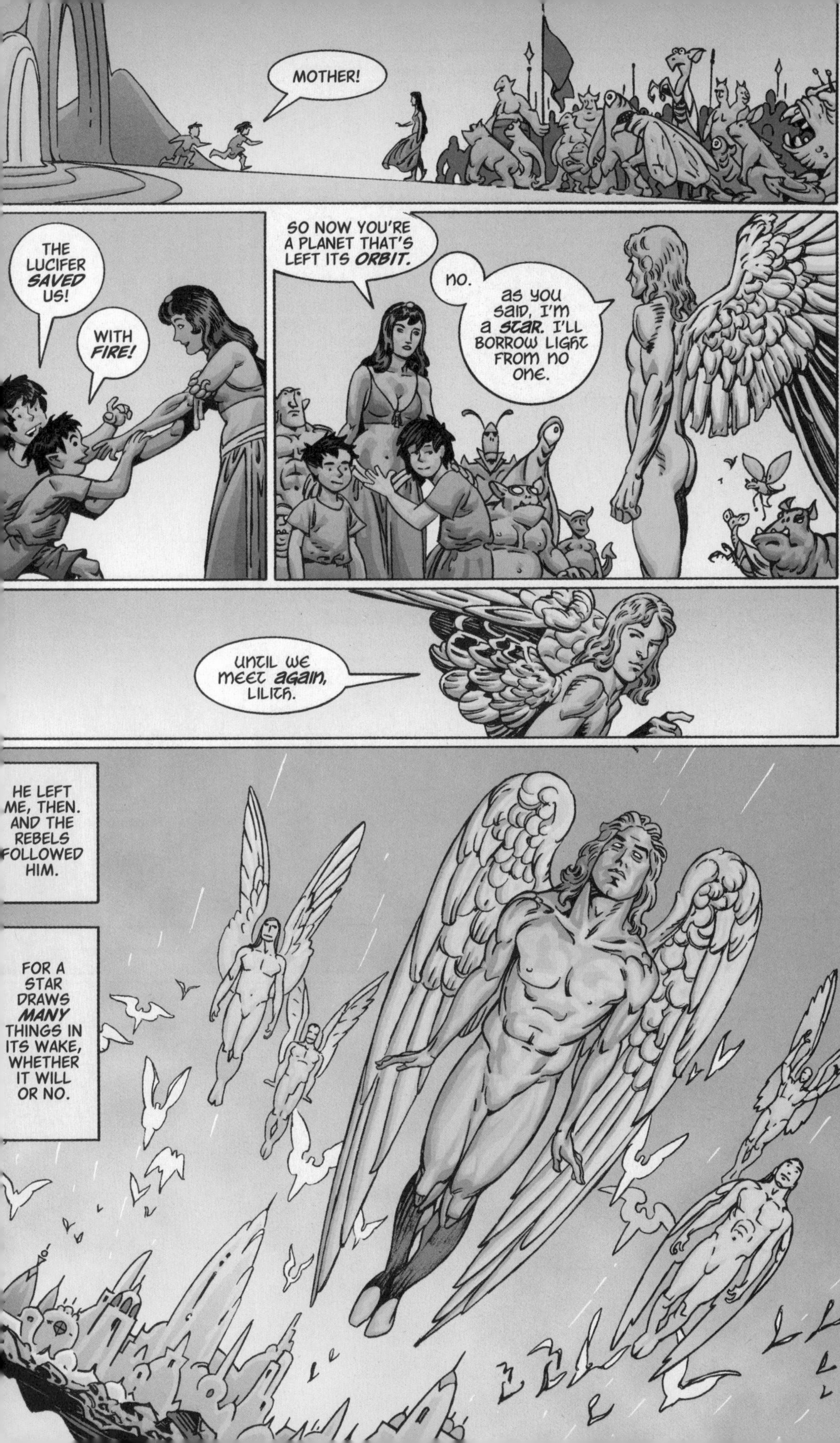
MOTHER!
THE LUCIFER SAVED US!
WITH FIRE!
SO NOW YOU'RE A PLANET THAT'S LEFT ITS ORBIT.
no.
as you said, I'm a star. I'll borrow light from no one.
until we meet again, Lilith.
HE LEFT ME, THEN. AND THE REBELS FOLLOWED HIM.
FOR A STAR DRAWS MANY THINGS IN ITS WAKE, WHETHER IT WILL OR NO.

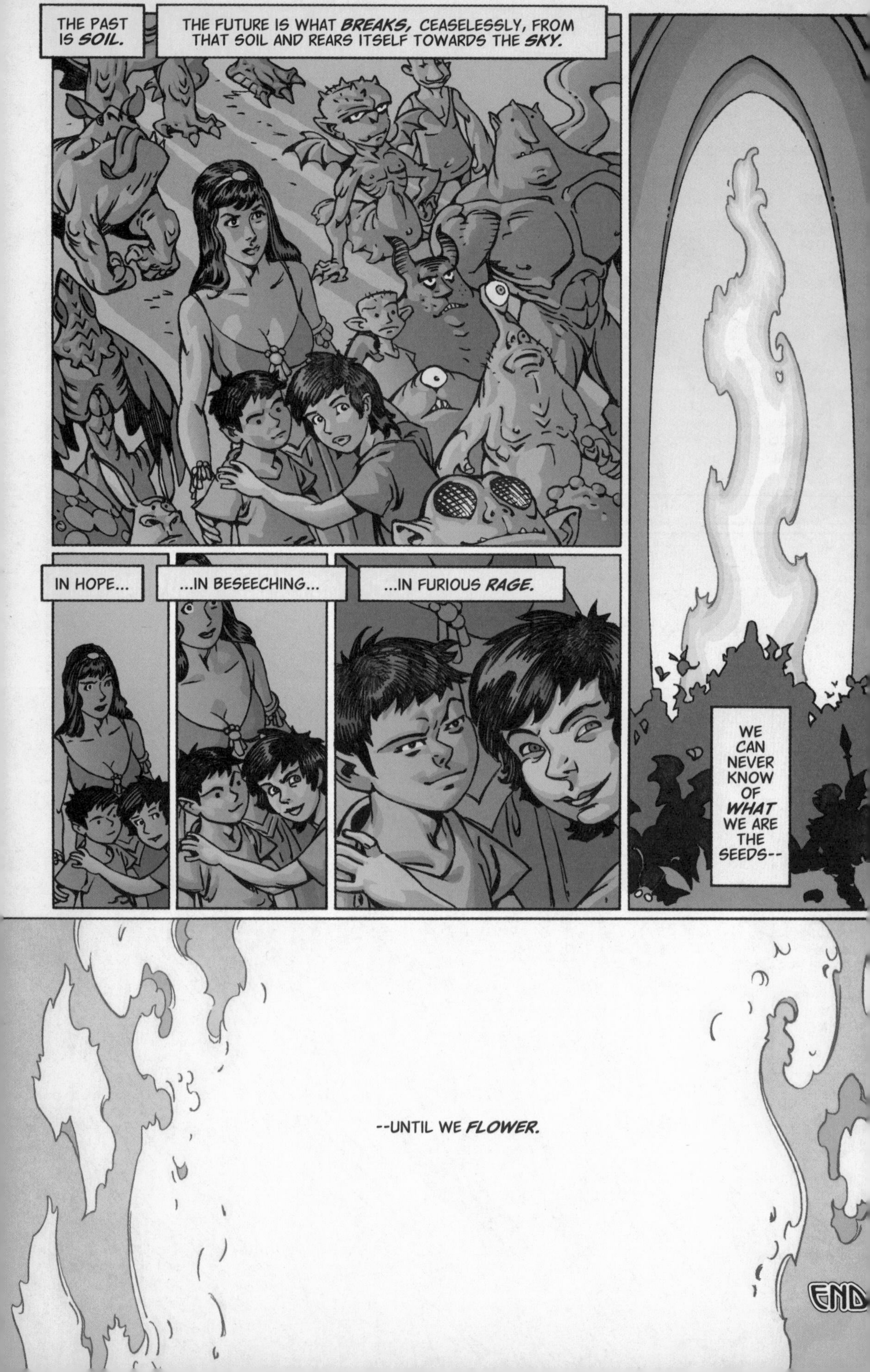
THE PAST IS SOIL.
THE FUTURE IS WHAT BREAKS, CEASELESSLY, FROM THAT SOIL AND REARS ITSELF TOWARDS THE SKY.
IN HOPE...
...IN BESEECHING...
...IN FURIOUS RAGE.
WE CAN NEVER KNOW OF WHAT WE ARE THE SEEDS--
--UNTIL WE FLOWER.
END

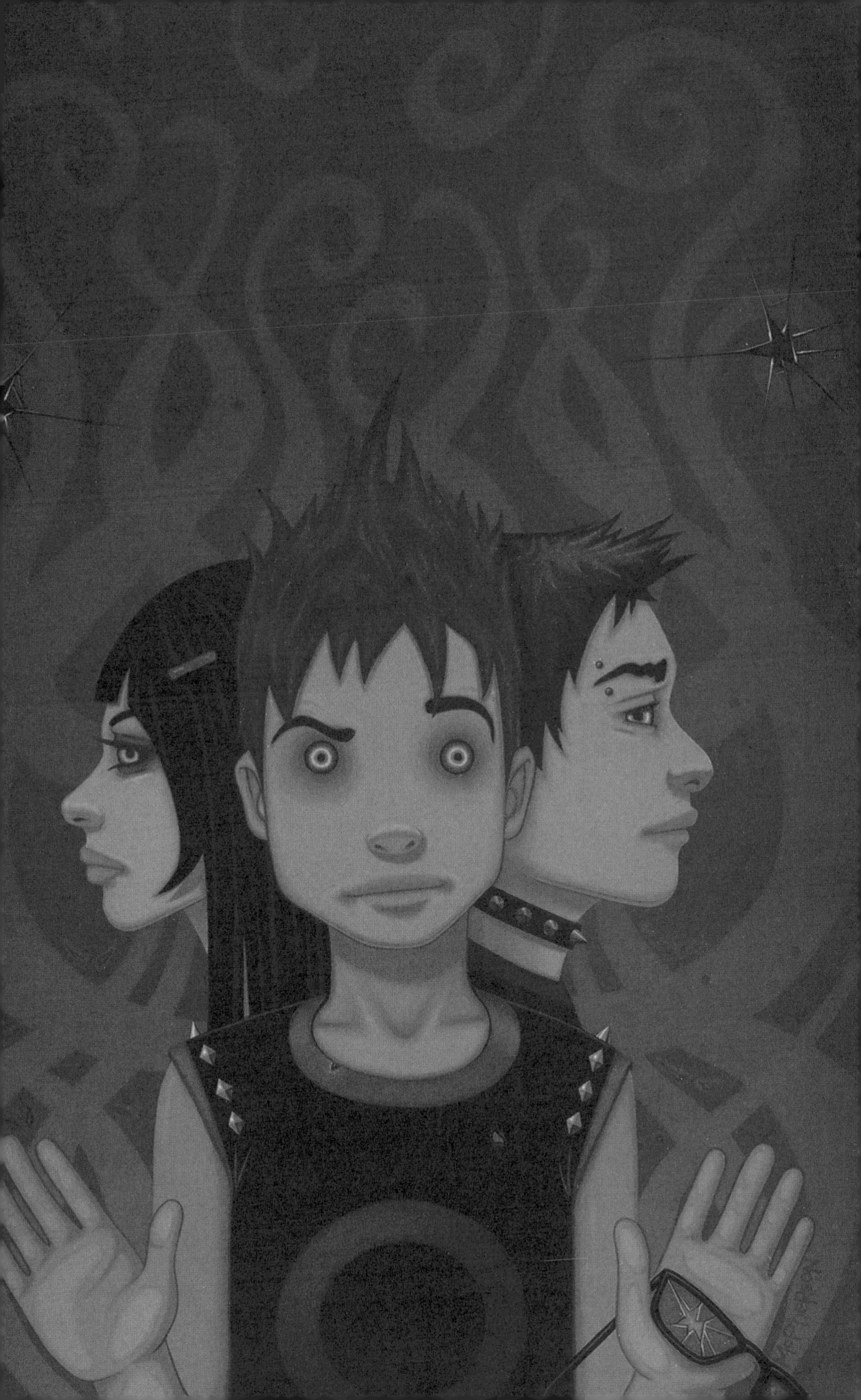

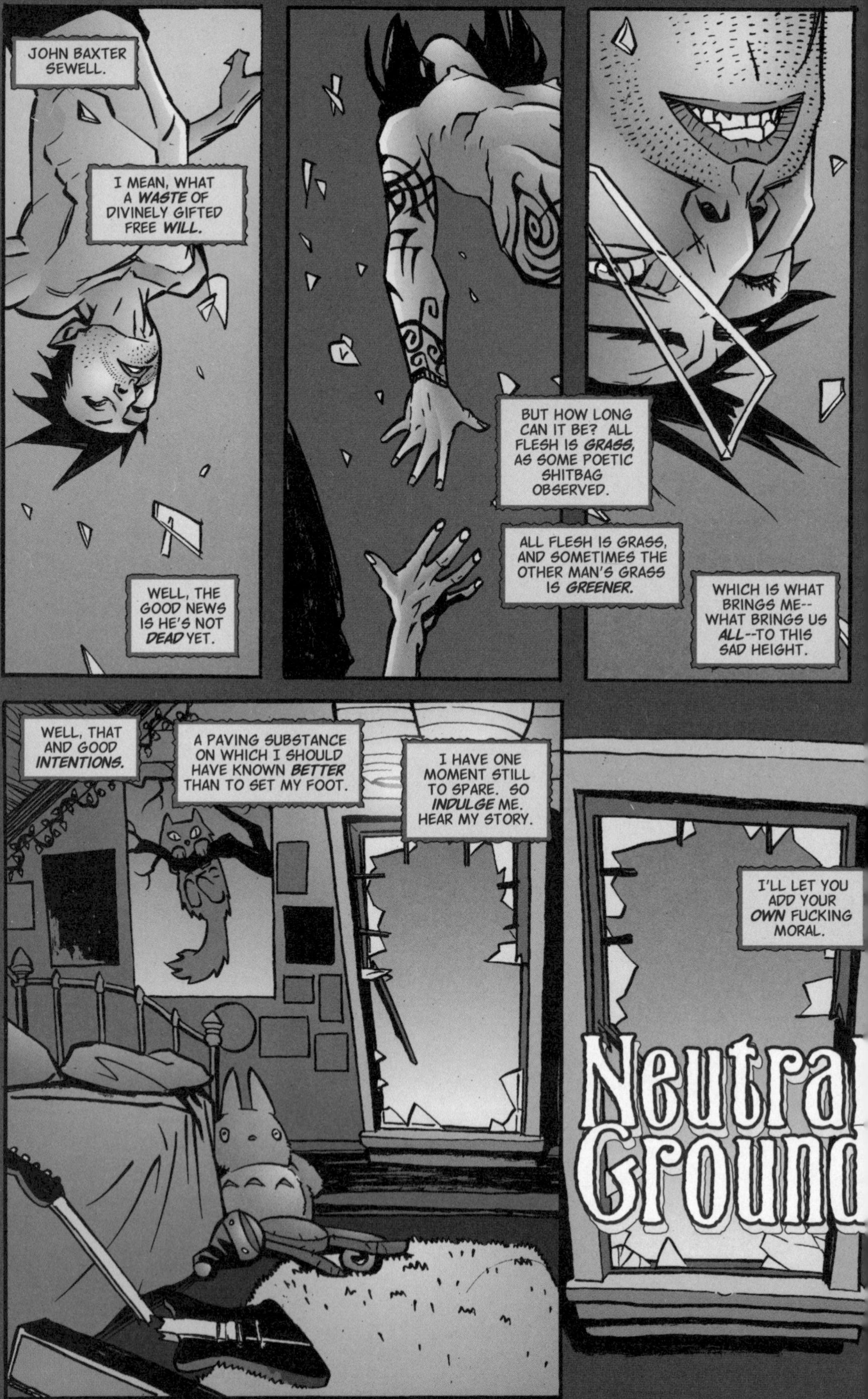
JOHN BAXTER SEWELL.
I MEAN, WHAT A WASTE OF DIVINELY GIFTED FREE WILL.
WELL, THE GOOD NEWS IS HE'S NOT DEAD YET.
BUT HOW LONG CAN IT BE? ALL FLESH IS GRASS, AS SOME POETIC SHITBAG OBSERVED.
ALL FLESH IS GRASS, AND SOMETIMES THE OTHER MAN'S GRASS IS GREENER.
WHICH IS WHAT BRINGS ME-- WHAT BRINGS US ALL--TO THIS SAD HEIGHT.
WELL, THAT AND GOOD INTENTIONS.
A PAVING SUBSTANCE ON WHICH I SHOULD HAVE KNOWN BETTER THAN TO SET MY FOOT.
I HAVE ONE MOMENT STILL TO SPARE. SO INDULGE ME. HEAR MY STORY.
I'LL LET YOU ADD YOUR OWN FUCKING MORAL.
Neutral Ground

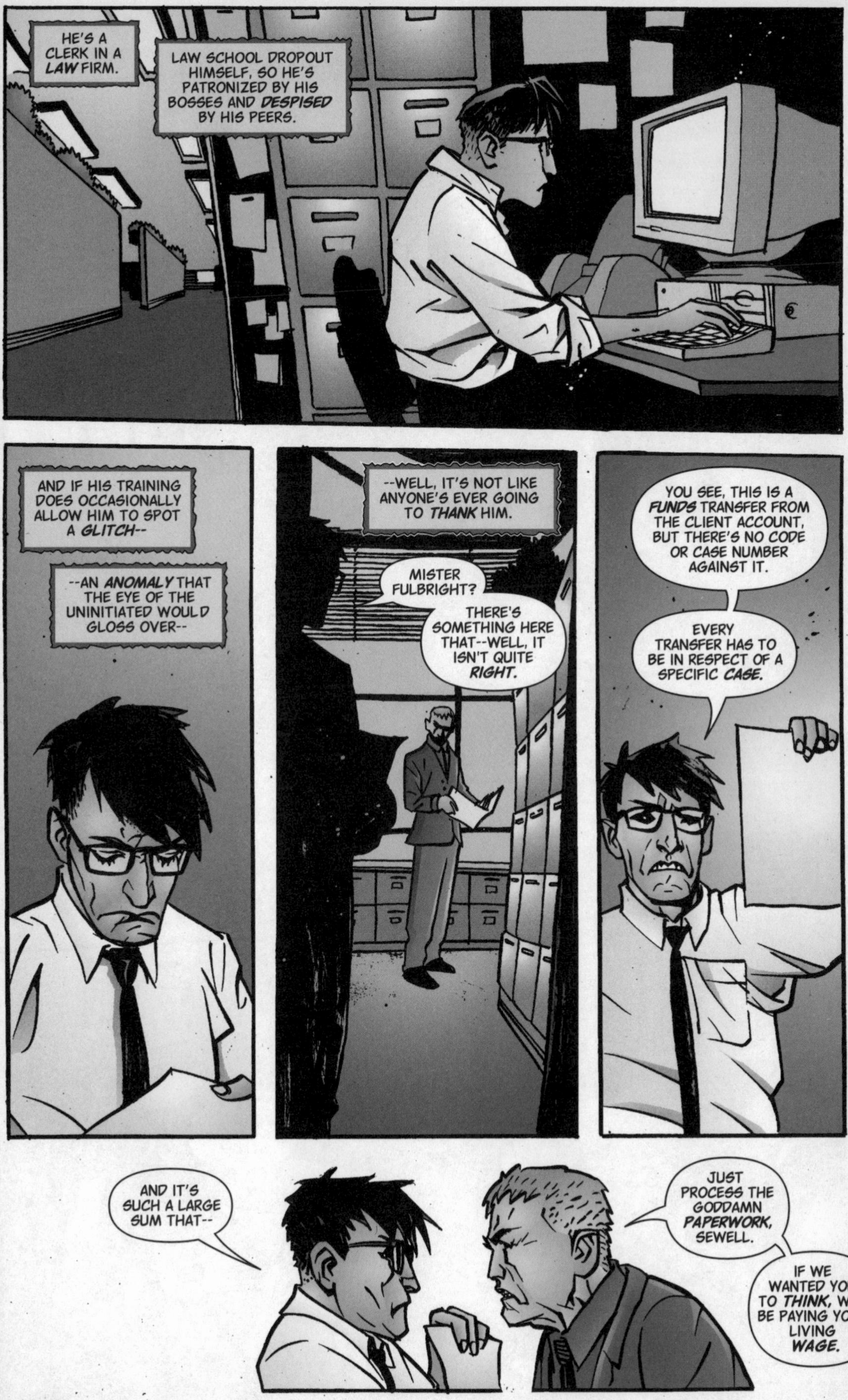
HE'S A CLERK IN A LAW FIRM.
LAW SCHOOL DROPOUT HIMSELF, SO HE'S PATRONIZED BY HIS BOSSES AND DESPISED BY HIS PEERS.
AND IF HIS TRAINING DOES OCCASIONALLY ALLOW HIM TO SPOT A GLITCH--
--AN ANOMALY THAT THE EYE OF THE UNINITIATED WOULD GLOSS OVER--
--WELL, IT'S NOT LIKE ANYONE'S EVER GOING TO THANK HIM.
MISTER FULBRIGHT?
THERE'S SOMETHING HERE THAT--WELL, IT ISN'T QUITE RIGHT.
YOU SEE, THIS IS A FUNDS TRANSFER FROM THE CLIENT ACCOUNT, BUT THERE'S NO CODE OR CASE NUMBER AGAINST IT.
EVERY TRANSFER HAS TO BE IN RESPECT OF A SPECIFIC CASE.
AND IT'S SUCH A LARGE SUM THAT--
JUST PROCESS THE GODDAMN PAPERWORK, SEWELL.
IF WE WANTED YOU TO THINK, WE'D BE PAYING YOU A LIVING WAGE.

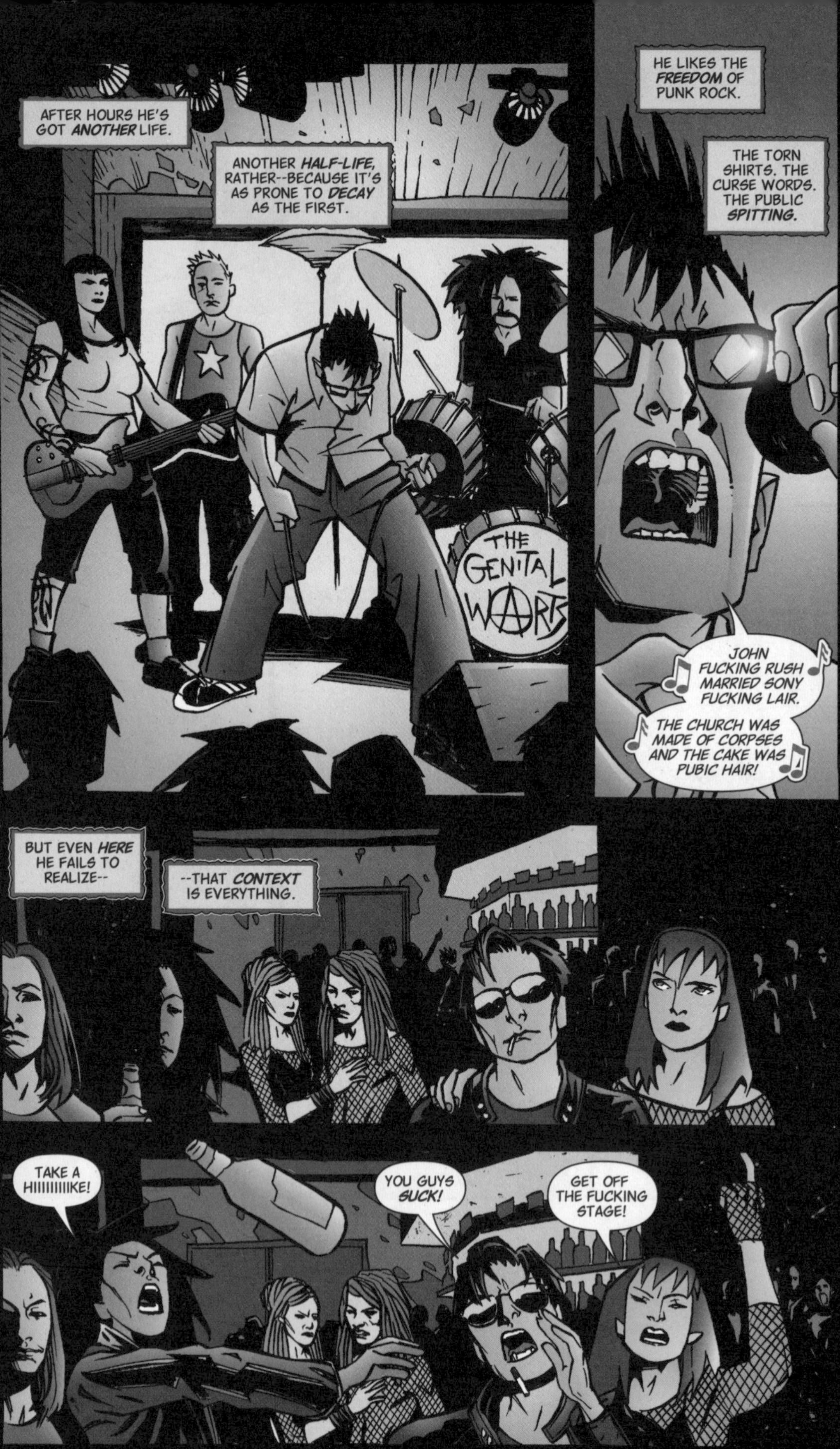
AFTER HOURS HE'S GOT ANOTHER LIFE.
ANOTHER HALF-LIFE, RATHER--BECAUSE IT'S AS PRONE TO DECAY AS THE FIRST.
THE GENITAL WARTS
HE LIKES THE FREEDOM OF PUNK ROCK.
THE TORN SHIRTS. THE CURSE WORDS. THE PUBLIC SPITTING.
JOHN FUCKING RUSH MARRIED SONY FUCKING LAIR.
THE CHURCH WAS MADE OF CORPSES AND THE CAKE WAS PUBIC HAIR!
BUT EVEN HERE HE FAILS TO REALIZE--
--THAT CONTEXT IS EVERYTHING.
TAKE A HIIIIIIIIKE!
YOU GUYS SUCK!
GET OFF THE FUCKING STAGE!

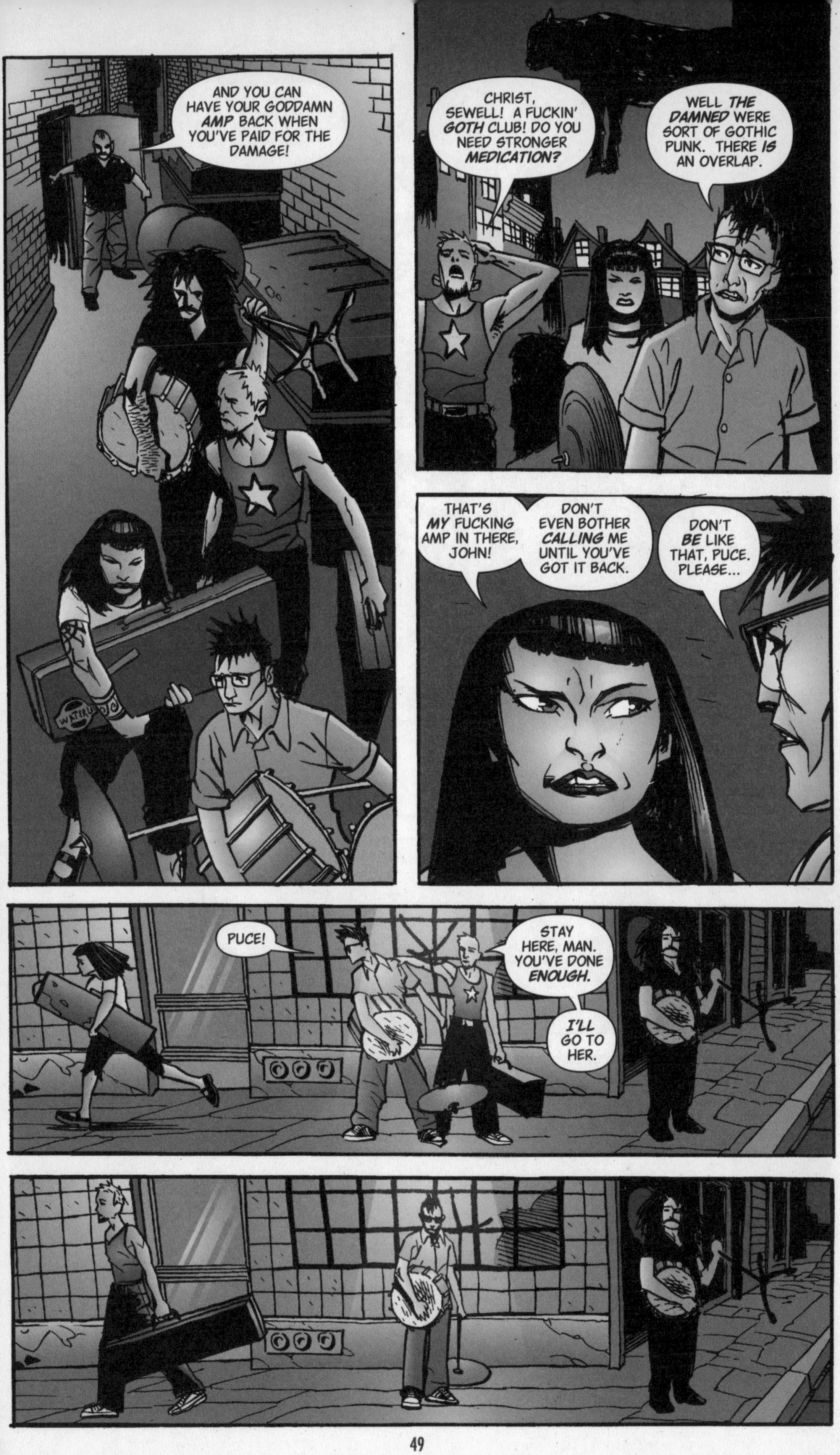
AND YOU CAN HAVE YOUR GODDAMN AMP BACK WHEN YOU'VE PAID FOR THE DAMAGE!
CHRIST, SEWELL! A FUCKIN' GOTH CLUB! DO YOU NEED STRONGER MEDICATION?
WELL THE DAMNED WERE SORT OF GOTHIC PUNK. THERE IS AN OVERLAP.
THAT'S MY FUCKING AMP IN THERE, JOHN!
DON'T EVEN BOTHER CALLING ME UNTIL YOU'VE GOT IT BACK.
DON'T BE LIKE THAT, PUCE. PLEASE...
PUCE!
STAY HERE, MAN. YOU'VE DONE ENOUGH.
I'LL GO TO HER.

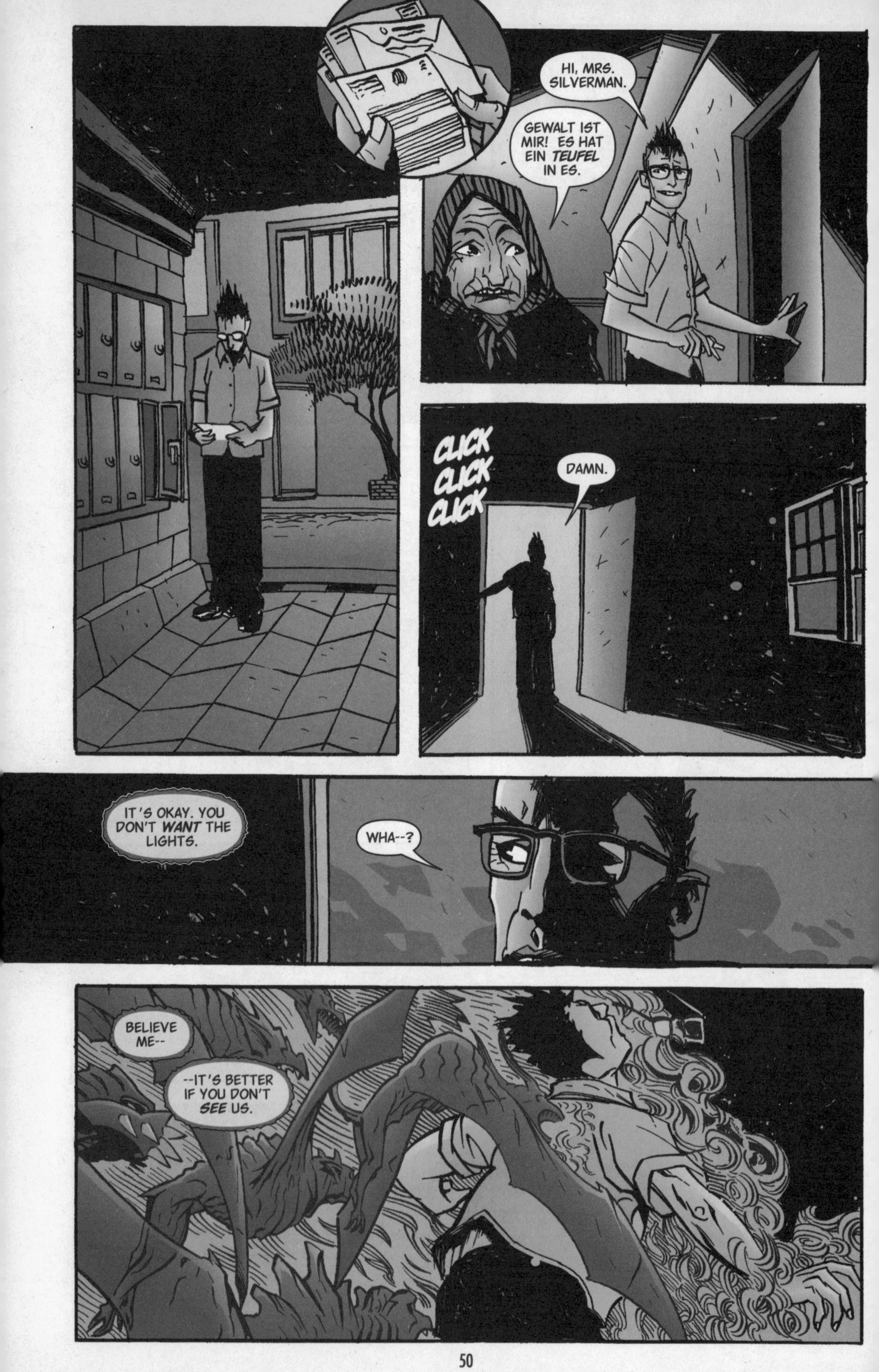

HI, MRS. SILVERMAN.
GEWALT IST MIR! ES HAT EIN *TEUFEL* IN ES.
CLICK CLICK CLICK
DAMN.
IT'S OKAY. YOU DON'T *WANT* THE LIGHTS.
WHA--?
BELIEVE ME--
--IT'S BETTER IF YOU DON'T *SEE* US.

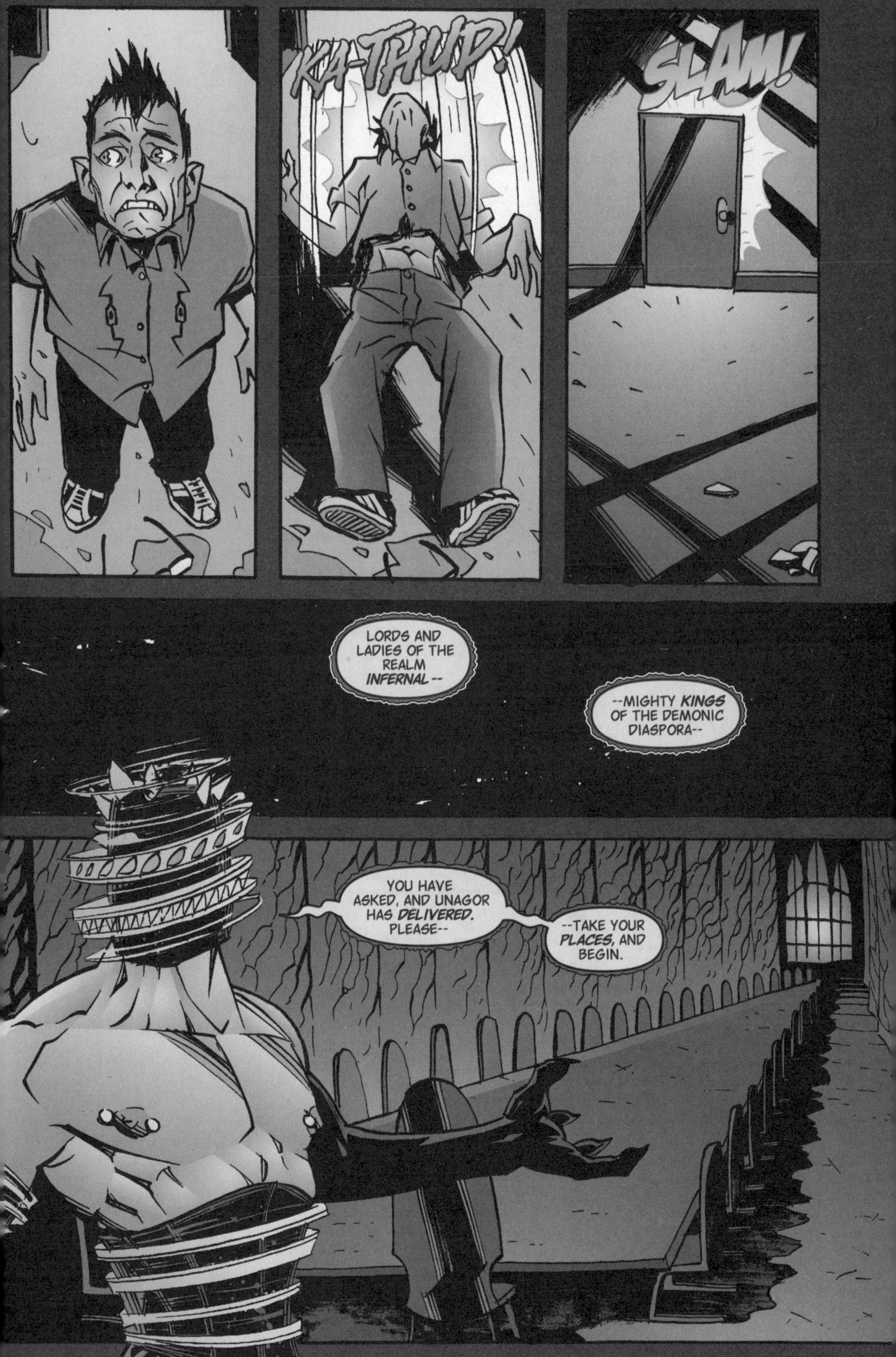
KA-THUD!
SLAM!
LORDS AND LADIES OF THE REALM INFERNAL--
--MIGHTY KINGS OF THE DEMONIC DIASPORA--
YOU HAVE ASKED, AND UNAGOR HAS DELIVERED. PLEASE--
--TAKE YOUR PLACES, AND BEGIN.

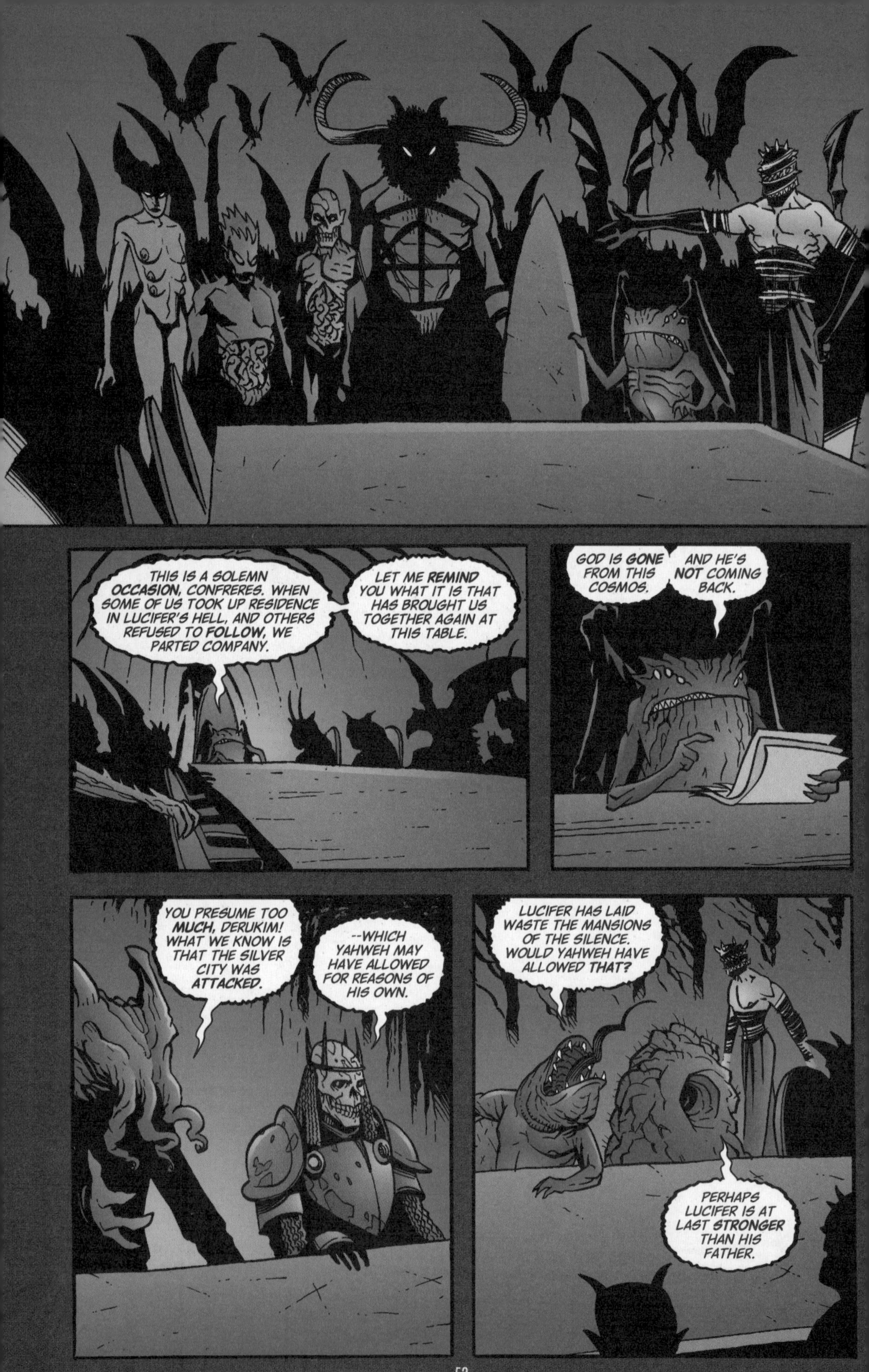

THIS IS A SOLEMN OCCASION, CONFRERES. WHEN SOME OF US TOOK UP RESIDENCE IN LUCIFER'S HELL, AND OTHERS REFUSED TO FOLLOW, WE PARTED COMPANY.
LET ME REMIND YOU WHAT IT IS THAT HAS BROUGHT US TOGETHER AGAIN AT THIS TABLE.
GOD IS GONE FROM THIS COSMOS.
AND HE'S NOT COMING BACK.
YOU PRESUME TOO MUCH, DERUKIM! WHAT WE KNOW IS THAT THE SILVER CITY WAS ATTACKED.
--WHICH YAHWEH MAY HAVE ALLOWED FOR REASONS OF HIS OWN.
LUCIFER HAS LAID WASTE THE MANSIONS OF THE SILENCE. WOULD YAHWEH HAVE ALLOWED THAT?
PERHAPS LUCIFER IS AT LAST STRONGER THAN HIS FATHER.

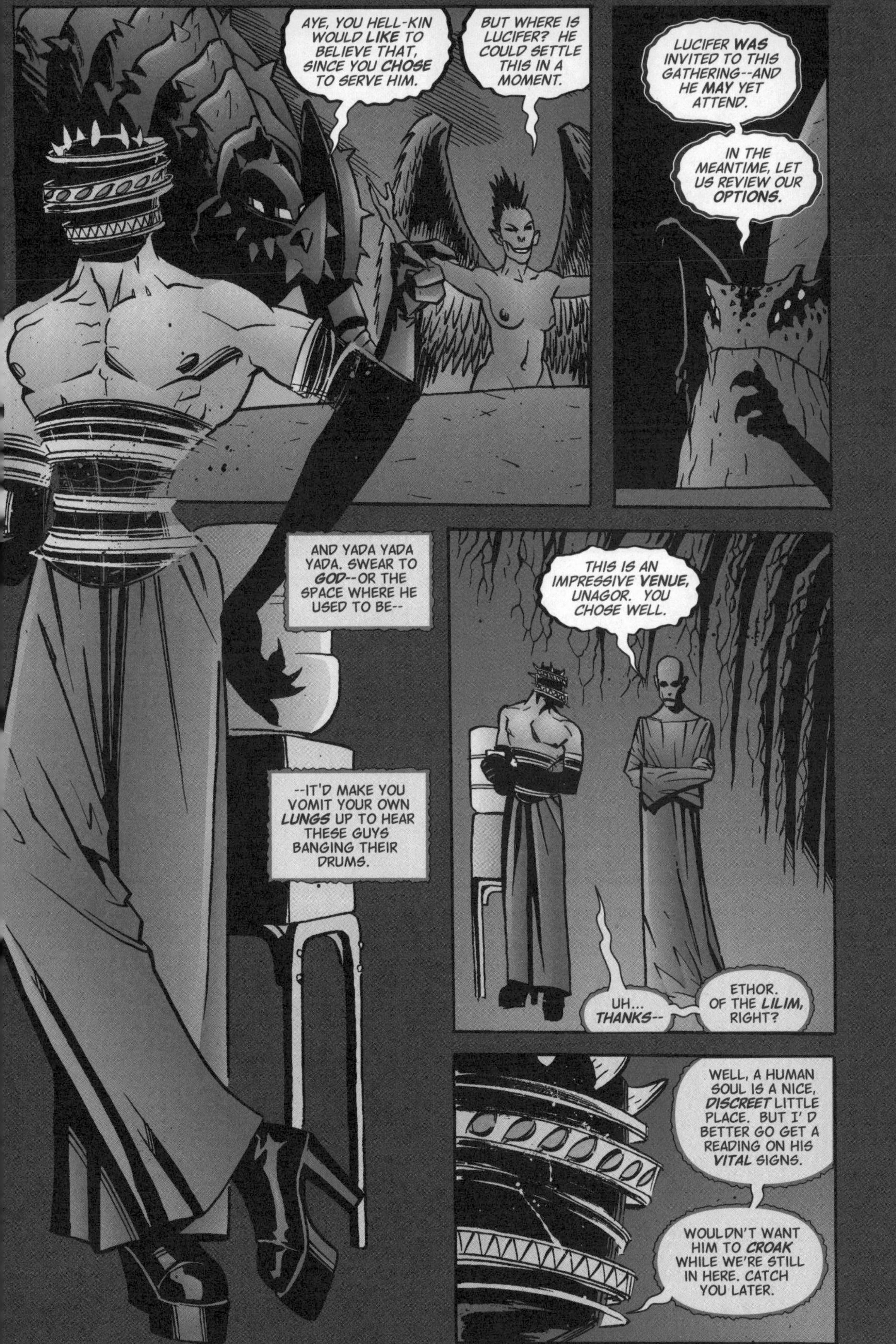
AYE, YOU HELL-KIN WOULD LIKE TO BELIEVE THAT, SINCE YOU CHOSE TO SERVE HIM.
BUT WHERE IS LUCIFER? HE COULD SETTLE THIS IN A MOMENT.
LUCIFER WAS INVITED TO THIS GATHERING--AND HE MAY YET ATTEND.
IN THE MEANTIME, LET US REVIEW OUR OPTIONS.
AND YADA YADA YADA. SWEAR TO GOD--OR THE SPACE WHERE HE USED TO BE--
--IT'D MAKE YOU VOMIT YOUR OWN LUNGS UP TO HEAR THESE GUYS BANGING THEIR DRUMS.
THIS IS AN IMPRESSIVE VENUE, UNAGOR. YOU CHOSE WELL.
UH... THANKS--
ETHOR. OF THE LILIM, RIGHT?
WELL, A HUMAN SOUL IS A NICE, DISCREET LITTLE PLACE. BUT I'D BETTER GO GET A READING ON HIS VITAL SIGNS.
WOULDN'T WANT HIM TO CROAK WHILE WE'RE STILL IN HERE. CATCH YOU LATER.

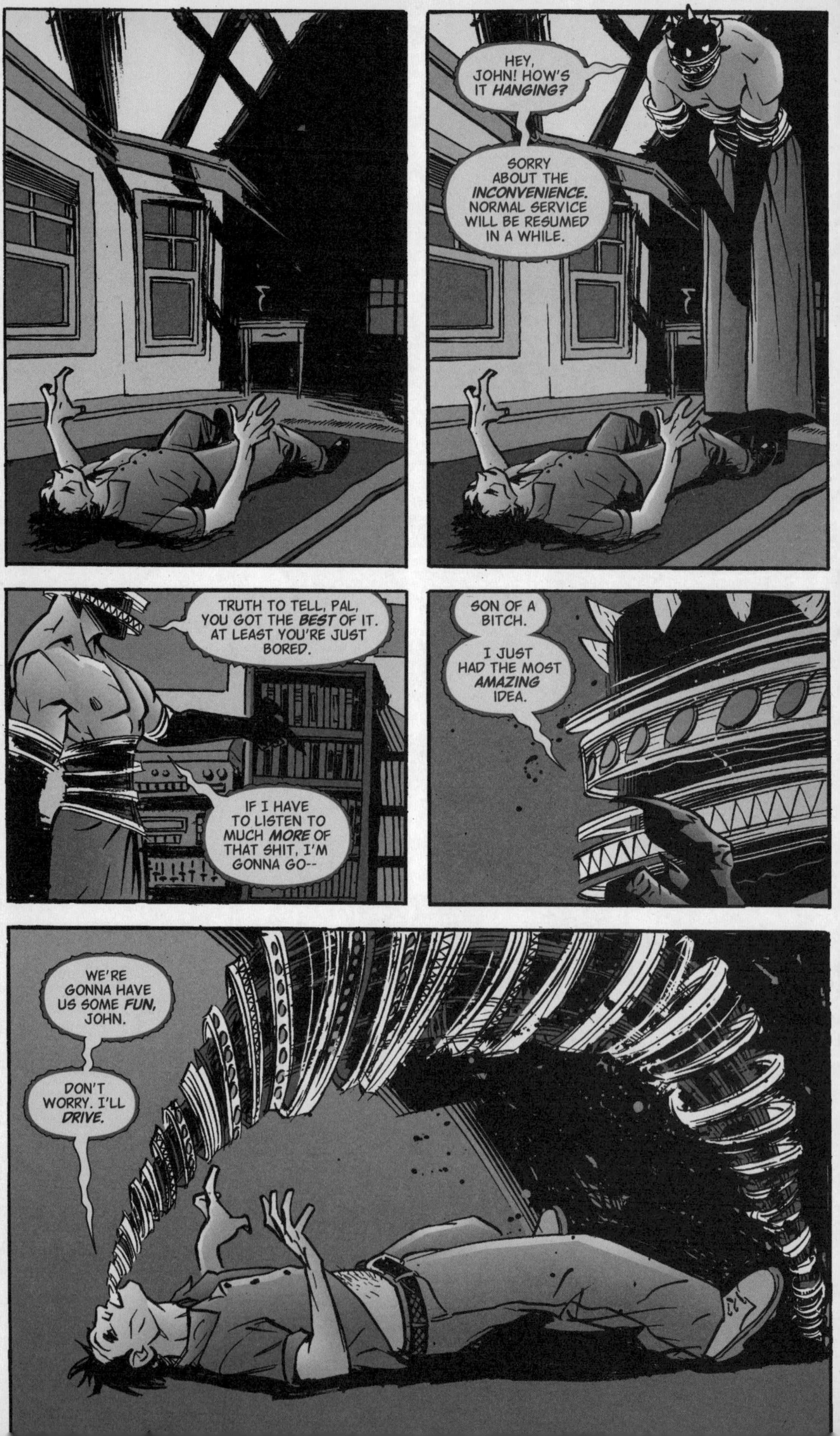
HEY, JOHN! HOW'S IT HANGING?
SORRY ABOUT THE INCONVENIENCE. NORMAL SERVICE WILL BE RESUMED IN A WHILE.
TRUTH TO TELL, PAL, YOU GOT THE BEST OF IT. AT LEAST YOU'RE JUST BORED.
IF I HAVE TO LISTEN TO MUCH MORE OF THAT SHIT, I'M GONNA GO--
SON OF A BITCH.
I JUST HAD THE MOST AMAZING IDEA.
WE'RE GONNA HAVE US SOME FUN, JOHN.
DON'T WORRY. I'LL DRIVE.

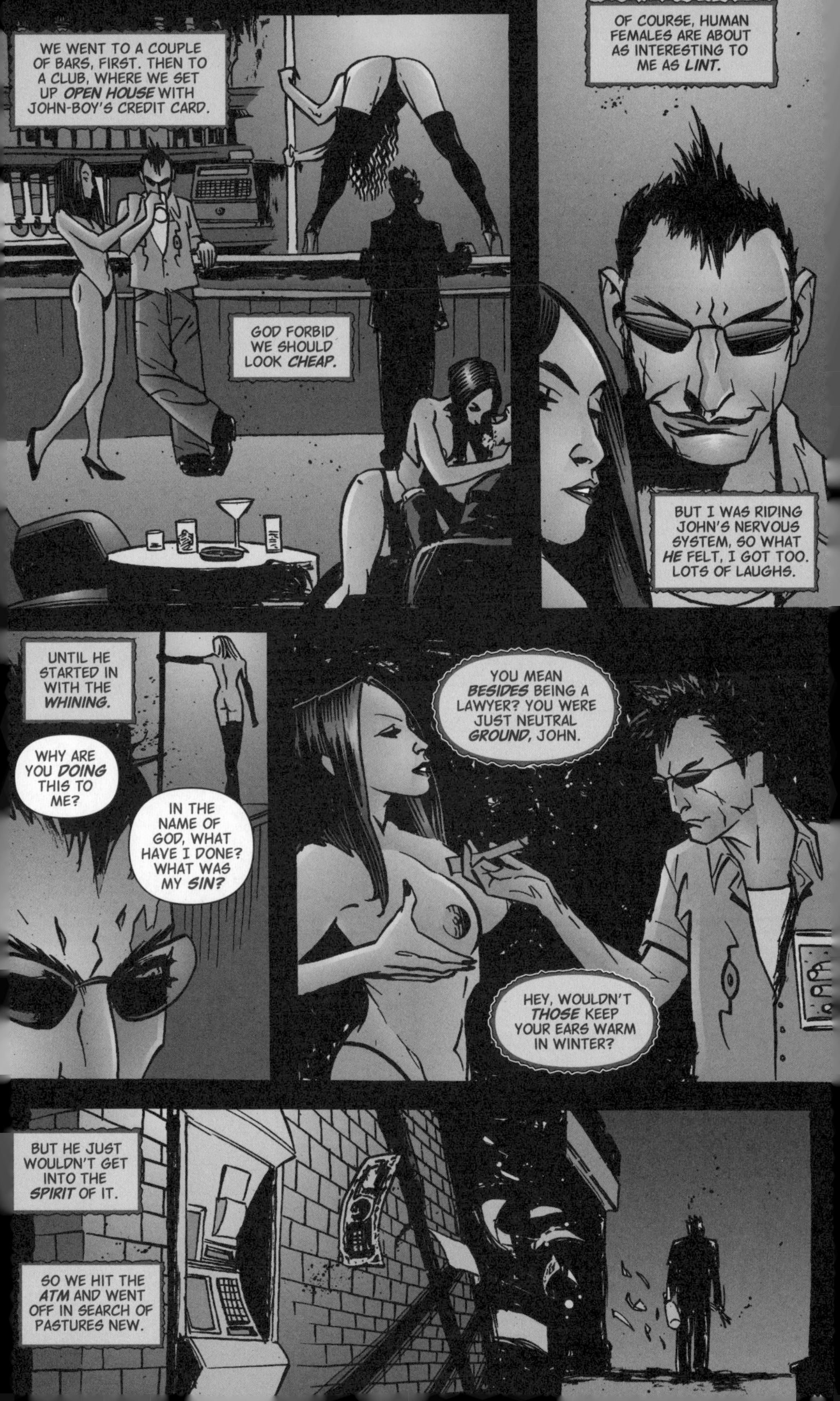
WE WENT TO A COUPLE OF BARS, FIRST. THEN TO A CLUB, WHERE WE SET UP OPEN HOUSE WITH JOHN-BOY'S CREDIT CARD.
GOD FORBID WE SHOULD LOOK CHEAP.
OF COURSE, HUMAN FEMALES ARE ABOUT AS INTERESTING TO ME AS LINT.
BUT I WAS RIDING JOHN'S NERVOUS SYSTEM, SO WHAT HE FELT, I GOT TOO. LOTS OF LAUGHS.
UNTIL HE STARTED IN WITH THE WHINING.
WHY ARE YOU DOING THIS TO ME?
IN THE NAME OF GOD, WHAT HAVE I DONE? WHAT WAS MY SIN?
YOU MEAN BESIDES BEING A LAWYER? YOU WERE JUST NEUTRAL GROUND, JOHN.
HEY, WOULDN'T THOSE KEEP YOUR EARS WARM IN WINTER?
BUT HE JUST WOULDN'T GET INTO THE SPIRIT OF IT.
SO WE HIT THE ATM AND WENT OFF IN SEARCH OF PASTURES NEW.

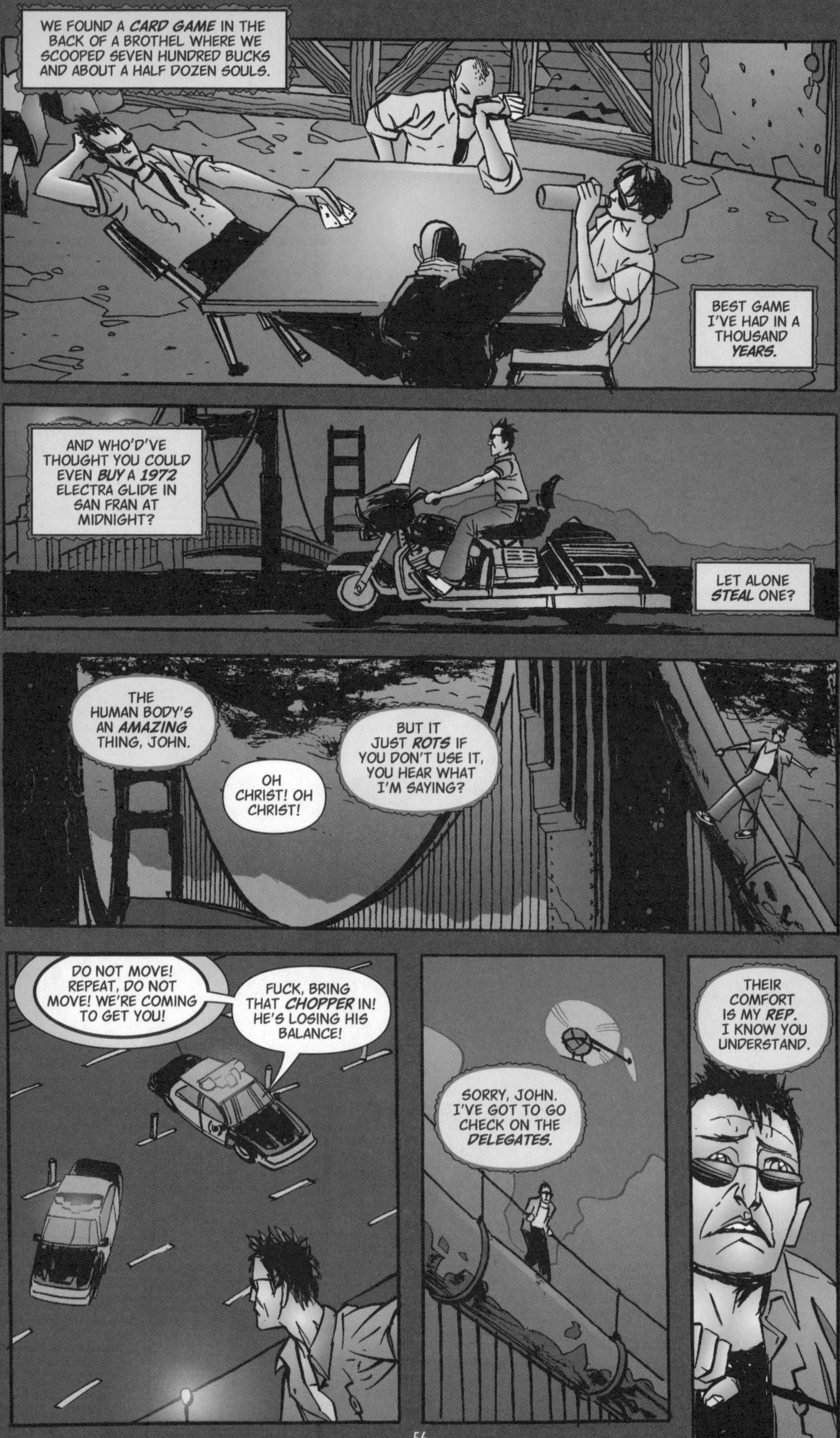

WE FOUND A CARD GAME IN THE BACK OF A BROTHEL WHERE WE SCOOPED SEVEN HUNDRED BUCKS AND ABOUT A HALF DOZEN SOULS.
BEST GAME I'VE HAD IN A THOUSAND YEARS.
AND WHO'D'VE THOUGHT YOU COULD EVEN BUY A 1972 ELECTRA GLIDE IN SAN FRAN AT MIDNIGHT?
LET ALONE STEAL ONE?
THE HUMAN BODY'S AN AMAZING THING, JOHN.
OH CHRIST! OH CHRIST!
BUT IT JUST ROTS IF YOU DON'T USE IT, YOU HEAR WHAT I'M SAYING?
DO NOT MOVE! REPEAT, DO NOT MOVE! WE'RE COMING TO GET YOU!
FUCK, BRING THAT CHOPPER IN! HE'S LOSING HIS BALANCE!
SORRY, JOHN. I'VE GOT TO GO CHECK ON THE DELEGATES.
THEIR COMFORT IS MY REP. I KNOW YOU UNDERSTAND.

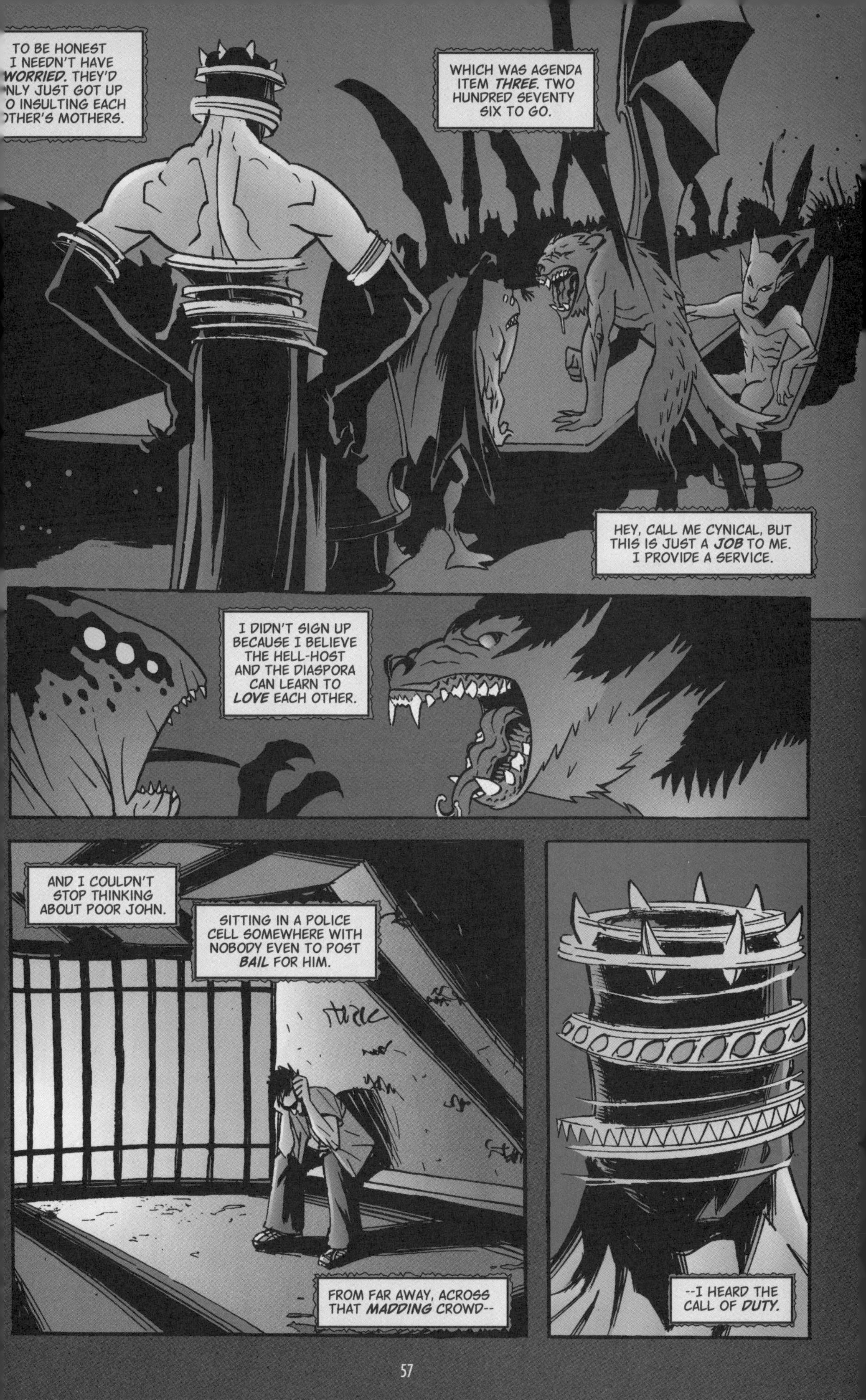

TO BE HONEST I NEEDN'T HAVE WORRIED. THEY'D NLY JUST GOT UP O INSULTING EACH THER'S MOTHERS.
WHICH WAS AGENDA ITEM THREE. TWO HUNDRED SEVENTY SIX TO GO.
HEY, CALL ME CYNICAL, BUT THIS IS JUST A JOB TO ME. I PROVIDE A SERVICE.
I DIDN'T SIGN UP BECAUSE I BELIEVE THE HELL-HOST AND THE DIASPORA CAN LEARN TO LOVE EACH OTHER.
AND I COULDN'T STOP THINKING ABOUT POOR JOHN.
SITTING IN A POLICE CELL SOMEWHERE WITH NOBODY EVEN TO POST BAIL FOR HIM.
FROM FAR AWAY, ACROSS THAT MADDING CROWD--
--I HEARD THE CALL OF DUTY.

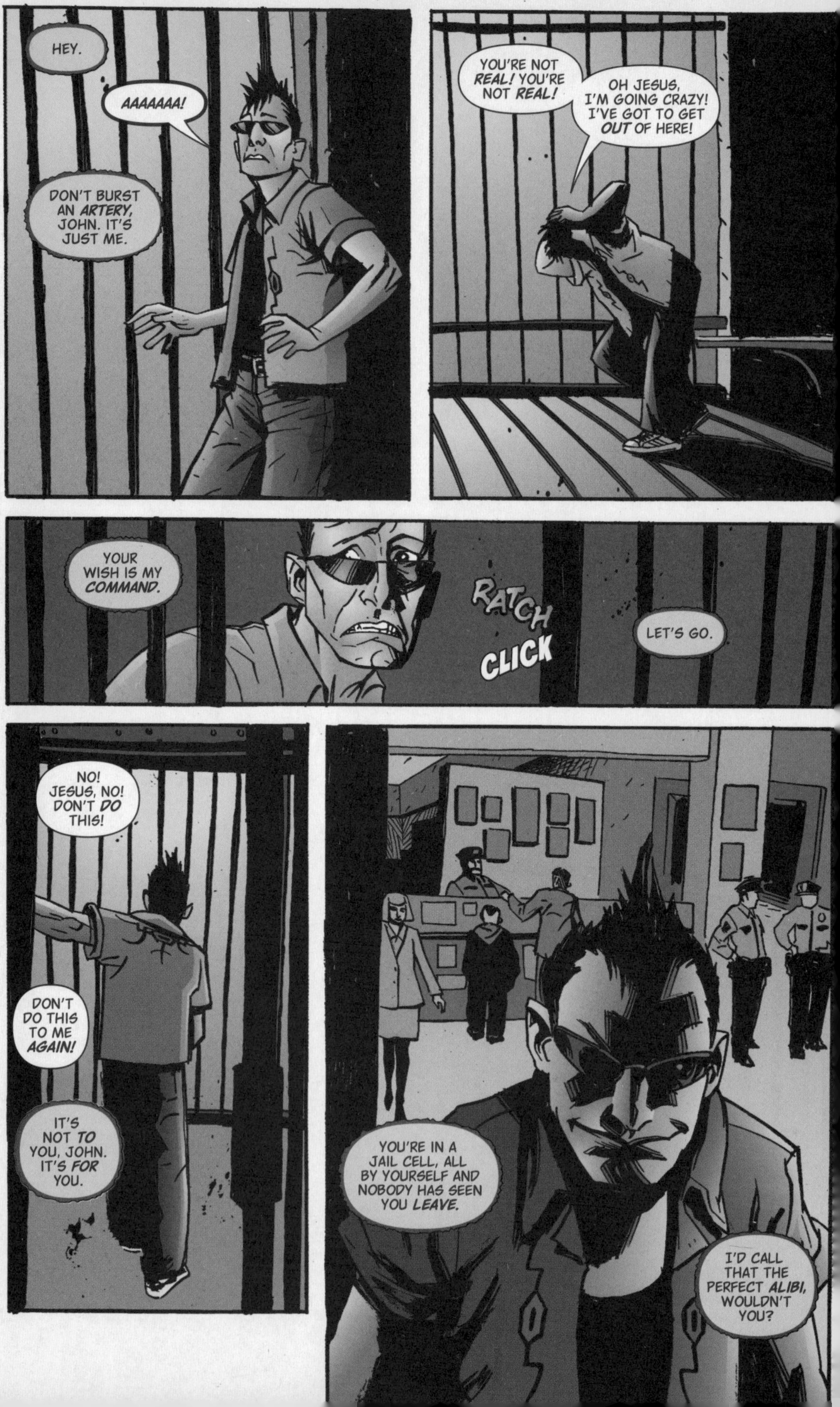
HEY.
AAAAAAA!
DON'T BURST AN ARTERY, JOHN. IT'S JUST ME.
YOU'RE NOT REAL! YOU'RE NOT REAL!
OH JESUS, I'M GOING CRAZY! I'VE GOT TO GET OUT OF HERE!
YOUR WISH IS MY COMMAND.
RATCH
CLICK
LET'S GO.
NO! JESUS, NO! DON'T DO THIS!
DON'T DO THIS TO ME AGAIN!
IT'S NOT TO YOU, JOHN. IT'S FOR YOU.
YOU'RE IN A JAIL CELL, ALL BY YOURSELF AND NOBODY HAS SEEN YOU LEAVE.
I'D CALL THAT THE PERFECT ALIBI, WOULDN'T YOU?

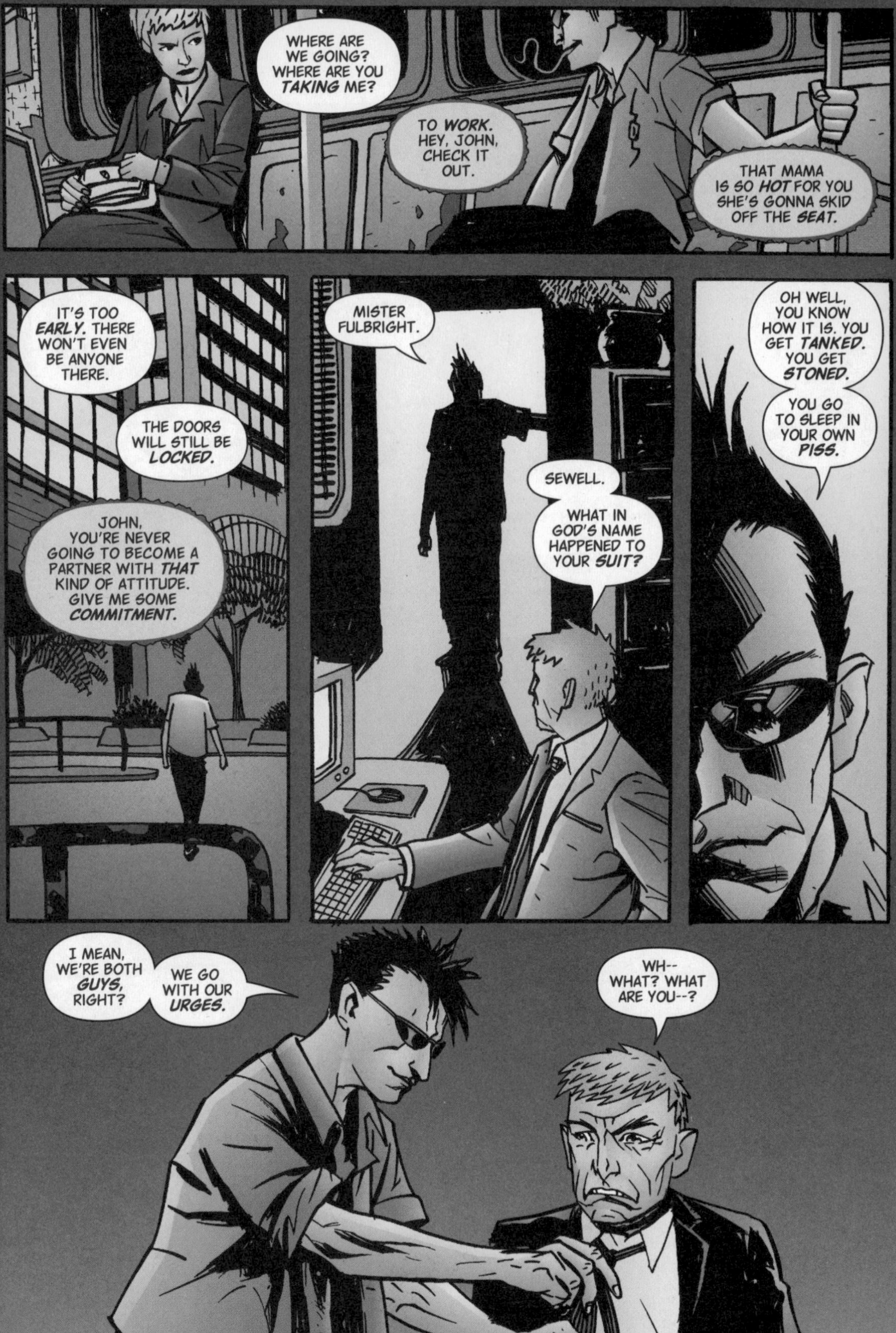
WHERE ARE WE GOING? WHERE ARE YOU TAKING ME?
TO WORK. HEY, JOHN, CHECK IT OUT.
THAT MAMA IS SO HOT FOR YOU SHE'S GONNA SKID OFF THE SEAT.
IT'S TOO EARLY. THERE WON'T EVEN BE ANYONE THERE.
THE DOORS WILL STILL BE LOCKED.
JOHN, YOU'RE NEVER GOING TO BECOME A PARTNER WITH THAT KIND OF ATTITUDE. GIVE ME SOME COMMITMENT.
MISTER FULBRIGHT.
SEWELL.
WHAT IN GOD'S NAME HAPPENED TO YOUR SUIT?
OH WELL, YOU KNOW HOW IT IS. YOU GET TANKED. YOU GET STONED.
YOU GO TO SLEEP IN YOUR OWN PISS.
I MEAN, WE'RE BOTH GUYS, RIGHT?
WE GO WITH OUR URGES.
WH-- WHAT? WHAT ARE YOU--?

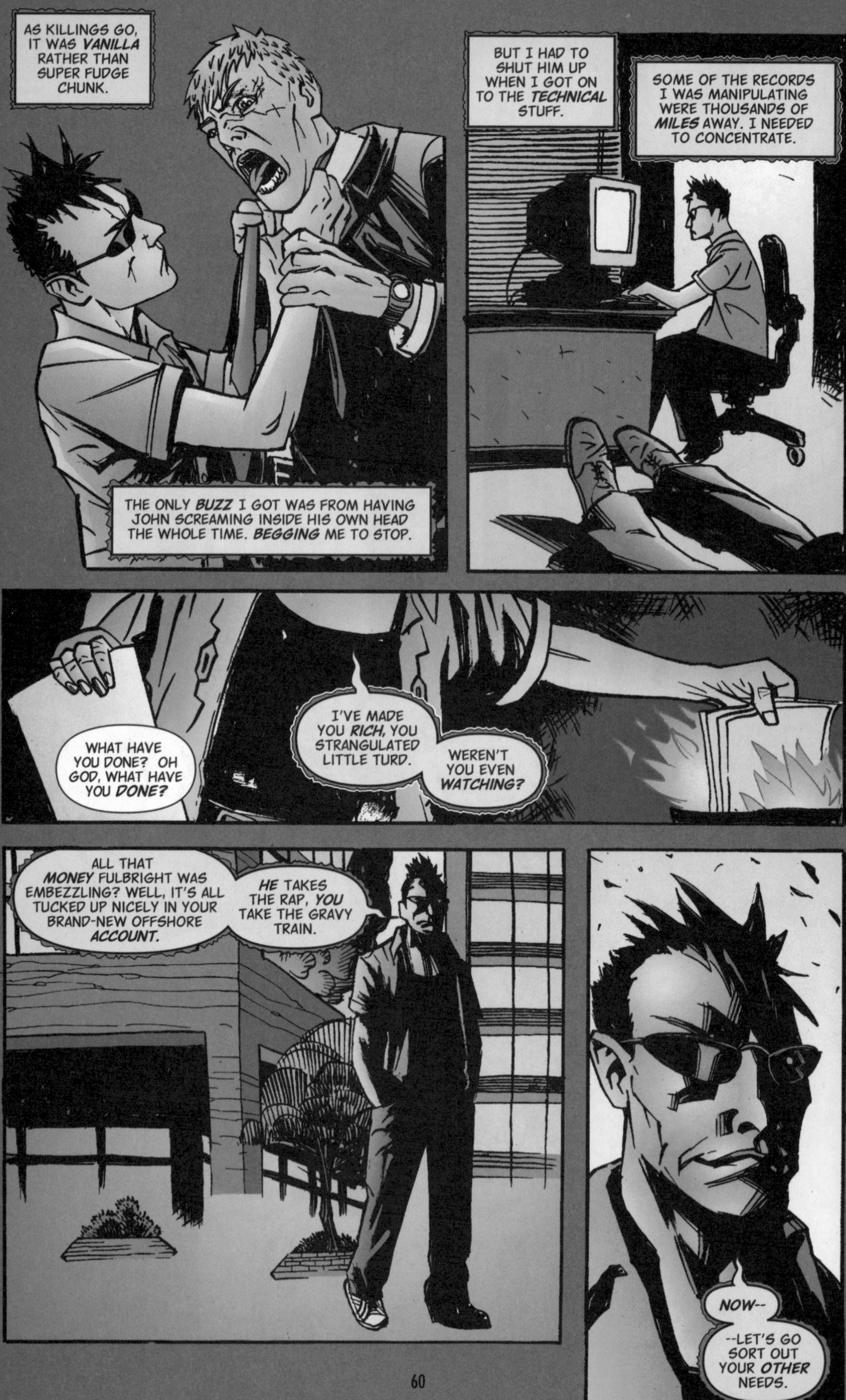
AS KILLINGS GO, IT WAS VANILLA RATHER THAN SUPER FUDGE CHUNK.
THE ONLY BUZZ I GOT WAS FROM HAVING JOHN SCREAMING INSIDE HIS OWN HEAD THE WHOLE TIME. BEGGING ME TO STOP.
BUT I HAD TO SHUT HIM UP WHEN I GOT ON TO THE TECHNICAL STUFF.
SOME OF THE RECORDS I WAS MANIPULATING WERE THOUSANDS OF MILES AWAY. I NEEDED TO CONCENTRATE.
WHAT HAVE YOU DONE? OH GOD, WHAT HAVE YOU DONE?
I'VE MADE YOU RICH, YOU STRANGULATED LITTLE TURD.
WEREN'T YOU EVEN WATCHING?
ALL THAT MONEY FULBRIGHT WAS EMBEZZLING? WELL, IT'S ALL TUCKED UP NICELY IN YOUR BRAND-NEW OFFSHORE ACCOUNT.
HE TAKES THE RAP, YOU TAKE THE GRAVY TRAIN.
NOW--
--LET'S GO SORT OUT YOUR OTHER NEEDS.

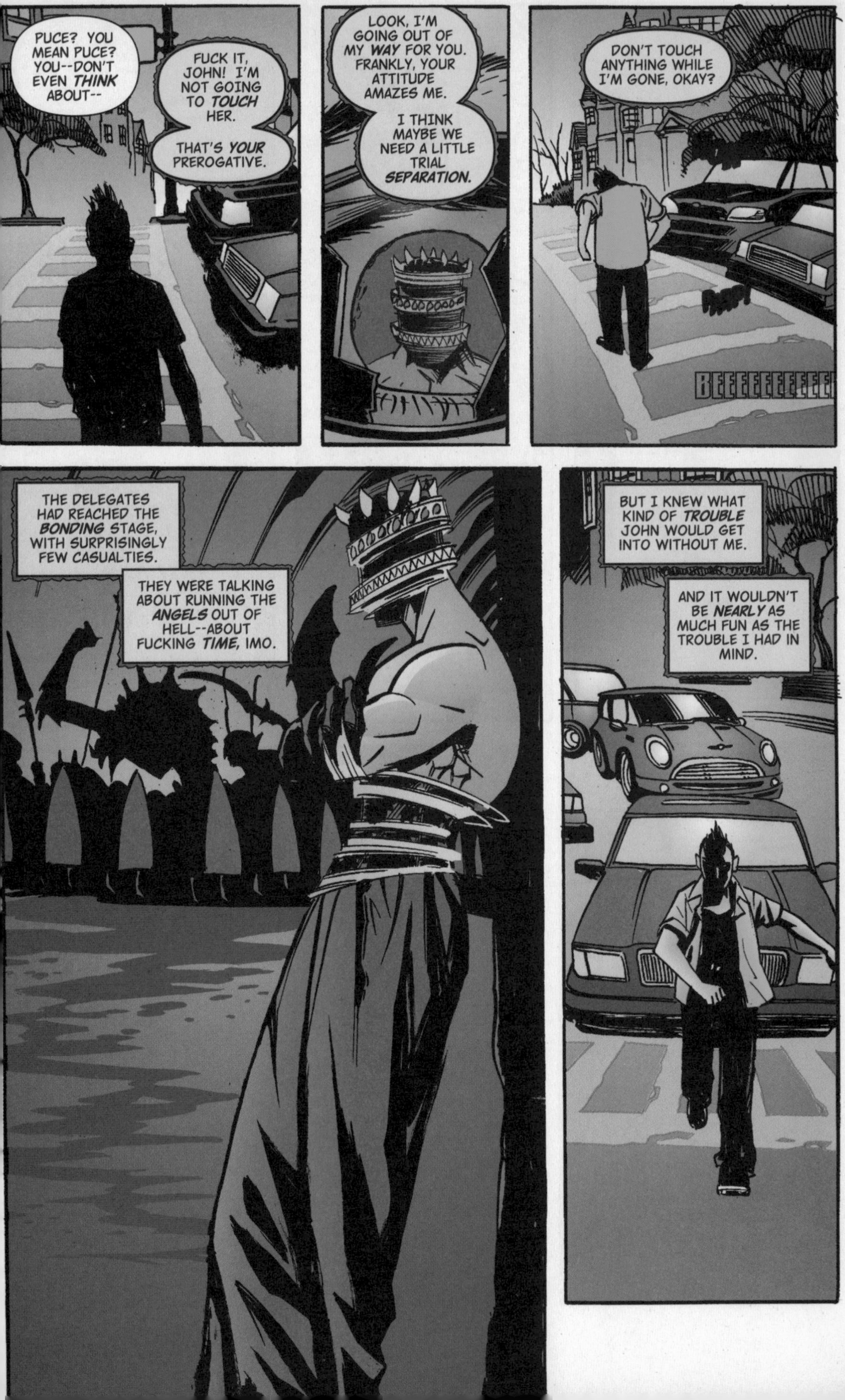
PUCE? YOU MEAN PUCE? YOU--DON'T EVEN *THINK* ABOUT--
FUCK IT, JOHN! I'M NOT GOING TO *TOUCH* HER.
THAT'S *YOUR* PREROGATIVE.
LOOK, I'M GOING OUT OF MY *WAY* FOR YOU. FRANKLY, YOUR ATTITUDE AMAZES ME.
I THINK MAYBE WE NEED A LITTLE TRIAL *SEPARATION.*
DON'T TOUCH ANYTHING WHILE I'M GONE, OKAY?
BEEEEEEEEEEE
THE DELEGATES HAD REACHED THE *BONDING* STAGE, WITH SURPRISINGLY FEW CASUALTIES.
THEY WERE TALKING ABOUT RUNNING THE *ANGELS* OUT OF HELL--ABOUT FUCKING *TIME,* IMO.
BUT I KNEW WHAT KIND OF *TROUBLE* JOHN WOULD GET INTO WITHOUT ME.
AND IT WOULDN'T BE *NEARLY* AS MUCH FUN AS THE TROUBLE I HAD IN MIND.

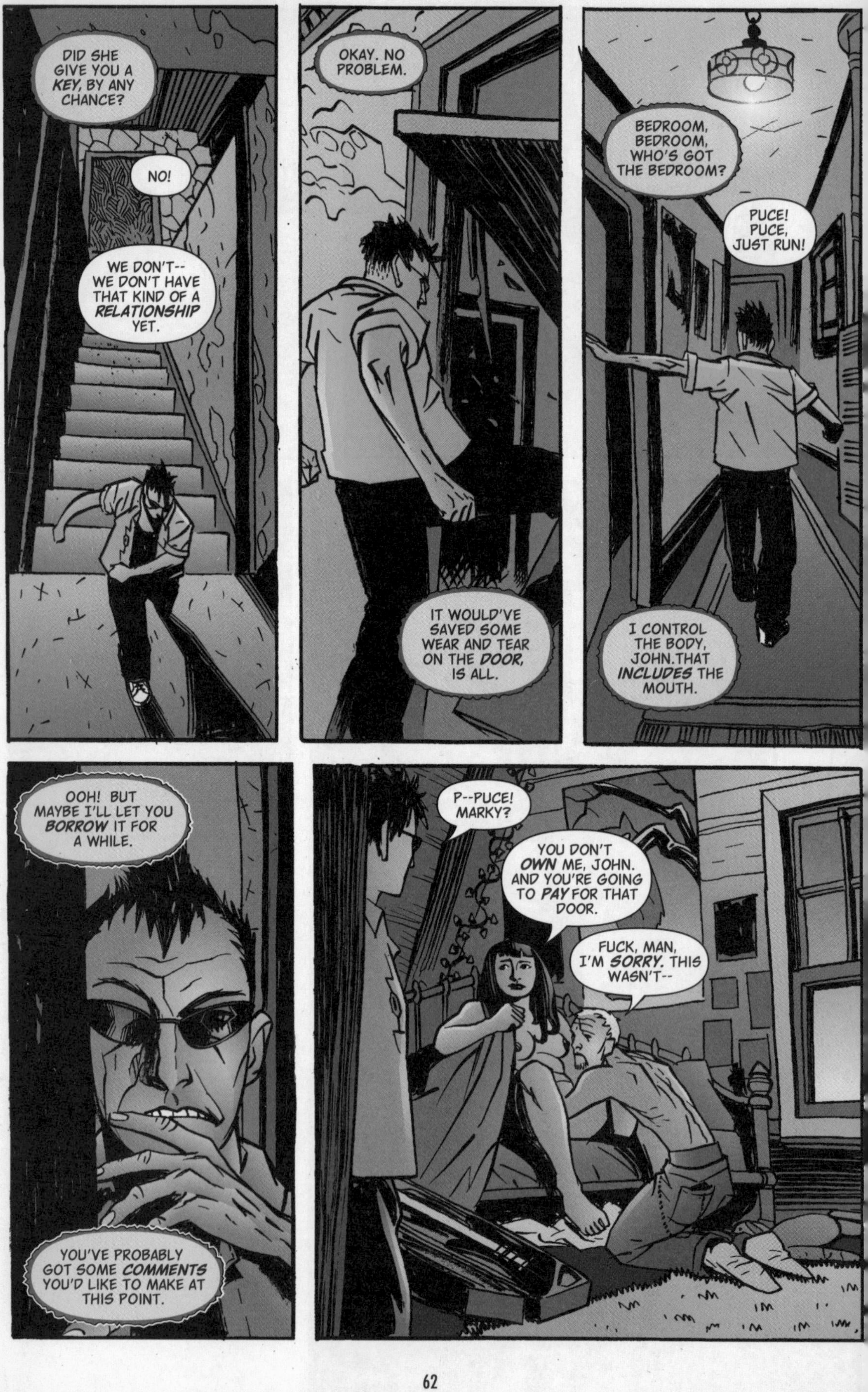
DID SHE GIVE YOU A KEY, BY ANY CHANCE?
NO!
WE DON'T-- WE DON'T HAVE THAT KIND OF A RELATIONSHIP YET.
OKAY. NO PROBLEM.
IT WOULD'VE SAVED SOME WEAR AND TEAR ON THE DOOR, IS ALL.
BEDROOM, BEDROOM, WHO'S GOT THE BEDROOM?
PUCE! PUCE, JUST RUN!
I CONTROL THE BODY, JOHN.THAT INCLUDES THE MOUTH.
OOH! BUT MAYBE I'LL LET YOU BORROW IT FOR A WHILE.
YOU'VE PROBABLY GOT SOME COMMENTS YOU'D LIKE TO MAKE AT THIS POINT.
P--PUCE! MARKY?
YOU DON'T OWN ME, JOHN. AND YOU'RE GOING TO PAY FOR THAT DOOR.
FUCK, MAN, I'M SORRY. THIS WASN'T--

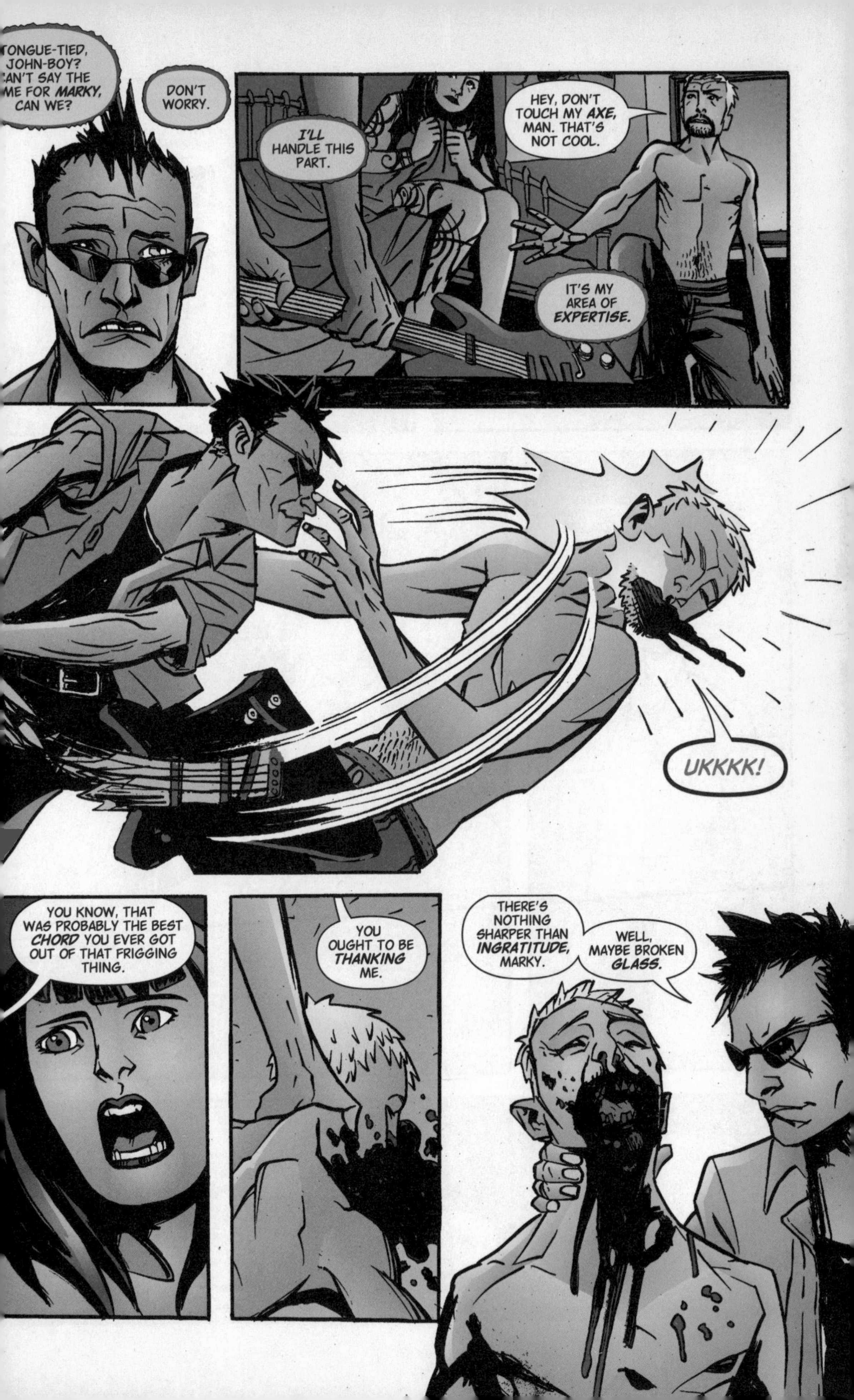
TONGUE-TIED, JOHN-BOY? CAN'T SAY THE SAME FOR MARKY, CAN WE?
DON'T WORRY.
I'LL HANDLE THIS PART.
HEY, DON'T TOUCH MY AXE, MAN. THAT'S NOT COOL.
IT'S MY AREA OF EXPERTISE.
UKKKK!
YOU KNOW, THAT WAS PROBABLY THE BEST CHORD YOU EVER GOT OUT OF THAT FRIGGING THING.
YOU OUGHT TO BE THANKING ME.
THERE'S NOTHING SHARPER THAN INGRATITUDE, MARKY.
WELL, MAYBE BROKEN GLASS.

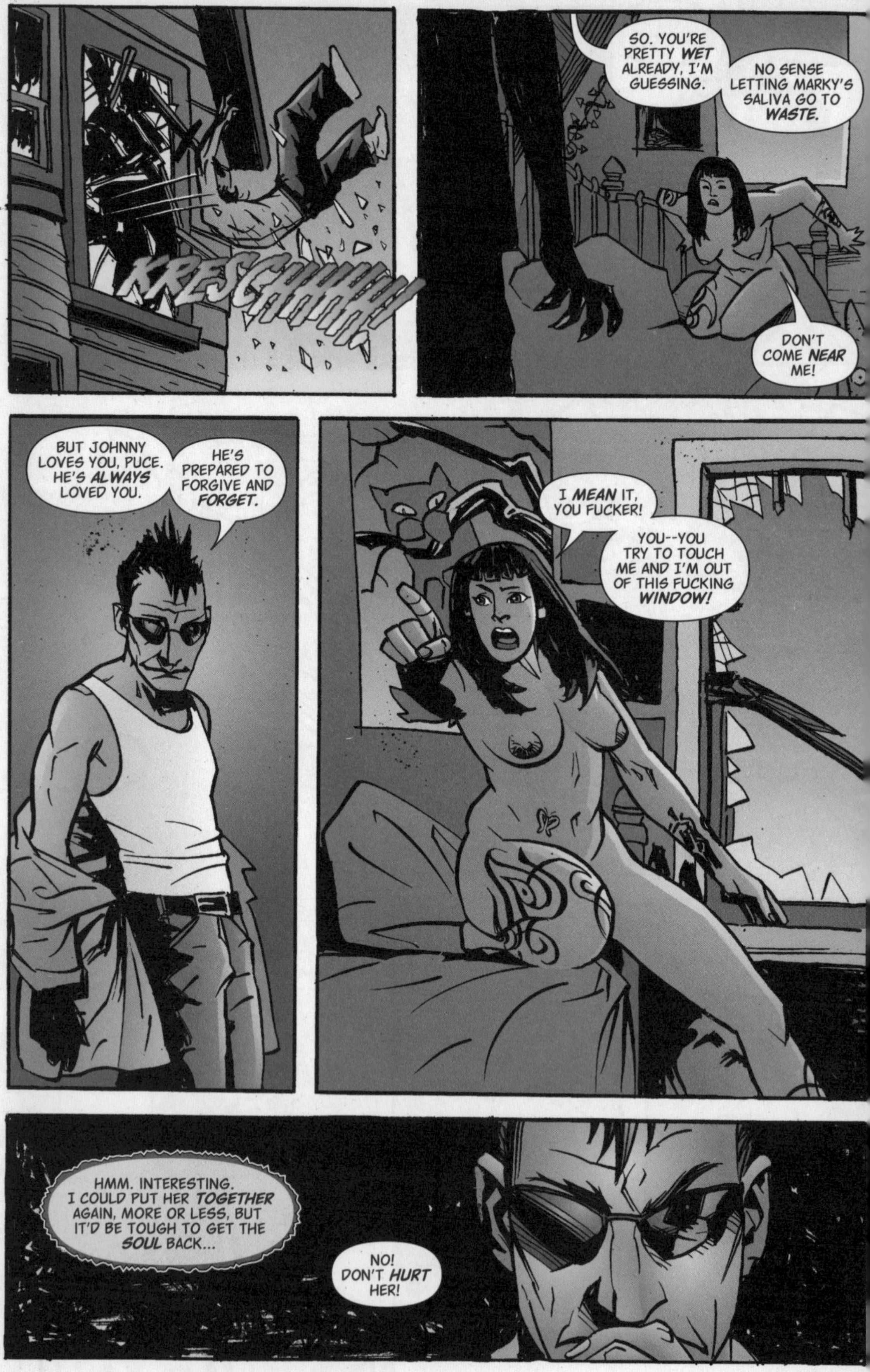
KRESCHHHH!!
SO. YOU'RE PRETTY WET ALREADY, I'M GUESSING.
NO SENSE LETTING MARKY'S SALIVA GO TO WASTE.
DON'T COME NEAR ME!
BUT JOHNNY LOVES YOU, PUCE. HE'S ALWAYS LOVED YOU.
HE'S PREPARED TO FORGIVE AND FORGET.
I MEAN IT, YOU FUCKER!
YOU--YOU TRY TO TOUCH ME AND I'M OUT OF THIS FUCKING WINDOW!
HMM. INTERESTING. I COULD PUT HER TOGETHER AGAIN, MORE OR LESS, BUT IT'D BE TOUGH TO GET THE SOUL BACK...
NO! DON'T HURT HER!

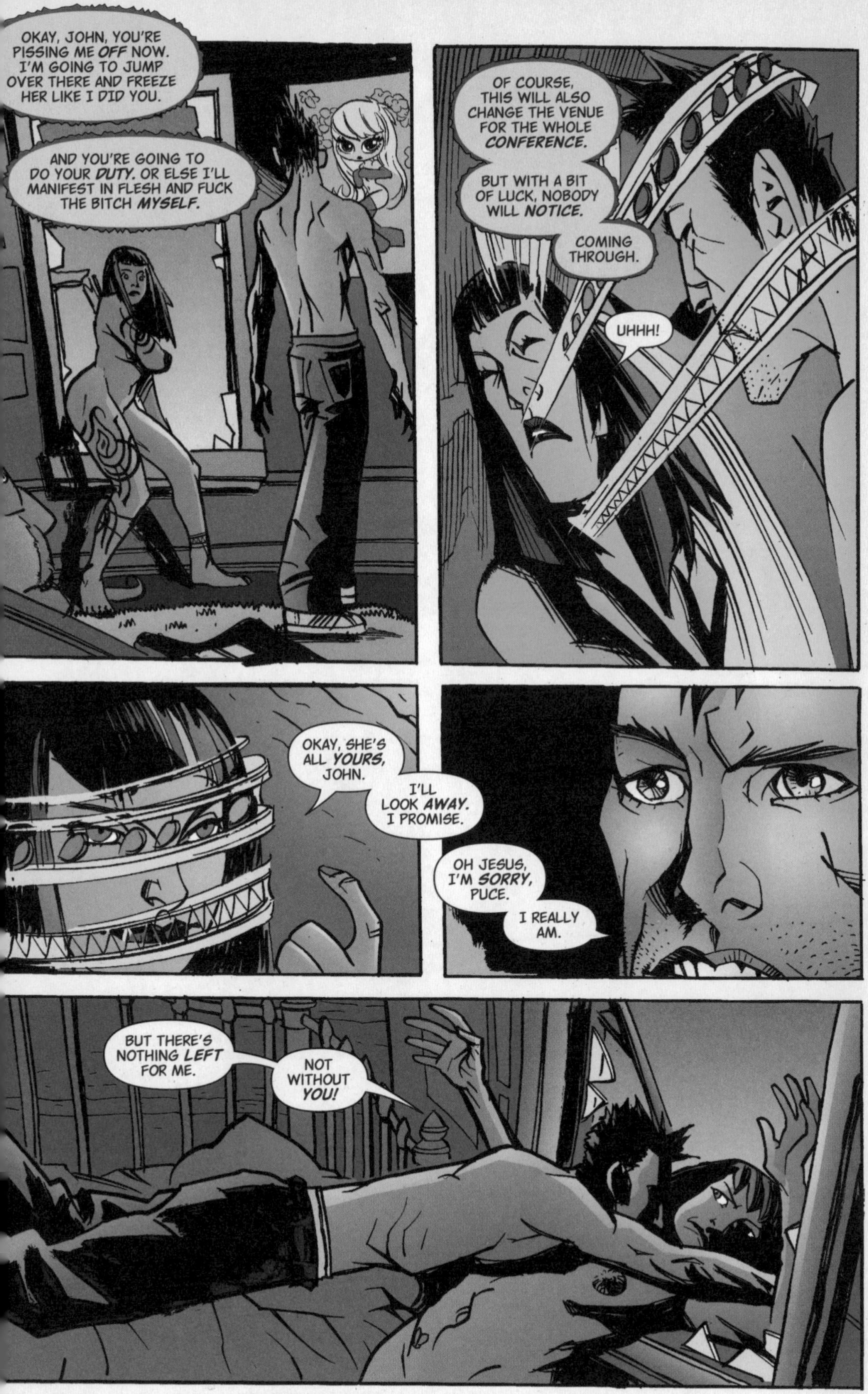
OKAY, JOHN, YOU'RE PISSING ME OFF NOW. I'M GOING TO JUMP OVER THERE AND FREEZE HER LIKE I DID YOU.
AND YOU'RE GOING TO DO YOUR DUTY. OR ELSE I'LL MANIFEST IN FLESH AND FUCK THE BITCH MYSELF.
OF COURSE, THIS WILL ALSO CHANGE THE VENUE FOR THE WHOLE CONFERENCE.
BUT WITH A BIT OF LUCK, NOBODY WILL NOTICE.
COMING THROUGH.
UHHH!
OKAY, SHE'S ALL YOURS, JOHN.
I'LL LOOK AWAY. I PROMISE.
OH JESUS, I'M SORRY, PUCE.
I REALLY AM.
BUT THERE'S NOTHING LEFT FOR ME.
NOT WITHOUT YOU!

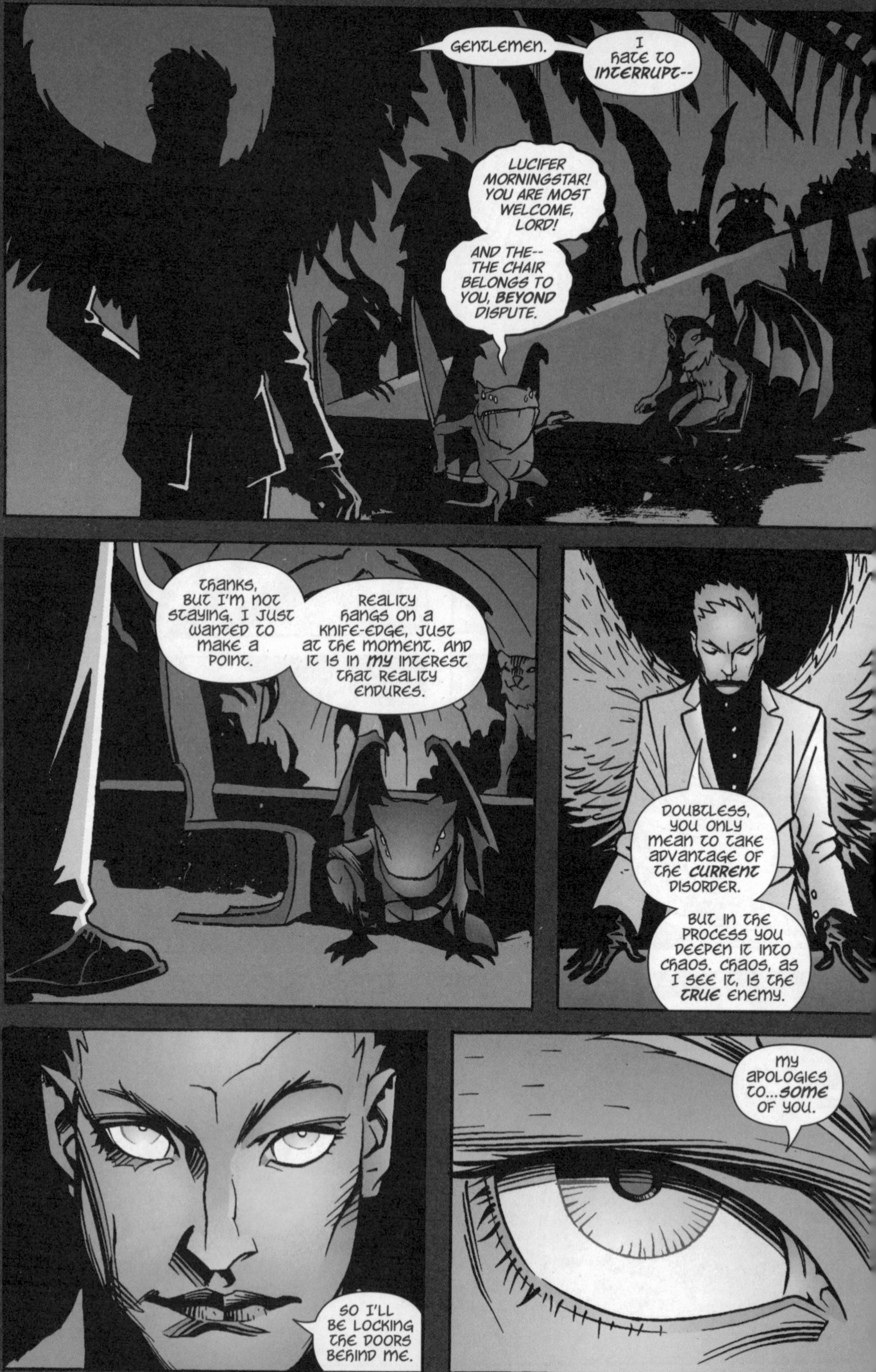
GENTLEMEN.
I HATE TO INTERRUPT--
LUCIFER MORNINGSTAR! YOU ARE MOST WELCOME, LORD!
AND THE-- THE CHAIR BELONGS TO YOU, BEYOND DISPUTE.
THANKS, BUT I'M NOT STAYING. I JUST WANTED TO MAKE A POINT.
REALITY HANGS ON A KNIFE-EDGE, JUST AT THE MOMENT. AND IT IS IN MY INTEREST THAT REALITY ENDURES.
DOUBTLESS, YOU ONLY MEAN TO TAKE ADVANTAGE OF THE CURRENT DISORDER.
BUT IN THE PROCESS YOU DEEPEN IT INTO CHAOS. CHAOS, AS I SEE IT, IS THE TRUE ENEMY.
SO I'LL BE LOCKING THE DOORS BEHIND ME.
MY APOLOGIES TO...SOME OF YOU.

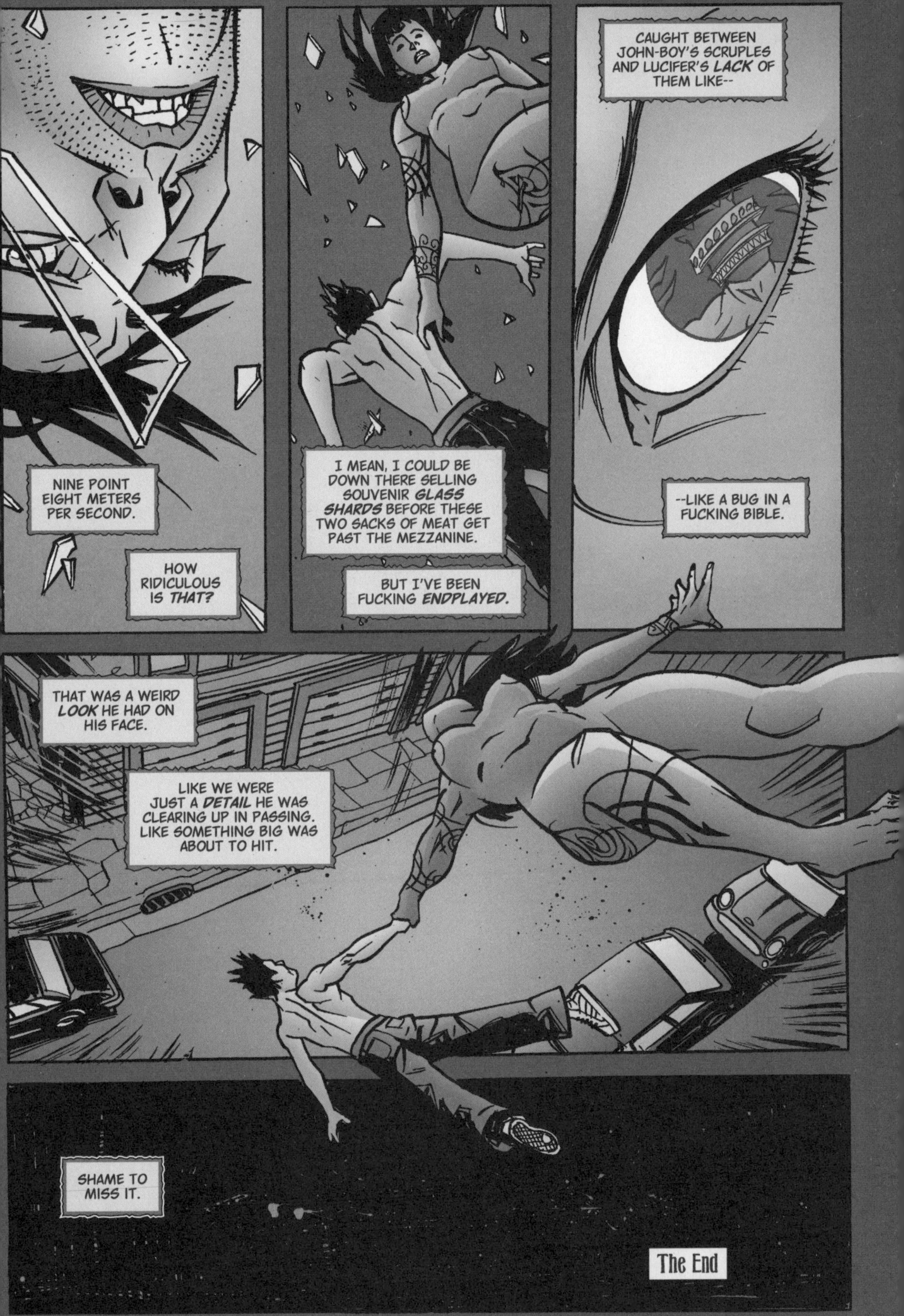
NINE POINT EIGHT METERS PER SECOND.
HOW RIDICULOUS IS THAT?
I MEAN, I COULD BE DOWN THERE SELLING SOUVENIR GLASS SHARDS BEFORE THESE TWO SACKS OF MEAT GET PAST THE MEZZANINE.
BUT I'VE BEEN FUCKING ENDPLAYED.
CAUGHT BETWEEN JOHN-BOY'S SCRUPLES AND LUCIFER'S LACK OF THEM LIKE--
--LIKE A BUG IN A FUCKING BIBLE.
THAT WAS A WEIRD LOOK HE HAD ON HIS FACE.
LIKE WE WERE JUST A DETAIL HE WAS CLEARING UP IN PASSING. LIKE SOMETHING BIG WAS ABOUT TO HIT.
SHAME TO MISS IT.
The End

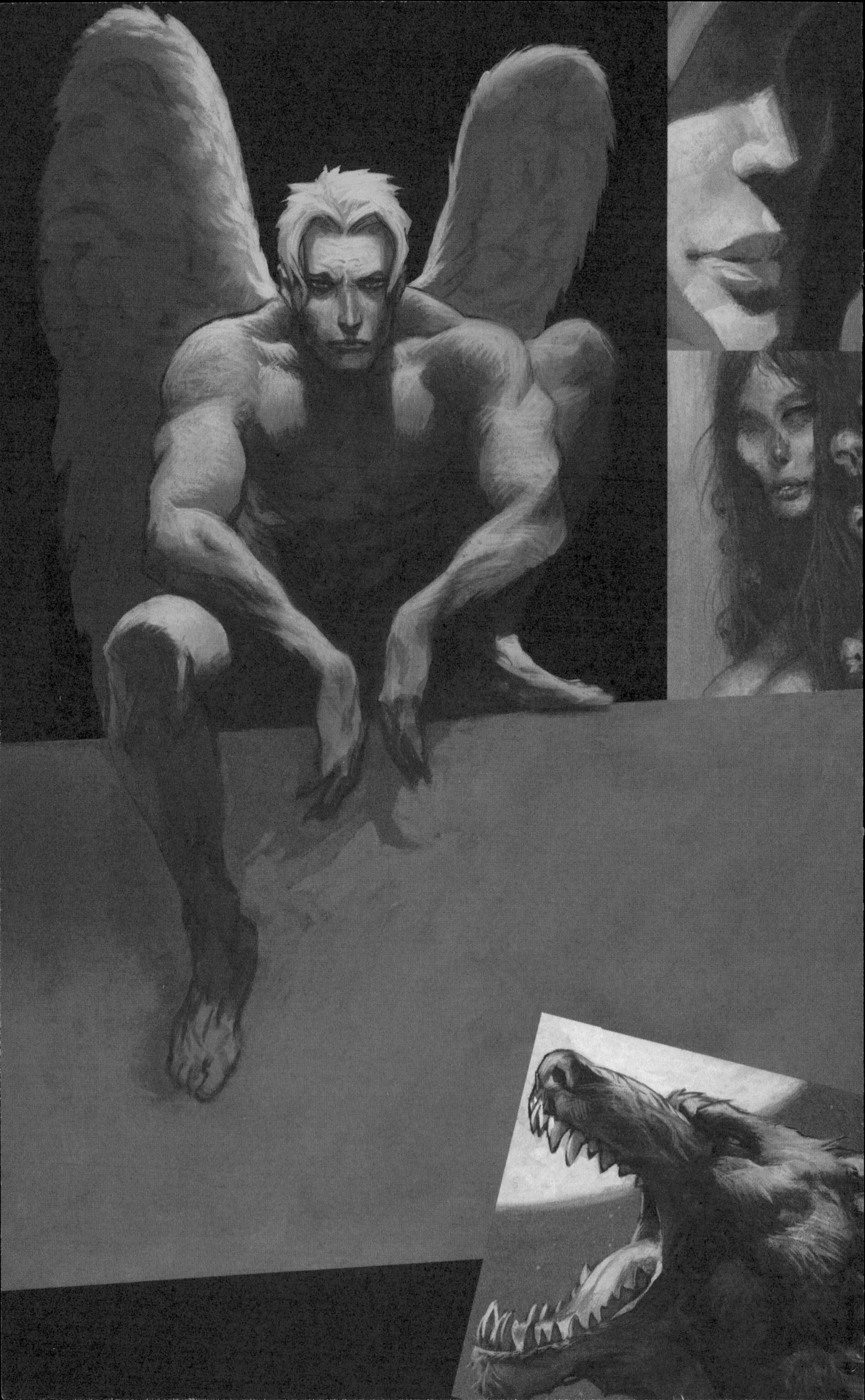

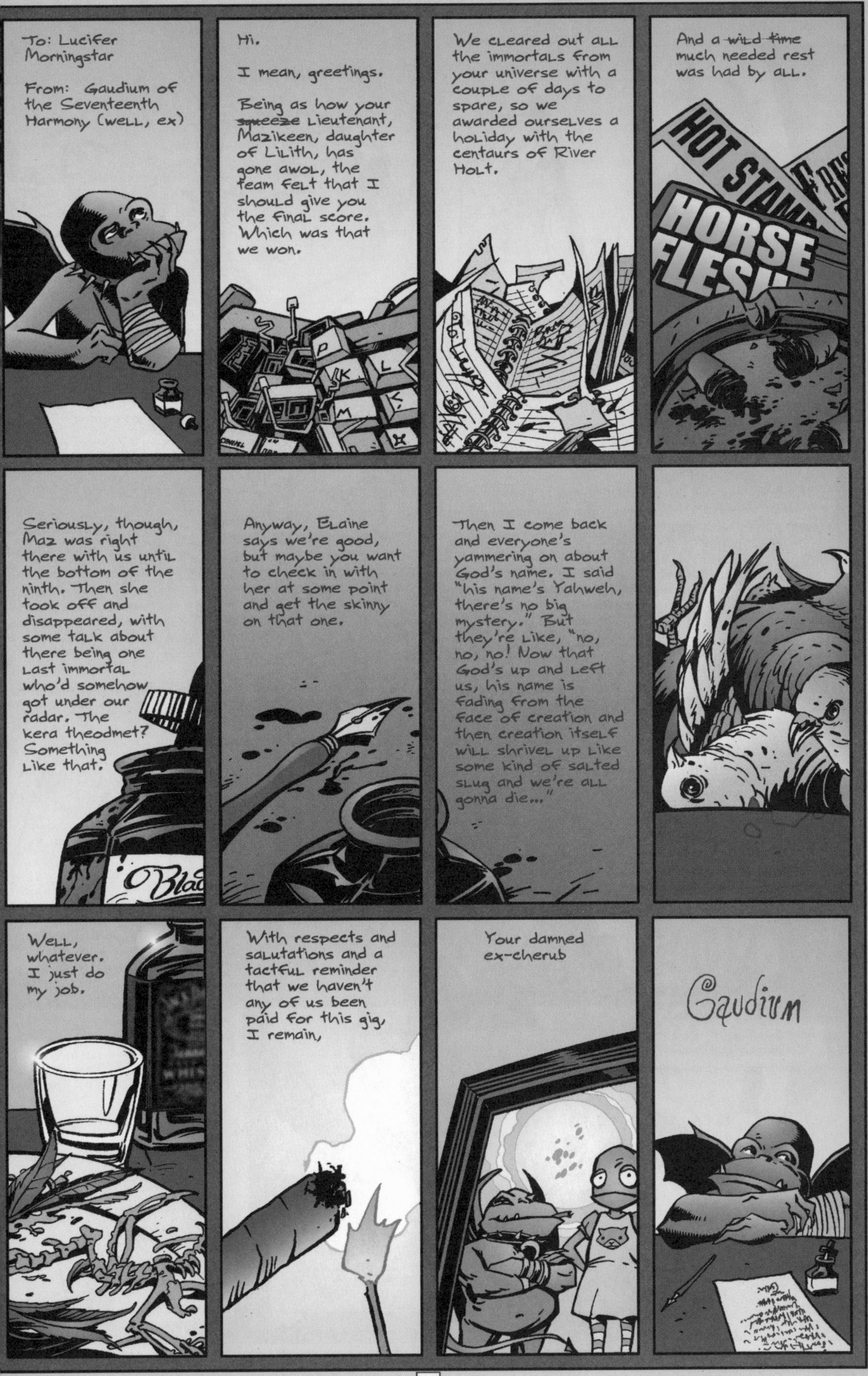
To: Lucifer Morningstar
From: Gaudium of the Seventeenth Harmony (well, ex)
Hi.
I mean, greetings.
Being as how your ~~squeeze~~ Lieutenant, Mazikeen, daughter of Lilith, has gone awol, the team felt that I should give you the final score. Which was that we won.
We cleared out all the immortals from your universe with a couple of days to spare, so we awarded ourselves a holiday with the centaurs of River Holt.
And a ~~wild time~~ much needed rest was had by all.
HOT STAM
HORSE
Seriously, though, Maz was right there with us until the bottom of the ninth. Then she took off and disappeared, with some talk about there being one last immortal who'd somehow got under our radar. The kera theodmet? Something like that.
Anyway, Elaine says we're good, but maybe you want to check in with her at some point and get the skinny on that one.
Then I come back and everyone's yammering on about God's name. I said "his name's Yahweh, there's no big mystery." But they're like, "no, no, no! Now that God's up and left us, his name is fading from the face of creation and then creation itself will shrivel up like some kind of salted slug and we're all gonna die..."
Well, whatever. I just do my job.
With respects and salutations and a tactful reminder that we haven't any of us been paid for this gig, I remain,
Your damned ex-cherub
Gaudium

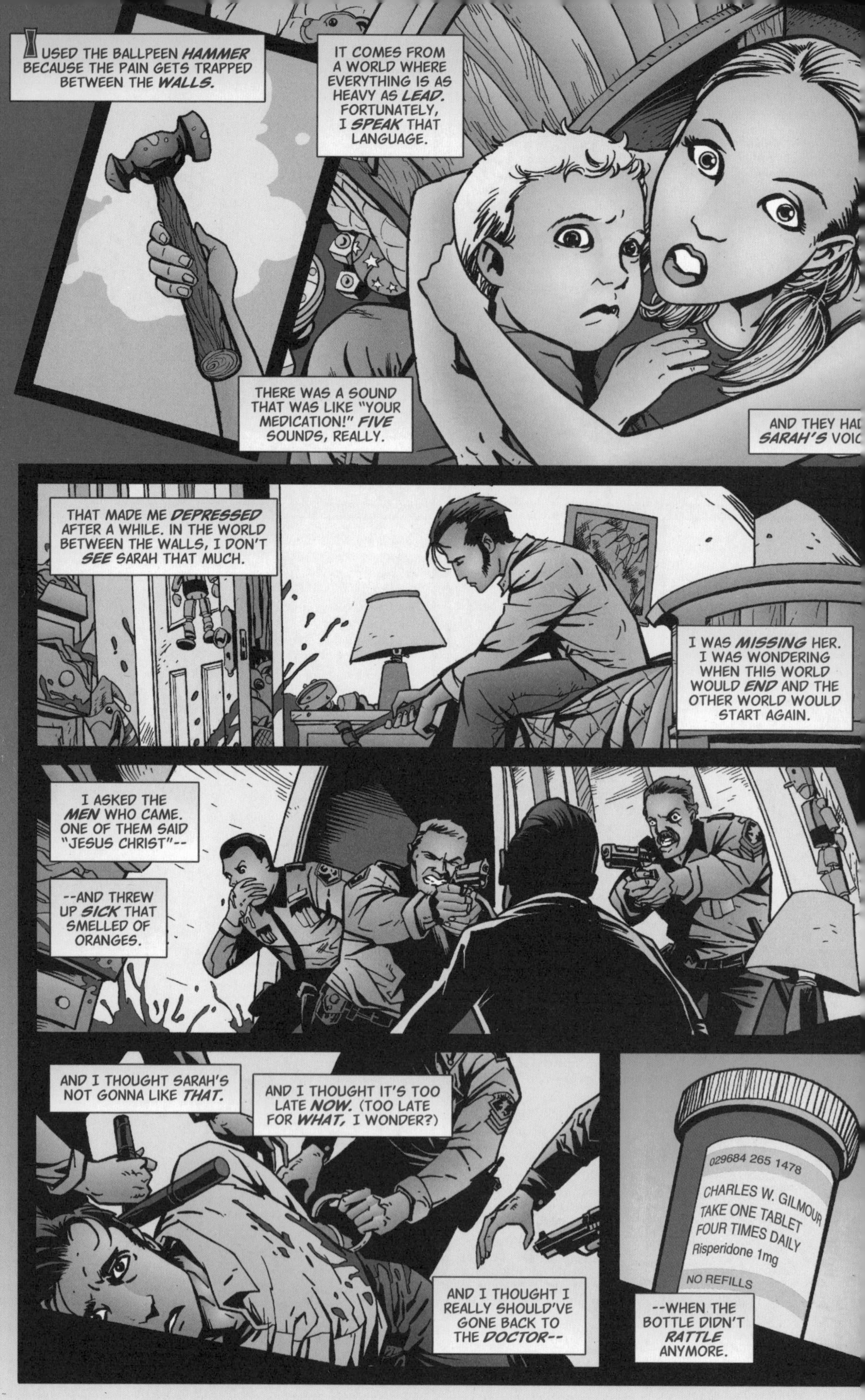
I USED THE BALLPEEN HAMMER BECAUSE THE PAIN GETS TRAPPED BETWEEN THE WALLS.
IT COMES FROM A WORLD WHERE EVERYTHING IS AS HEAVY AS LEAD. FORTUNATELY, I SPEAK THAT LANGUAGE.
THERE WAS A SOUND THAT WAS LIKE "YOUR MEDICATION!" FIVE SOUNDS, REALLY.
AND THEY HAD SARAH'S VOIC
THAT MADE ME DEPRESSED AFTER A WHILE. IN THE WORLD BETWEEN THE WALLS, I DON'T SEE SARAH THAT MUCH.
I WAS MISSING HER. I WAS WONDERING WHEN THIS WORLD WOULD END AND THE OTHER WORLD WOULD START AGAIN.
I ASKED THE MEN WHO CAME. ONE OF THEM SAID "JESUS CHRIST"--
--AND THREW UP SICK THAT SMELLED OF ORANGES.
AND I THOUGHT SARAH'S NOT GONNA LIKE THAT.
AND I THOUGHT IT'S TOO LATE NOW. (TOO LATE FOR WHAT, I WONDER?)
AND I THOUGHT I REALLY SHOULD'VE GONE BACK TO THE DOCTOR--
029684 265 1478
CHARLES W. GILMOUR
TAKE ONE TABLET FOUR TIMES DAILY
Risperidone 1mg
NO REFILLS
--WHEN THE BOTTLE DIDN'T RATTLE ANYMORE.

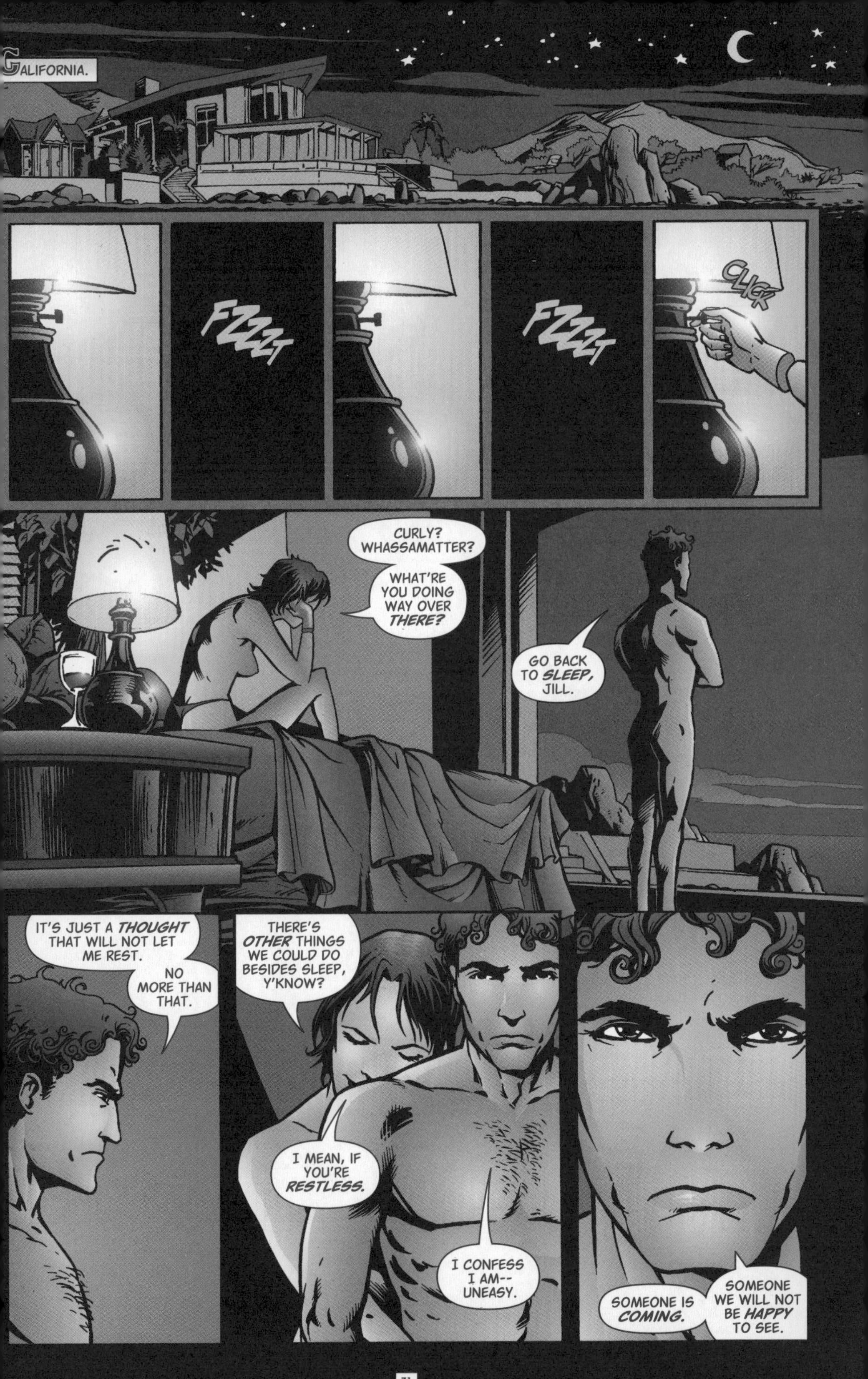
CALIFORNIA.
FZZZT
FZZZT
CLICK
CURLY? WHASSAMATTER?
WHAT'RE YOU DOING WAY OVER THERE?
GO BACK TO SLEEP, JILL.
IT'S JUST A THOUGHT THAT WILL NOT LET ME REST.
NO MORE THAN THAT.
THERE'S OTHER THINGS WE COULD DO BESIDES SLEEP, Y'KNOW?
I MEAN, IF YOU'RE RESTLESS.
I CONFESS I AM-- UNEASY.
SOMEONE IS COMING.
SOMEONE WE WILL NOT BE HAPPY TO SEE.

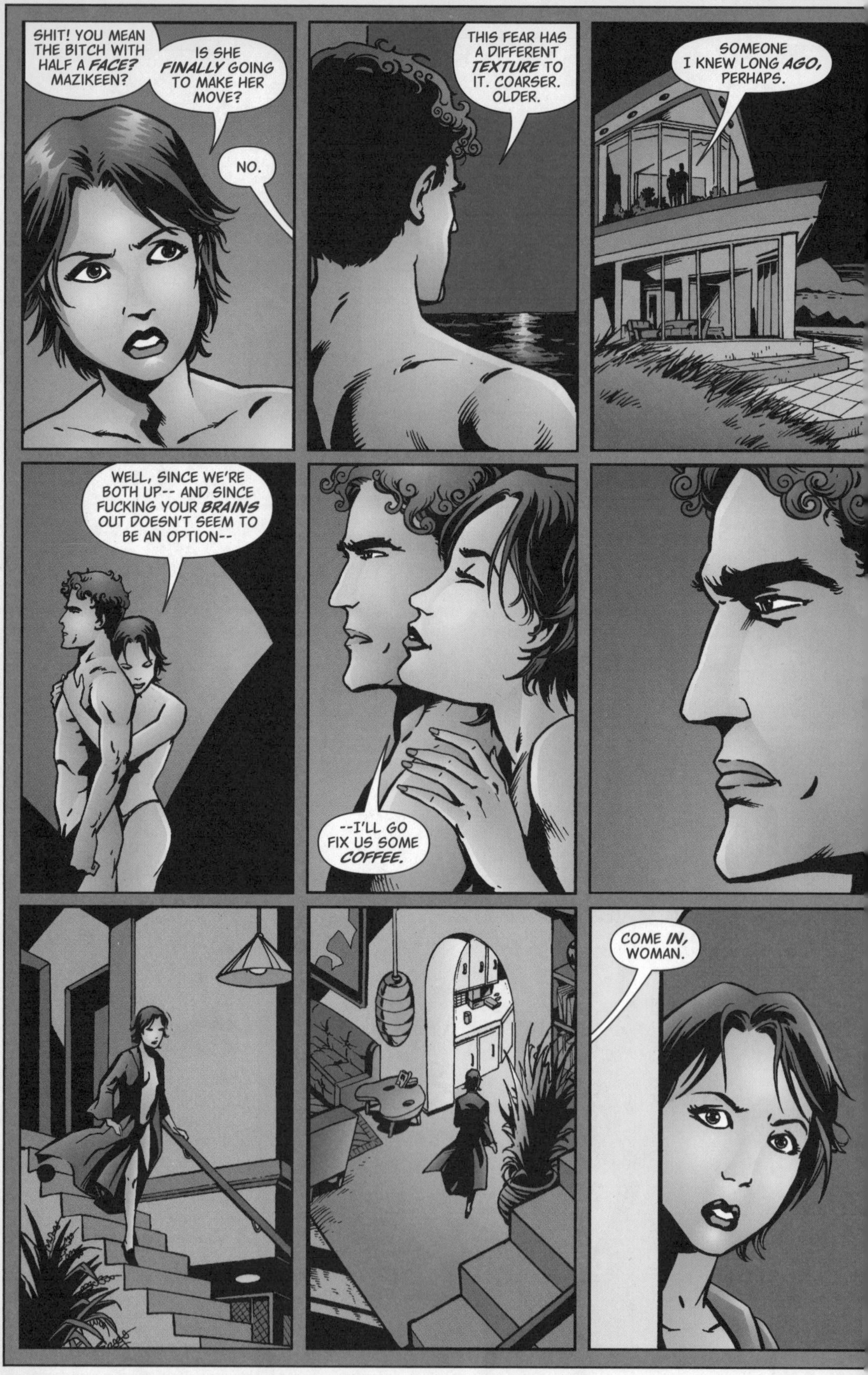
SHIT! YOU MEAN THE BITCH WITH HALF A *FACE?* MAZIKEEN?
IS SHE *FINALLY* GOING TO MAKE HER MOVE?
NO.
THIS FEAR HAS A DIFFERENT *TEXTURE* TO IT. COARSER. OLDER.
SOMEONE I KNEW LONG *AGO,* PERHAPS.
WELL, SINCE WE'RE BOTH UP-- AND SINCE FUCKING YOUR *BRAINS* OUT DOESN'T SEEM TO BE AN OPTION--
--I'LL GO FIX US SOME *COFFEE.*
COME *IN,* WOMAN.

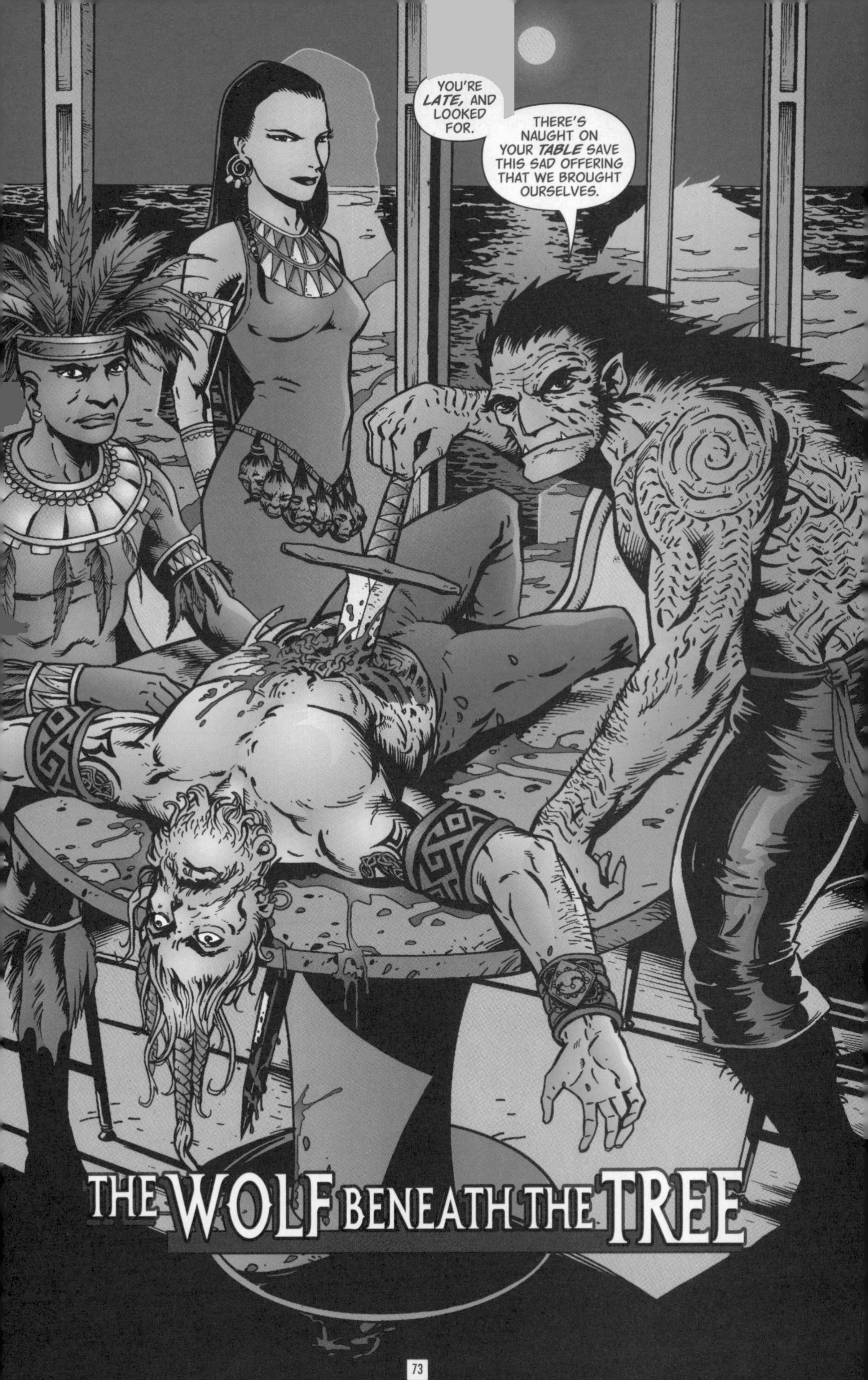
YOU'RE LATE, AND LOOKED FOR.
THERE'S NAUGHT ON YOUR TABLE SAVE THIS SAD OFFERING THAT WE BROUGHT OURSELVES.
THE WOLF BENEATH THE TREE

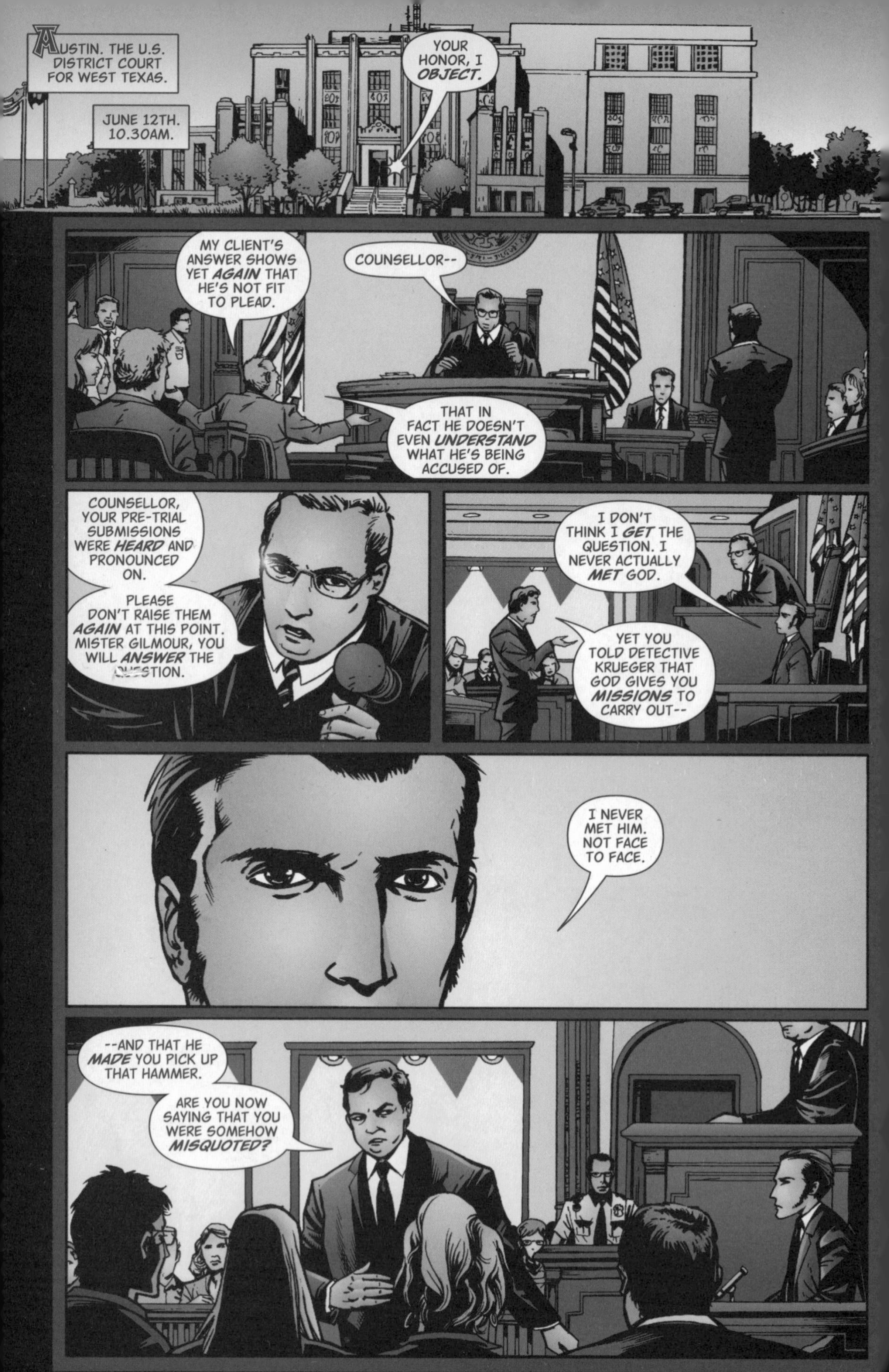
AUSTIN. THE U.S. DISTRICT COURT FOR WEST TEXAS.
JUNE 12TH. 10.30AM.
YOUR HONOR, I OBJECT.
MY CLIENT'S ANSWER SHOWS YET AGAIN THAT HE'S NOT FIT TO PLEAD.
COUNSELLOR--
THAT IN FACT HE DOESN'T EVEN UNDERSTAND WHAT HE'S BEING ACCUSED OF.
COUNSELLOR, YOUR PRE-TRIAL SUBMISSIONS WERE HEARD AND PRONOUNCED ON.
PLEASE DON'T RAISE THEM AGAIN AT THIS POINT. MISTER GILMOUR, YOU WILL ANSWER THE QUESTION.
I DON'T THINK I GET THE QUESTION. I NEVER ACTUALLY MET GOD.
YET YOU TOLD DETECTIVE KRUEGER THAT GOD GIVES YOU MISSIONS TO CARRY OUT--
I NEVER MET HIM. NOT FACE TO FACE.
--AND THAT HE MADE YOU PICK UP THAT HAMMER.
ARE YOU NOW SAYING THAT YOU WERE SOMEHOW MISQUOTED?

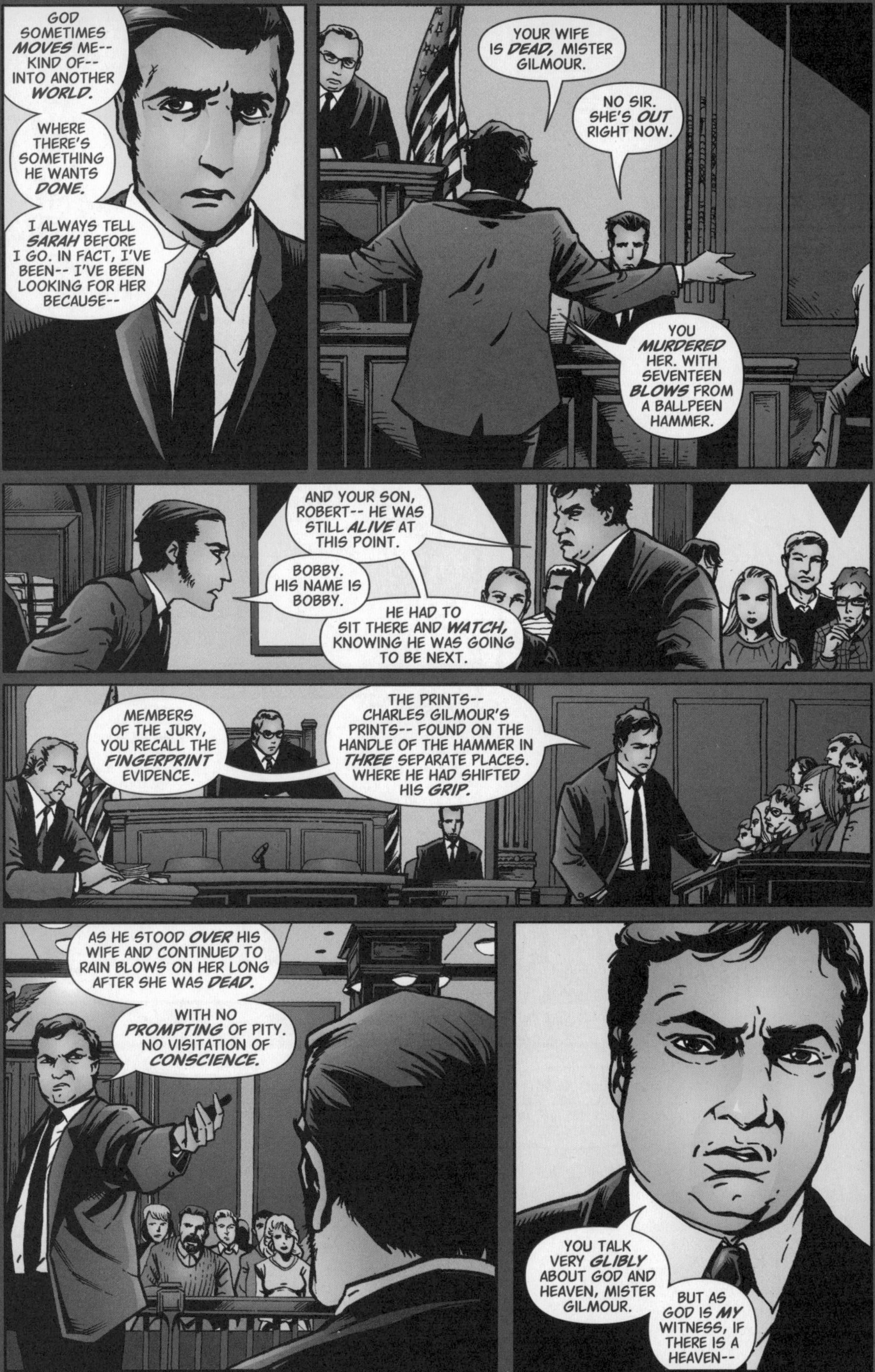
GOD SOMETIMES MOVES ME-- KIND OF-- INTO ANOTHER WORLD.
WHERE THERE'S SOMETHING HE WANTS DONE.
I ALWAYS TELL SARAH BEFORE I GO. IN FACT, I'VE BEEN-- I'VE BEEN LOOKING FOR HER BECAUSE--
YOUR WIFE IS DEAD, MISTER GILMOUR.
NO SIR. SHE'S OUT RIGHT NOW.
YOU MURDERED HER. WITH SEVENTEEN BLOWS FROM A BALLPEEN HAMMER.
AND YOUR SON, ROBERT-- HE WAS STILL ALIVE AT THIS POINT.
BOBBY. HIS NAME IS BOBBY.
HE HAD TO SIT THERE AND WATCH, KNOWING HE WAS GOING TO BE NEXT.
MEMBERS OF THE JURY, YOU RECALL THE FINGERPRINT EVIDENCE.
THE PRINTS-- CHARLES GILMOUR'S PRINTS-- FOUND ON THE HANDLE OF THE HAMMER IN THREE SEPARATE PLACES. WHERE HE HAD SHIFTED HIS GRIP.
AS HE STOOD OVER HIS WIFE AND CONTINUED TO RAIN BLOWS ON HER LONG AFTER SHE WAS DEAD.
WITH NO PROMPTING OF PITY. NO VISITATION OF CONSCIENCE.
YOU TALK VERY GLIBLY ABOUT GOD AND HEAVEN, MISTER GILMOUR.
BUT AS GOD IS MY WITNESS, IF THERE IS A HEAVEN--

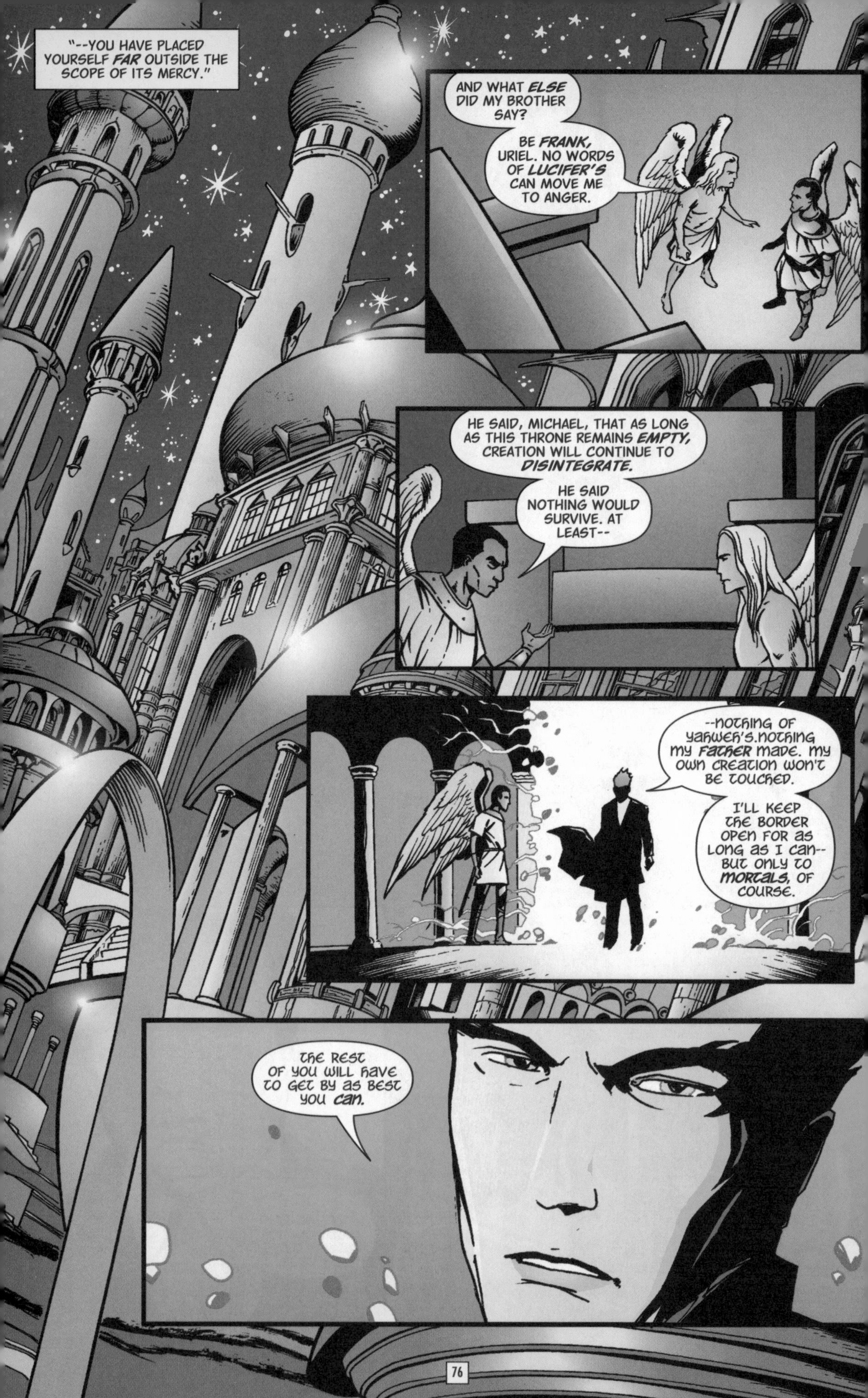
"--YOU HAVE PLACED YOURSELF FAR OUTSIDE THE SCOPE OF ITS MERCY."
AND WHAT ELSE DID MY BROTHER SAY?
BE FRANK, URIEL. NO WORDS OF LUCIFER'S CAN MOVE ME TO ANGER.
HE SAID, MICHAEL, THAT AS LONG AS THIS THRONE REMAINS EMPTY, CREATION WILL CONTINUE TO DISINTEGRATE.
HE SAID NOTHING WOULD SURVIVE. AT LEAST--
--NOTHING OF YAHWEH'S. NOTHING MY FATHER MADE. MY OWN CREATION WON'T BE TOUCHED.
I'LL KEEP THE BORDER OPEN FOR AS LONG AS I CAN--BUT ONLY TO MORTALS, OF COURSE.
THE REST OF YOU WILL HAVE TO GET BY AS BEST YOU CAN.

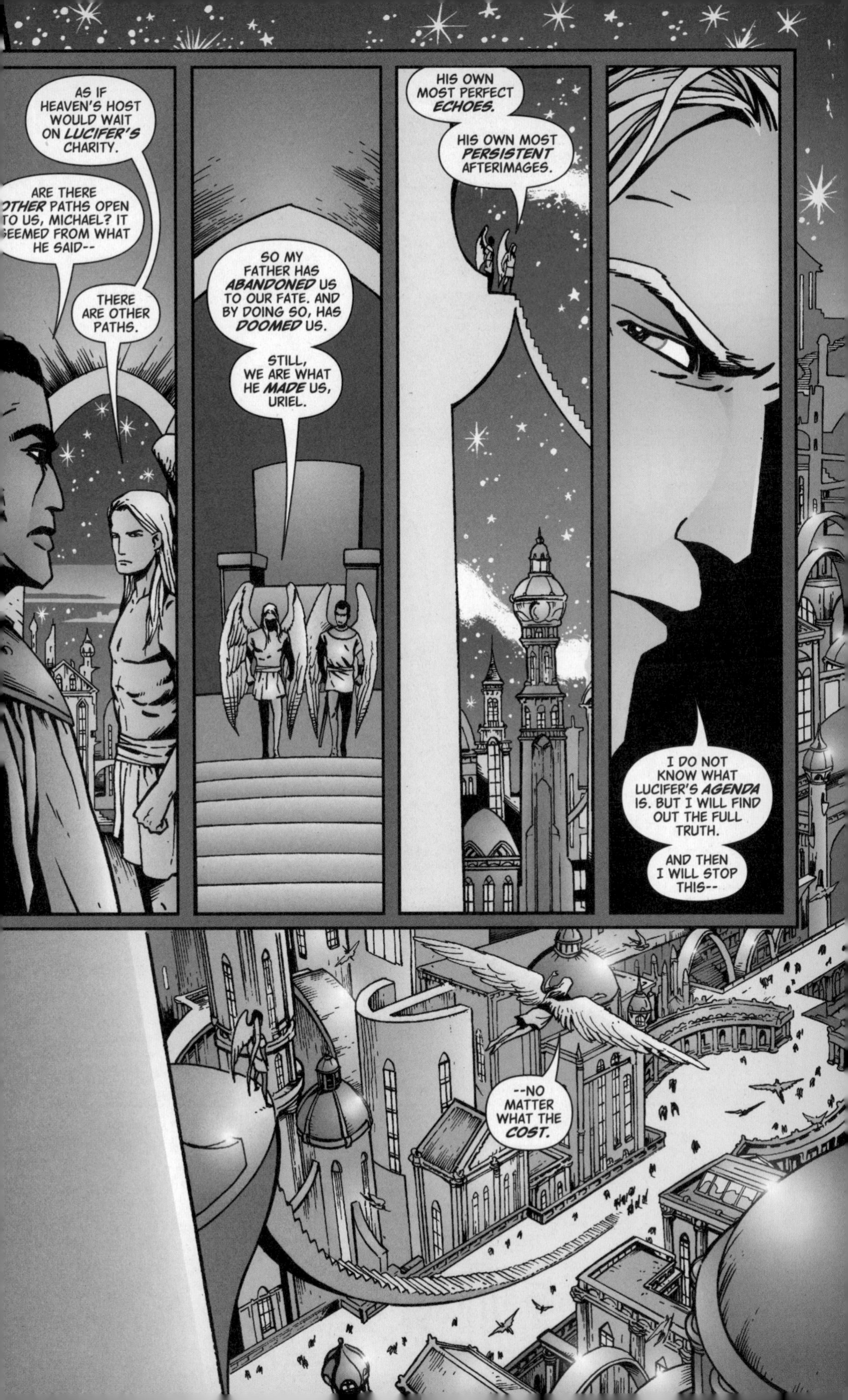
AS IF HEAVEN'S HOST WOULD WAIT ON *LUCIFER'S* CHARITY.
ARE THERE *OTHER* PATHS OPEN TO US, MICHAEL? IT SEEMED FROM WHAT HE SAID--
THERE ARE OTHER PATHS.
SO MY FATHER HAS *ABANDONED* US TO OUR FATE. AND BY DOING SO, HAS *DOOMED* US.
STILL, WE ARE WHAT HE *MADE* US, URIEL.
HIS OWN MOST PERFECT *ECHOES.*
HIS OWN MOST *PERSISTENT* AFTERIMAGES.
I DO NOT KNOW WHAT LUCIFER'S *AGENDA* IS. BUT I WILL FIND OUT THE FULL TRUTH.
AND THEN I WILL STOP THIS--
--NO MATTER WHAT THE *COST.*

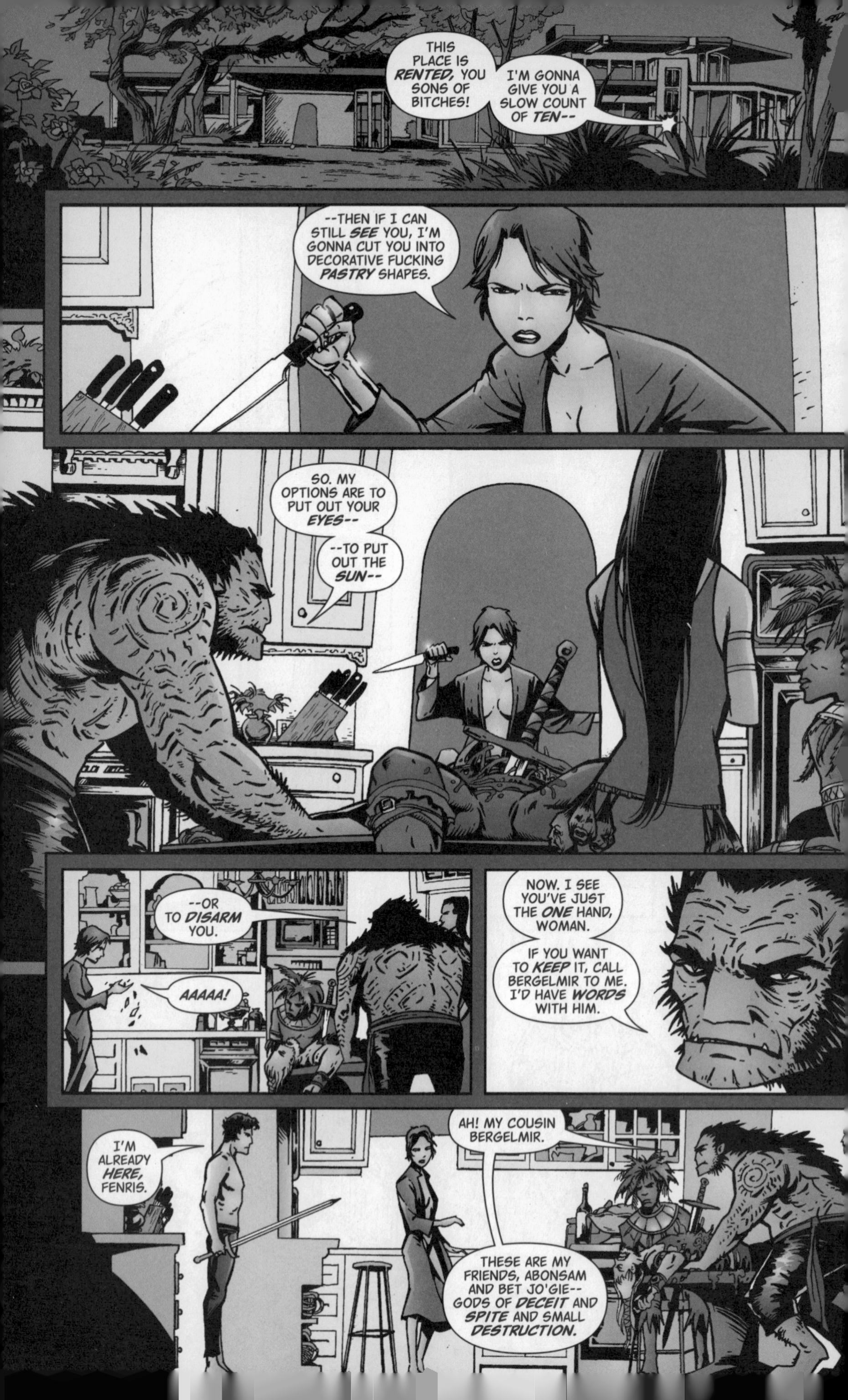
THIS PLACE IS RENTED, YOU SONS OF BITCHES!
I'M GONNA GIVE YOU A SLOW COUNT OF TEN--
--THEN IF I CAN STILL SEE YOU, I'M GONNA CUT YOU INTO DECORATIVE FUCKING PASTRY SHAPES.
SO. MY OPTIONS ARE TO PUT OUT YOUR EYES--
--TO PUT OUT THE SUN--
--OR TO DISARM YOU.
AAAAA!
NOW. I SEE YOU'VE JUST THE ONE HAND, WOMAN.
IF YOU WANT TO KEEP IT, CALL BERGELMIR TO ME. I'D HAVE WORDS WITH HIM.
I'M ALREADY HERE, FENRIS.
AH! MY COUSIN BERGELMIR.
THESE ARE MY FRIENDS, ABONSAM AND BET JO'GIE-- GODS OF DECEIT AND SPITE AND SMALL DESTRUCTION.

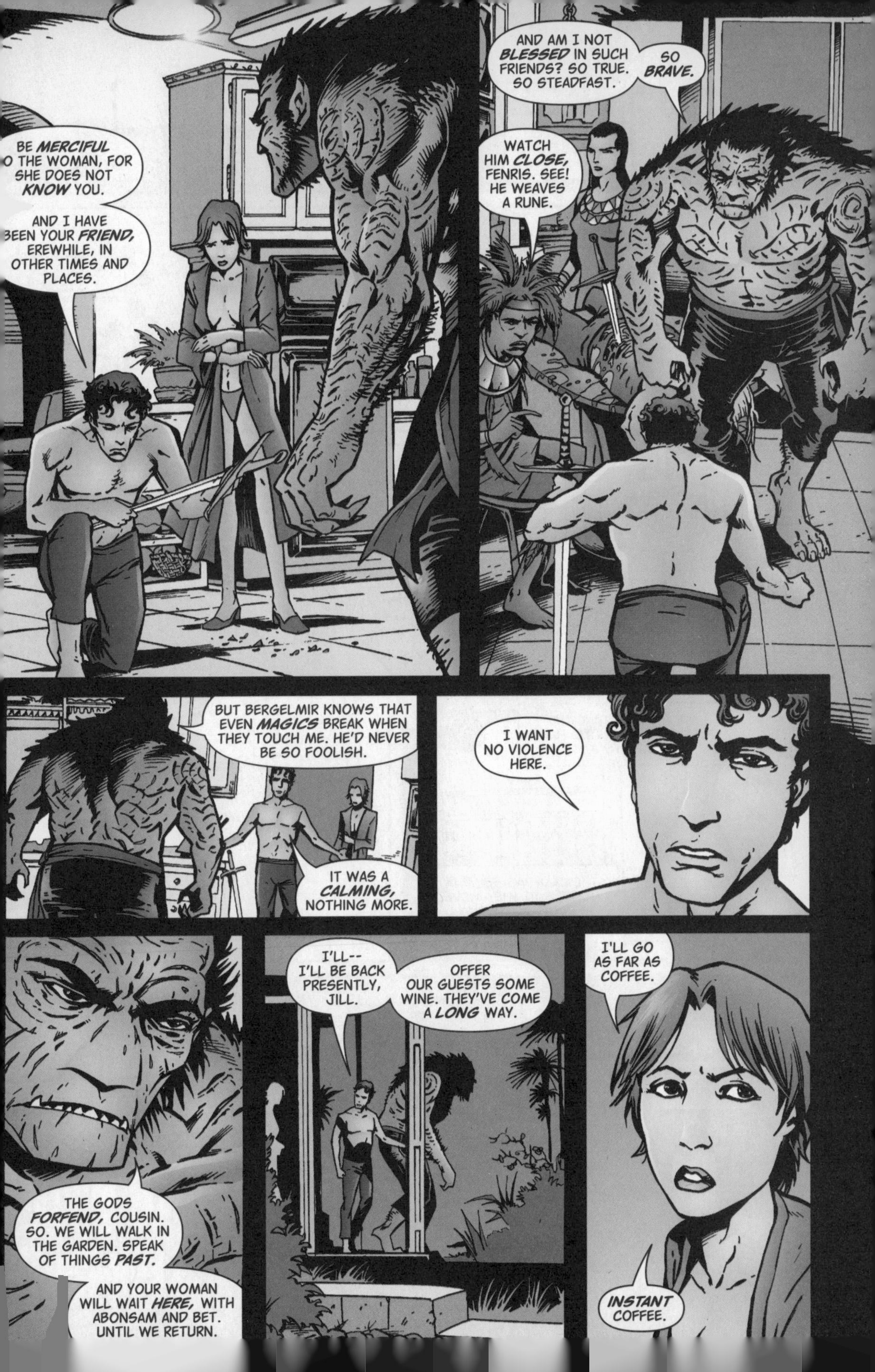
BE MERCIFUL
O THE WOMAN, FOR SHE DOES NOT KNOW YOU.
AND I HAVE BEEN YOUR FRIEND, EREWHILE, IN OTHER TIMES AND PLACES.
AND AM I NOT BLESSED IN SUCH FRIENDS? SO TRUE. SO STEADFAST.
SO BRAVE.
WATCH HIM CLOSE, FENRIS. SEE! HE WEAVES A RUNE.
BUT BERGELMIR KNOWS THAT EVEN MAGICS BREAK WHEN THEY TOUCH ME. HE'D NEVER BE SO FOOLISH.
IT WAS A CALMING, NOTHING MORE.
I WANT NO VIOLENCE HERE.
THE GODS FORFEND, COUSIN. SO. WE WILL WALK IN THE GARDEN. SPEAK OF THINGS PAST.
AND YOUR WOMAN WILL WAIT HERE, WITH ABONSAM AND BET. UNTIL WE RETURN.
I'LL-- I'LL BE BACK PRESENTLY, JILL.
OFFER OUR GUESTS SOME WINE. THEY'VE COME A LONG WAY.
I'LL GO AS FAR AS COFFEE.
INSTANT COFFEE.

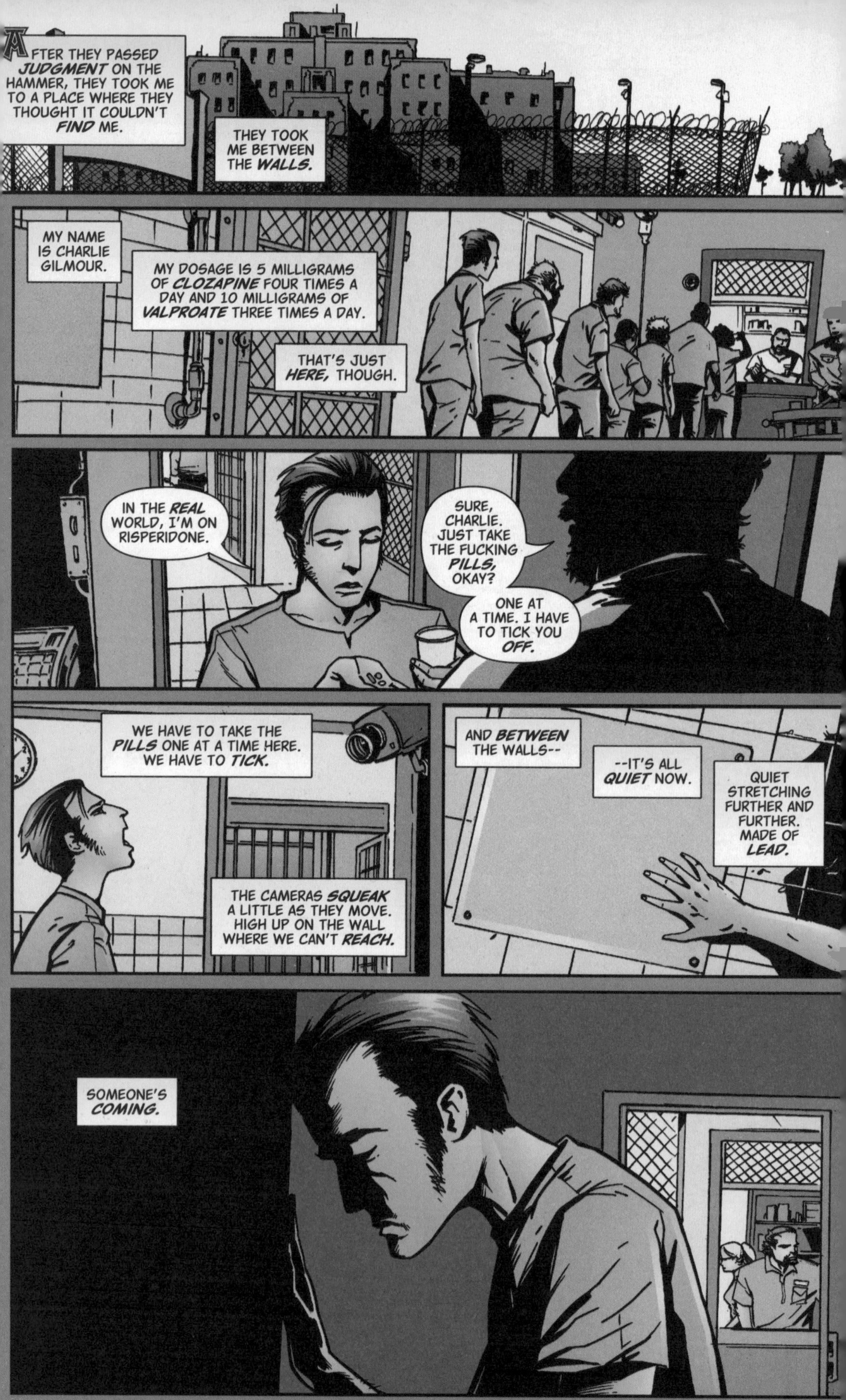
AFTER THEY PASSED JUDGMENT ON THE HAMMER, THEY TOOK ME TO A PLACE WHERE THEY THOUGHT IT COULDN'T FIND ME.
THEY TOOK ME BETWEEN THE WALLS.
MY NAME IS CHARLIE GILMOUR.
MY DOSAGE IS 5 MILLIGRAMS OF CLOZAPINE FOUR TIMES A DAY AND 10 MILLIGRAMS OF VALPROATE THREE TIMES A DAY.
THAT'S JUST HERE, THOUGH.
IN THE REAL WORLD, I'M ON RISPERIDONE.
SURE, CHARLIE. JUST TAKE THE FUCKING PILLS, OKAY?
ONE AT A TIME. I HAVE TO TICK YOU OFF.
WE HAVE TO TAKE THE PILLS ONE AT A TIME HERE. WE HAVE TO TICK.
THE CAMERAS SQUEAK A LITTLE AS THEY MOVE. HIGH UP ON THE WALL WHERE WE CAN'T REACH.
AND BETWEEN THE WALLS--
--IT'S ALL QUIET NOW.
QUIET STRETCHING FURTHER AND FURTHER. MADE OF LEAD.
SOMEONE'S COMING.

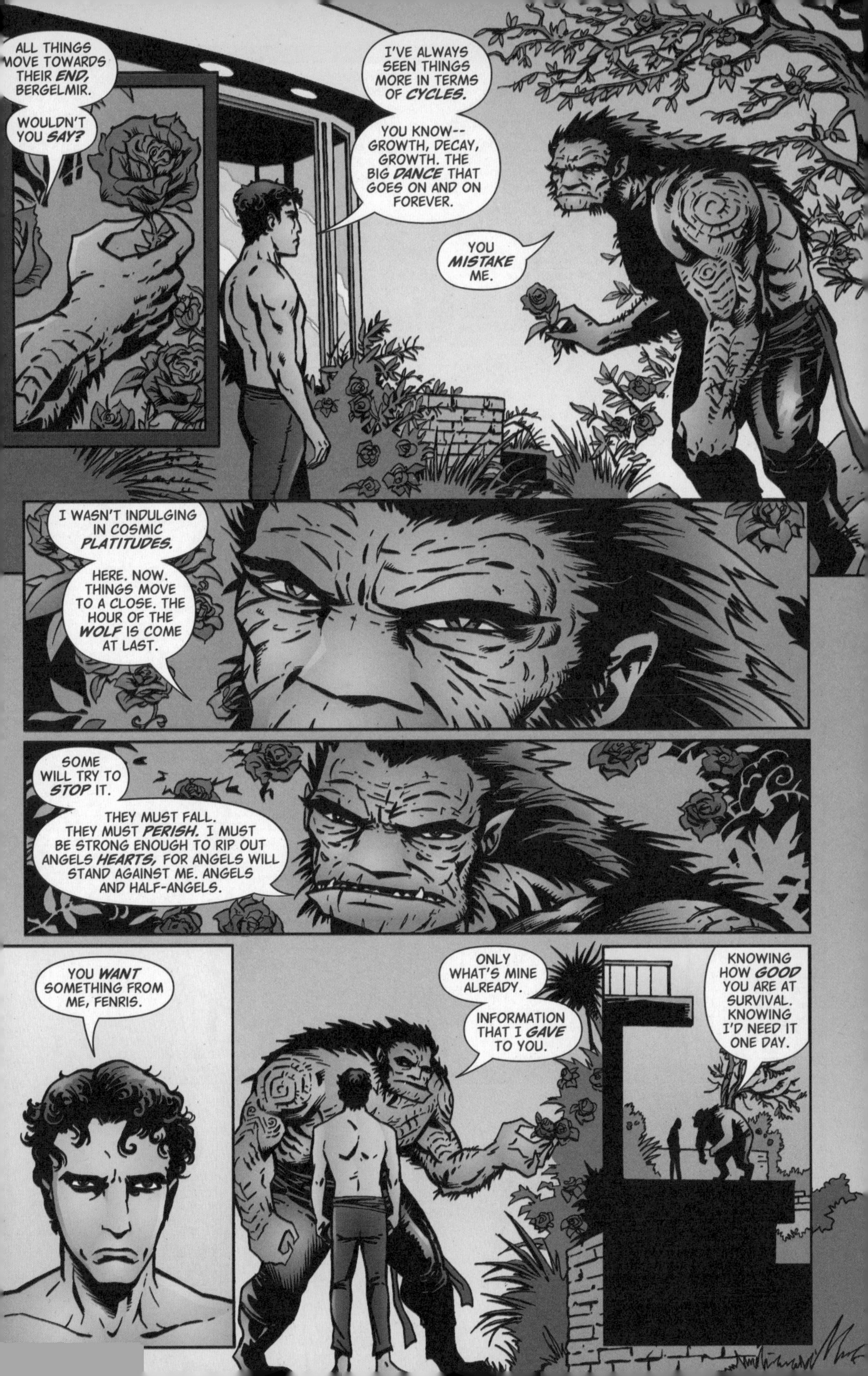
ALL THINGS MOVE TOWARDS THEIR END, BERGELMIR.
WOULDN'T YOU SAY?
I'VE ALWAYS SEEN THINGS MORE IN TERMS OF CYCLES.
YOU KNOW-- GROWTH, DECAY, GROWTH. THE BIG DANCE THAT GOES ON AND ON FOREVER.
YOU MISTAKE ME.
I WASN'T INDULGING IN COSMIC PLATITUDES.
HERE. NOW. THINGS MOVE TO A CLOSE. THE HOUR OF THE WOLF IS COME AT LAST.
SOME WILL TRY TO STOP IT.
THEY MUST FALL. THEY MUST PERISH. I MUST BE STRONG ENOUGH TO RIP OUT ANGELS HEARTS, FOR ANGELS WILL STAND AGAINST ME. ANGELS AND HALF-ANGELS.
YOU WANT SOMETHING FROM ME, FENRIS.
ONLY WHAT'S MINE ALREADY.
INFORMATION THAT I GAVE TO YOU.
KNOWING HOW GOOD YOU ARE AT SURVIVAL. KNOWING I'D NEED IT ONE DAY.

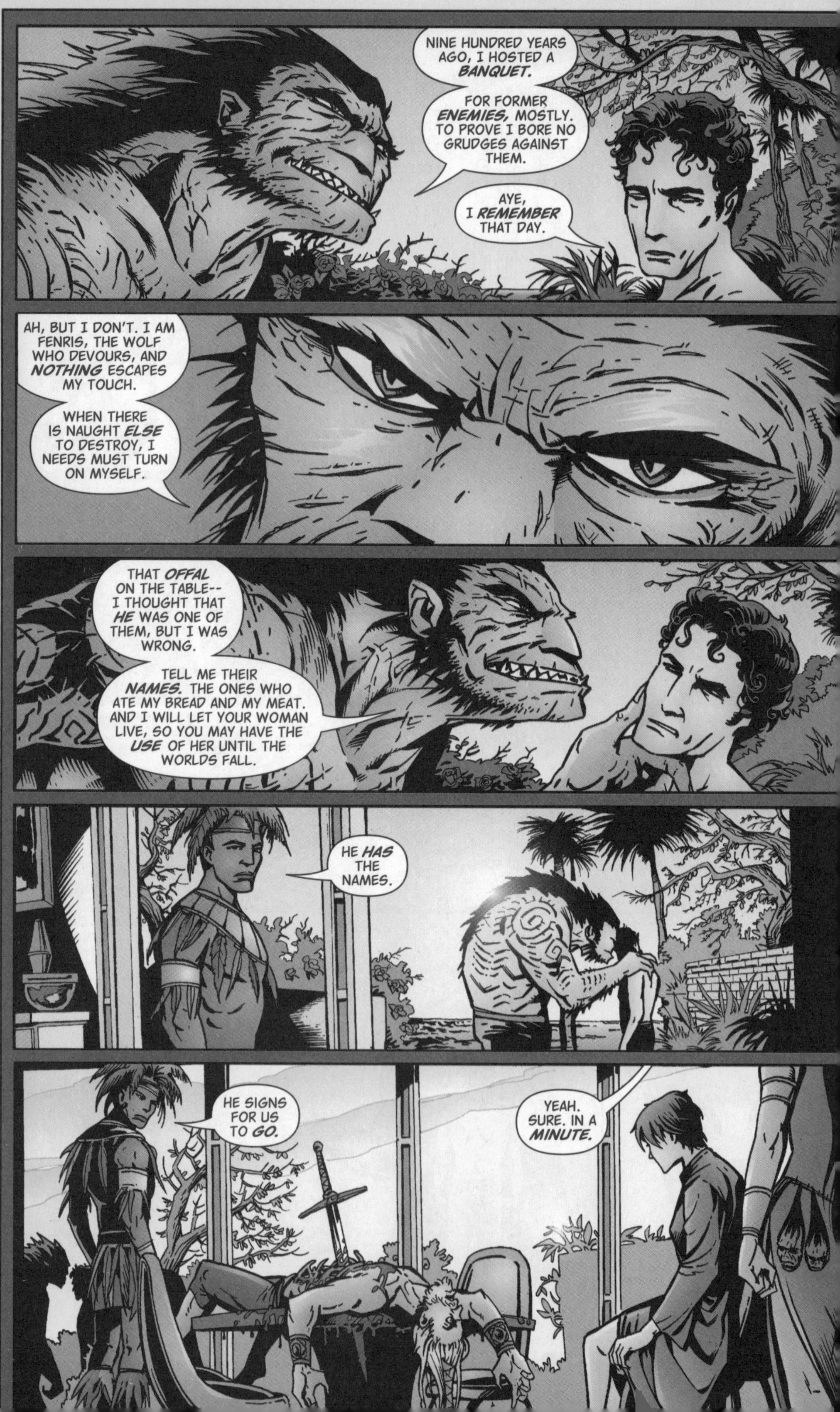
NINE HUNDRED YEARS AGO, I HOSTED A **BANQUET.**
FOR FORMER **ENEMIES,** MOSTLY. TO PROVE I BORE NO GRUDGES AGAINST THEM.
AYE, I **REMEMBER** THAT DAY.
AH, BUT I DON'T. I AM FENRIS, THE WOLF WHO DEVOURS, AND **NOTHING** ESCAPES MY TOUCH.
WHEN THERE IS NAUGHT **ELSE** TO DESTROY, I NEEDS MUST TURN ON MYSELF.
THAT **OFFAL** ON THE TABLE-- I THOUGHT THAT **HE** WAS ONE OF THEM, BUT I WAS WRONG.
TELL ME THEIR **NAMES.** THE ONES WHO ATE MY BREAD AND MY MEAT. AND I WILL LET YOUR WOMAN LIVE, SO YOU MAY HAVE THE **USE** OF HER UNTIL THE WORLDS FALL.
HE **HAS** THE NAMES.
HE SIGNS FOR US TO **GO.**
YEAH. SURE. IN A **MINUTE.**

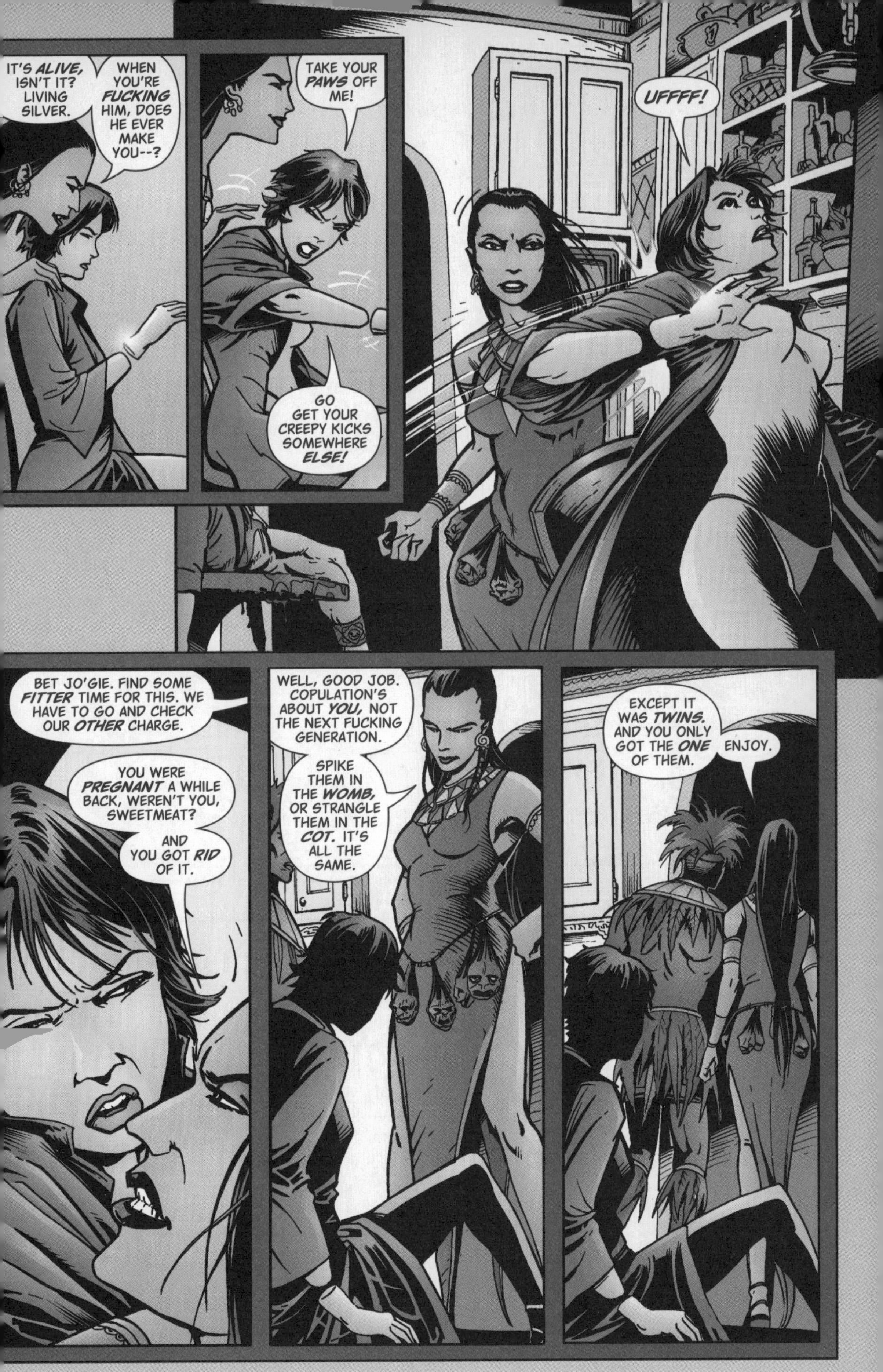
IT'S ALIVE, ISN'T IT? LIVING SILVER.
WHEN YOU'RE FUCKING HIM, DOES HE EVER MAKE YOU--?
TAKE YOUR PAWS OFF ME!
GO GET YOUR CREEPY KICKS SOMEWHERE ELSE!
UFFFF!
BET JO'GIE. FIND SOME FITTER TIME FOR THIS. WE HAVE TO GO AND CHECK OUR OTHER CHARGE.
YOU WERE PREGNANT A WHILE BACK, WEREN'T YOU, SWEETMEAT?
AND YOU GOT RID OF IT.
WELL, GOOD JOB. COPULATION'S ABOUT YOU, NOT THE NEXT FUCKING GENERATION.
SPIKE THEM IN THE WOMB, OR STRANGLE THEM IN THE COT. IT'S ALL THE SAME.
EXCEPT IT WAS TWINS. AND YOU ONLY GOT THE ONE OF THEM.
ENJOY.

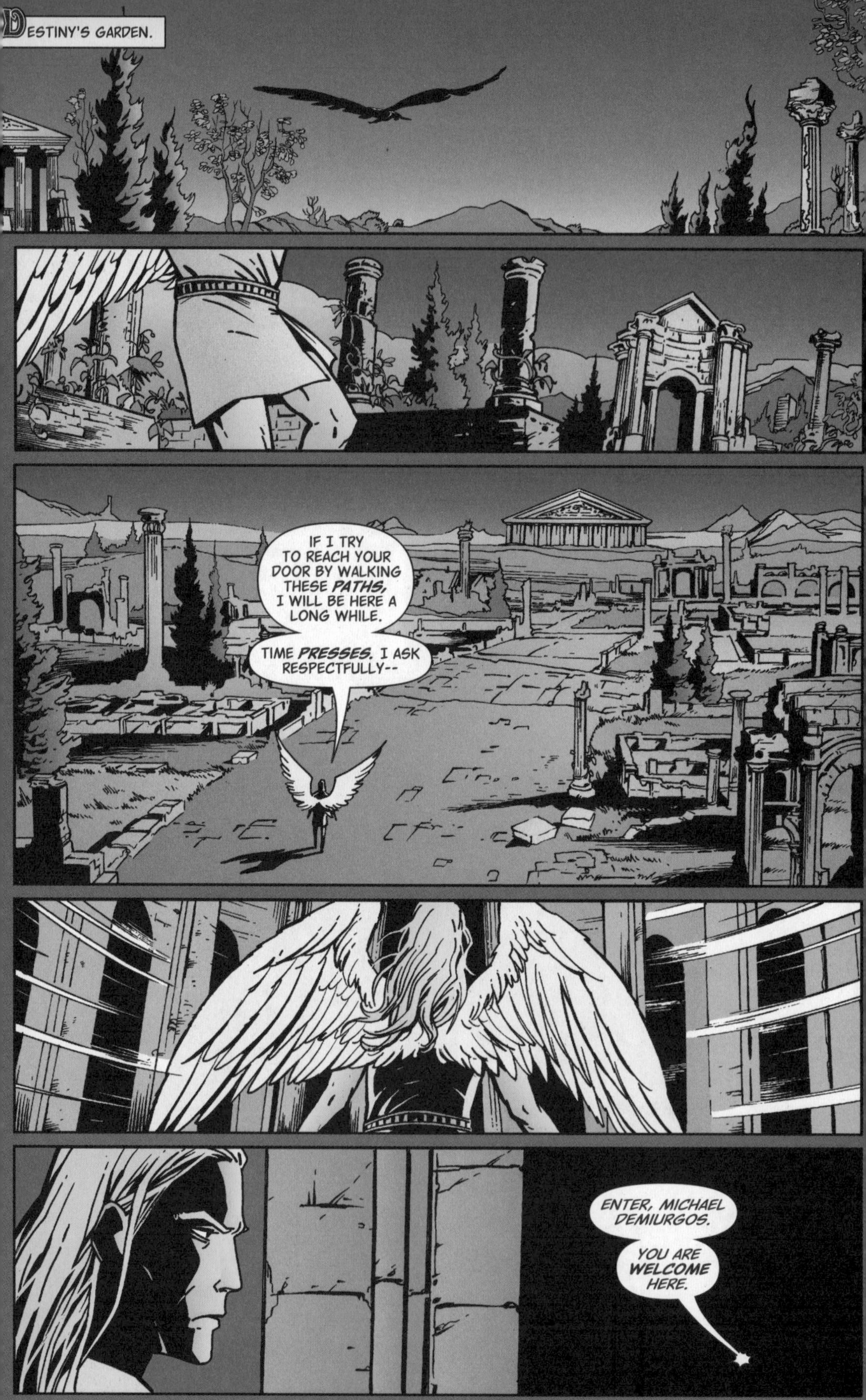
DESTINY'S GARDEN.
IF I TRY TO REACH YOUR DOOR BY WALKING THESE PATHS, I WILL BE HERE A LONG WHILE.
TIME PRESSES. I ASK RESPECTFULLY--
ENTER, MICHAEL DEMIURGOS.
YOU ARE WELCOME HERE.

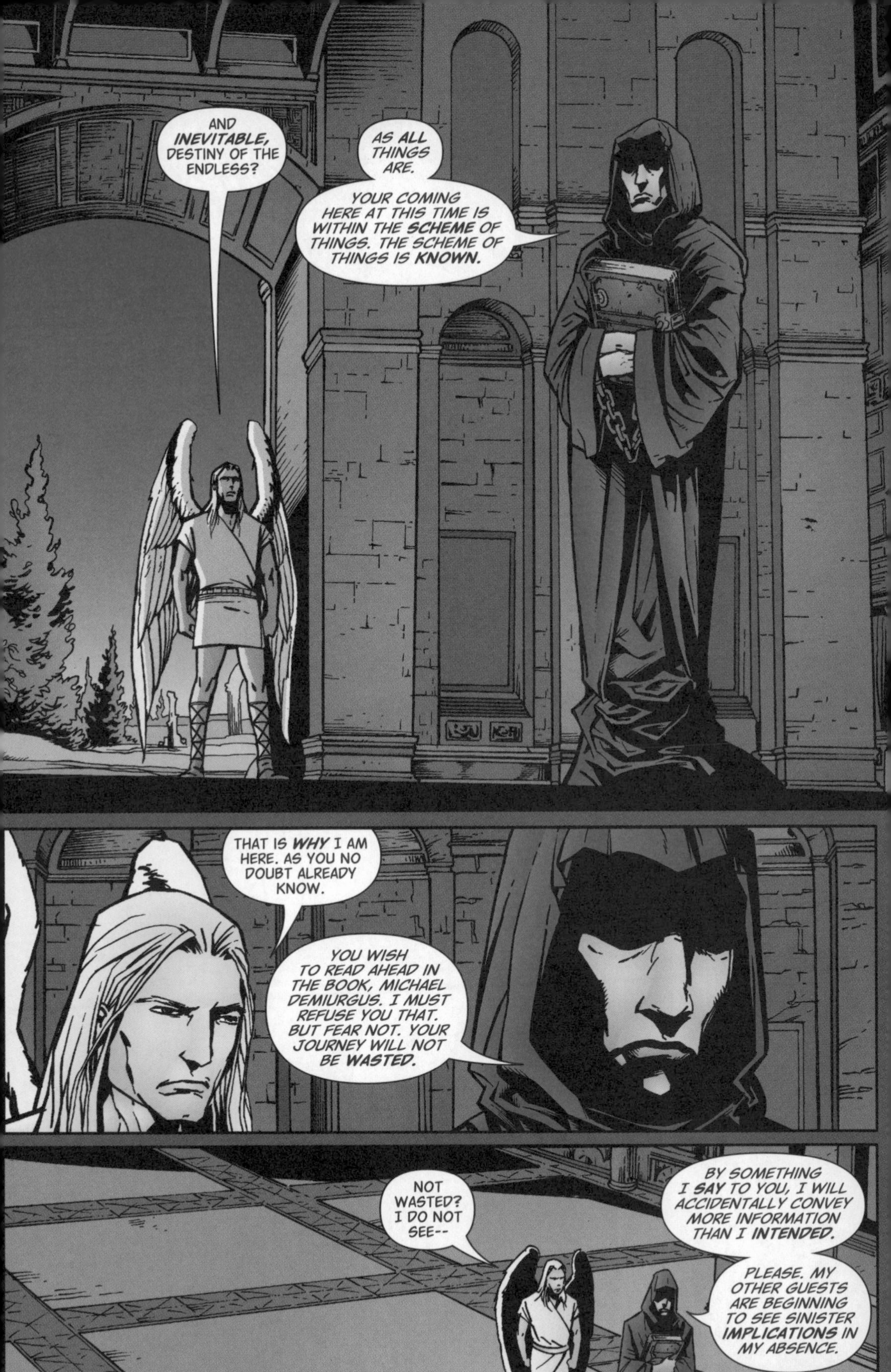
AND INEVITABLE, DESTINY OF THE ENDLESS?
AS ALL THINGS ARE.
YOUR COMING HERE AT THIS TIME IS WITHIN THE SCHEME OF THINGS. THE SCHEME OF THINGS IS KNOWN.
THAT IS WHY I AM HERE. AS YOU NO DOUBT ALREADY KNOW.
YOU WISH TO READ AHEAD IN THE BOOK, MICHAEL DEMIURGUS. I MUST REFUSE YOU THAT. BUT FEAR NOT. YOUR JOURNEY WILL NOT BE WASTED.
NOT WASTED? I DO NOT SEE--
BY SOMETHING I SAY TO YOU, I WILL ACCIDENTALLY CONVEY MORE INFORMATION THAN I INTENDED.
PLEASE. MY OTHER GUESTS ARE BEGINNING TO SEE SINISTER IMPLICATIONS IN MY ABSENCE.

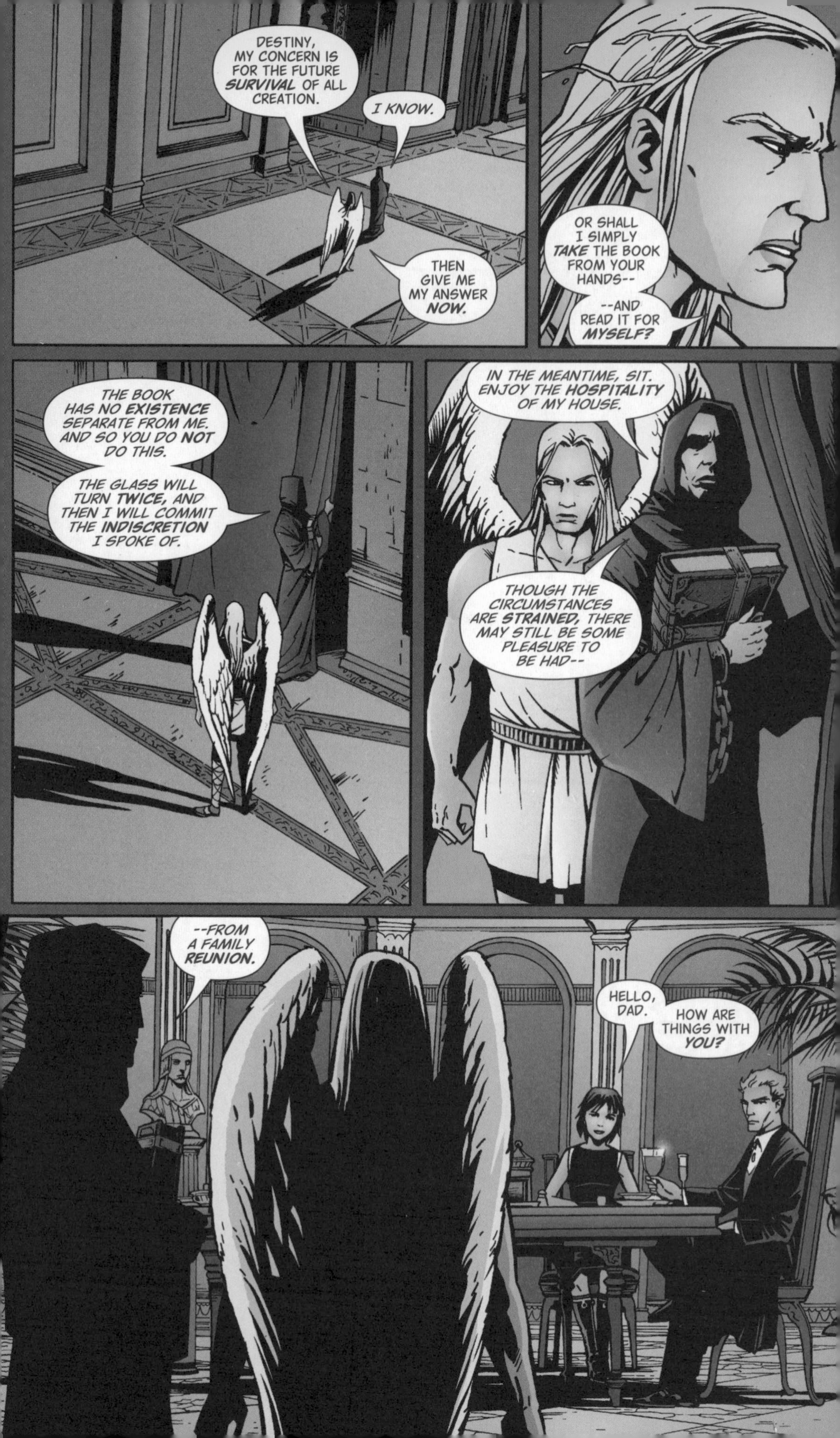
DESTINY, MY CONCERN IS FOR THE FUTURE SURVIVAL OF ALL CREATION.
I KNOW.
THEN GIVE ME MY ANSWER NOW.
OR SHALL I SIMPLY TAKE THE BOOK FROM YOUR HANDS--
--AND READ IT FOR MYSELF?
THE BOOK HAS NO EXISTENCE SEPARATE FROM ME. AND SO YOU DO NOT DO THIS.
THE GLASS WILL TURN TWICE, AND THEN I WILL COMMIT THE INDISCRETION I SPOKE OF.
IN THE MEANTIME, SIT. ENJOY THE HOSPITALITY OF MY HOUSE.
THOUGH THE CIRCUMSTANCES ARE STRAINED, THERE MAY STILL BE SOME PLEASURE TO BE HAD--
--FROM A FAMILY REUNION.
HELLO, DAD.
HOW ARE THINGS WITH YOU?

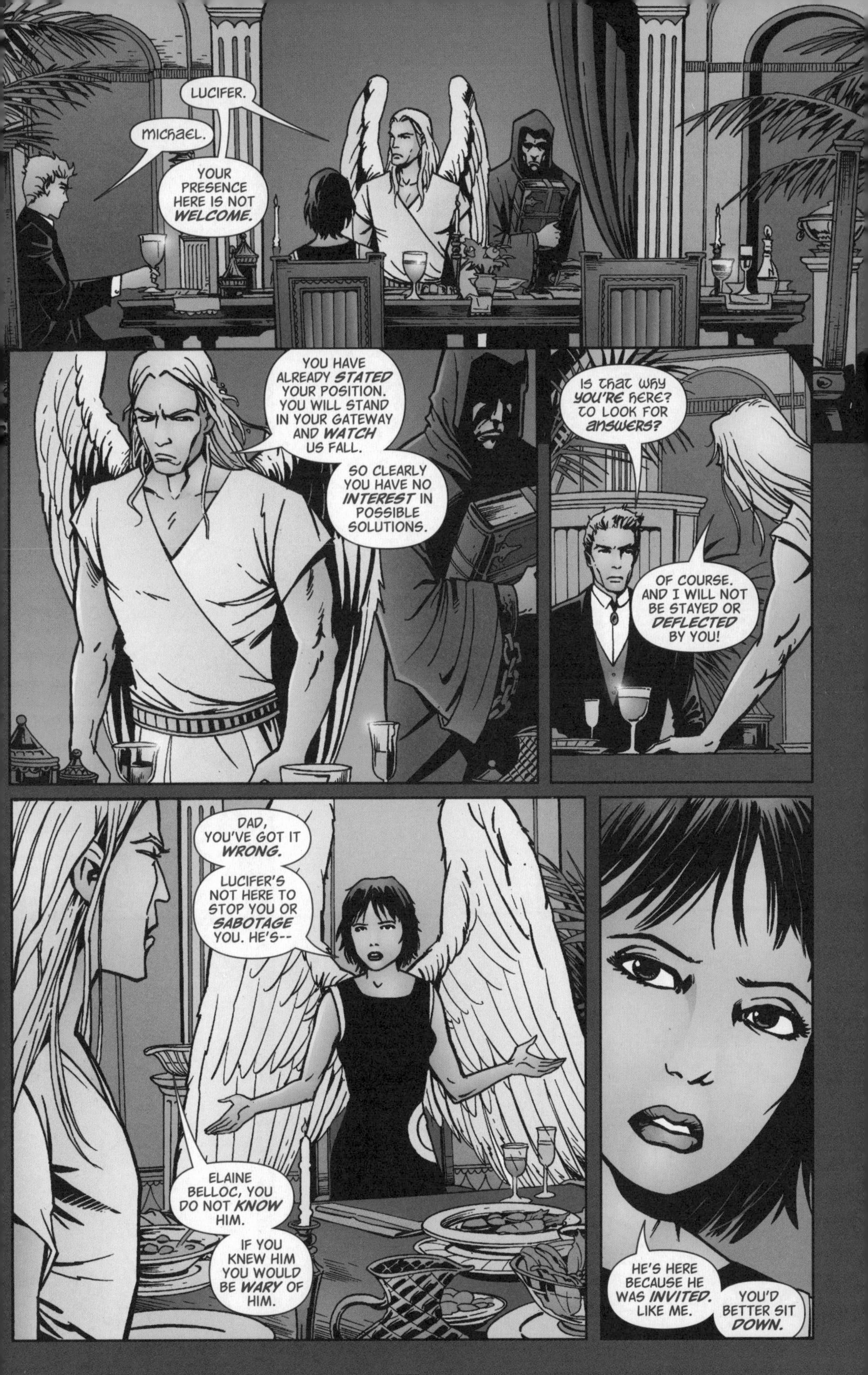
LUCIFER.
MICHAEL.
YOUR PRESENCE HERE IS NOT WELCOME.
YOU HAVE ALREADY STATED YOUR POSITION. YOU WILL STAND IN YOUR GATEWAY AND WATCH US FALL.
SO CLEARLY YOU HAVE NO INTEREST IN POSSIBLE SOLUTIONS.
IS THAT WHY YOU'RE HERE? TO LOOK FOR ANSWERS?
OF COURSE. AND I WILL NOT BE STAYED OR DEFLECTED BY YOU!
DAD, YOU'VE GOT IT WRONG.
LUCIFER'S NOT HERE TO STOP YOU OR SABOTAGE YOU. HE'S--
ELAINE BELLOC, YOU DO NOT KNOW HIM.
IF YOU KNEW HIM YOU WOULD BE WARY OF HIM.
HE'S HERE BECAUSE HE WAS INVITED. LIKE ME.
YOU'D BETTER SIT DOWN.

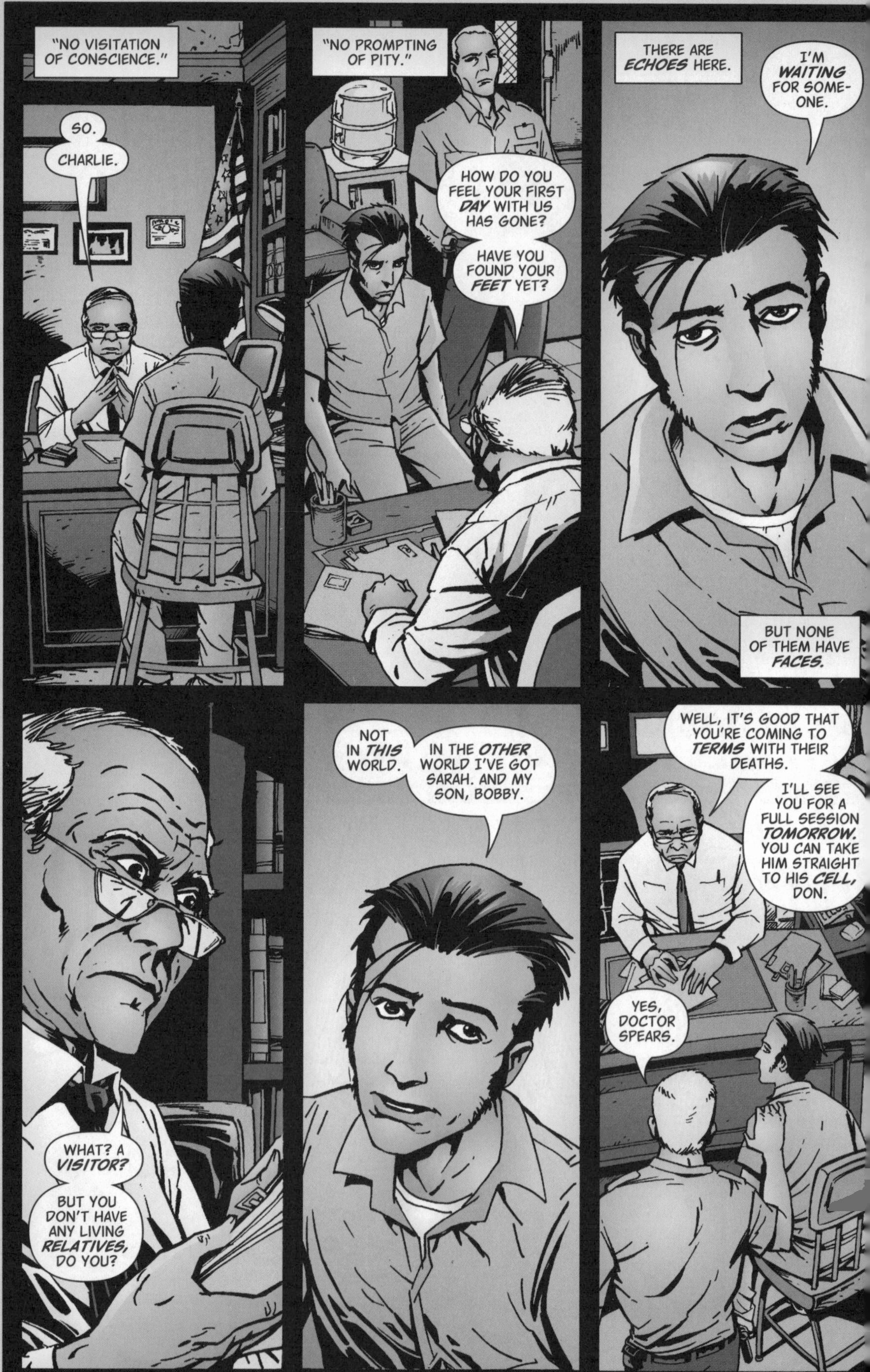
"NO VISITATION OF CONSCIENCE."
SO.
CHARLIE.
"NO PROMPTING OF PITY."
HOW DO YOU FEEL YOUR FIRST DAY WITH US HAS GONE?
HAVE YOU FOUND YOUR FEET YET?
THERE ARE ECHOES HERE.
I'M WAITING FOR SOME-ONE.
BUT NONE OF THEM HAVE FACES.
WHAT? A VISITOR?
BUT YOU DON'T HAVE ANY LIVING RELATIVES, DO YOU?
NOT IN THIS WORLD.
IN THE OTHER WORLD I'VE GOT SARAH. AND MY SON, BOBBY.
WELL, IT'S GOOD THAT YOU'RE COMING TO TERMS WITH THEIR DEATHS.
I'LL SEE YOU FOR A FULL SESSION TOMORROW. YOU CAN TAKE HIM STRAIGHT TO HIS CELL, DON.
YES, DOCTOR SPEARS.

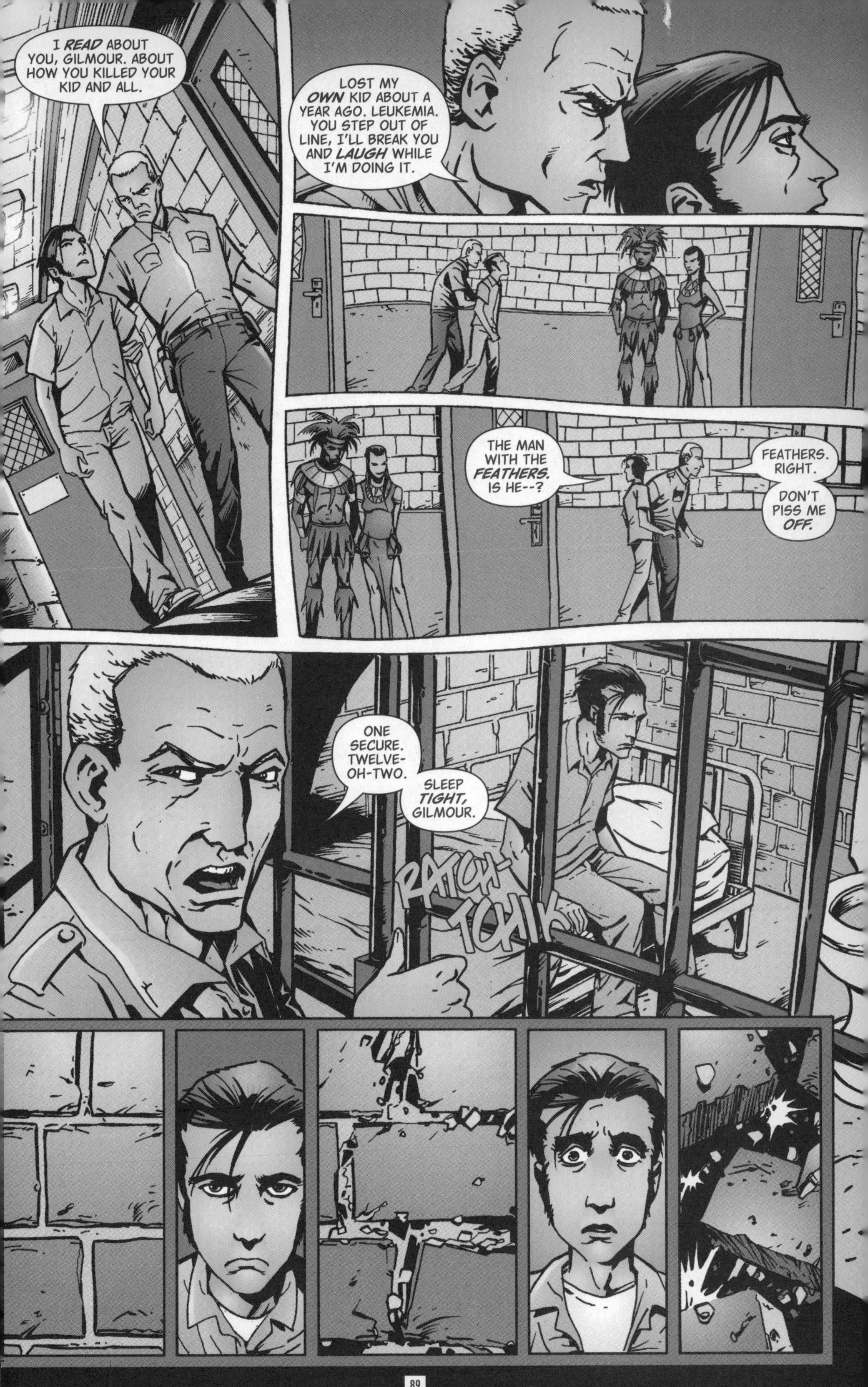
I READ ABOUT YOU, GILMOUR. ABOUT HOW YOU KILLED YOUR KID AND ALL.
LOST MY OWN KID ABOUT A YEAR AGO. LEUKEMIA. YOU STEP OUT OF LINE, I'LL BREAK YOU AND LAUGH WHILE I'M DOING IT.
THE MAN WITH THE FEATHERS. IS HE--?
FEATHERS. RIGHT.
DON'T PISS ME OFF.
ONE SECURE. TWELVE-OH-TWO.
SLEEP TIGHT, GILMOUR.
RATCH-TCHIK

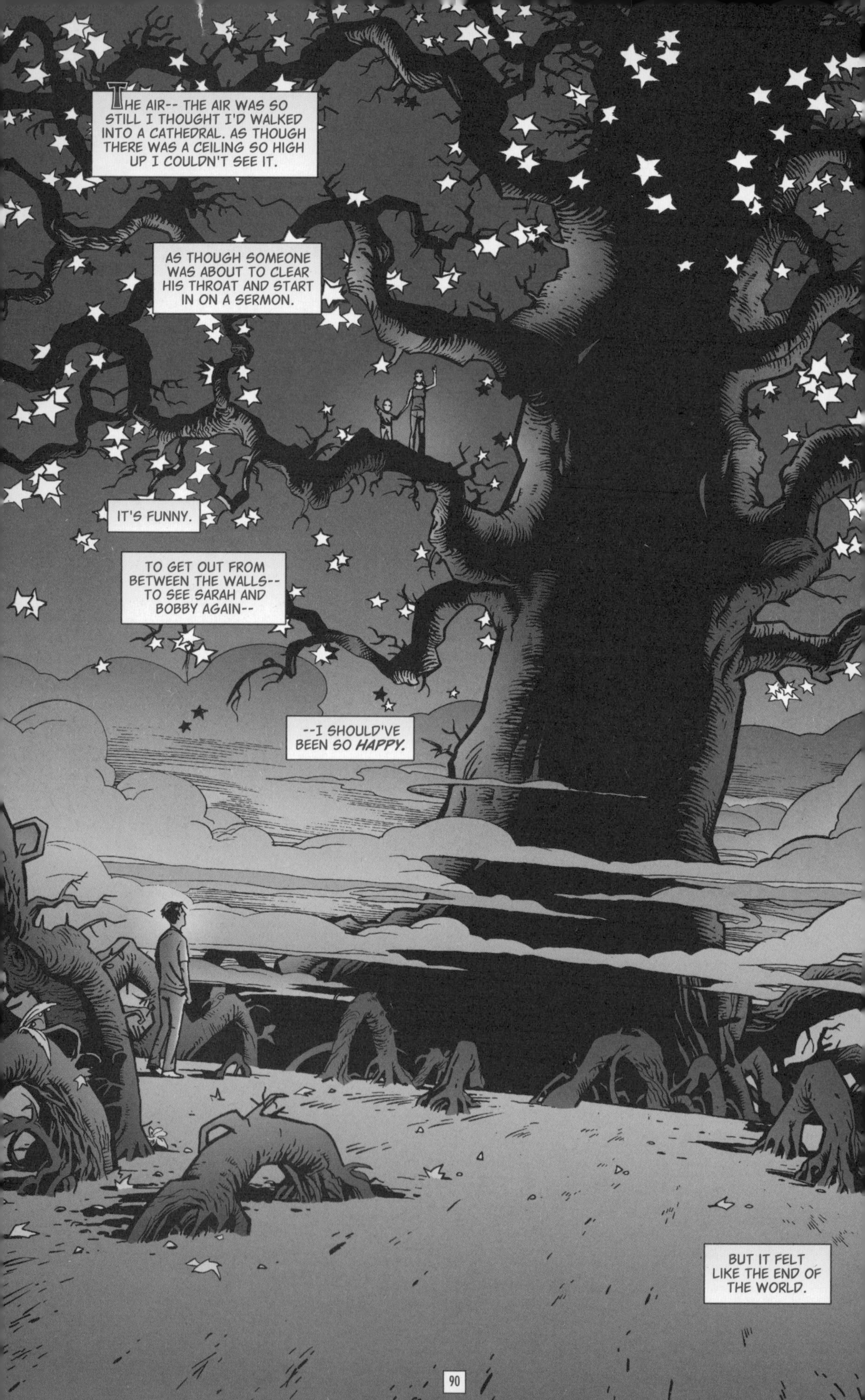
THE AIR-- THE AIR WAS SO STILL I THOUGHT I'D WALKED INTO A CATHEDRAL. AS THOUGH THERE WAS A CEILING SO HIGH UP I COULDN'T SEE IT.
AS THOUGH SOMEONE WAS ABOUT TO CLEAR HIS THROAT AND START IN ON A SERMON.
IT'S FUNNY.
TO GET OUT FROM BETWEEN THE WALLS-- TO SEE SARAH AND BOBBY AGAIN--
--I SHOULD'VE BEEN SO *HAPPY.*
BUT IT FELT LIKE THE END OF THE WORLD.

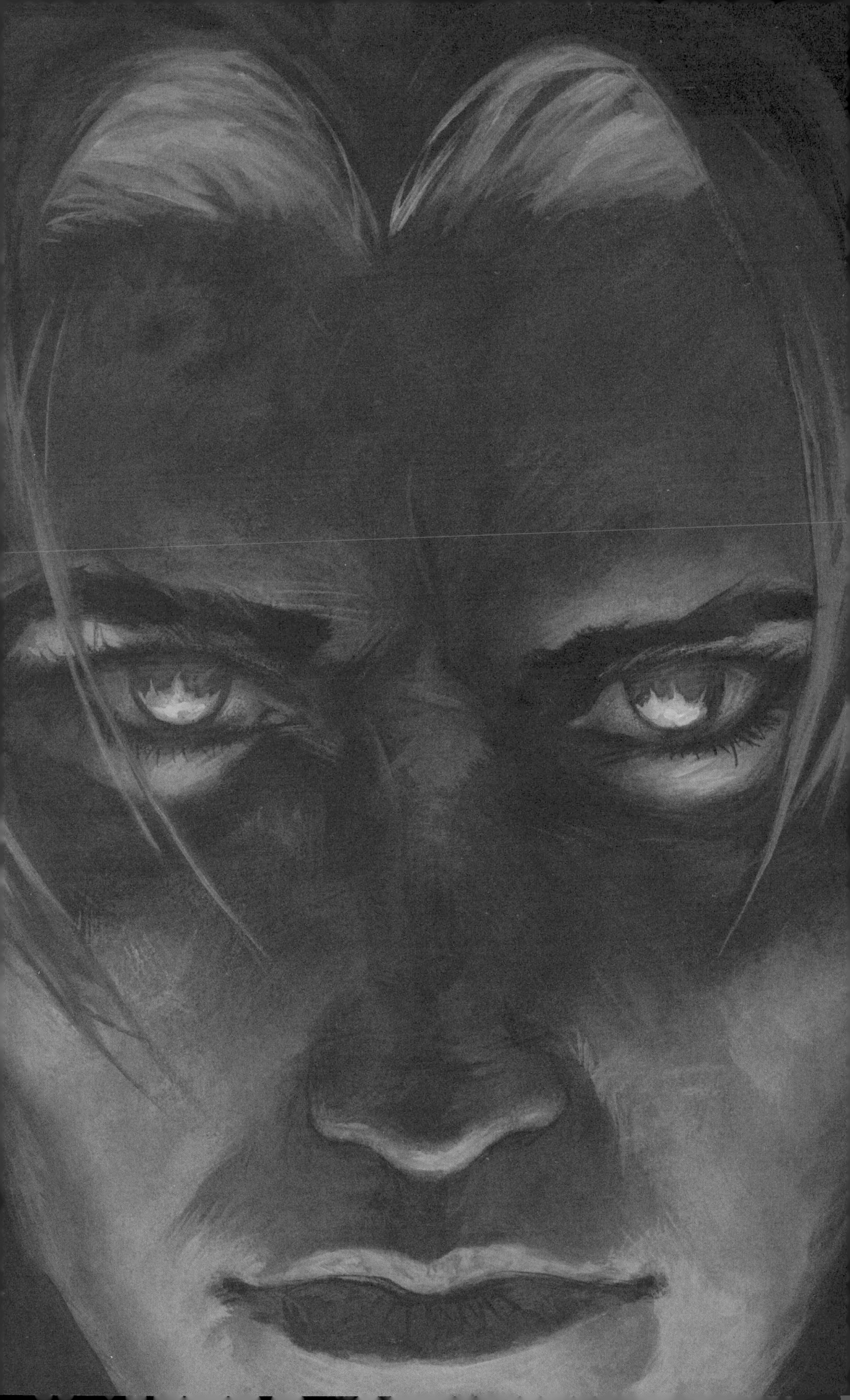

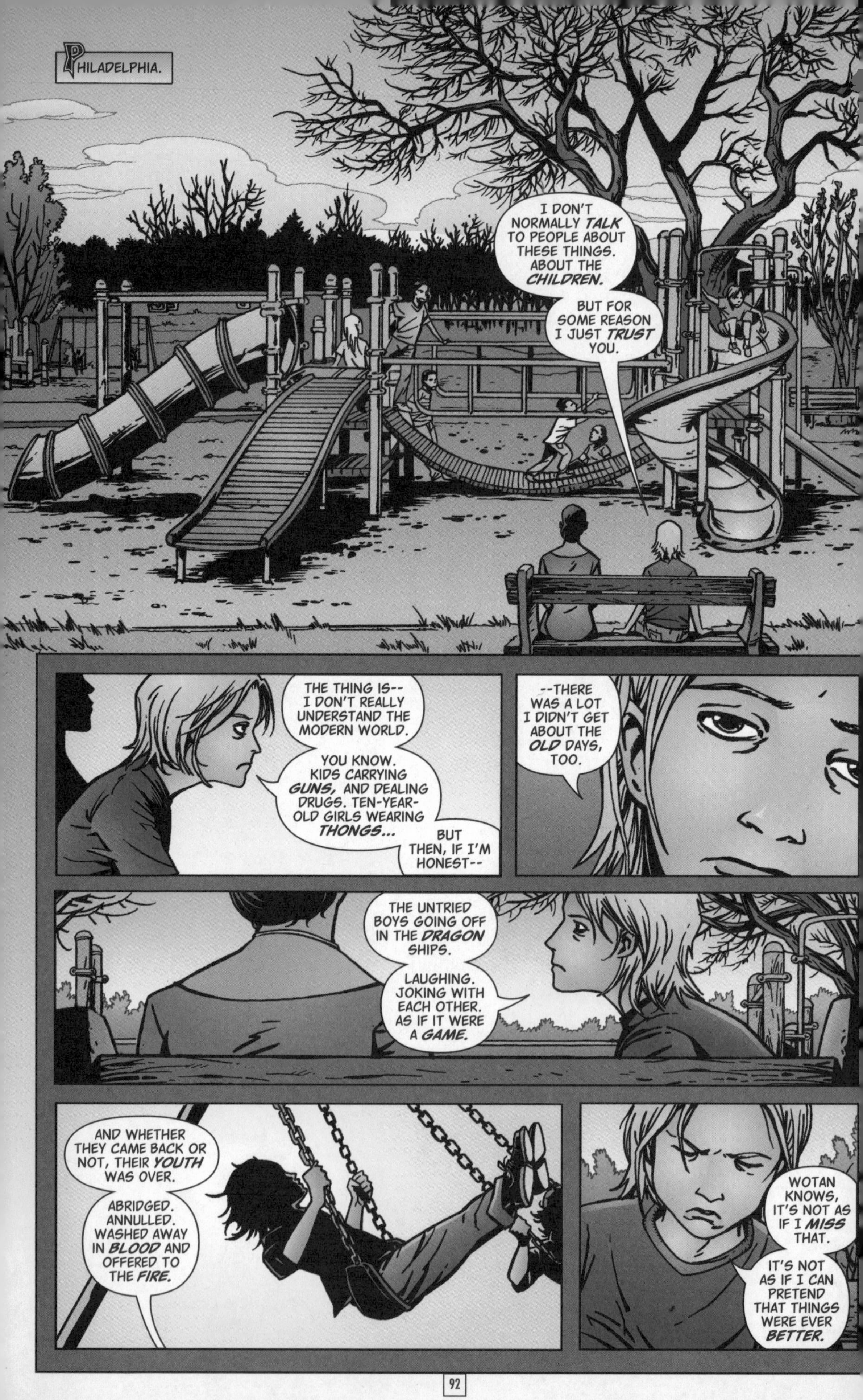
PHILADELPHIA.
I DON'T NORMALLY TALK TO PEOPLE ABOUT THESE THINGS. ABOUT THE CHILDREN.
BUT FOR SOME REASON I JUST TRUST YOU.
THE THING IS-- I DON'T REALLY UNDERSTAND THE MODERN WORLD.
YOU KNOW. KIDS CARRYING GUNS, AND DEALING DRUGS. TEN-YEAR-OLD GIRLS WEARING THONGS...
BUT THEN, IF I'M HONEST--
--THERE WAS A LOT I DIDN'T GET ABOUT THE OLD DAYS, TOO.
THE UNTRIED BOYS GOING OFF IN THE DRAGON SHIPS.
LAUGHING. JOKING WITH EACH OTHER. AS IF IT WERE A GAME.
AND WHETHER THEY CAME BACK OR NOT, THEIR YOUTH WAS OVER.
ABRIDGED. ANNULLED. WASHED AWAY IN BLOOD AND OFFERED TO THE FIRE.
WOTAN KNOWS, IT'S NOT AS IF I MISS THAT.
IT'S NOT AS IF I CAN PRETEND THAT THINGS WERE EVER BETTER.

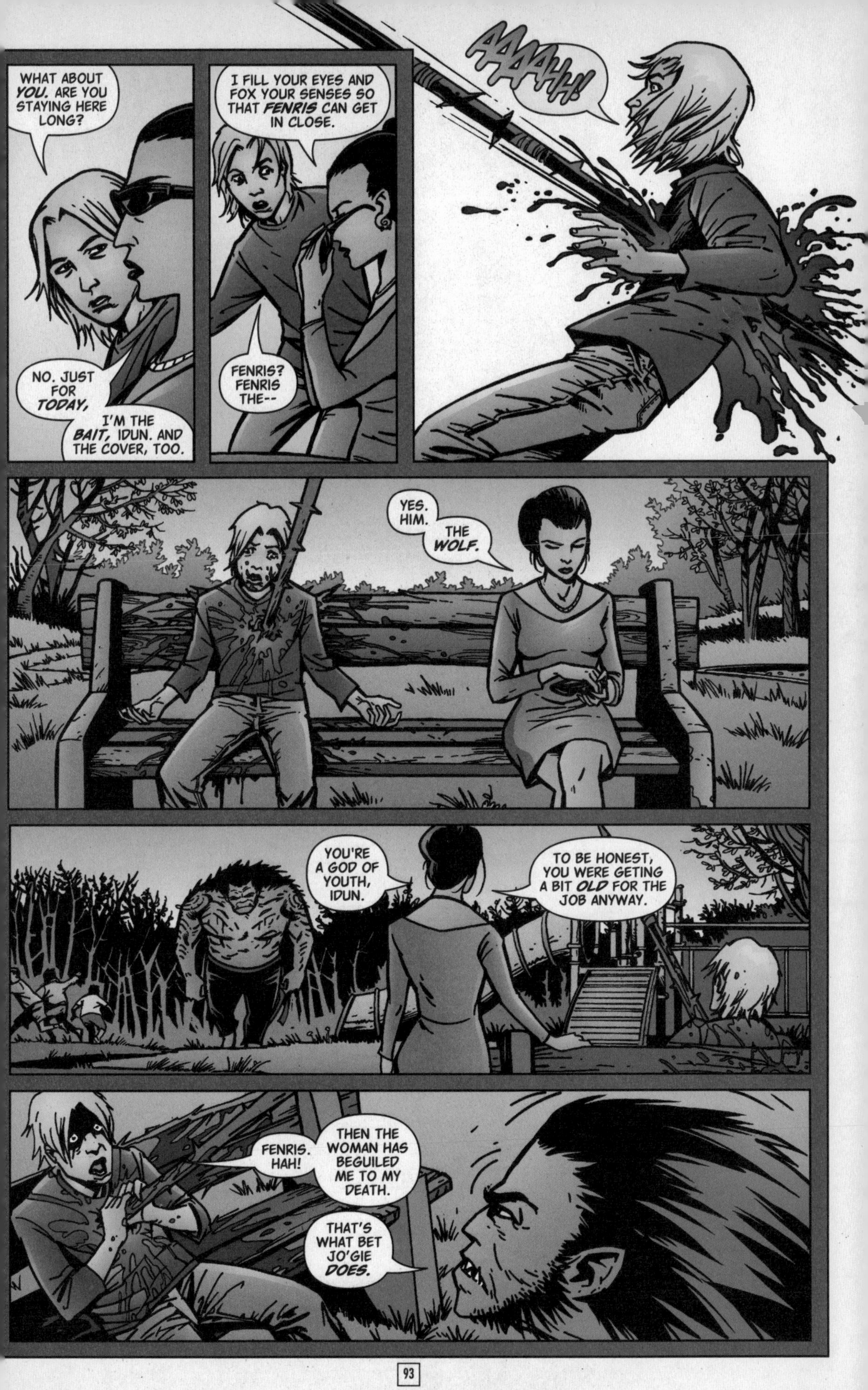
WHAT ABOUT YOU. ARE YOU STAYING HERE LONG?
NO. JUST FOR TODAY,
I'M THE BAIT, IDUN. AND THE COVER, TOO.
I FILL YOUR EYES AND FOX YOUR SENSES SO THAT FENRIS CAN GET IN CLOSE.
FENRIS? FENRIS THE--
AAAAHH!
YES. HIM.
THE WOLF.
YOU'RE A GOD OF YOUTH, IDUN.
TO BE HONEST, YOU WERE GETING A BIT OLD FOR THE JOB ANYWAY.
FENRIS. HAH!
THEN THE WOMAN HAS BEGUILED ME TO MY DEATH.
THAT'S WHAT BET JO'GIE DOES.

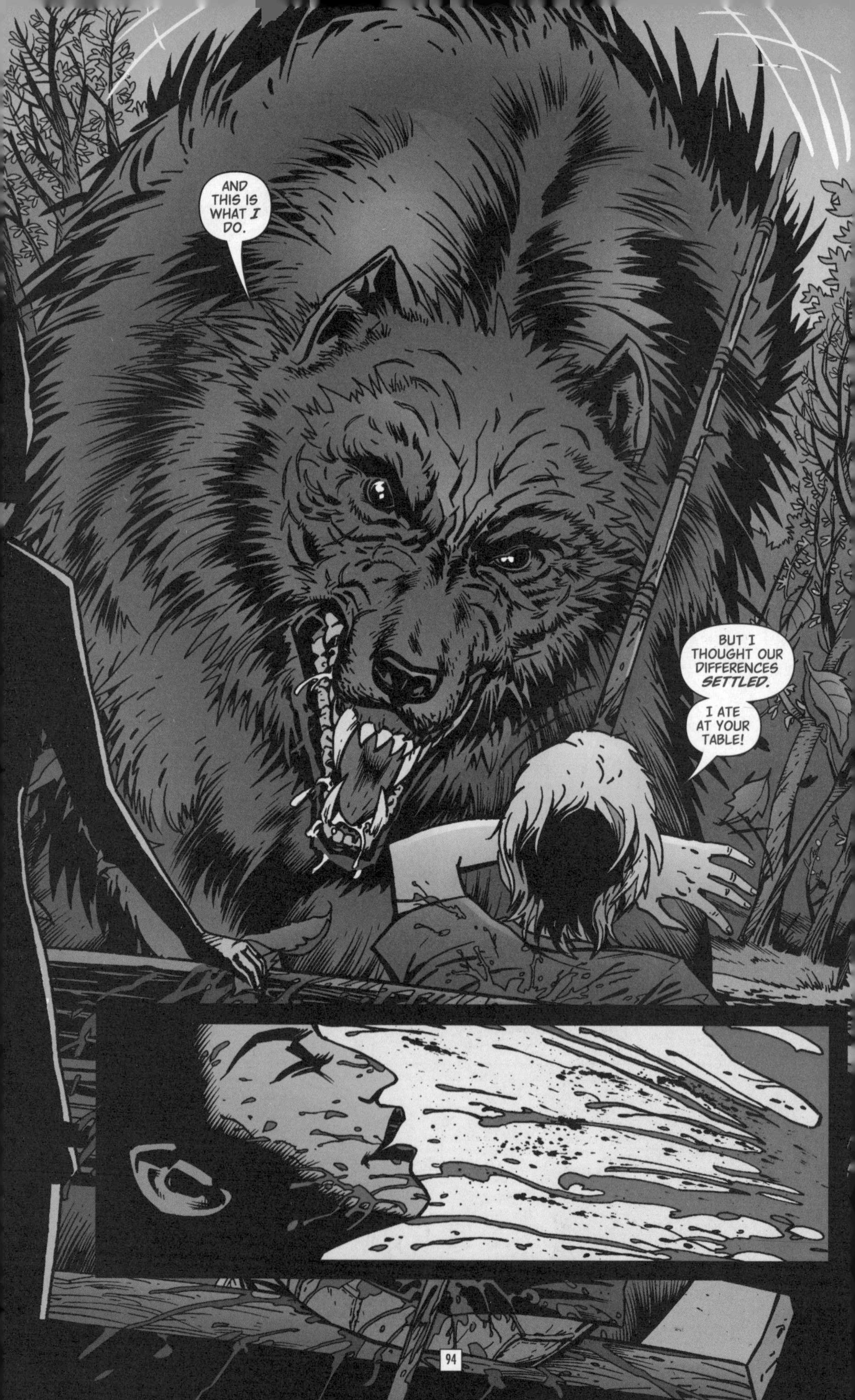
AND THIS IS WHAT I DO.
BUT I THOUGHT OUR DIFFERENCES SETTLED.
I ATE AT YOUR TABLE!

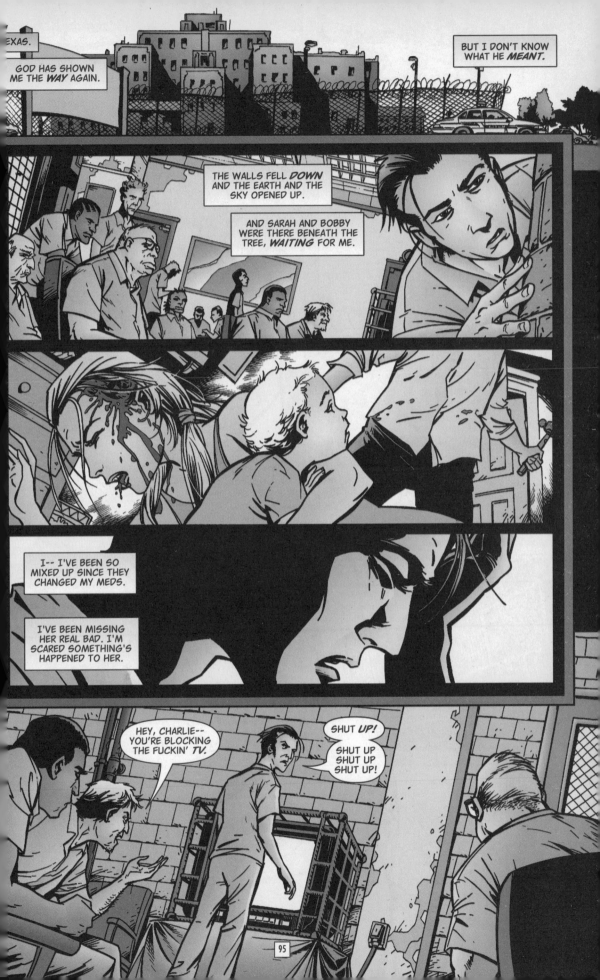

XAS.

GOD HAS SHOWN ME THE *WAY* AGAIN.

BUT I DON'T KNOW WHAT HE *MEANT*.

THE WALLS FELL *DOWN* AND THE EARTH AND THE SKY OPENED UP.

AND SARAH AND BOBBY WERE THERE BENEATH THE TREE, *WAITING* FOR ME.

I-- I'VE BEEN SO MIXED UP SINCE THEY CHANGED MY MEDS.

I'VE BEEN MISSING HER REAL BAD. I'M SCARED SOMETHING'S HAPPENED TO HER.

HEY, CHARLIE-- YOU'RE BLOCKING THE FUCKIN' *TV.*

SHUT *UP!*

SHUT UP SHUT UP SHUT UP!

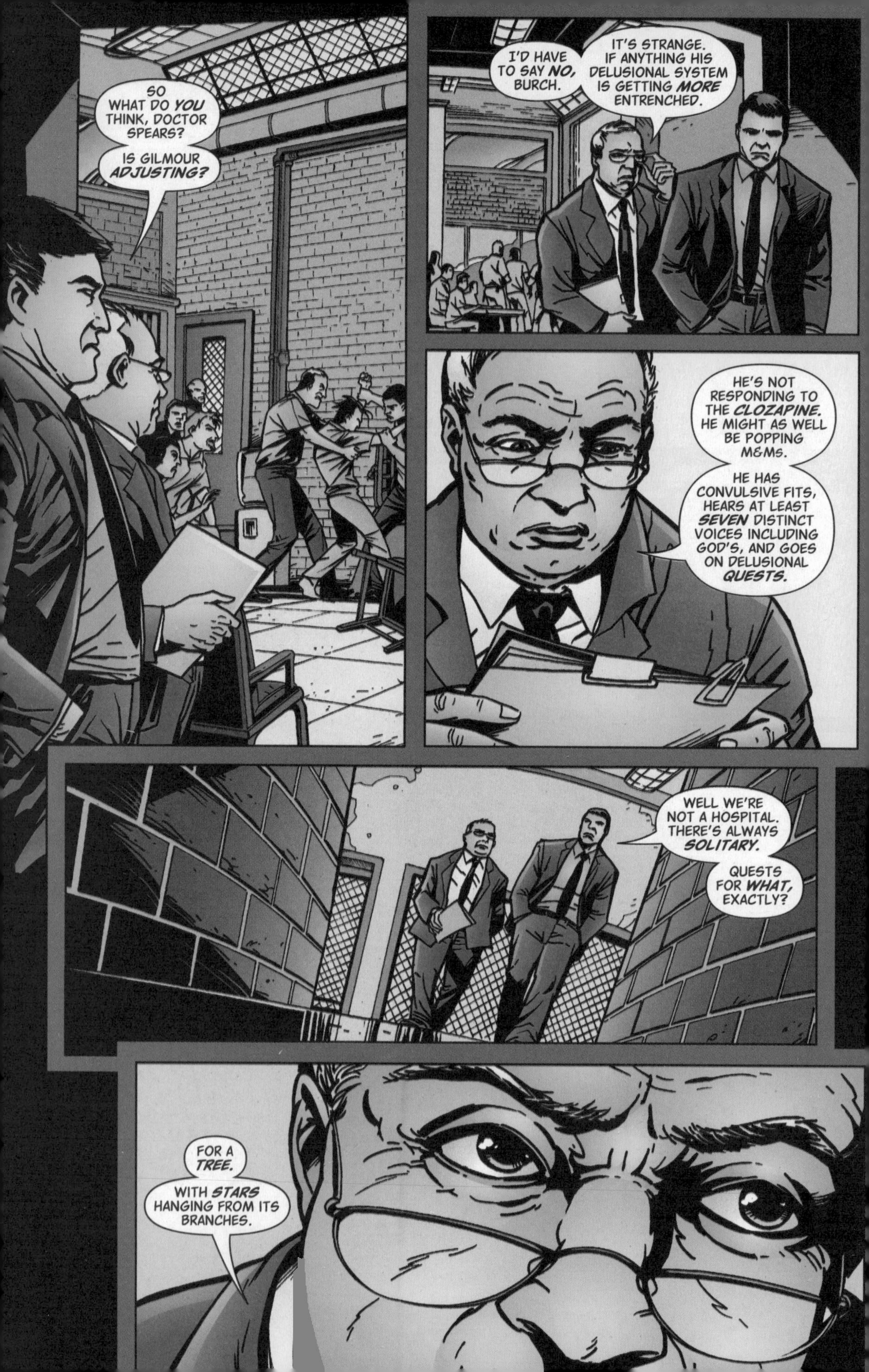
SO WHAT DO YOU THINK, DOCTOR SPEARS?
IS GILMOUR ADJUSTING?
I'D HAVE TO SAY NO, BURCH.
IT'S STRANGE. IF ANYTHING HIS DELUSIONAL SYSTEM IS GETTING MORE ENTRENCHED.
HE'S NOT RESPONDING TO THE CLOZAPINE. HE MIGHT AS WELL BE POPPING M&Ms.
HE HAS CONVULSIVE FITS, HEARS AT LEAST SEVEN DISTINCT VOICES INCLUDING GOD'S, AND GOES ON DELUSIONAL QUESTS.
WELL WE'RE NOT A HOSPITAL. THERE'S ALWAYS SOLITARY.
QUESTS FOR WHAT, EXACTLY?
FOR A TREE.
WITH STARS HANGING FROM ITS BRANCHES.

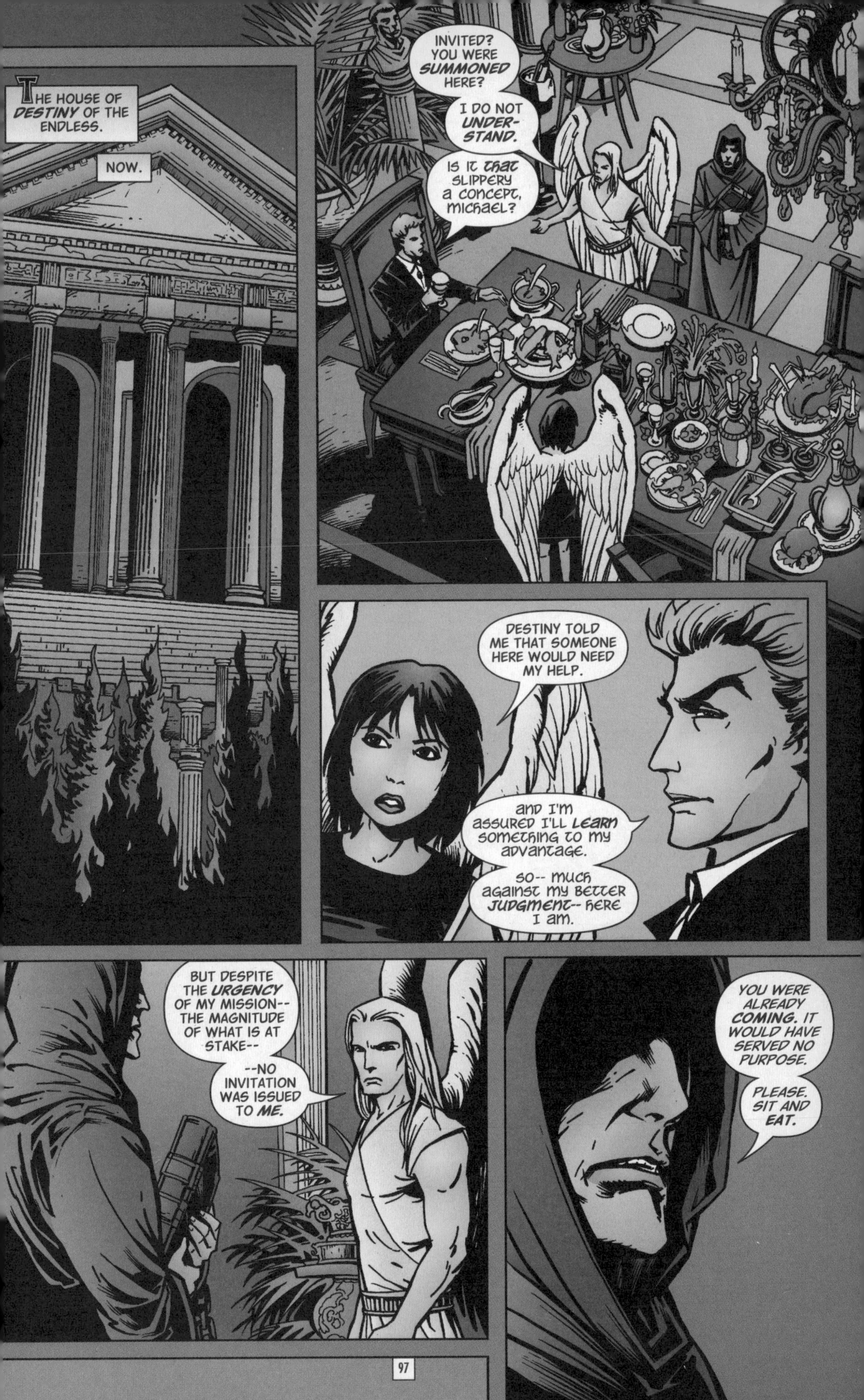
THE HOUSE OF DESTINY OF THE ENDLESS.
NOW.
INVITED? YOU WERE SUMMONED HERE?
I DO NOT UNDER-STAND.
IS IT THAT SLIPPERY A CONCEPT, MICHAEL?
DESTINY TOLD ME THAT SOMEONE HERE WOULD NEED MY HELP.
AND I'M ASSURED I'LL LEARN SOMETHING TO MY ADVANTAGE.
SO-- MUCH AGAINST MY BETTER JUDGMENT-- HERE I AM.
BUT DESPITE THE URGENCY OF MY MISSION-- THE MAGNITUDE OF WHAT IS AT STAKE--
--NO INVITATION WAS ISSUED TO ME.
YOU WERE ALREADY COMING. IT WOULD HAVE SERVED NO PURPOSE.
PLEASE. SIT AND EAT.

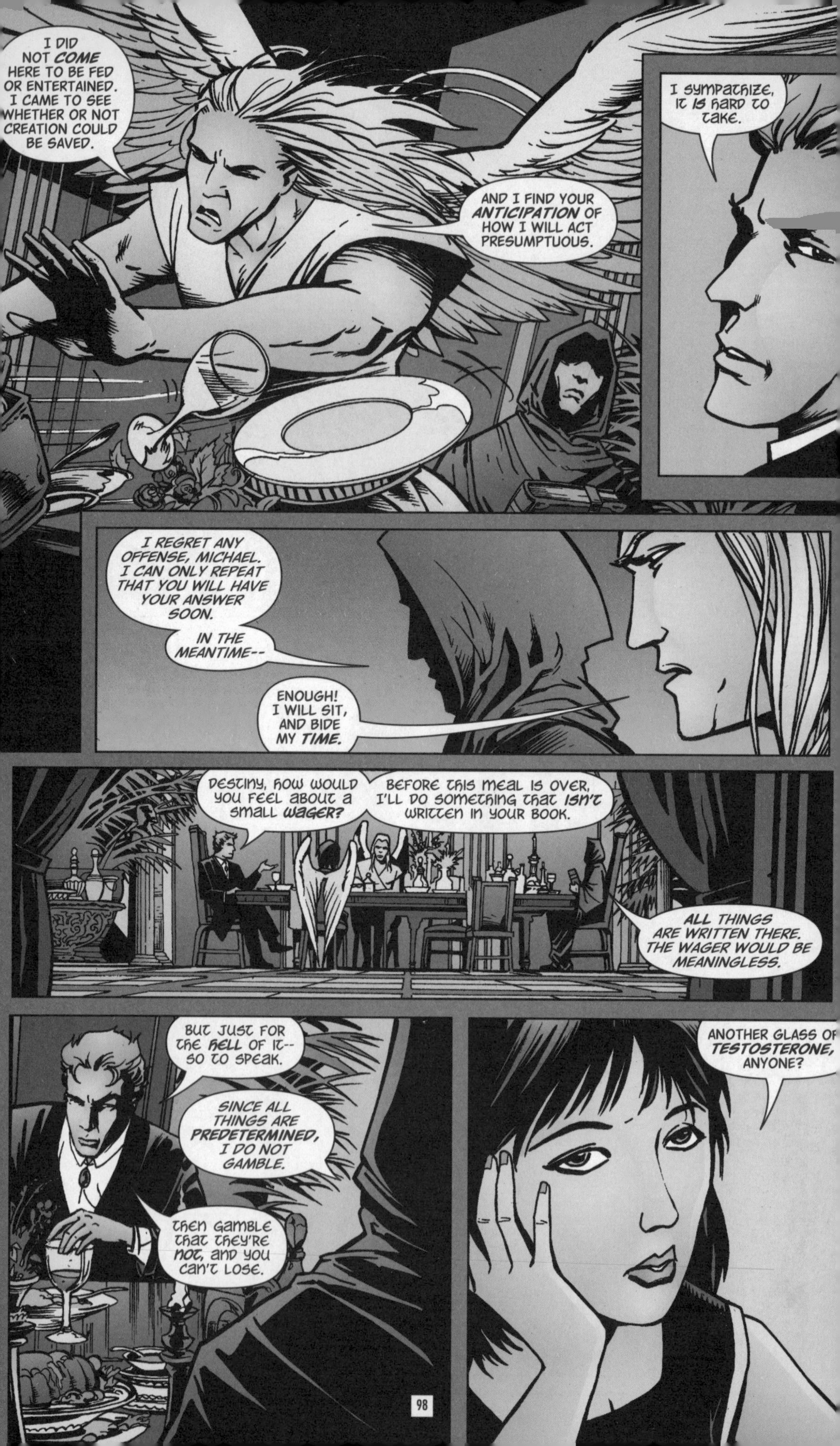
I DID NOT COME HERE TO BE FED OR ENTERTAINED. I CAME TO SEE WHETHER OR NOT CREATION COULD BE SAVED.
AND I FIND YOUR ANTICIPATION OF HOW I WILL ACT PRESUMPTUOUS.
I SYMPATHIZE, IT IS HARD TO TAKE.
I REGRET ANY OFFENSE, MICHAEL. I CAN ONLY REPEAT THAT YOU WILL HAVE YOUR ANSWER SOON.
IN THE MEANTIME--
ENOUGH! I WILL SIT, AND BIDE MY TIME.
DESTINY, HOW WOULD YOU FEEL ABOUT A SMALL WAGER?
BEFORE THIS MEAL IS OVER, I'LL DO SOMETHING THAT ISN'T WRITTEN IN YOUR BOOK.
ALL THINGS ARE WRITTEN THERE. THE WAGER WOULD BE MEANINGLESS.
BUT JUST FOR THE HELL OF IT-- SO TO SPEAK.
SINCE ALL THINGS ARE PREDETERMINED, I DO NOT GAMBLE.
THEN GAMBLE THAT THEY'RE NOT, AND YOU CAN'T LOSE.
ANOTHER GLASS OF TESTOSTERONE, ANYONE?

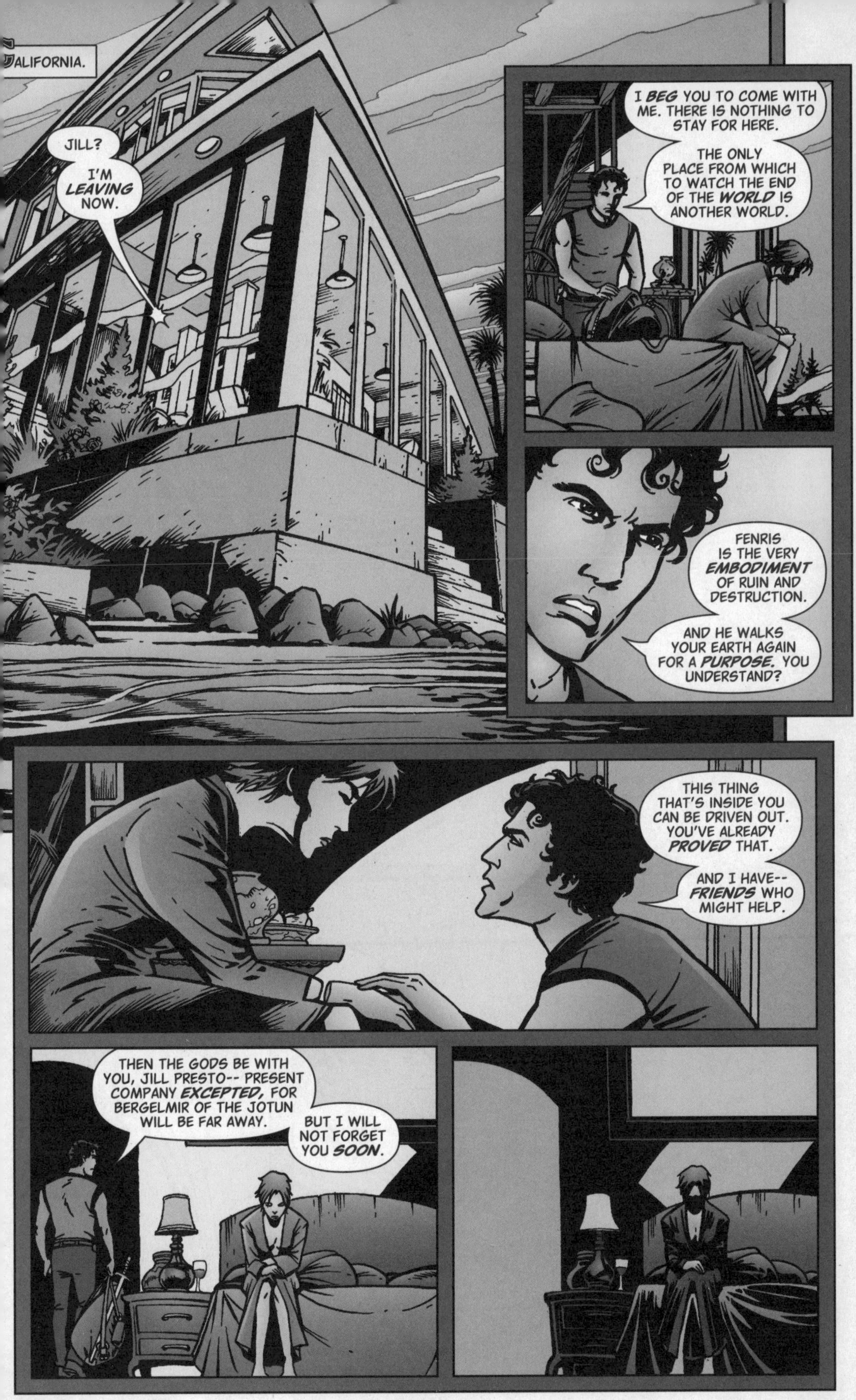
CALIFORNIA.
JILL?
I'M LEAVING NOW.
I BEG YOU TO COME WITH ME. THERE IS NOTHING TO STAY FOR HERE.
THE ONLY PLACE FROM WHICH TO WATCH THE END OF THE WORLD IS ANOTHER WORLD.
FENRIS IS THE VERY EMBODIMENT OF RUIN AND DESTRUCTION.
AND HE WALKS YOUR EARTH AGAIN FOR A PURPOSE. YOU UNDERSTAND?
THIS THING THAT'S INSIDE YOU CAN BE DRIVEN OUT. YOU'VE ALREADY PROVED THAT.
AND I HAVE-- FRIENDS WHO MIGHT HELP.
THEN THE GODS BE WITH YOU, JILL PRESTO-- PRESENT COMPANY EXCEPTED, FOR BERGELMIR OF THE JOTUN WILL BE FAR AWAY.
BUT I WILL NOT FORGET YOU SOON.

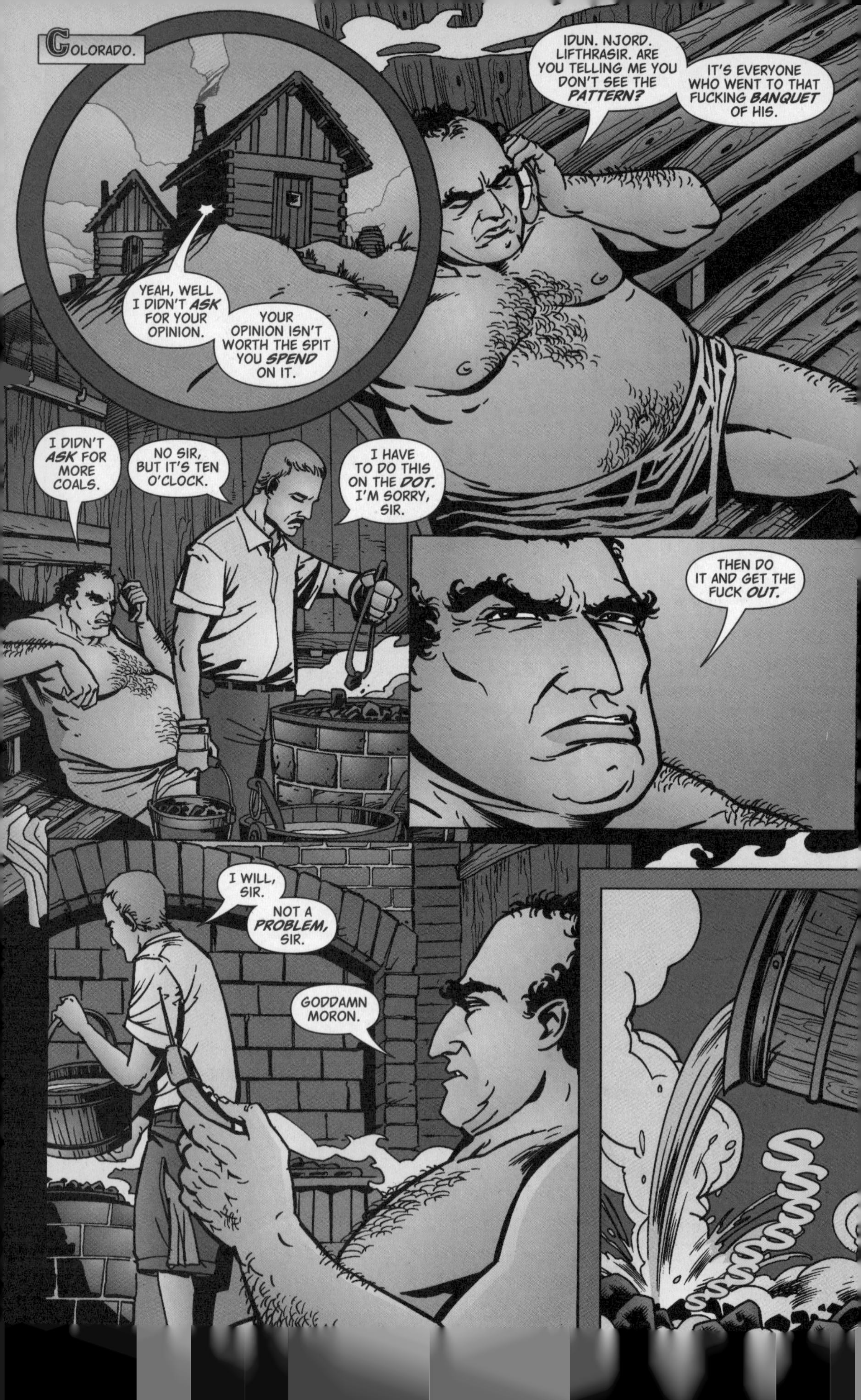
COLORADO.
IDUN. NJORD. LIFTHRASIR. ARE YOU TELLING ME YOU DON'T SEE THE PATTERN?
IT'S EVERYONE WHO WENT TO THAT FUCKING BANQUET OF HIS.
YEAH, WELL I DIDN'T ASK FOR YOUR OPINION.
YOUR OPINION ISN'T WORTH THE SPIT YOU SPEND ON IT.
I DIDN'T ASK FOR MORE COALS.
NO SIR, BUT IT'S TEN O'CLOCK.
I HAVE TO DO THIS ON THE DOT. I'M SORRY, SIR.
THEN DO IT AND GET THE FUCK OUT.
I WILL, SIR.
NOT A PROBLEM, SIR.
GODDAMN MORON.
SSSSSSSSS

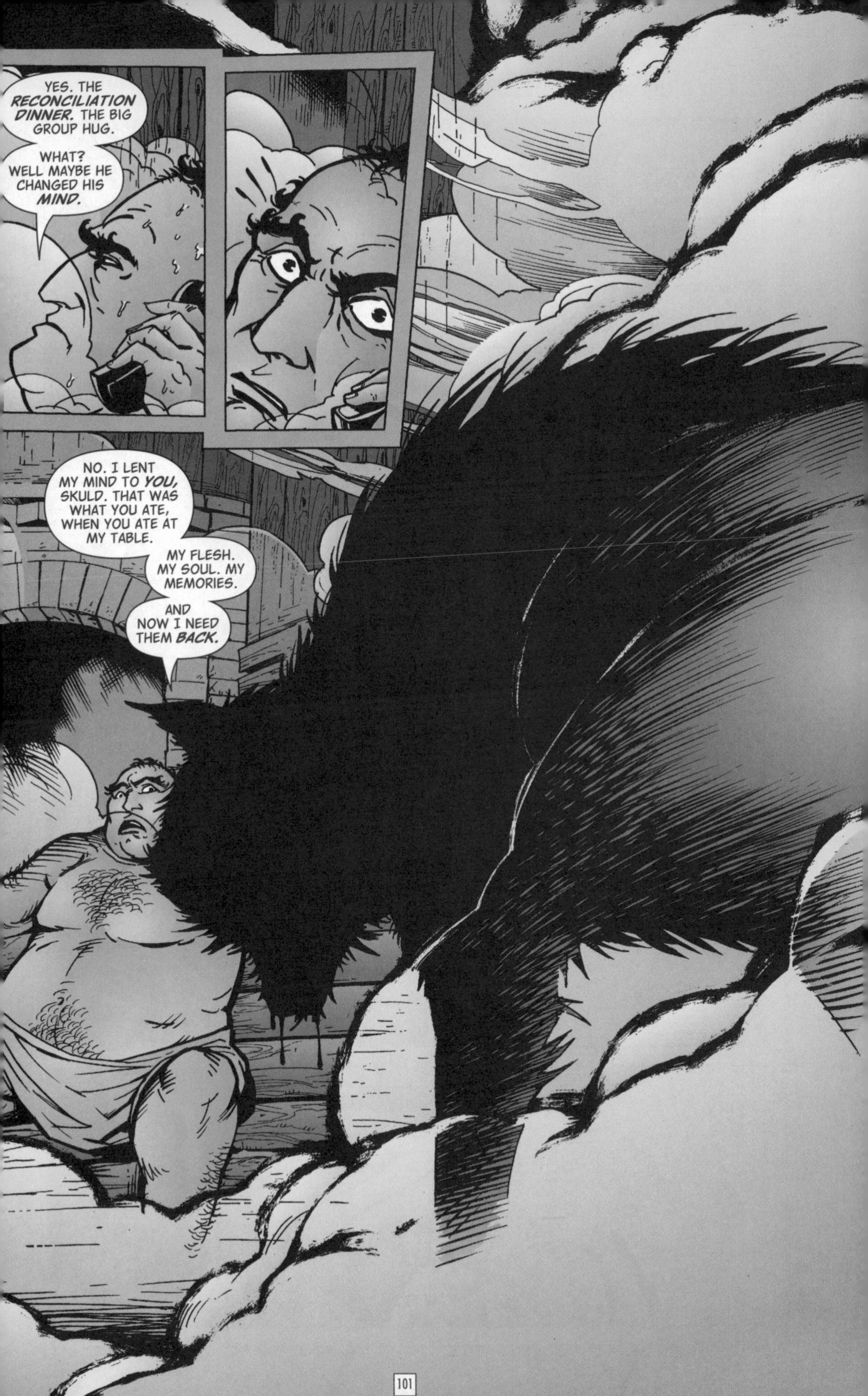
YES. THE **RECONCILIATION DINNER.** THE BIG GROUP HUG.
WHAT? WELL MAYBE HE CHANGED HIS **MIND.**
NO. I LENT MY MIND TO **YOU,** SKULD. THAT WAS WHAT YOU ATE, WHEN YOU ATE AT MY TABLE.
MY FLESH. MY SOUL. MY MEMORIES.
AND NOW I NEED THEM **BACK.**

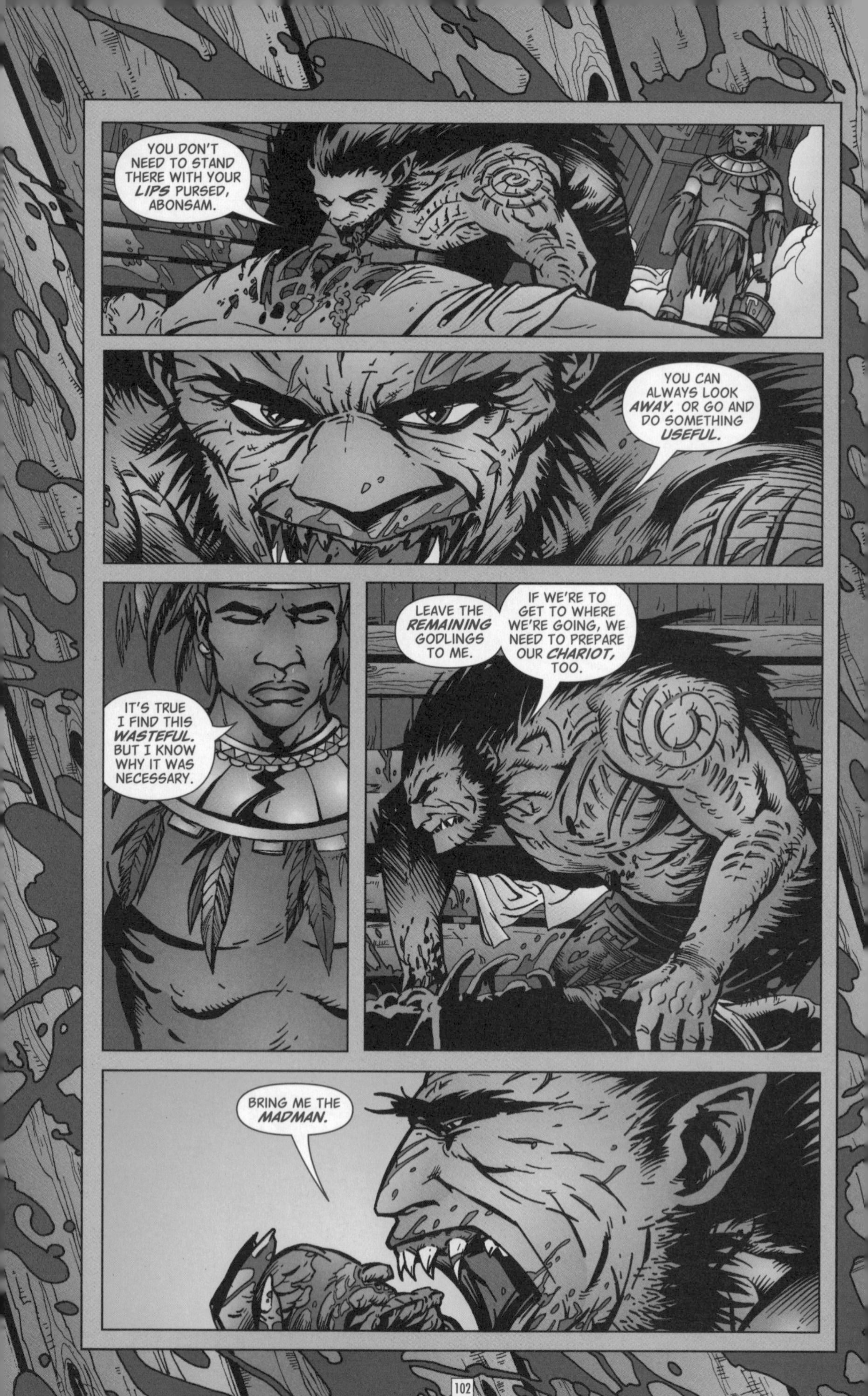
YOU DON'T NEED TO STAND THERE WITH YOUR LIPS PURSED, ABONSAM.
YOU CAN ALWAYS LOOK AWAY. OR GO AND DO SOMETHING USEFUL.
IT'S TRUE I FIND THIS WASTEFUL. BUT I KNOW WHY IT WAS NECESSARY.
LEAVE THE REMAINING GODLINGS TO ME.
IF WE'RE TO GET TO WHERE WE'RE GOING, WE NEED TO PREPARE OUR CHARIOT, TOO.
BRING ME THE MADMAN.

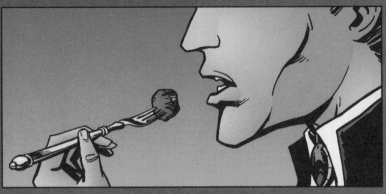

SO-- UMM-- ARE THINGS GETTING BACK TO *NORMAL* NOW IN THE SILVER CITY?

I MEAN, AFTER THE DAMAGE THE *TITANS* CAUSED?

THE TERM *NORMAL* NO LONGER HAS A MEANING, ELAINE.

GOD HAS ABANDONED US, AND AS A RESULT THE WHOLE OF *CREATION* IS BEGINNING TO UNRAVEL.

IT-- IT IS? I DIDN'T *HEAR* ABOUT THAT.

IS THAT *TRUE?*

ONLY *YAHWEH'S* CREATION. IT DEPENDS ON THE *LOGOS*-- THE WORD OF GOD-- FOR ITS EXISTENCE.

MY *OWN* COSMOS WON'T BE AFFECTED.

AND THEREFORE IT DOES NOT *MATTER.*

AS ANY-THING THAT DOES NOT TOUCH *YOU* DOES NOT MATTER, LUCIFER.

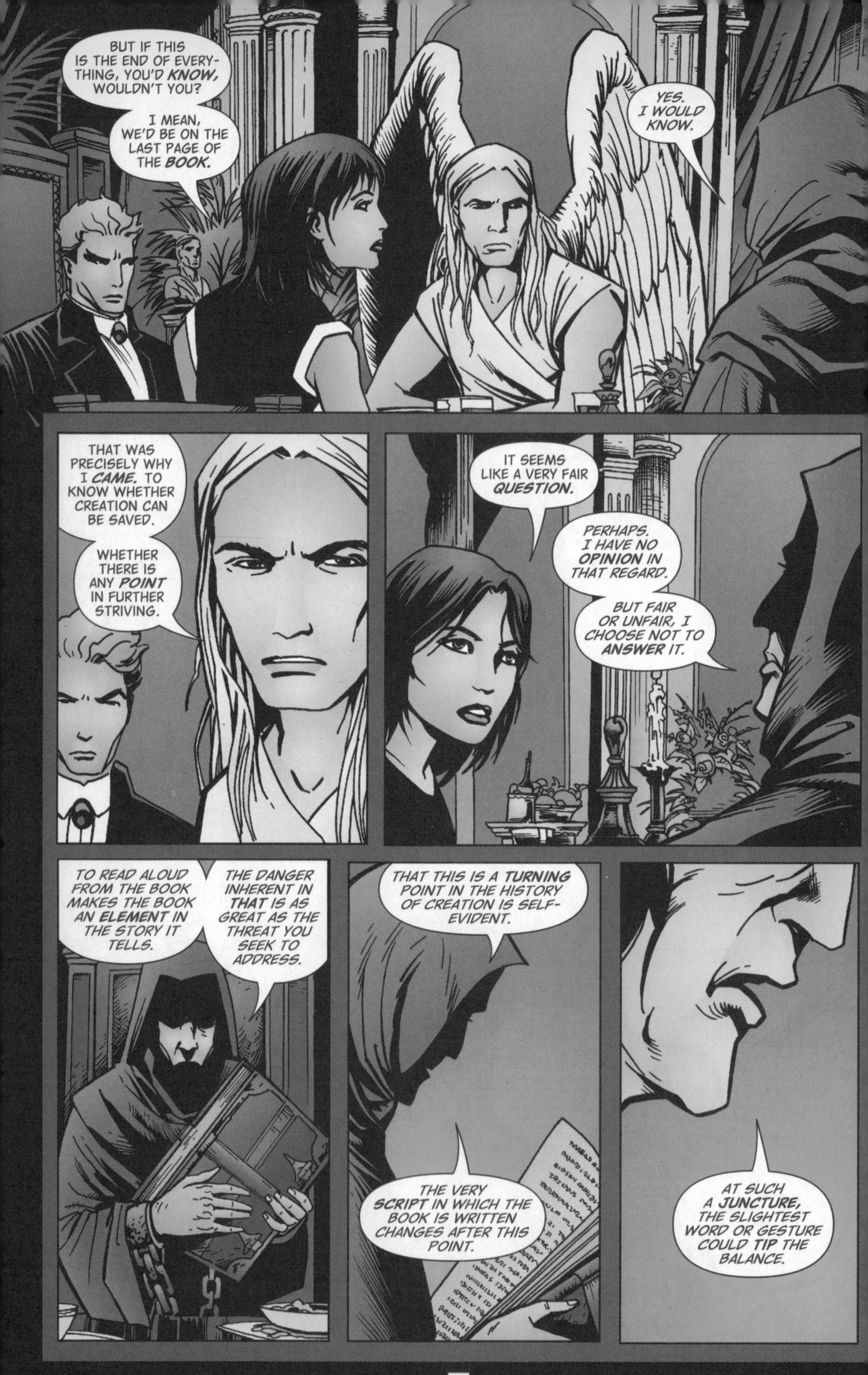

BUT IF THIS IS THE END OF EVERYTHING, YOU'D KNOW, WOULDN'T YOU?
I MEAN, WE'D BE ON THE LAST PAGE OF THE BOOK.
YES. I WOULD KNOW.
THAT WAS PRECISELY WHY I CAME. TO KNOW WHETHER CREATION CAN BE SAVED.
WHETHER THERE IS ANY POINT IN FURTHER STRIVING.
IT SEEMS LIKE A VERY FAIR QUESTION.
PERHAPS. I HAVE NO OPINION IN THAT REGARD.
BUT FAIR OR UNFAIR, I CHOOSE NOT TO ANSWER IT.
TO READ ALOUD FROM THE BOOK MAKES THE BOOK AN ELEMENT IN THE STORY IT TELLS.
THE DANGER INHERENT IN THAT IS AS GREAT AS THE THREAT YOU SEEK TO ADDRESS.
THAT THIS IS A TURNING POINT IN THE HISTORY OF CREATION IS SELF-EVIDENT.
THE VERY SCRIPT IN WHICH THE BOOK IS WRITTEN CHANGES AFTER THIS POINT.
AT SUCH A JUNCTURE, THE SLIGHTEST WORD OR GESTURE COULD TIP THE BALANCE.

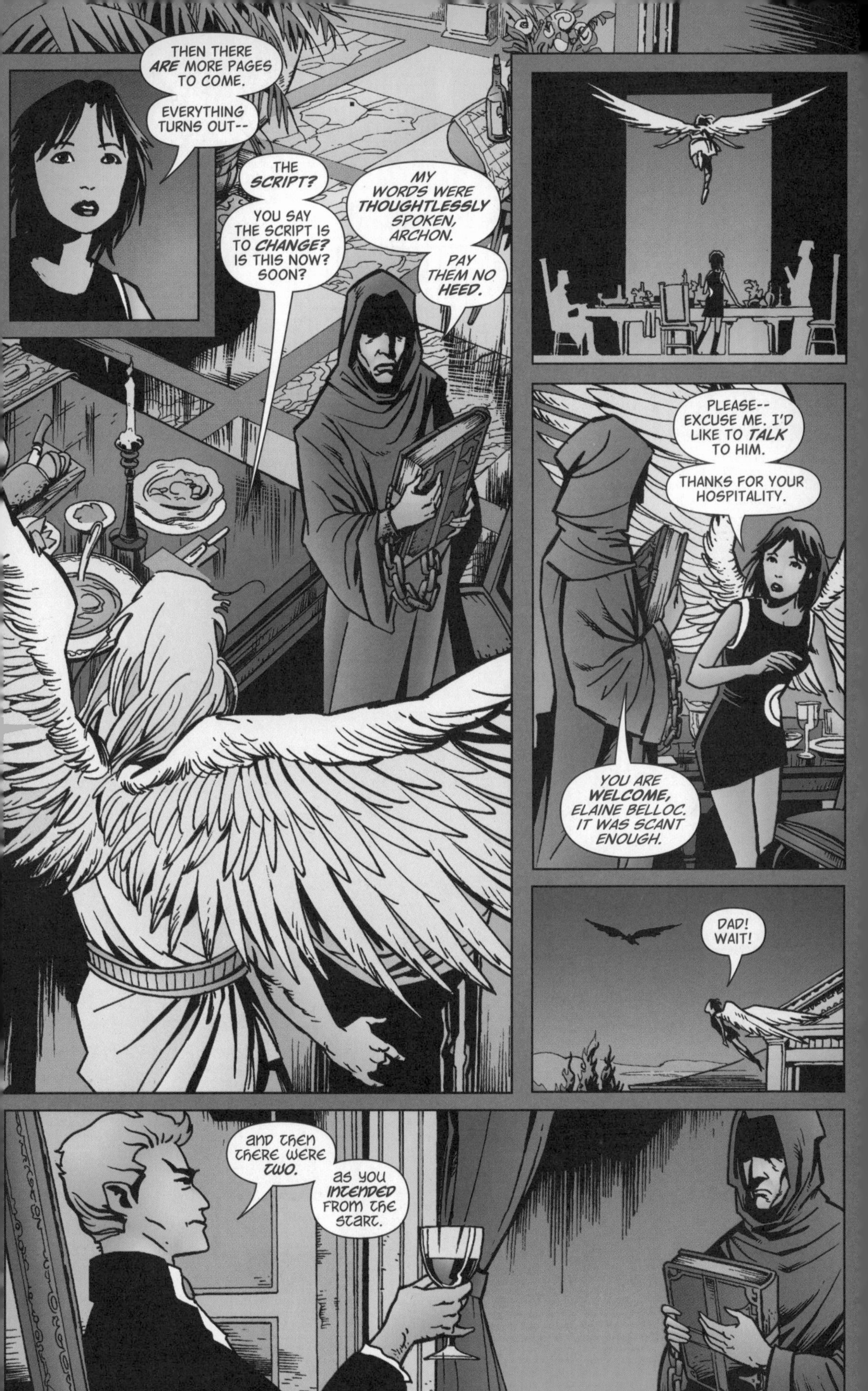
THEN THERE ARE MORE PAGES TO COME.
EVERYTHING TURNS OUT--
THE SCRIPT?
YOU SAY THE SCRIPT IS TO CHANGE? IS THIS NOW? SOON?
MY WORDS WERE THOUGHTLESSLY SPOKEN, ARCHON.
PAY THEM NO HEED.
PLEASE-- EXCUSE ME. I'D LIKE TO TALK TO HIM.
THANKS FOR YOUR HOSPITALITY.
YOU ARE WELCOME, ELAINE BELLOC. IT WAS SCANT ENOUGH.
DAD! WAIT!
and then there were two.
as you intended from the start.

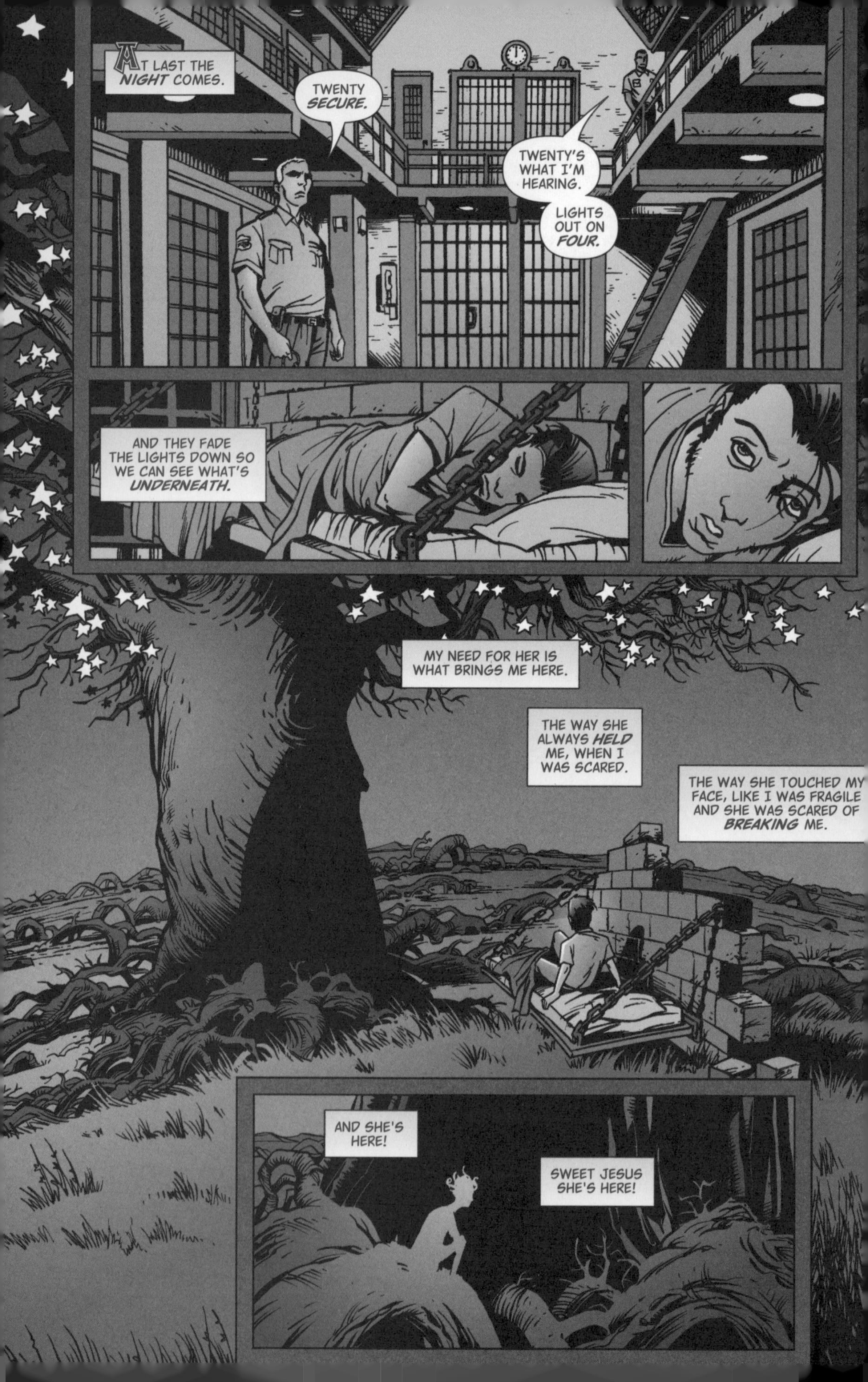
AT LAST THE NIGHT COMES.
TWENTY SECURE.
TWENTY'S WHAT I'M HEARING.
LIGHTS OUT ON FOUR.
AND THEY FADE THE LIGHTS DOWN SO WE CAN SEE WHAT'S UNDERNEATH.
MY NEED FOR HER IS WHAT BRINGS ME HERE.
THE WAY SHE ALWAYS HELD ME, WHEN I WAS SCARED.
THE WAY SHE TOUCHED MY FACE, LIKE I WAS FRAGILE AND SHE WAS SCARED OF BREAKING ME.
AND SHE'S HERE!
SWEET JESUS SHE'S HERE!

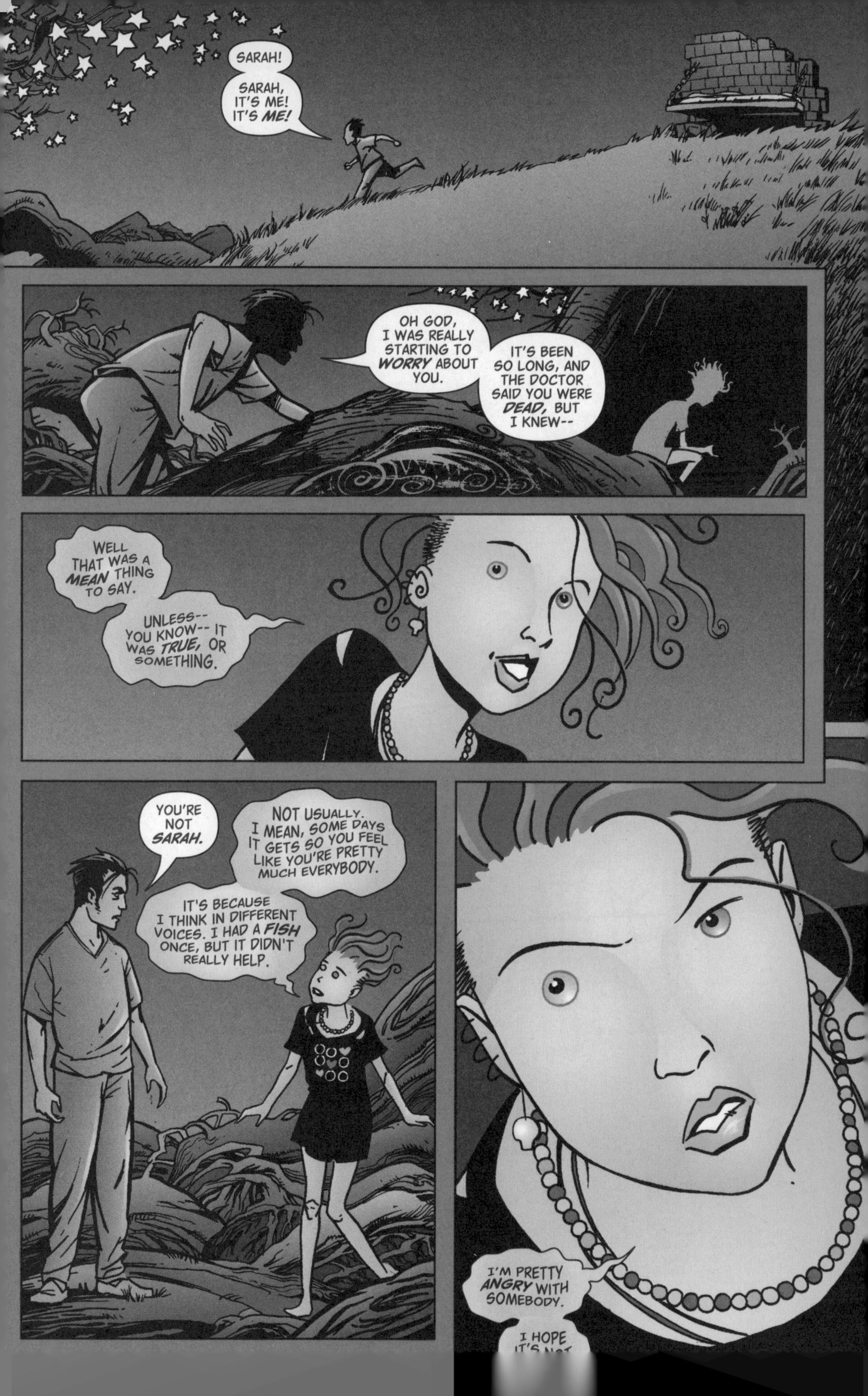
SARAH!
SARAH, IT'S ME! IT'S ME!
OH GOD, I WAS REALLY STARTING TO WORRY ABOUT YOU.
IT'S BEEN SO LONG, AND THE DOCTOR SAID YOU WERE DEAD, BUT I KNEW--
WELL THAT WAS A MEAN THING TO SAY.
UNLESS-- YOU KNOW-- IT WAS TRUE, OR SOMETHING.
YOU'RE NOT SARAH.
NOT USUALLY. I MEAN, SOME DAYS IT GETS SO YOU FEEL LIKE YOU'RE PRETTY MUCH EVERYBODY.
IT'S BECAUSE I THINK IN DIFFERENT VOICES. I HAD A FISH ONCE, BUT IT DIDN'T REALLY HELP.
I'M PRETTY ANGRY WITH SOMEBODY.
I HOPE

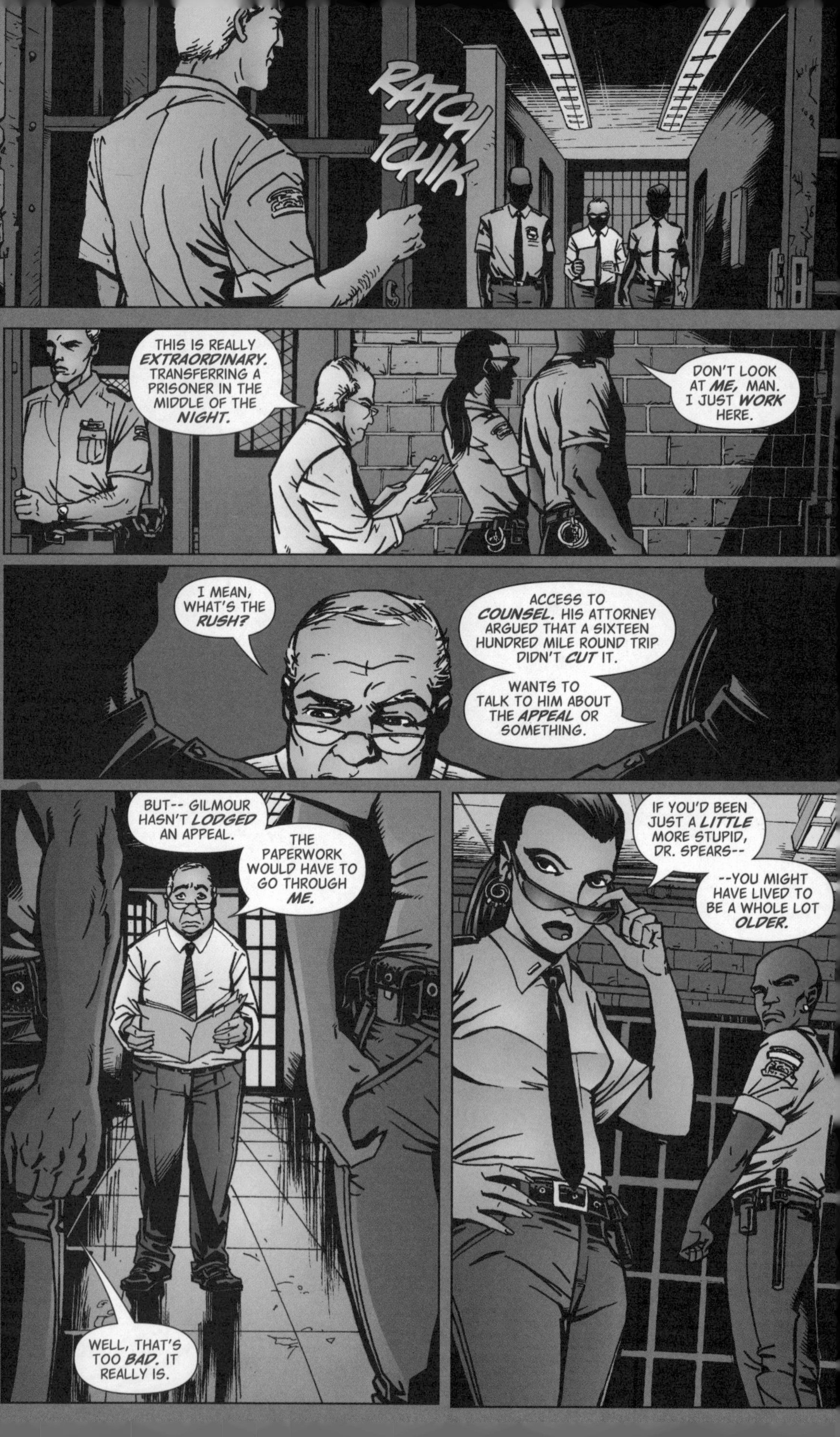

RATCH TCHIK
THIS IS REALLY EXTRAORDINARY. TRANSFERRING A PRISONER IN THE MIDDLE OF THE NIGHT.
DON'T LOOK AT ME, MAN. I JUST WORK HERE.
I MEAN, WHAT'S THE RUSH?
ACCESS TO COUNSEL. HIS ATTORNEY ARGUED THAT A SIXTEEN HUNDRED MILE ROUND TRIP DIDN'T CUT IT.
WANTS TO TALK TO HIM ABOUT THE APPEAL OR SOMETHING.
BUT-- GILMOUR HASN'T LODGED AN APPEAL.
THE PAPERWORK WOULD HAVE TO GO THROUGH ME.
WELL, THAT'S TOO BAD. IT REALLY IS.
IF YOU'D BEEN JUST A LITTLE MORE STUPID, DR. SPEARS--
--YOU MIGHT HAVE LIVED TO BE A WHOLE LOT OLDER.

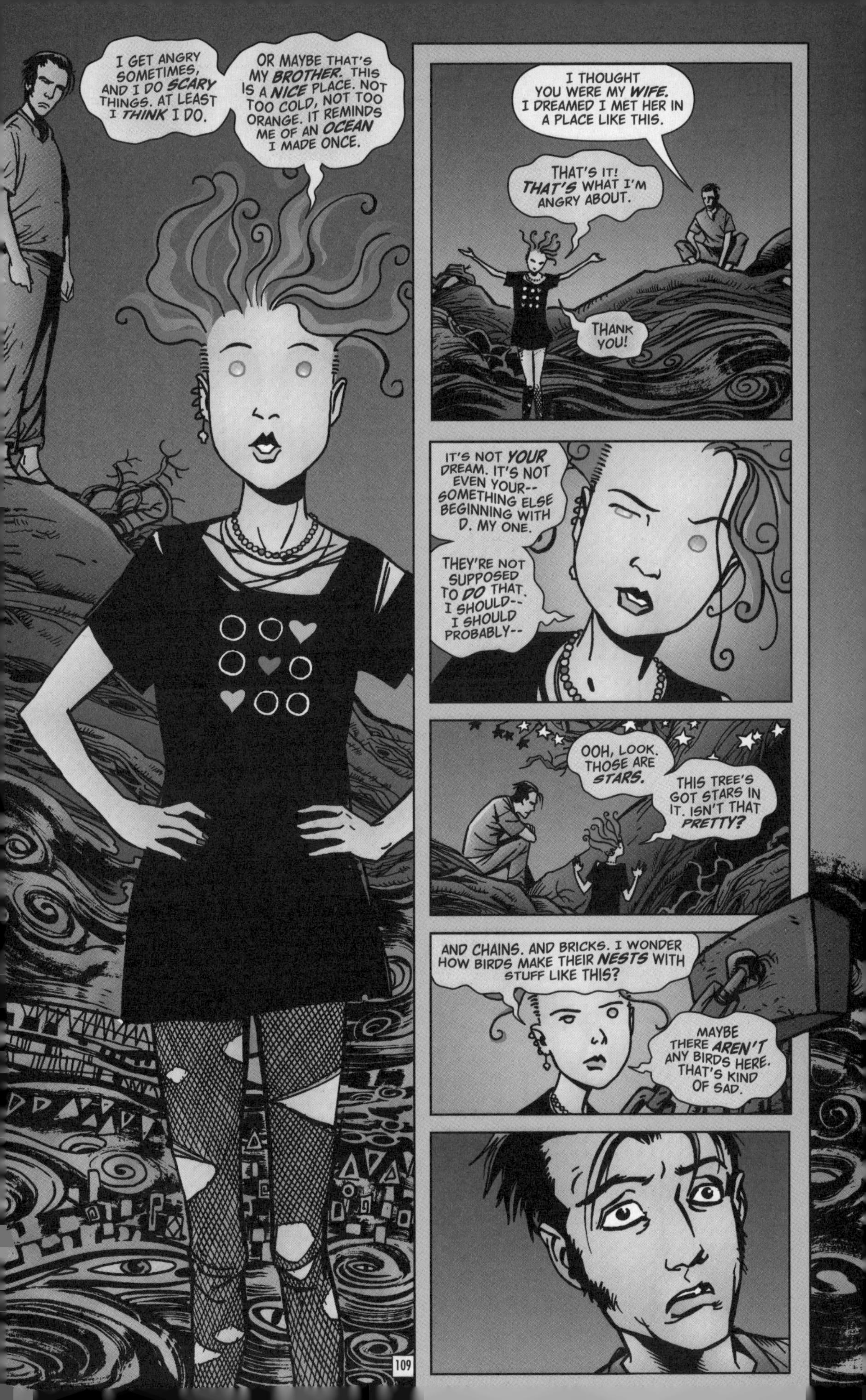
I GET ANGRY SOMETIMES, AND I DO SCARY THINGS. AT LEAST I THINK I DO.
OR MAYBE THAT'S MY BROTHER. THIS IS A NICE PLACE. NOT TOO COLD, NOT TOO ORANGE. IT REMINDS ME OF AN OCEAN I MADE ONCE.
I THOUGHT YOU WERE MY WIFE. I DREAMED I MET HER IN A PLACE LIKE THIS.
THAT'S IT! THAT'S WHAT I'M ANGRY ABOUT.
THANK YOU!
IT'S NOT YOUR DREAM. IT'S NOT EVEN YOUR-- SOMETHING ELSE BEGINNING WITH D. MY ONE.
THEY'RE NOT SUPPOSED TO DO THAT. I SHOULD-- I SHOULD PROBABLY--
OOH, LOOK. THOSE ARE STARS.
THIS TREE'S GOT STARS IN IT. ISN'T THAT PRETTY?
AND CHAINS. AND BRICKS. I WONDER HOW BIRDS MAKE THEIR NESTS WITH STUFF LIKE THIS?
MAYBE THERE AREN'T ANY BIRDS HERE. THAT'S KIND OF SAD.

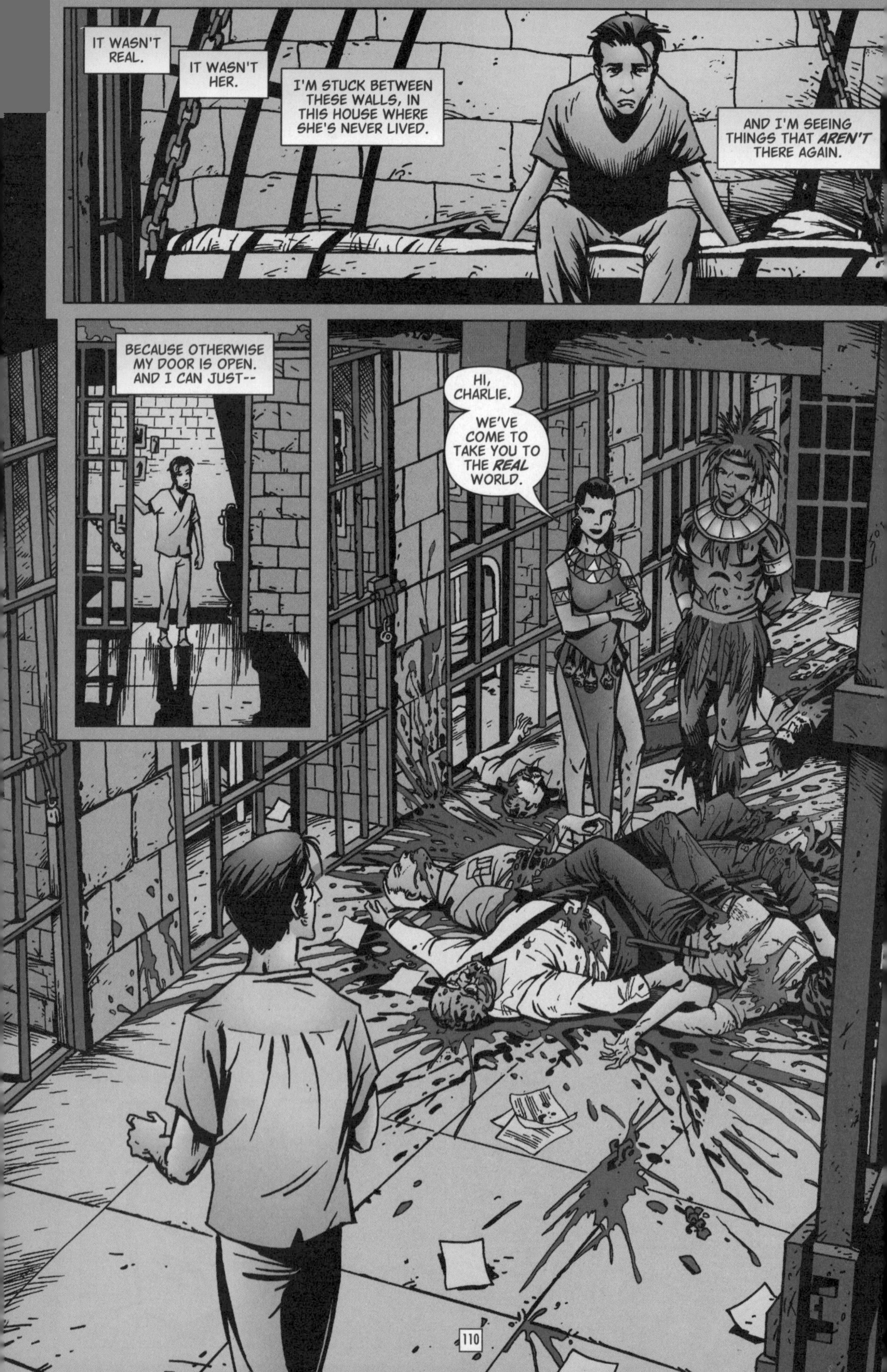
IT WASN'T REAL.
IT WASN'T HER.
I'M STUCK BETWEEN THESE WALLS, IN THIS HOUSE WHERE SHE'S NEVER LIVED.
AND I'M SEEING THINGS THAT *AREN'T* THERE AGAIN.
BECAUSE OTHERWISE MY DOOR IS OPEN. AND I CAN JUST--
HI, CHARLIE.
WE'VE COME TO TAKE YOU TO THE *REAL* WORLD.

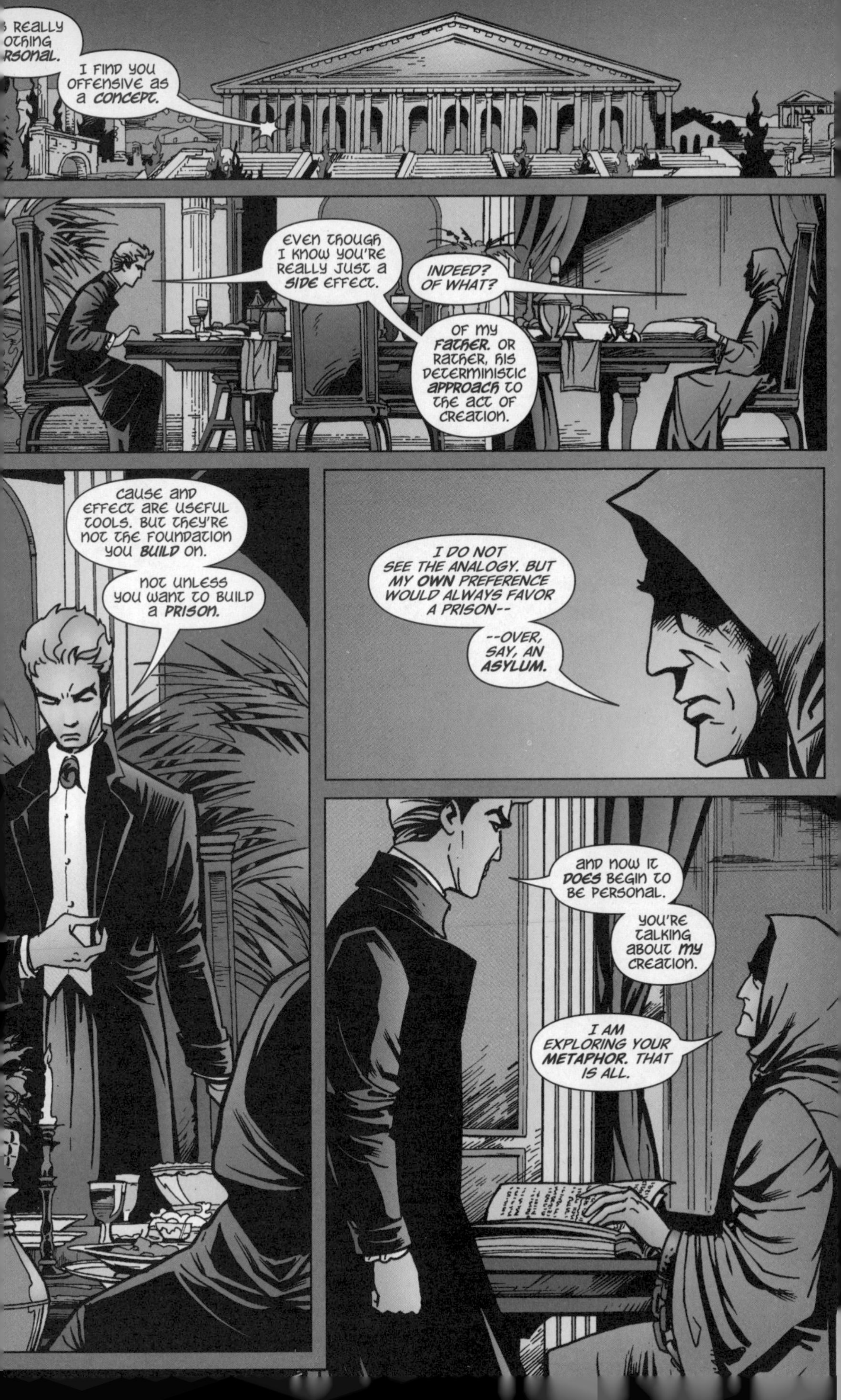

S REALLY
OTHING
RSONAL.
I FIND YOU OFFENSIVE AS A CONCEPT.
EVEN THOUGH I KNOW YOU'RE REALLY JUST A SIDE EFFECT.
INDEED? OF WHAT?
OF MY FATHER. OR RATHER, HIS DETERMINISTIC APPROACH TO THE ACT OF CREATION.
CAUSE AND EFFECT ARE USEFUL TOOLS. BUT THEY'RE NOT THE FOUNDATION YOU BUILD ON.
NOT UNLESS YOU WANT TO BUILD A PRISON.
I DO NOT SEE THE ANALOGY. BUT MY OWN PREFERENCE WOULD ALWAYS FAVOR A PRISON--
--OVER, SAY, AN ASYLUM.
AND NOW IT DOES BEGIN TO BE PERSONAL.
YOU'RE TALKING ABOUT MY CREATION.
I AM EXPLORING YOUR METAPHOR. THAT IS ALL.

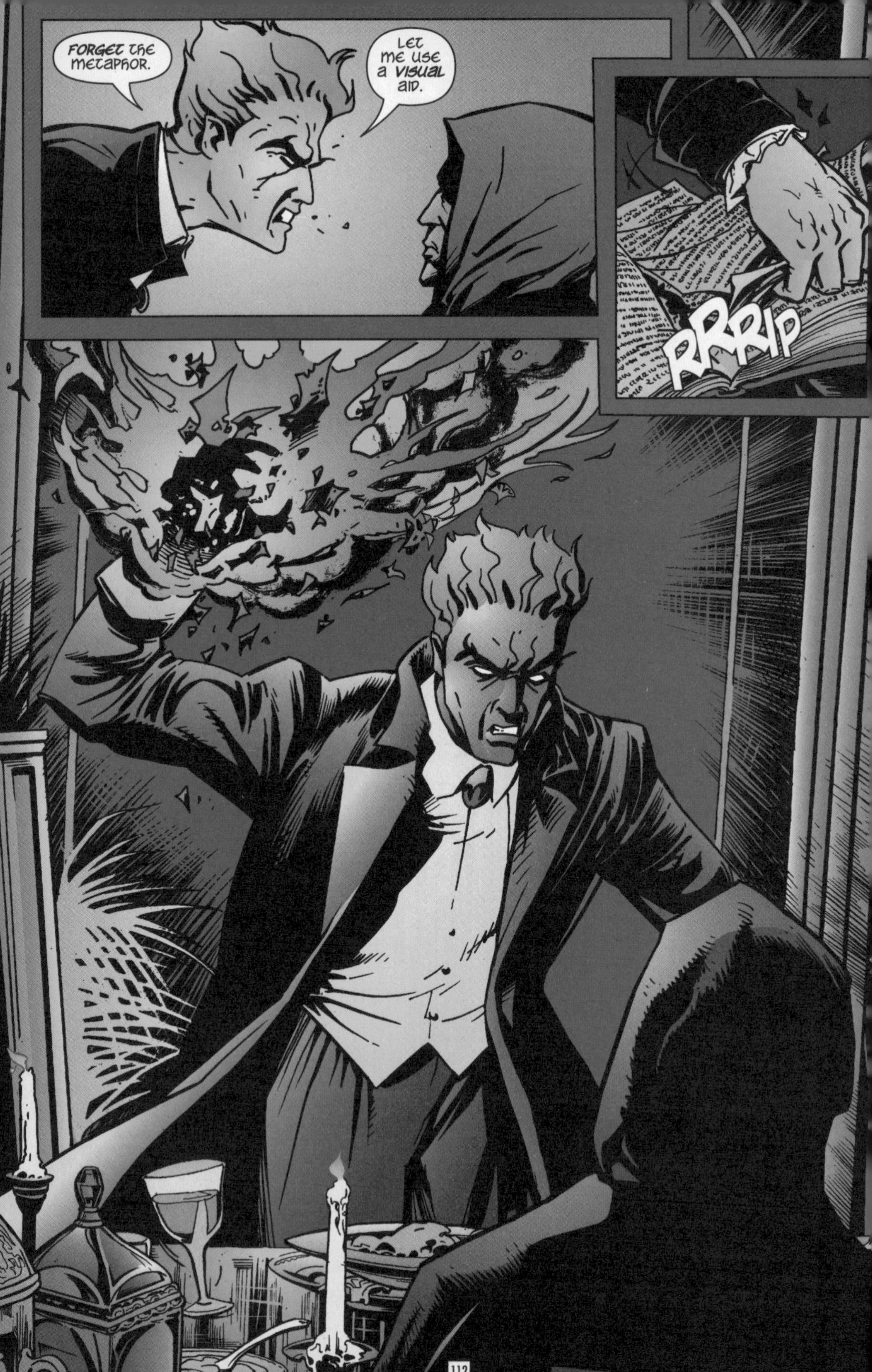
FORGET THE METAPHOR.
LET ME USE A VISUAL AID.
RRRIP

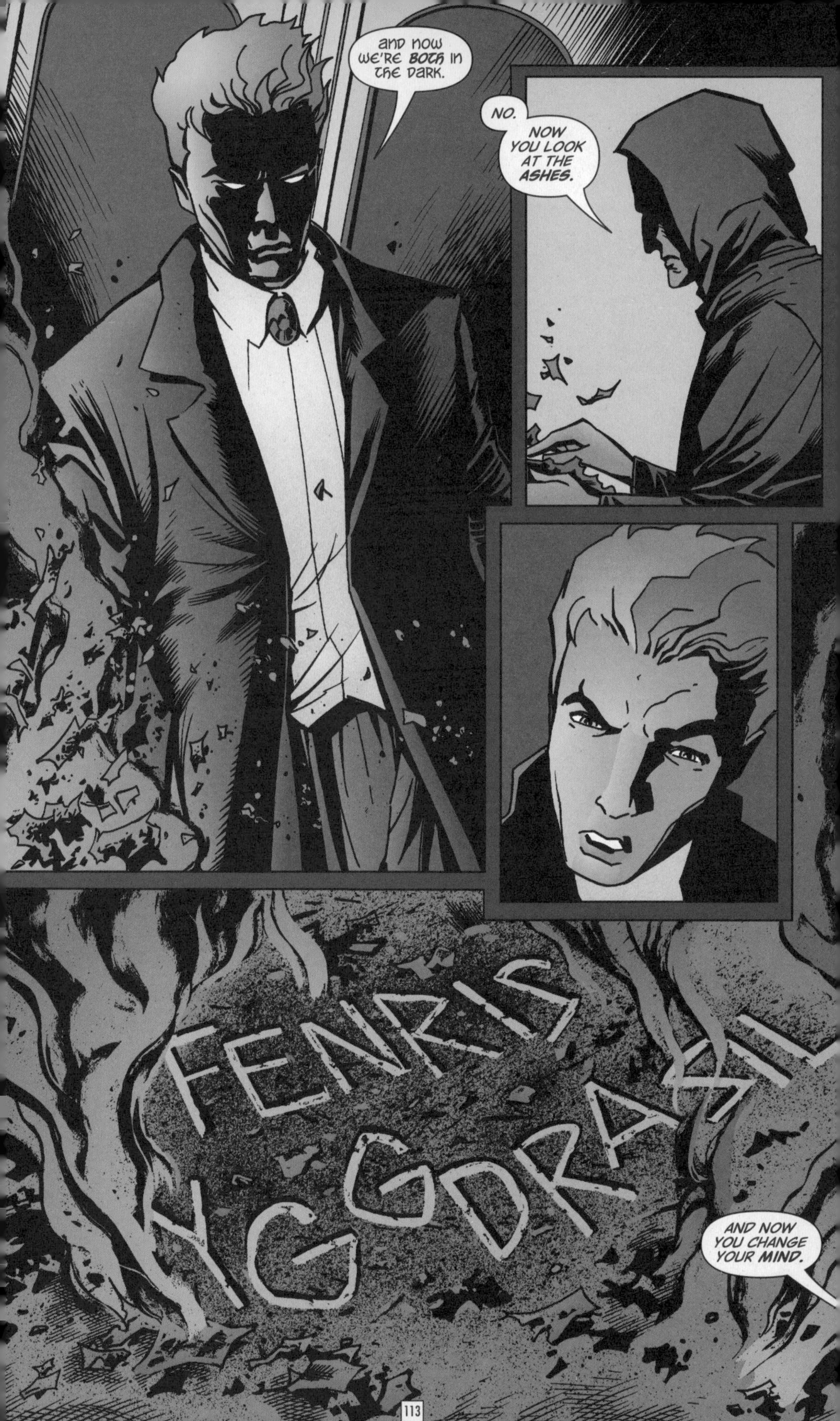
and now we're BOTH in the dark.
NO.
NOW YOU LOOK AT THE ASHES.
FENRIS
YGGDRASIL
AND NOW YOU CHANGE YOUR MIND.

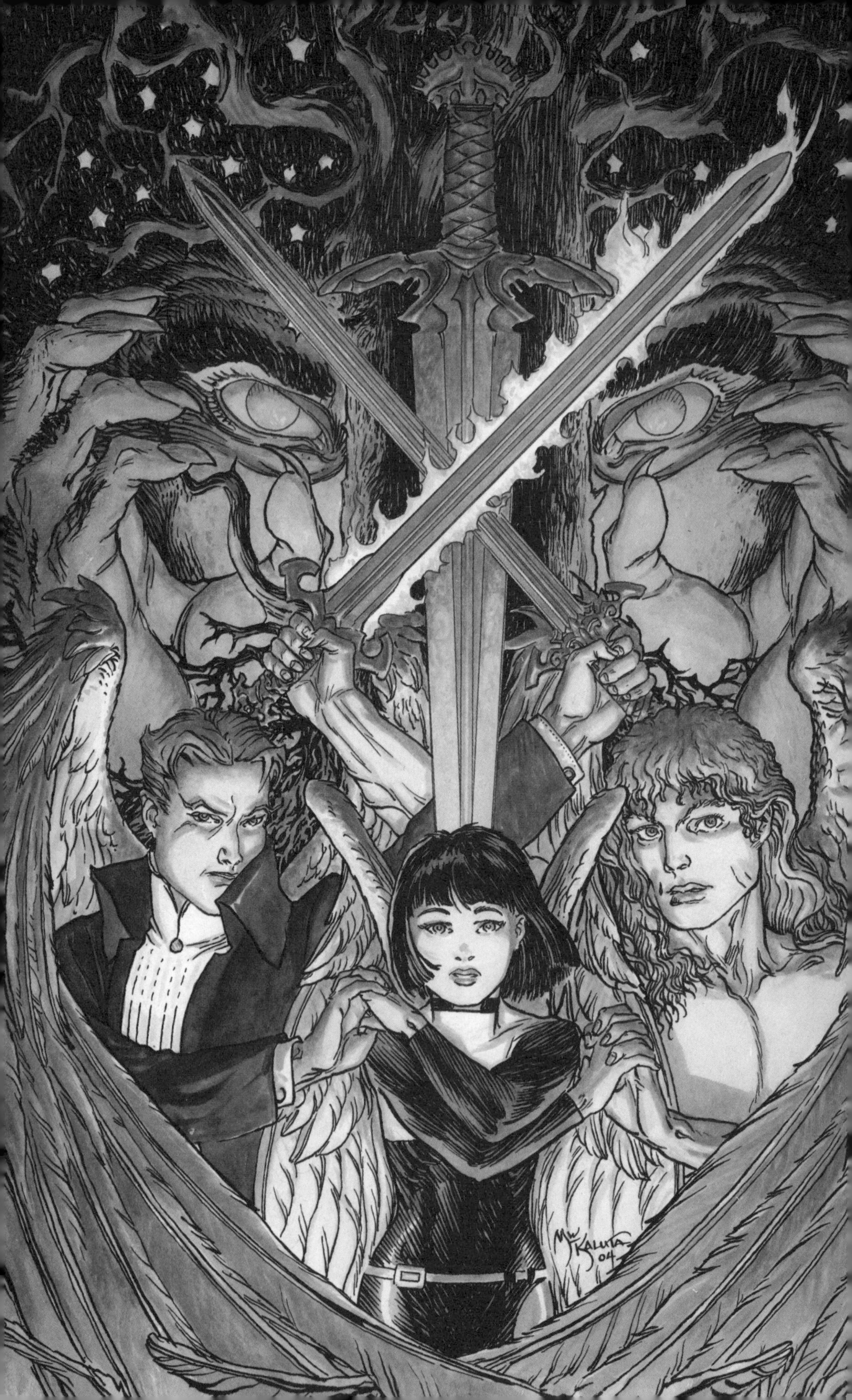
MW KALUTA
'04

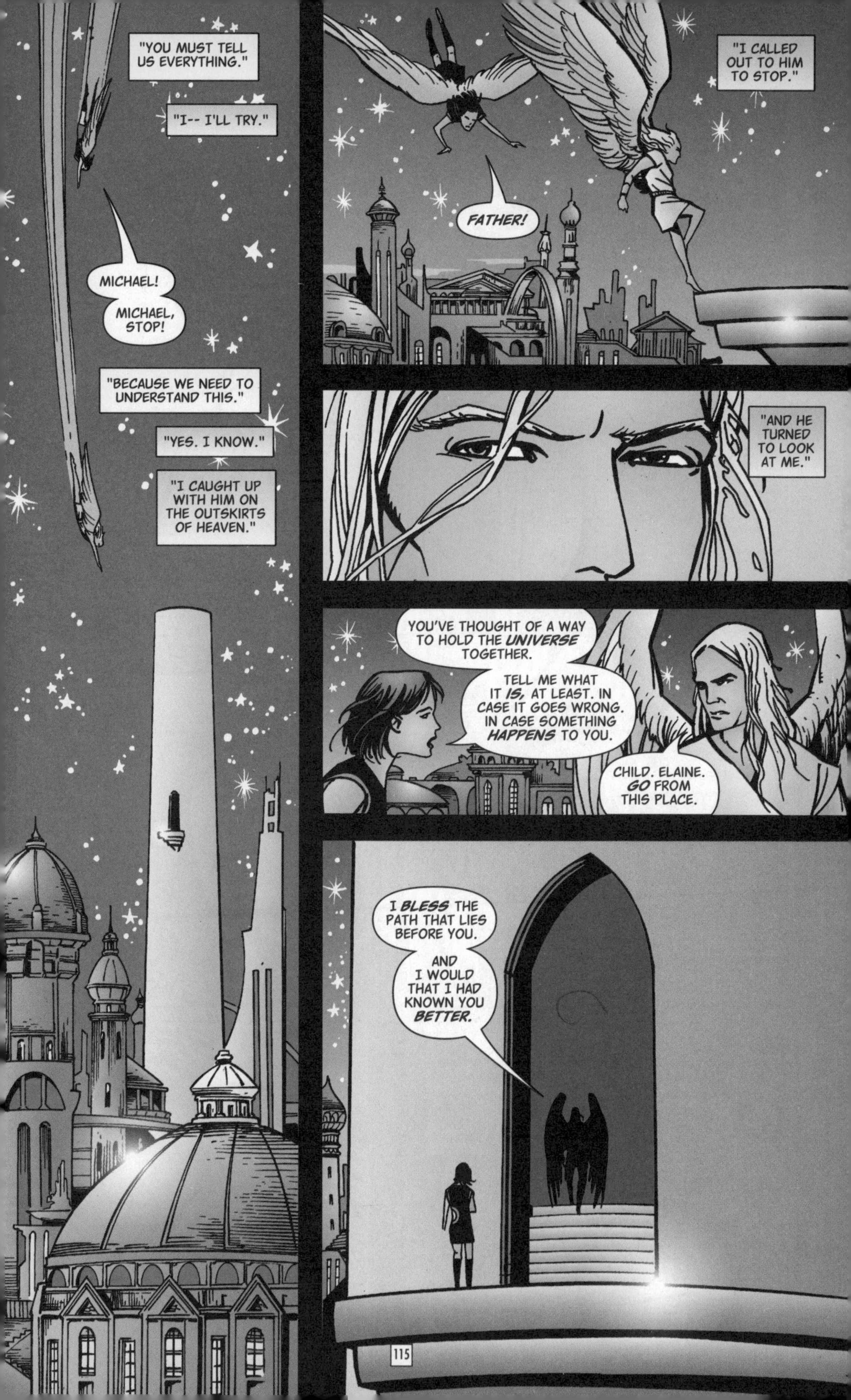
"YOU MUST TELL US EVERYTHING."
"I-- I'LL TRY."
MICHAEL!
MICHAEL, STOP!
"BECAUSE WE NEED TO UNDERSTAND THIS."
"YES. I KNOW."
"I CAUGHT UP WITH HIM ON THE OUTSKIRTS OF HEAVEN."
"I CALLED OUT TO HIM TO STOP."
FATHER!
"AND HE TURNED TO LOOK AT ME."
YOU'VE THOUGHT OF A WAY TO HOLD THE UNIVERSE TOGETHER.
TELL ME WHAT IT IS, AT LEAST. IN CASE IT GOES WRONG. IN CASE SOMETHING HAPPENS TO YOU.
CHILD. ELAINE. GO FROM THIS PLACE.
I BLESS THE PATH THAT LIES BEFORE YOU.
AND I WOULD THAT I HAD KNOWN YOU BETTER.

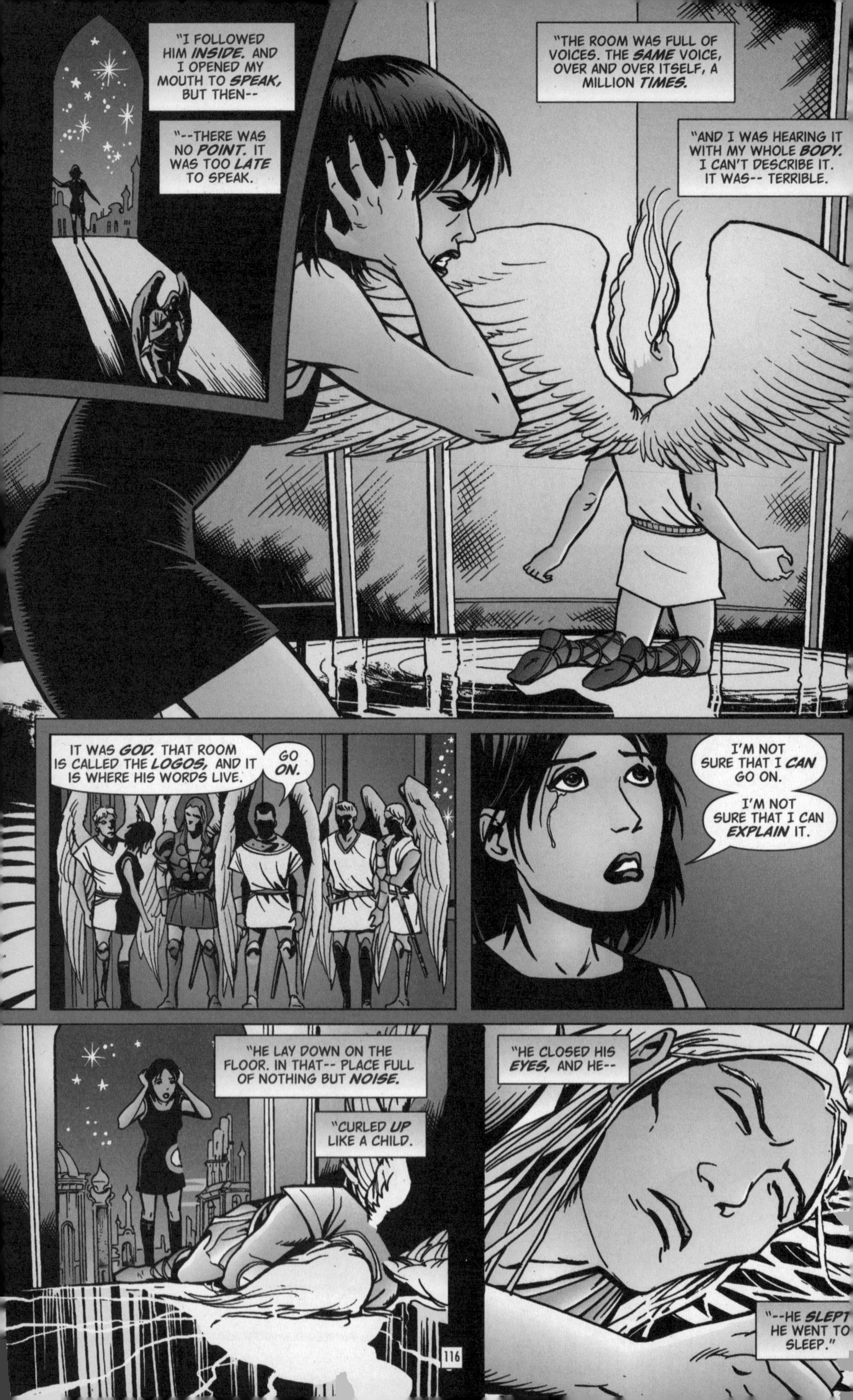

"I FOLLOWED HIM INSIDE. AND I OPENED MY MOUTH TO SPEAK, BUT THEN--
"--THERE WAS NO POINT. IT WAS TOO LATE TO SPEAK.
"THE ROOM WAS FULL OF VOICES. THE SAME VOICE, OVER AND OVER ITSELF, A MILLION TIMES.
"AND I WAS HEARING IT WITH MY WHOLE BODY. I CAN'T DESCRIBE IT. IT WAS-- TERRIBLE.
IT WAS GOD. THAT ROOM IS CALLED THE LOGOS, AND IT IS WHERE HIS WORDS LIVE.
GO ON.
I'M NOT SURE THAT I CAN GO ON.
I'M NOT SURE THAT I CAN EXPLAIN IT.
"HE LAY DOWN ON THE FLOOR. IN THAT-- PLACE FULL OF NOTHING BUT NOISE.
"CURLED UP LIKE A CHILD.
"HE CLOSED HIS EYES, AND HE--
"--HE SLEPT. HE WENT TO SLEEP."

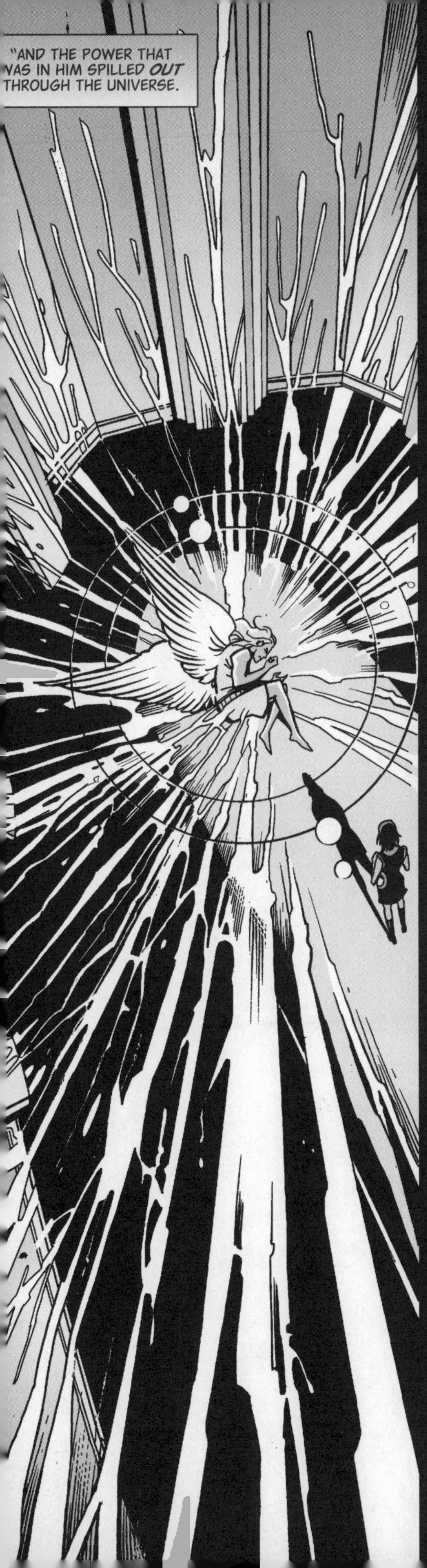
"AND THE POWER THAT
WAS IN HIM SPILLED OUT
THROUGH THE UNIVERSE.

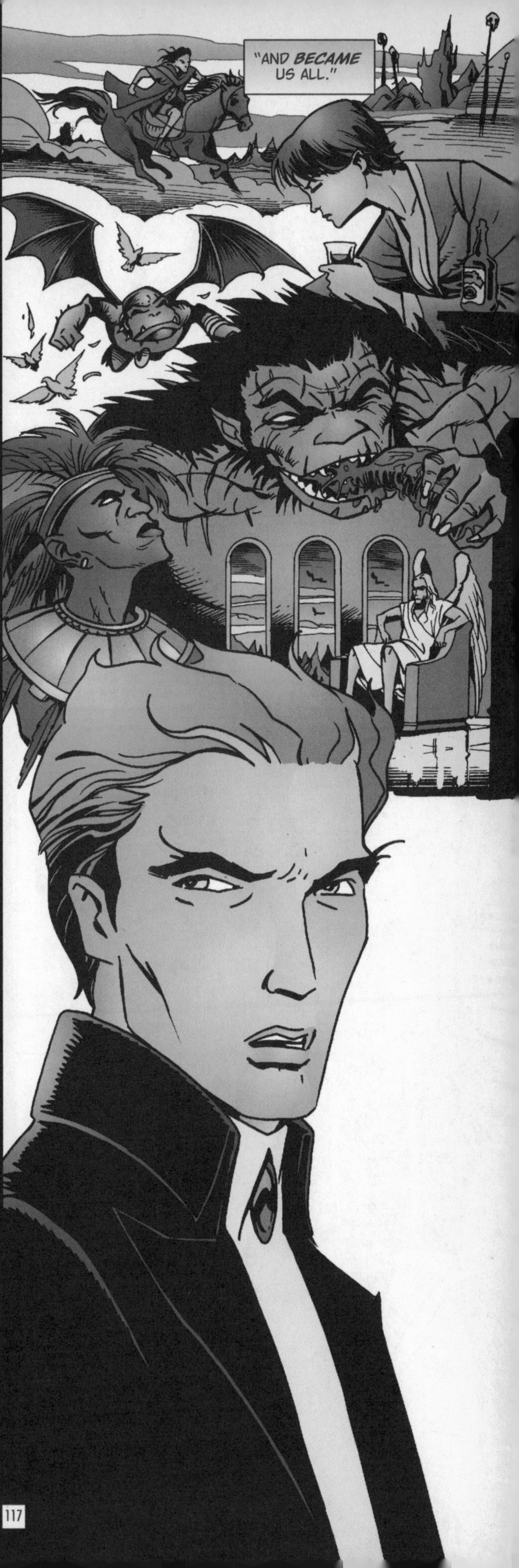
"AND BECAME
US ALL."

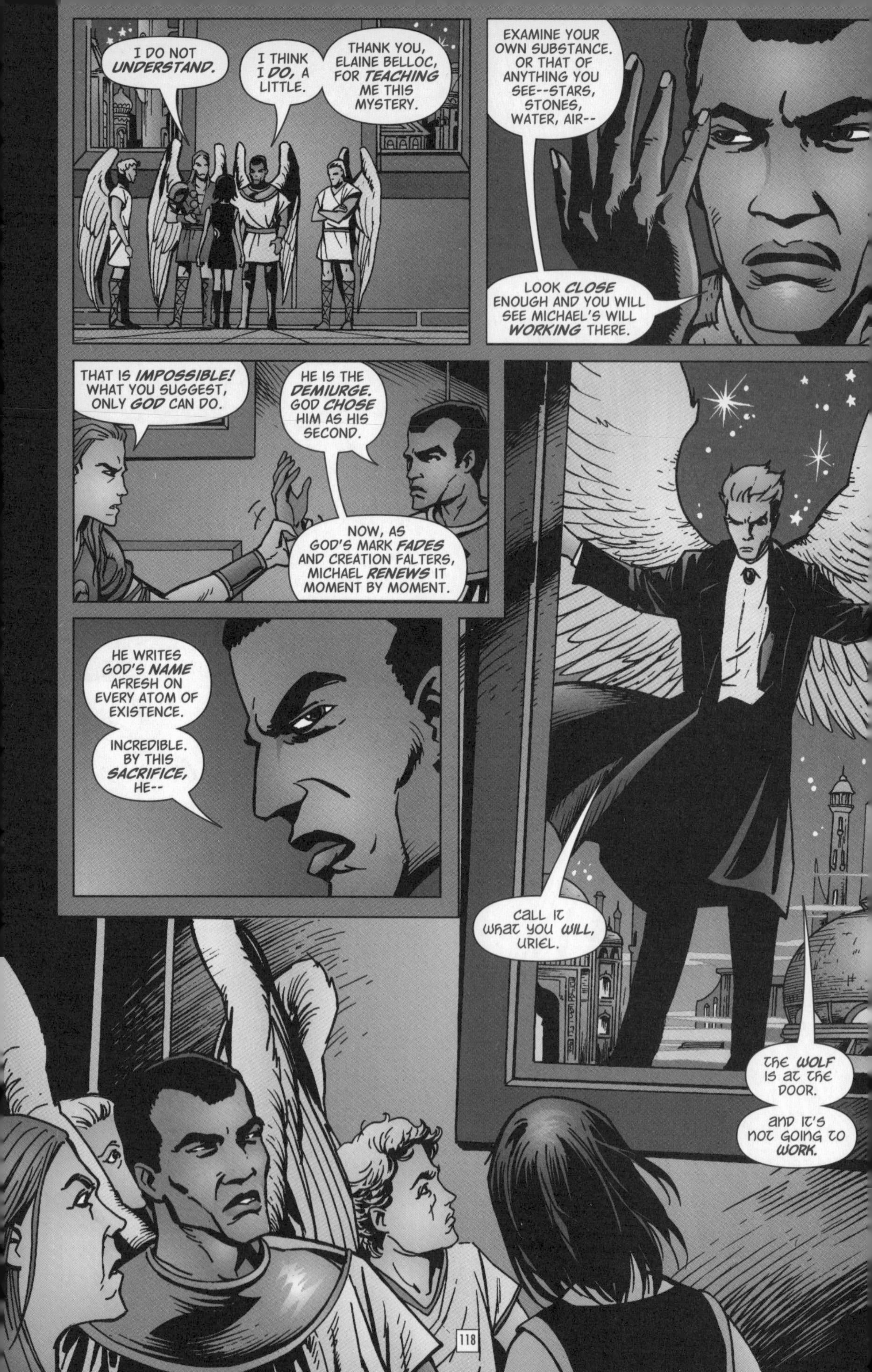

I DO NOT UNDERSTAND.
I THINK I DO, A LITTLE.
THANK YOU, ELAINE BELLOC, FOR TEACHING ME THIS MYSTERY.
EXAMINE YOUR OWN SUBSTANCE. OR THAT OF ANYTHING YOU SEE--STARS, STONES, WATER, AIR--
LOOK CLOSE ENOUGH AND YOU WILL SEE MICHAEL'S WILL WORKING THERE.
THAT IS IMPOSSIBLE! WHAT YOU SUGGEST, ONLY GOD CAN DO.
HE IS THE DEMIURGE. GOD CHOSE HIM AS HIS SECOND.
NOW, AS GOD'S MARK FADES AND CREATION FALTERS, MICHAEL RENEWS IT MOMENT BY MOMENT.
HE WRITES GOD'S NAME AFRESH ON EVERY ATOM OF EXISTENCE.
INCREDIBLE. BY THIS SACRIFICE, HE--
CALL IT WHAT YOU WILL, URIEL.
THE WOLF IS AT THE DOOR.
AND IT'S NOT GOING TO WORK.

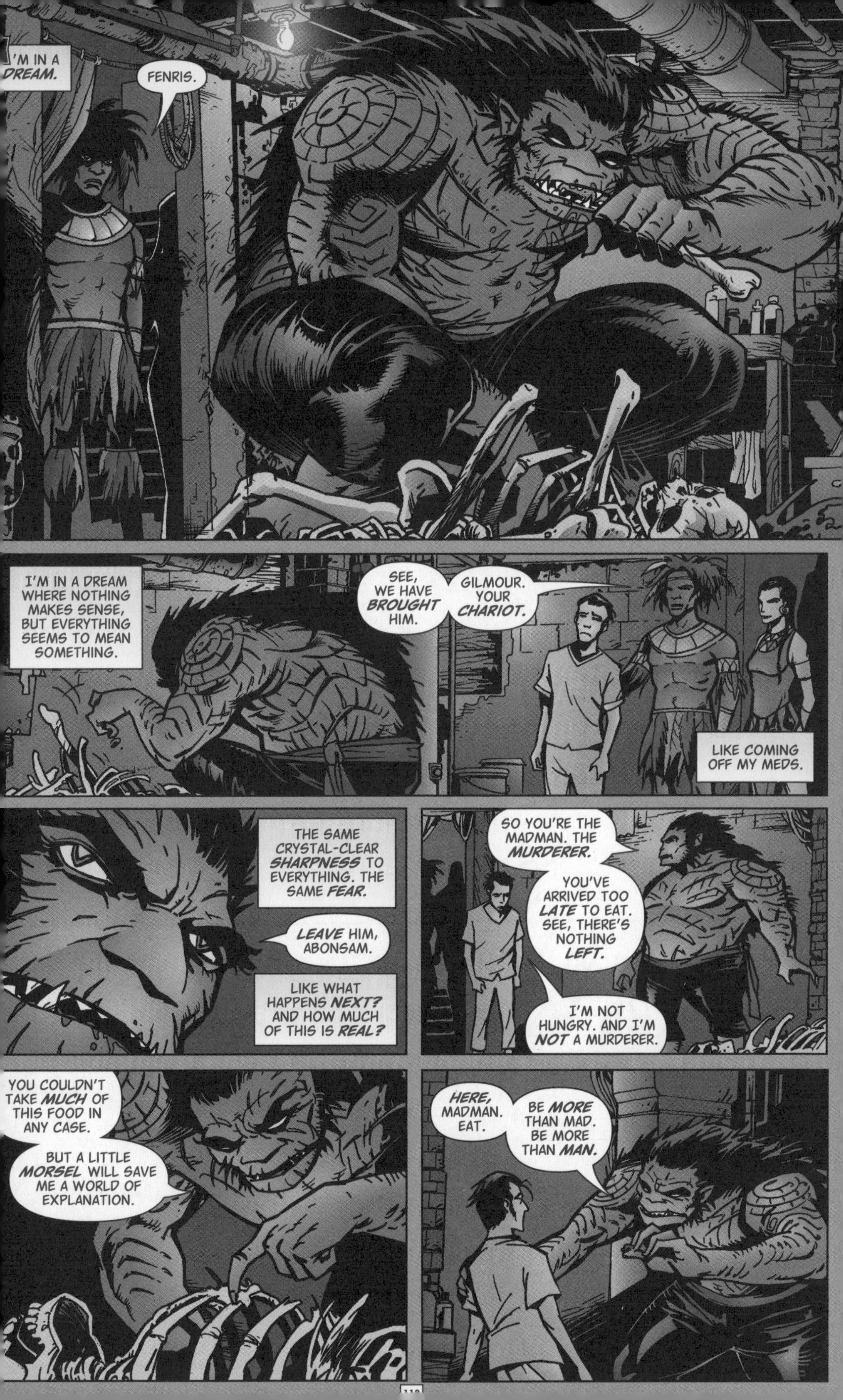
I'M IN A DREAM.
FENRIS.
I'M IN A DREAM WHERE NOTHING MAKES SENSE, BUT EVERYTHING SEEMS TO MEAN SOMETHING.
SEE, WE HAVE BROUGHT HIM.
GILMOUR. YOUR CHARIOT.
LIKE COMING OFF MY MEDS.
THE SAME CRYSTAL-CLEAR SHARPNESS TO EVERYTHING. THE SAME FEAR.
LEAVE HIM, ABONSAM.
LIKE WHAT HAPPENS NEXT? AND HOW MUCH OF THIS IS REAL?
SO YOU'RE THE MADMAN. THE MURDERER.
YOU'VE ARRIVED TOO LATE TO EAT. SEE, THERE'S NOTHING LEFT.
I'M NOT HUNGRY. AND I'M NOT A MURDERER.
YOU COULDN'T TAKE MUCH OF THIS FOOD IN ANY CASE.
BUT A LITTLE MORSEL WILL SAVE ME A WORLD OF EXPLANATION.
HERE, MADMAN. EAT.
BE MORE THAN MAD. BE MORE THAN MAN.

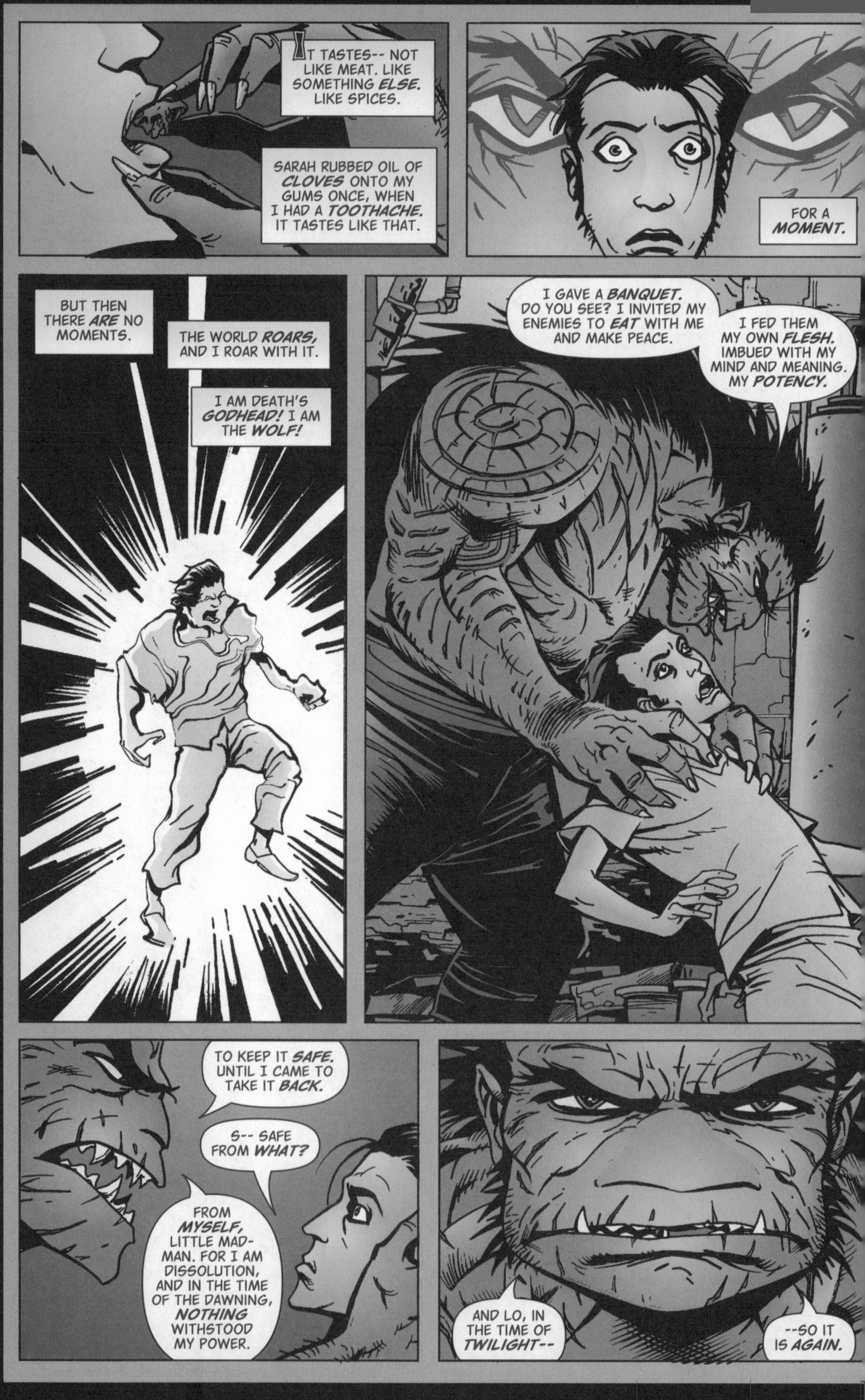
IT TASTES-- NOT LIKE MEAT. LIKE SOMETHING ELSE. LIKE SPICES.
SARAH RUBBED OIL OF CLOVES ONTO MY GUMS ONCE, WHEN I HAD A TOOTHACHE. IT TASTES LIKE THAT.
FOR A MOMENT.
BUT THEN THERE ARE NO MOMENTS.
THE WORLD ROARS, AND I ROAR WITH IT.
I AM DEATH'S GODHEAD! I AM THE WOLF!
I GAVE A BANQUET. DO YOU SEE? I INVITED MY ENEMIES TO EAT WITH ME AND MAKE PEACE.
I FED THEM MY OWN FLESH. IMBUED WITH MY MIND AND MEANING. MY POTENCY.
TO KEEP IT SAFE. UNTIL I CAME TO TAKE IT BACK.
S-- SAFE FROM WHAT?
FROM MYSELF, LITTLE MAD-MAN. FOR I AM DISSOLUTION, AND IN THE TIME OF THE DAWNING, NOTHING WITHSTOOD MY POWER.
AND LO, IN THE TIME OF TWILIGHT--
--SO IT IS AGAIN.

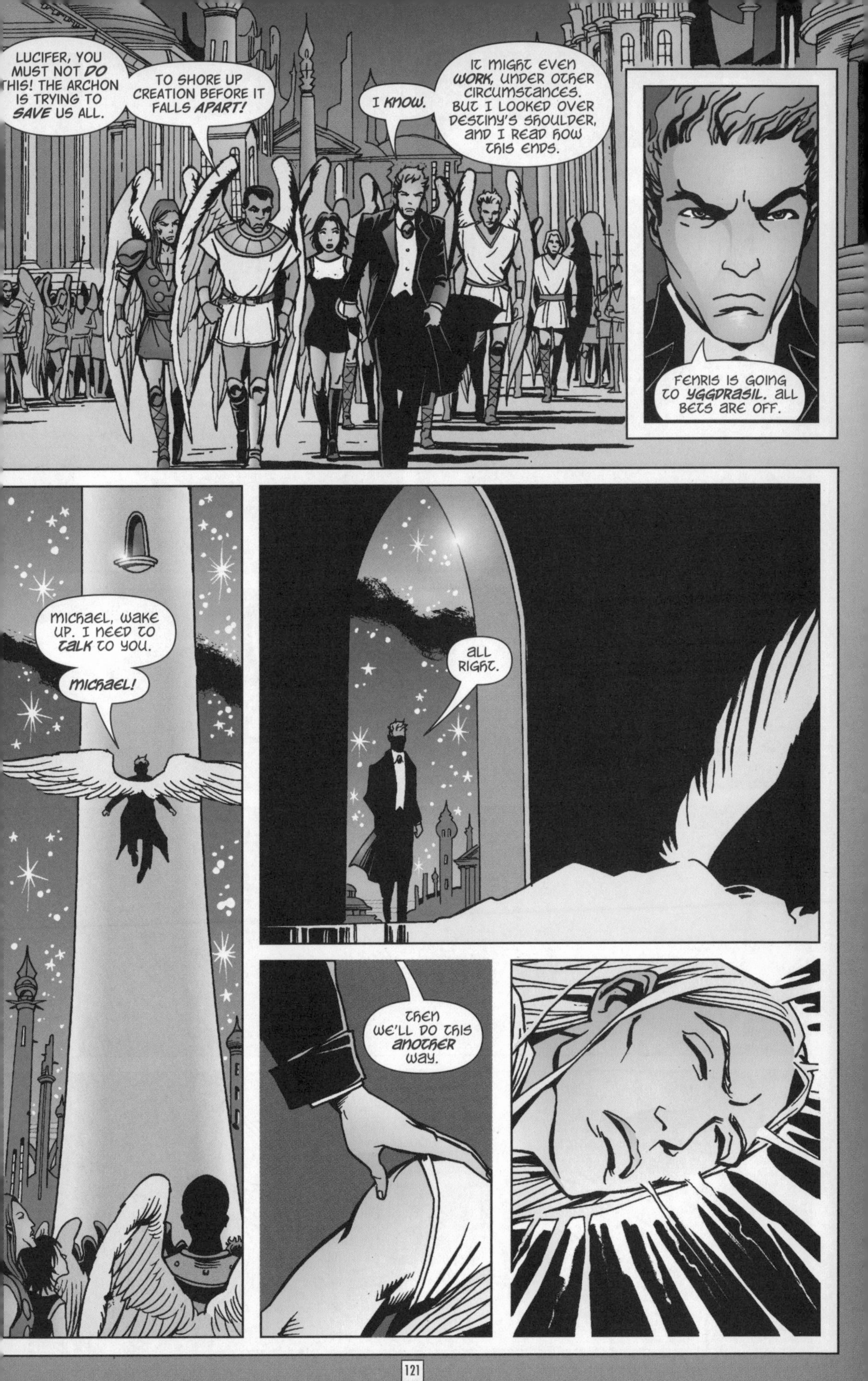
LUCIFER, YOU MUST NOT *DO* THIS! THE ARCHON IS TRYING TO *SAVE* US ALL.
TO SHORE UP CREATION BEFORE IT FALLS *APART!*
I *KNOW.*
IT MIGHT EVEN *WORK*, UNDER OTHER CIRCUMSTANCES. BUT I LOOKED OVER DESTINY'S SHOULDER, AND I READ HOW THIS ENDS.
FENRIS IS GOING TO *YGGDRASIL.* ALL BETS ARE OFF.
MICHAEL, WAKE UP. I NEED TO *TALK* TO YOU.
MICHAEL!
ALL RIGHT.
THEN WE'LL DO THIS *ANOTHER* WAY.

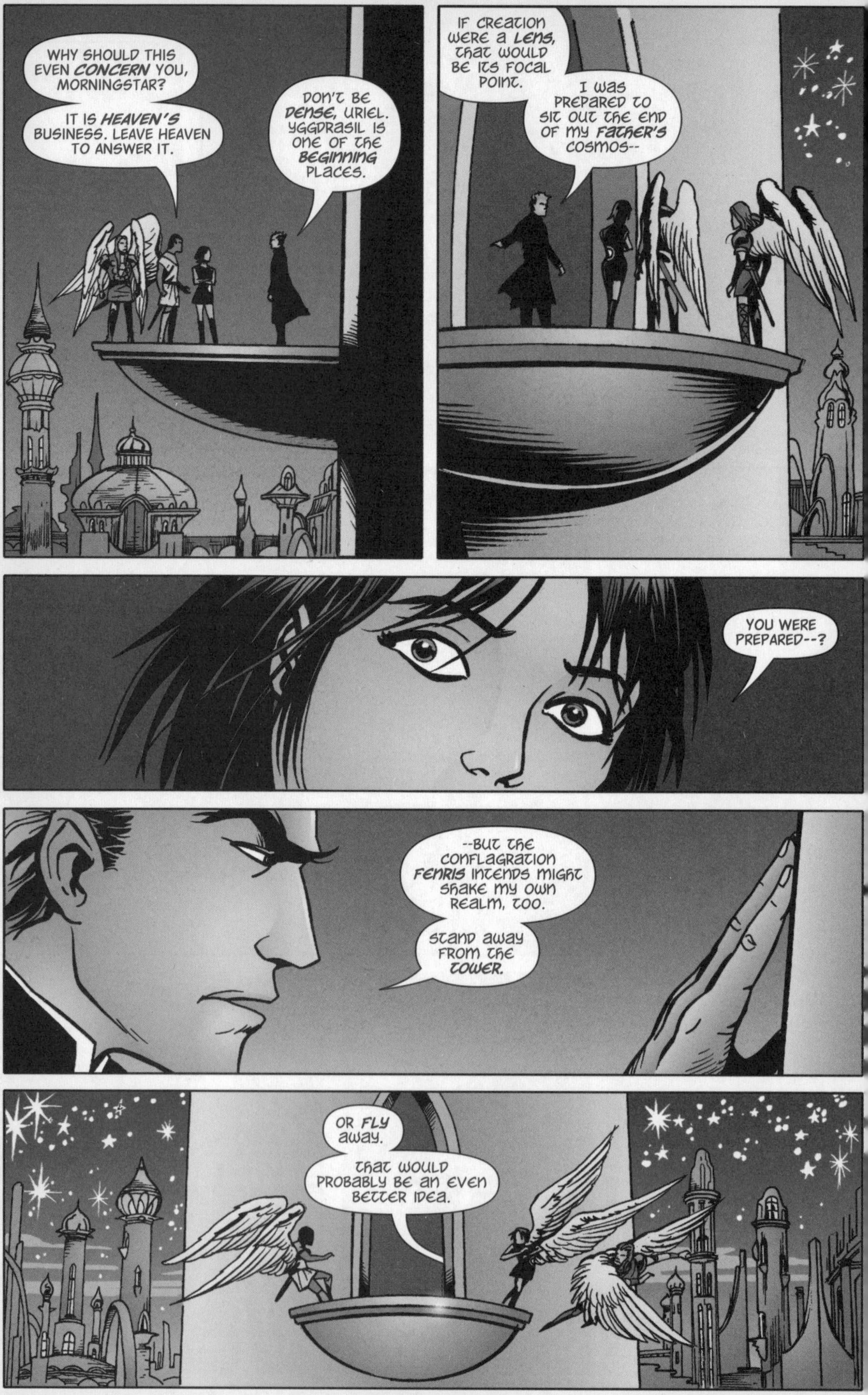
WHY SHOULD THIS EVEN CONCERN YOU, MORNINGSTAR?
IT IS HEAVEN'S BUSINESS. LEAVE HEAVEN TO ANSWER IT.
DON'T BE DENSE, URIEL. YGGDRASIL IS ONE OF THE BEGINNING PLACES.
IF CREATION WERE A LENS, THAT WOULD BE ITS FOCAL POINT.
I WAS PREPARED TO SIT OUT THE END OF MY FATHER'S COSMOS--
YOU WERE PREPARED--?
--BUT THE CONFLAGRATION FENRIS INTENDS MIGHT SHAKE MY OWN REALM, TOO.
STAND AWAY FROM THE TOWER.
OR FLY AWAY.
THAT WOULD PROBABLY BE AN EVEN BETTER IDEA.

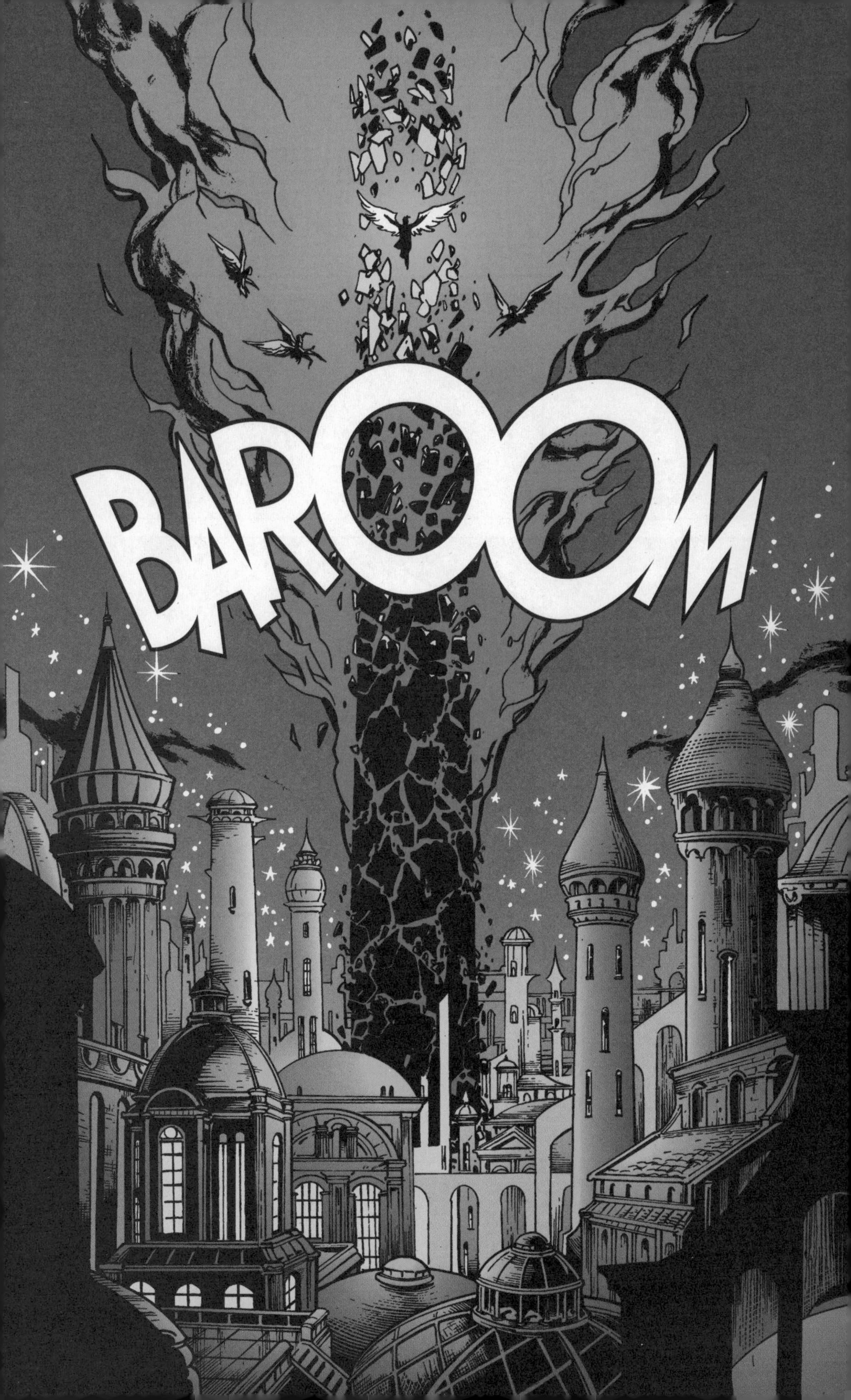
BAROOM

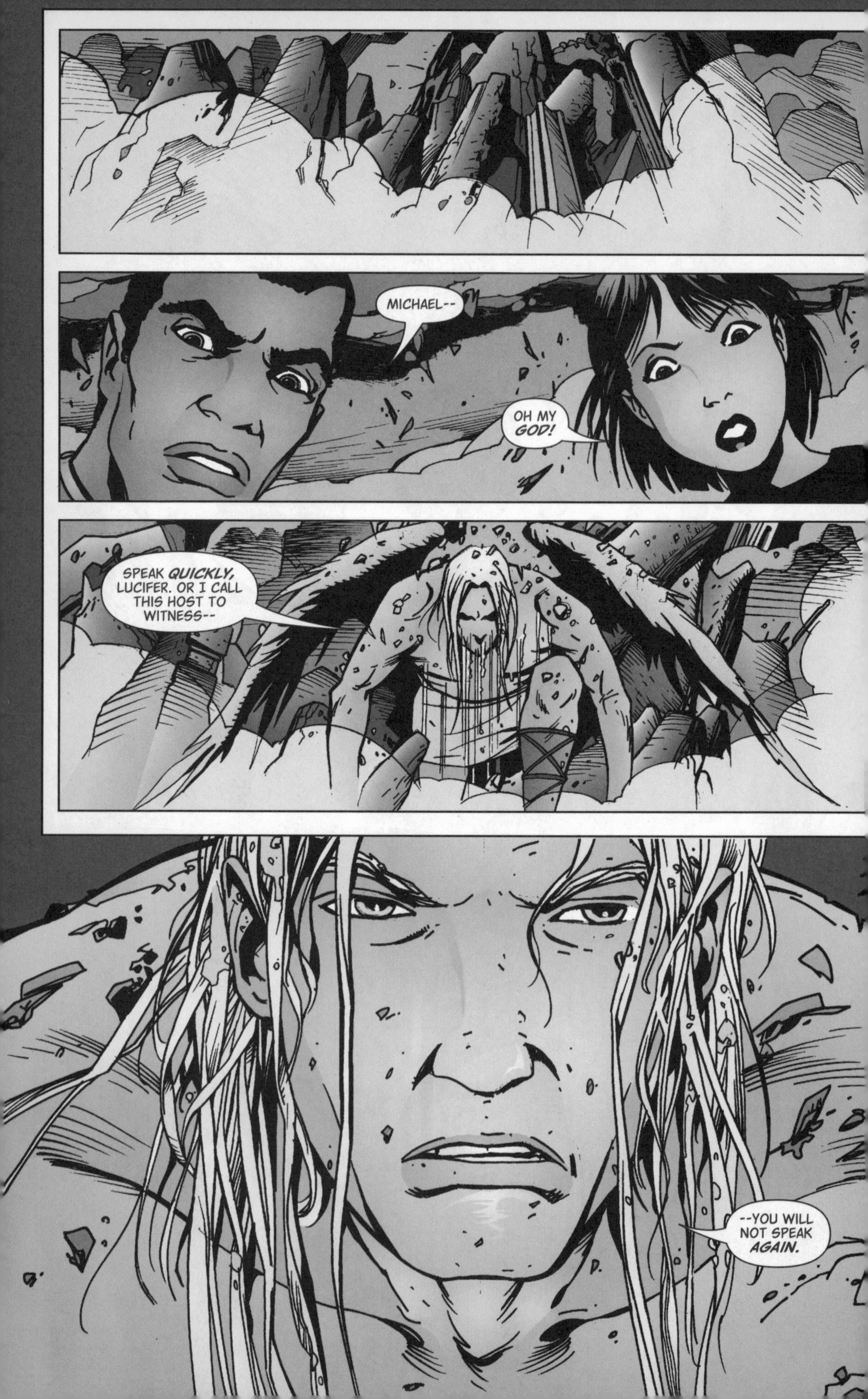
MICHAEL--
OH MY GOD!
SPEAK QUICKLY, LUCIFER. OR I CALL THIS HOST TO WITNESS--
--YOU WILL NOT SPEAK AGAIN.

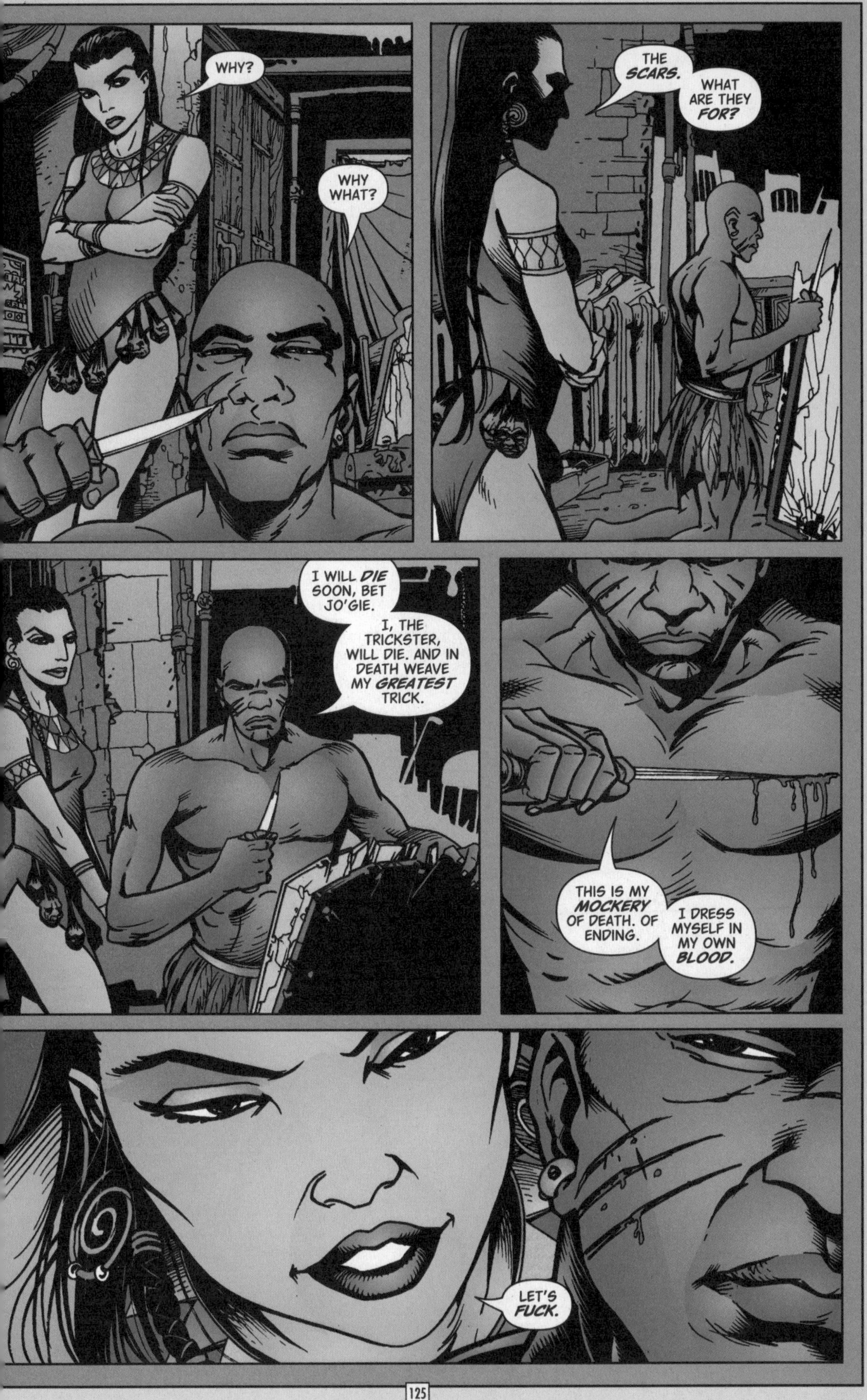
WHY?
WHY WHAT?
THE *SCARS.*
WHAT ARE THEY *FOR?*
I WILL *DIE* SOON, BET JO'GIE.
I, THE TRICKSTER, WILL DIE. AND IN DEATH WEAVE MY *GREATEST* TRICK.
THIS IS MY *MOCKERY* OF DEATH. OF ENDING.
I DRESS MYSELF IN MY OWN *BLOOD.*
LET'S *FUCK.*

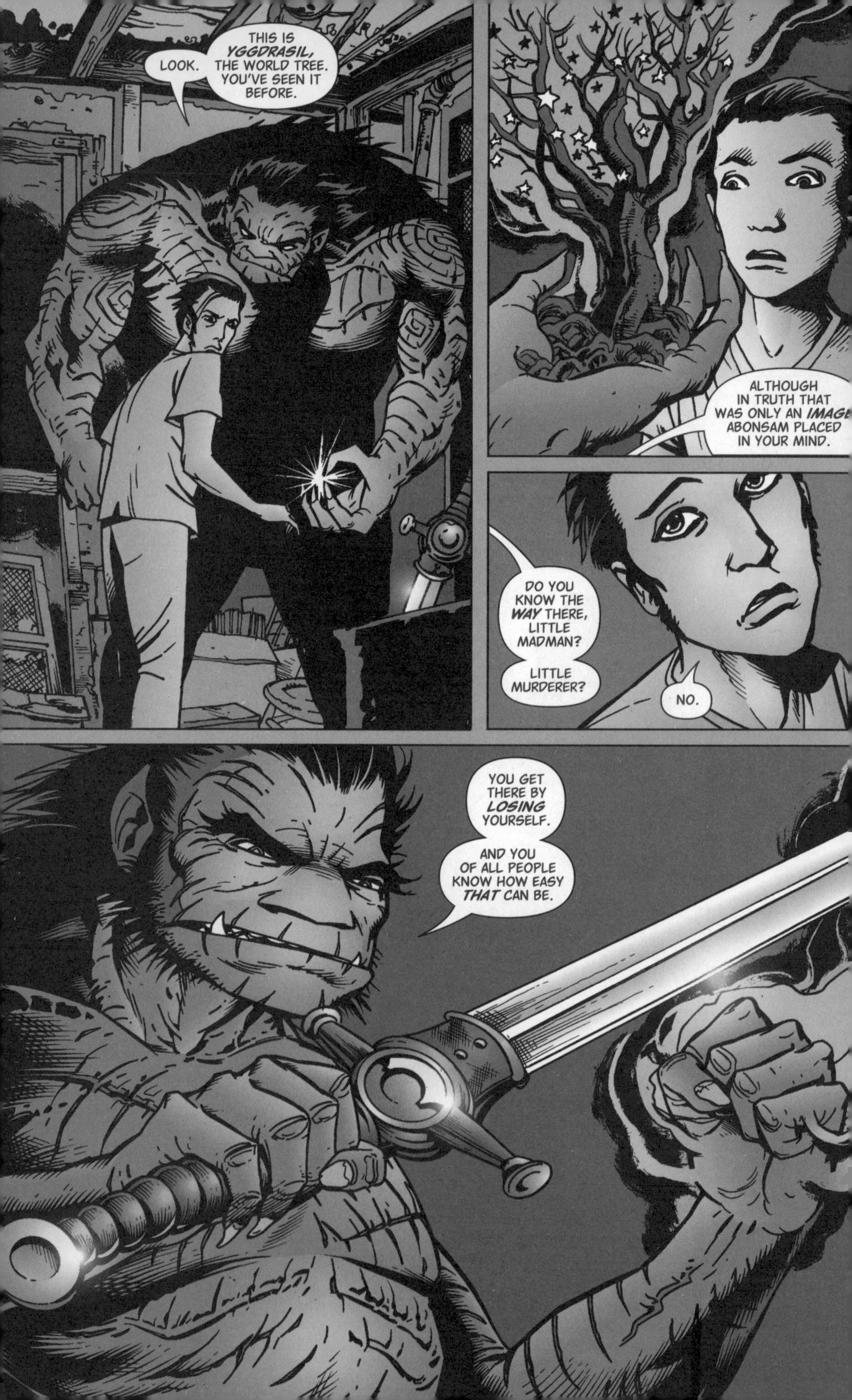
LOOK.
THIS IS YGGDRASIL, THE WORLD TREE. YOU'VE SEEN IT BEFORE.
ALTHOUGH IN TRUTH THAT WAS ONLY AN IMAGE ABONSAM PLACED IN YOUR MIND.
DO YOU KNOW THE WAY THERE, LITTLE MADMAN?
LITTLE MURDERER?
NO.
YOU GET THERE BY LOSING YOURSELF.
AND YOU OF ALL PEOPLE KNOW HOW EASY THAT CAN BE.

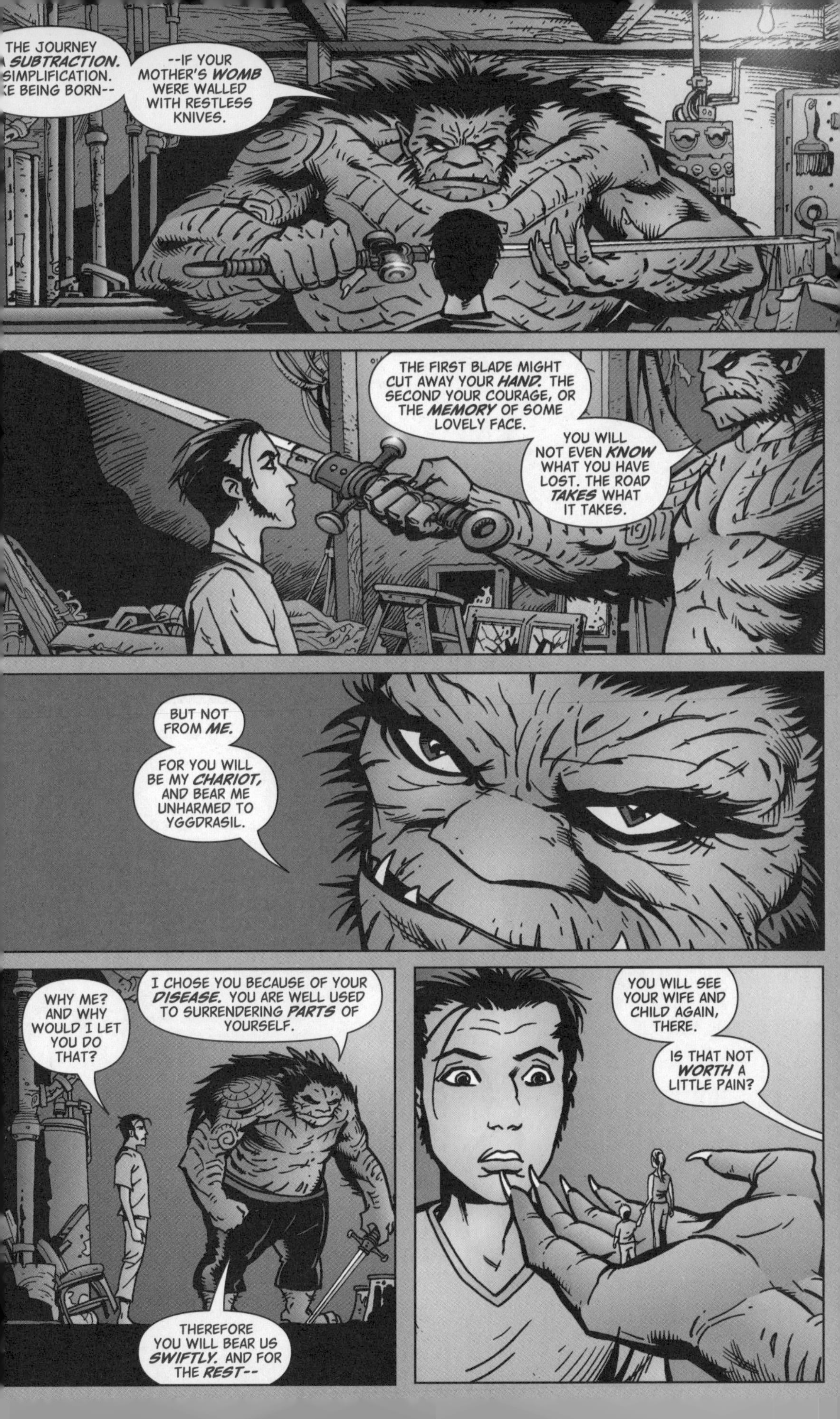

THE JOURNEY
A SUBTRACTION.
SIMPLIFICATION.
KE BEING BORN--
--IF YOUR MOTHER'S WOMB WERE WALLED WITH RESTLESS KNIVES.
THE FIRST BLADE MIGHT CUT AWAY YOUR HAND. THE SECOND YOUR COURAGE, OR THE MEMORY OF SOME LOVELY FACE.
YOU WILL NOT EVEN KNOW WHAT YOU HAVE LOST. THE ROAD TAKES WHAT IT TAKES.
BUT NOT FROM ME.
FOR YOU WILL BE MY CHARIOT, AND BEAR ME UNHARMED TO YGGDRASIL.
WHY ME? AND WHY WOULD I LET YOU DO THAT?
I CHOSE YOU BECAUSE OF YOUR DISEASE. YOU ARE WELL USED TO SURRENDERING PARTS OF YOURSELF.
THEREFORE YOU WILL BEAR US SWIFTLY. AND FOR THE REST--
YOU WILL SEE YOUR WIFE AND CHILD AGAIN, THERE.
IS THAT NOT WORTH A LITTLE PAIN?

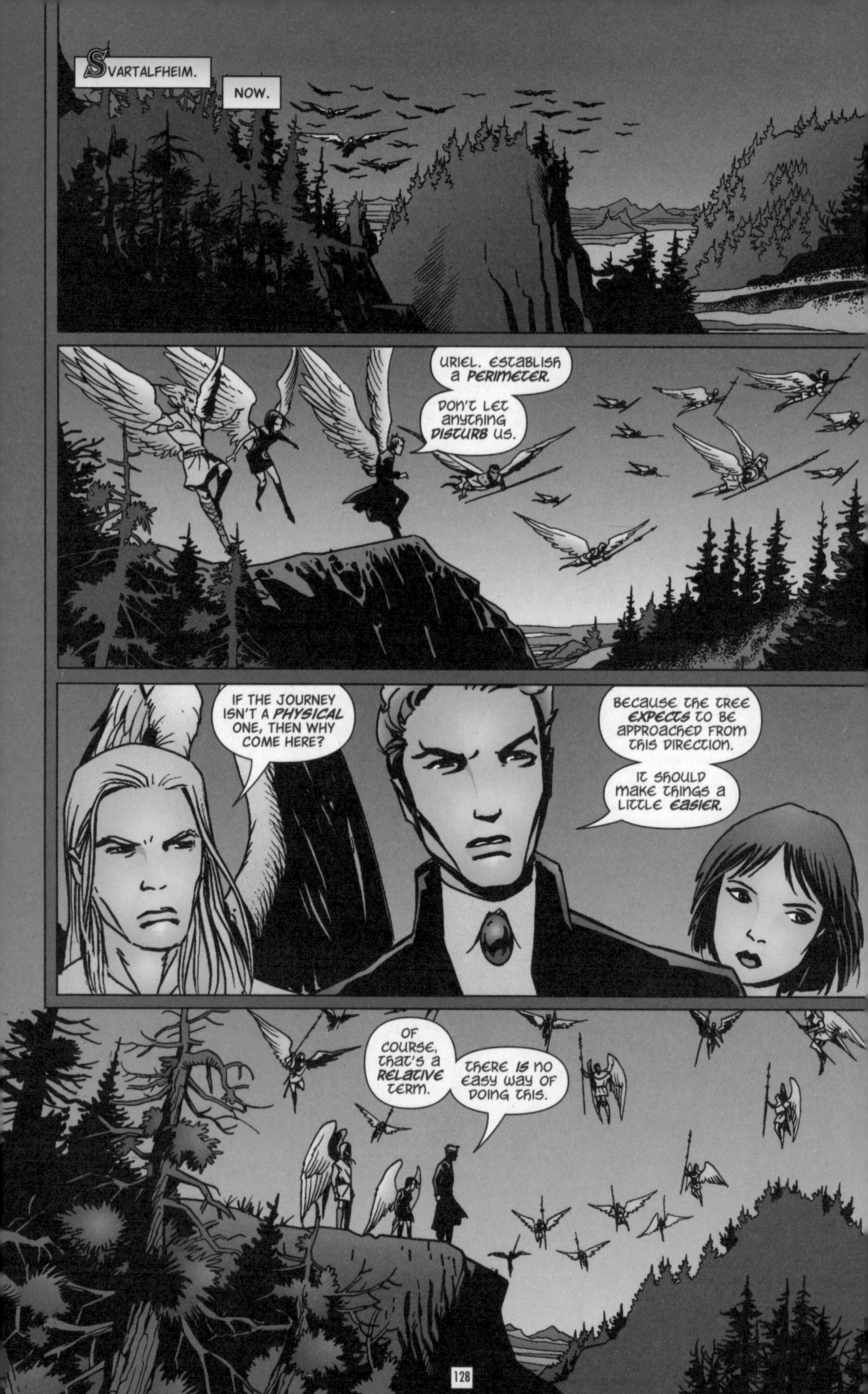
SVARTALFHEIM.
NOW.
URIEL. ESTABLISH A PERIMETER.
DON'T LET ANYTHING DISTURB US.
IF THE JOURNEY ISN'T A PHYSICAL ONE, THEN WHY COME HERE?
BECAUSE THE TREE EXPECTS TO BE APPROACHED FROM THIS DIRECTION.
IT SHOULD MAKE THINGS A LITTLE EASIER.
OF COURSE, THAT'S A RELATIVE TERM.
THERE IS NO EASY WAY OF DOING THIS.

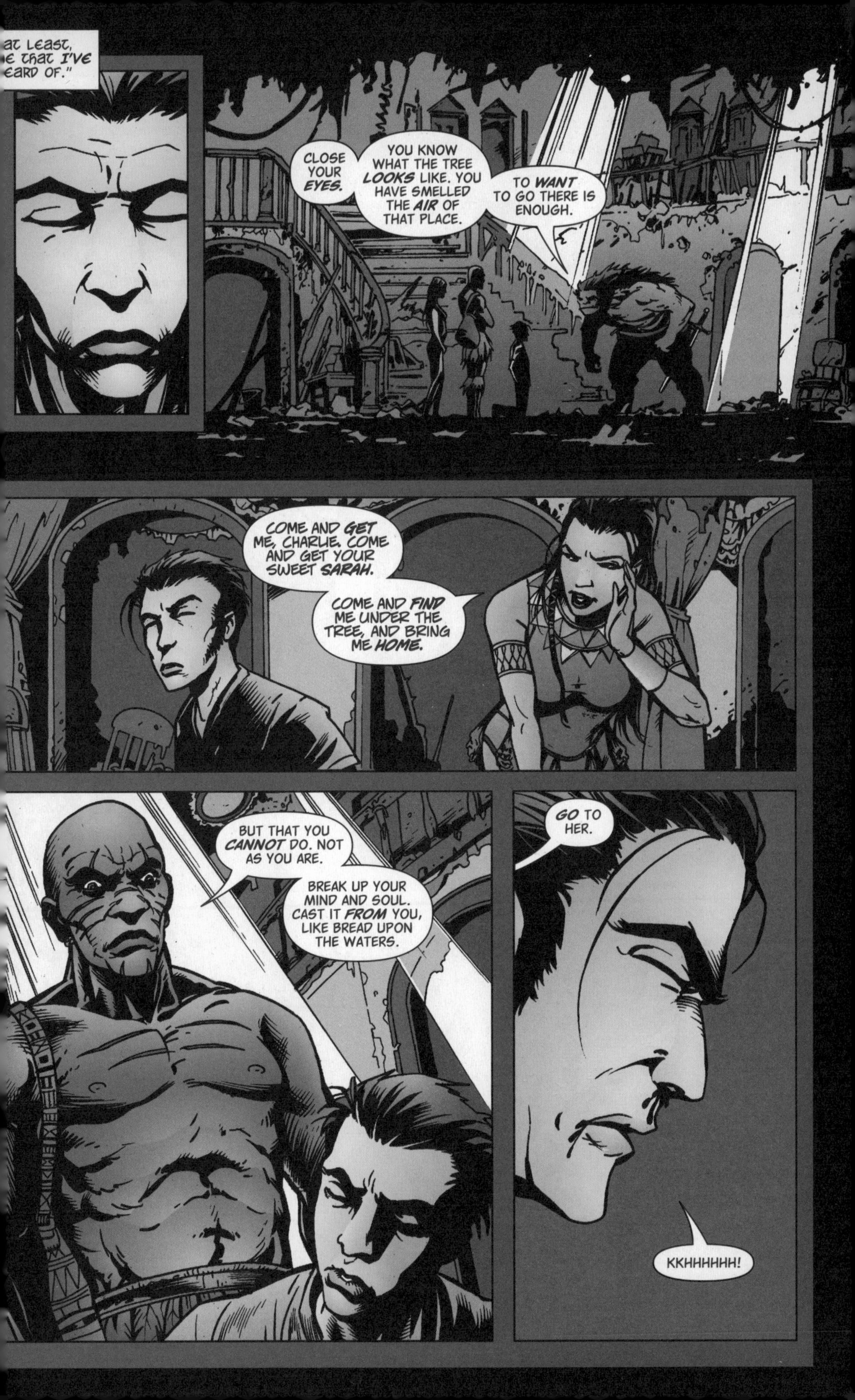

AT LEAST, E THAT I'VE EARD OF."
CLOSE YOUR EYES.
YOU KNOW WHAT THE TREE LOOKS LIKE. YOU HAVE SMELLED THE AIR OF THAT PLACE.
TO WANT TO GO THERE IS ENOUGH.
COME AND GET ME, CHARLIE. COME AND GET YOUR SWEET SARAH.
COME AND FIND ME UNDER THE TREE, AND BRING ME HOME.
BUT THAT YOU CANNOT DO. NOT AS YOU ARE.
BREAK UP YOUR MIND AND SOUL. CAST IT FROM YOU, LIKE BREAD UPON THE WATERS.
GO TO HER.
KKHHHHHH!

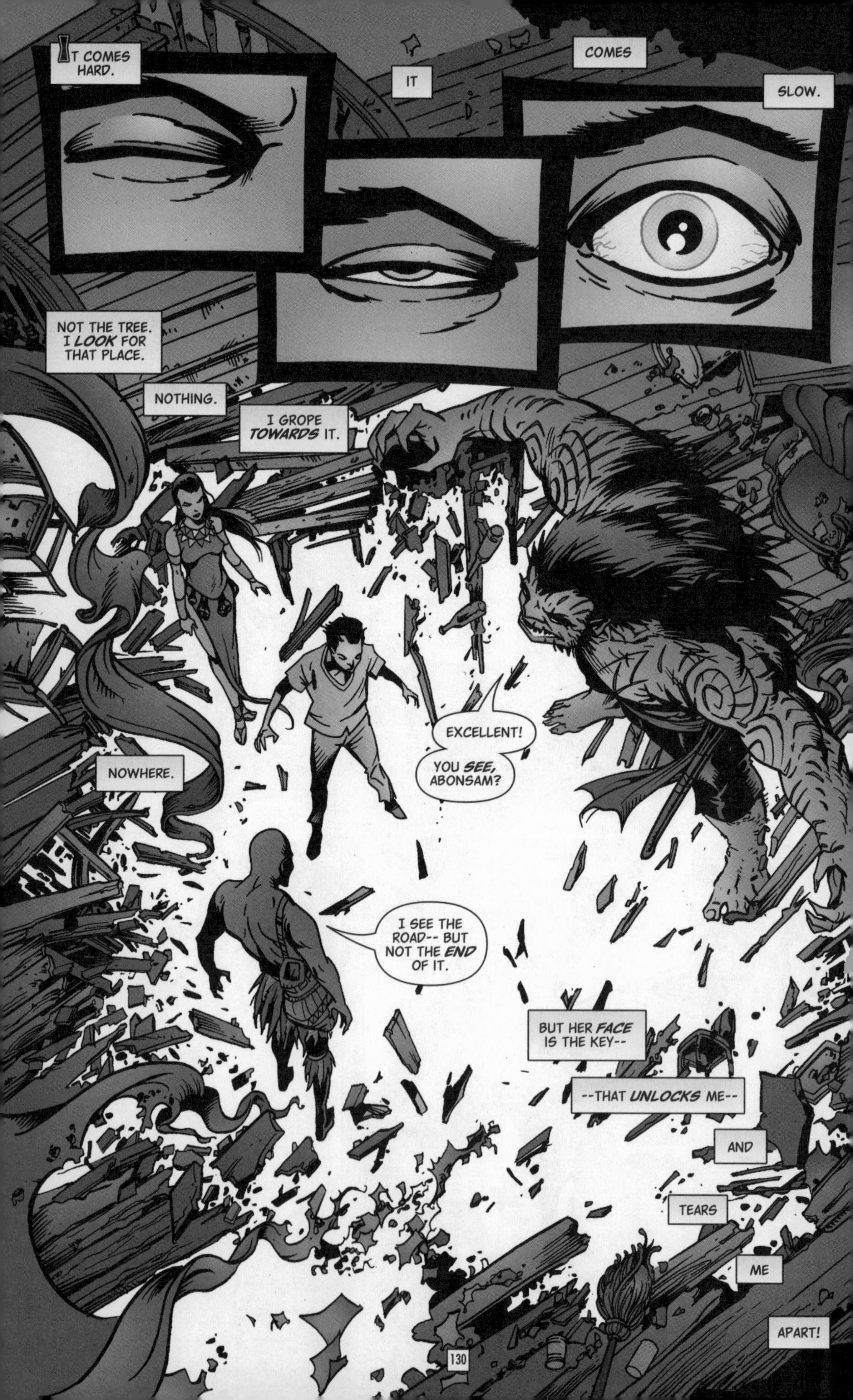
IT COMES HARD.
IT
COMES
SLOW.
NOT THE TREE. I LOOK FOR THAT PLACE.
NOTHING.
I GROPE TOWARDS IT.
EXCELLENT!
YOU SEE, ABONSAM?
NOWHERE.
I SEE THE ROAD-- BUT NOT THE END OF IT.
BUT HER FACE IS THE KEY--
--THAT UNLOCKS ME--
AND
TEARS
ME
APART!

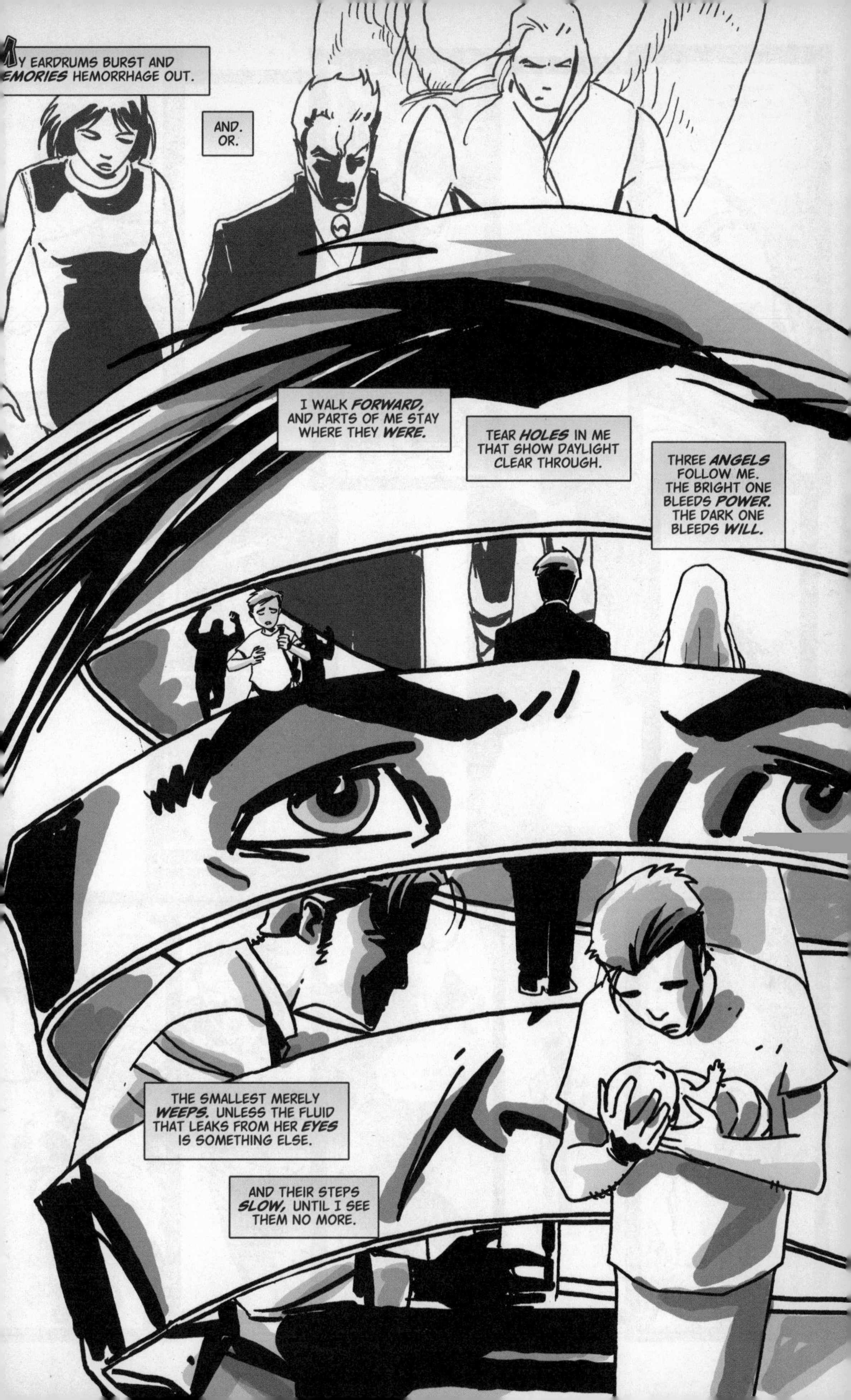
MY EARDRUMS BURST AND MEMORIES HEMORRHAGE OUT.
AND. OR.
I WALK FORWARD, AND PARTS OF ME STAY WHERE THEY WERE.
TEAR HOLES IN ME THAT SHOW DAYLIGHT CLEAR THROUGH.
THREE ANGELS FOLLOW ME. THE BRIGHT ONE BLEEDS POWER. THE DARK ONE BLEEDS WILL.
THE SMALLEST MERELY WEEPS. UNLESS THE FLUID THAT LEAKS FROM HER EYES IS SOMETHING ELSE.
AND THEIR STEPS SLOW, UNTIL I SEE THEM NO MORE.

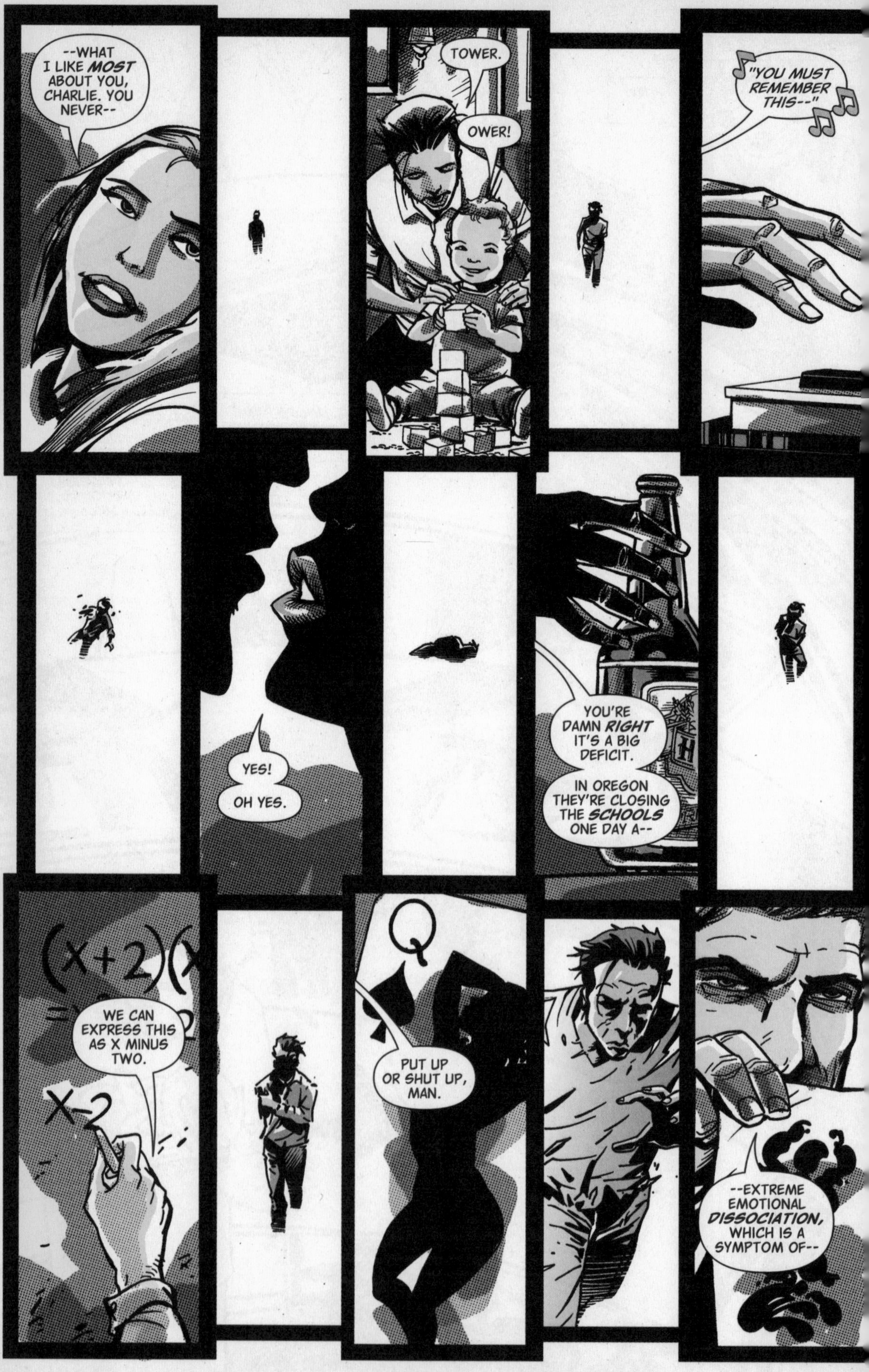
--WHAT I LIKE MOST ABOUT YOU, CHARLIE. YOU NEVER--
TOWER.
OWER!
"YOU MUST REMEMBER THIS--"
YES!
OH YES.
YOU'RE DAMN RIGHT IT'S A BIG DEFICIT.
IN OREGON THEY'RE CLOSING THE SCHOOLS ONE DAY A--
(X+2)(X
WE CAN EXPRESS THIS AS X MINUS TWO.
X-2
PUT UP OR SHUT UP, MAN.
--EXTREME EMOTIONAL DISSOCIATION, WHICH IS A SYMPTOM OF--

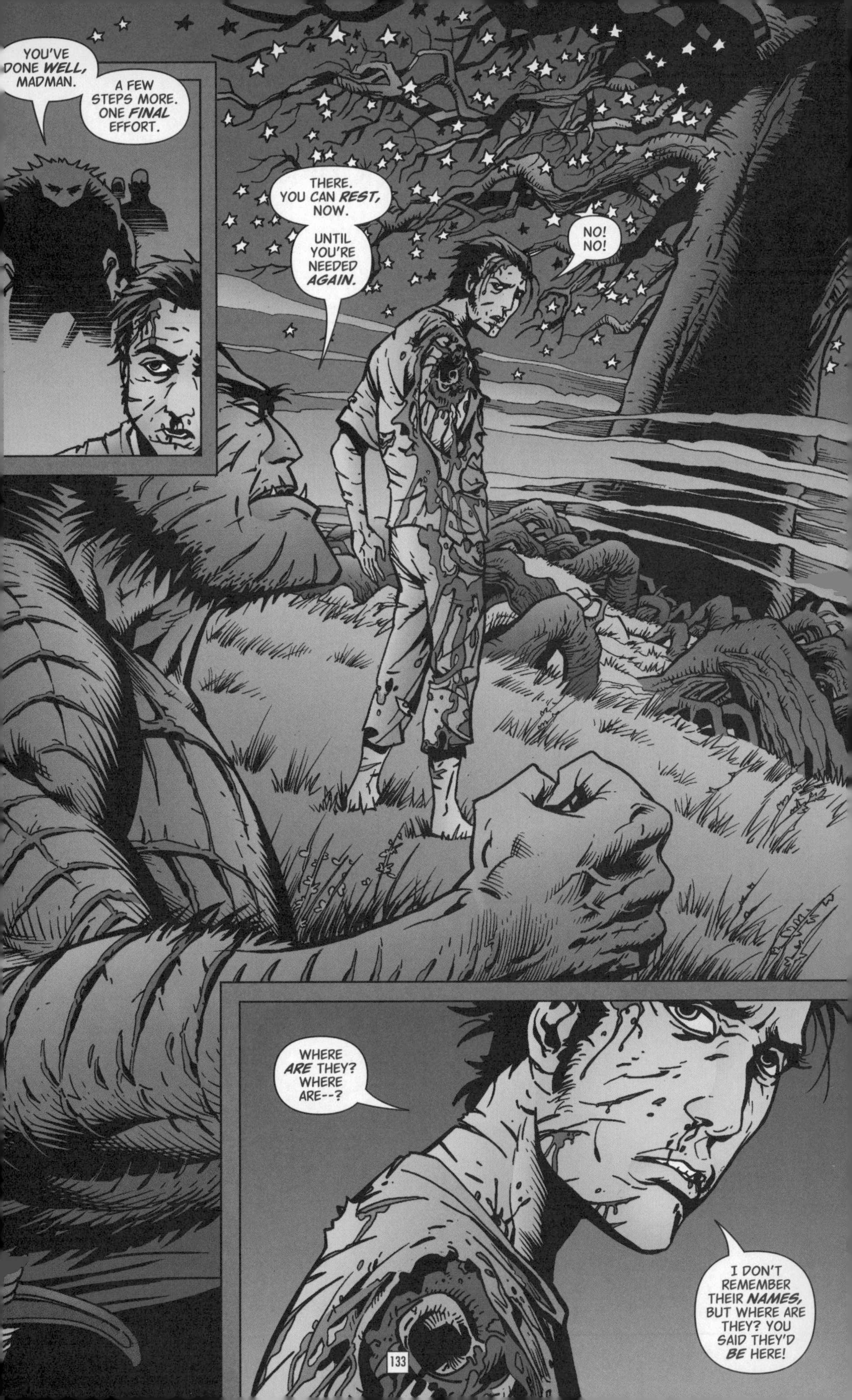
YOU'VE DONE WELL, MADMAN.
A FEW STEPS MORE. ONE FINAL EFFORT.
THERE. YOU CAN REST, NOW.
UNTIL YOU'RE NEEDED AGAIN.
NO! NO!
WHERE ARE THEY? WHERE ARE--?
I DON'T REMEMBER THEIR NAMES, BUT WHERE ARE THEY? YOU SAID THEY'D BE HERE!

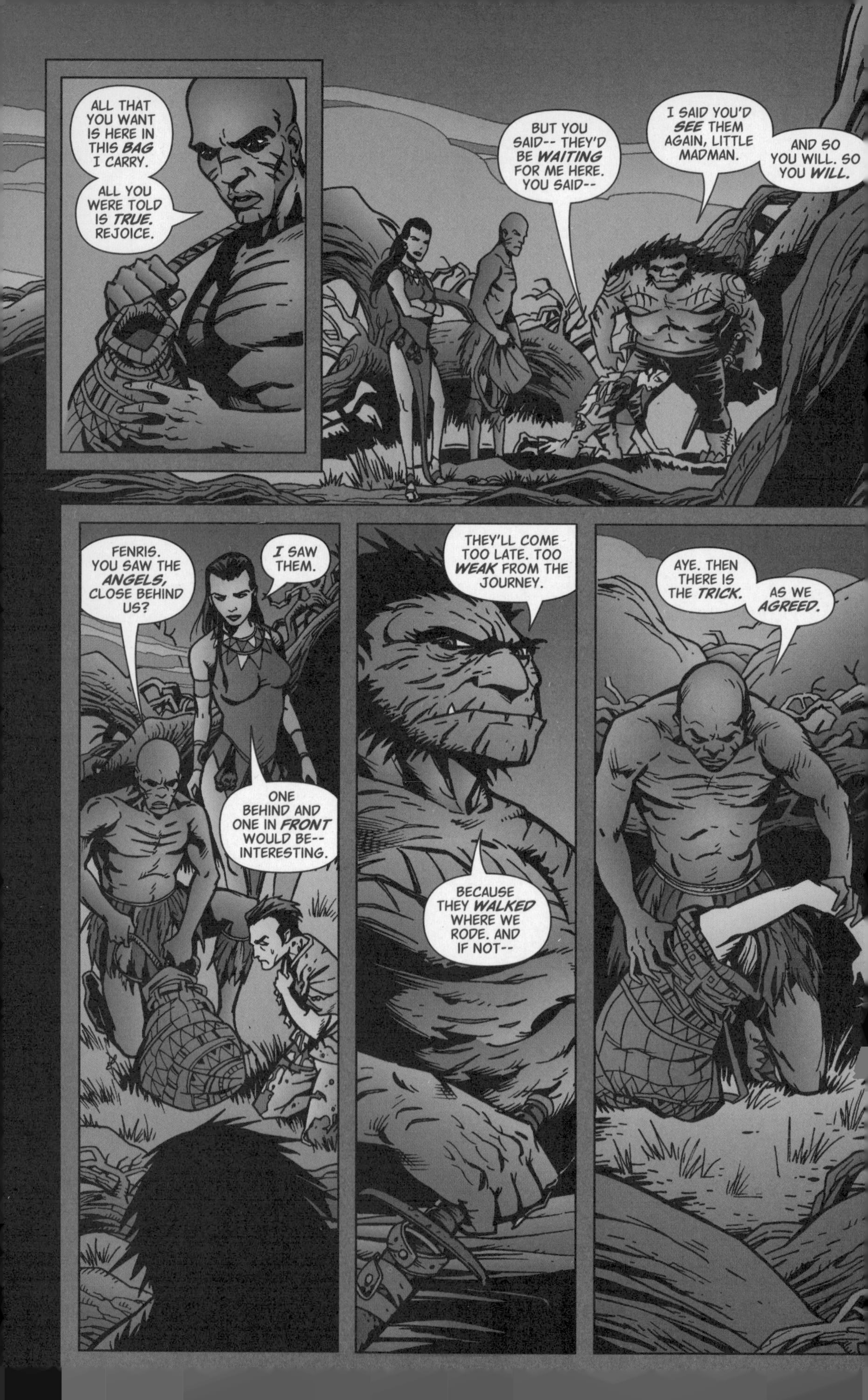
ALL THAT YOU WANT IS HERE IN THIS BAG I CARRY.
ALL YOU WERE TOLD IS TRUE. REJOICE.
BUT YOU SAID-- THEY'D BE WAITING FOR ME HERE. YOU SAID--
I SAID YOU'D SEE THEM AGAIN, LITTLE MADMAN.
AND SO YOU WILL. SO YOU WILL.
FENRIS. YOU SAW THE ANGELS, CLOSE BEHIND US?
I SAW THEM.
ONE BEHIND AND ONE IN FRONT WOULD BE-- INTERESTING.
THEY'LL COME TOO LATE. TOO WEAK FROM THE JOURNEY.
BECAUSE THEY WALKED WHERE WE RODE. AND IF NOT--
AYE. THEN THERE IS THE TRICK.
AS WE AGREED.

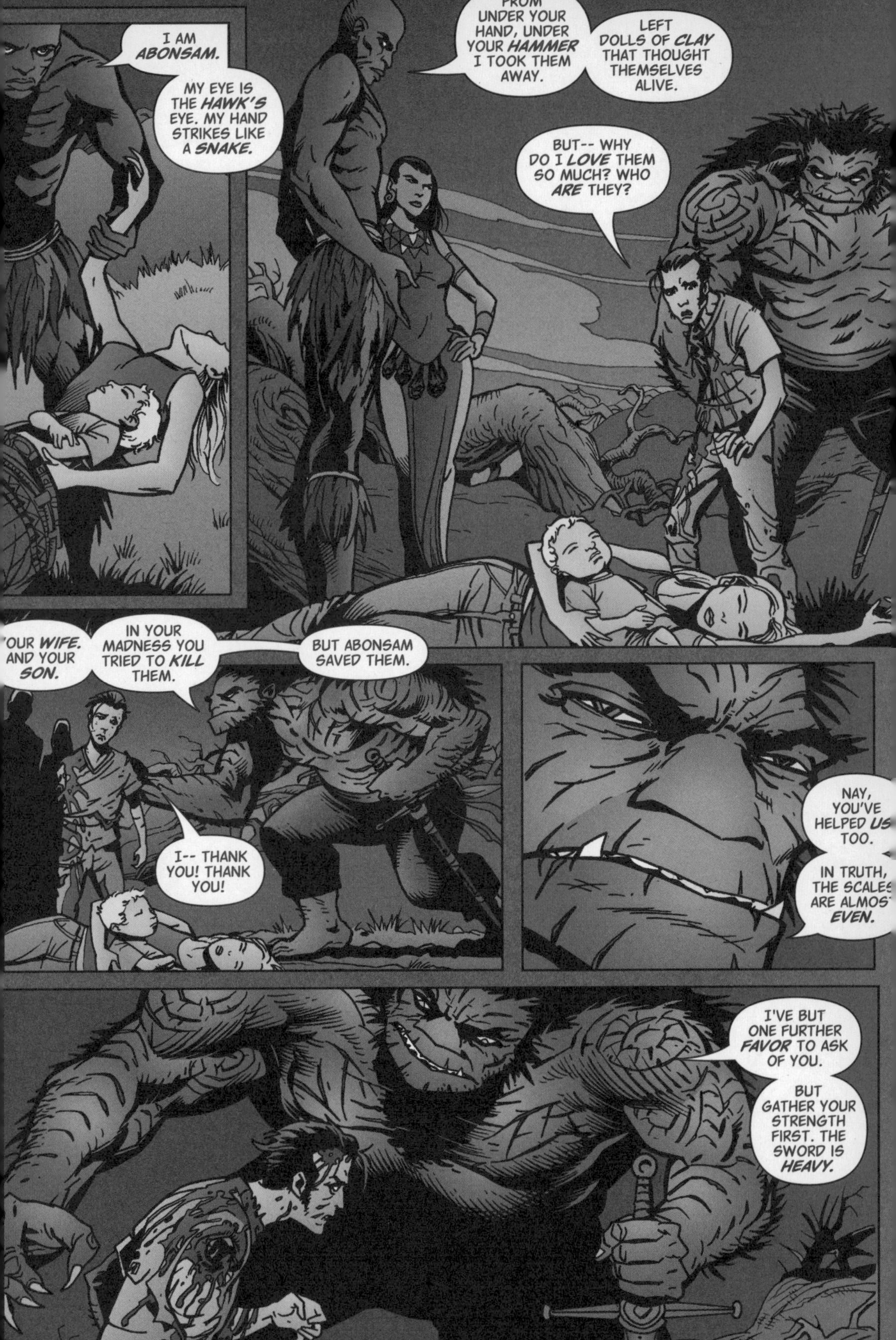
I AM ABONSAM.
MY EYE IS THE HAWK'S EYE. MY HAND STRIKES LIKE A SNAKE.
FROM UNDER YOUR HAND, UNDER YOUR HAMMER I TOOK THEM AWAY.
LEFT DOLLS OF CLAY THAT THOUGHT THEMSELVES ALIVE.
BUT-- WHY DO I LOVE THEM SO MUCH? WHO ARE THEY?
OUR WIFE. AND YOUR SON.
IN YOUR MADNESS YOU TRIED TO KILL THEM.
BUT ABONSAM SAVED THEM.
I-- THANK YOU! THANK YOU!
NAY, YOU'VE HELPED US TOO.
IN TRUTH, THE SCALES ARE ALMOST EVEN.
I'VE BUT ONE FURTHER FAVOR TO ASK OF YOU.
BUT GATHER YOUR STRENGTH FIRST. THE SWORD IS HEAVY.

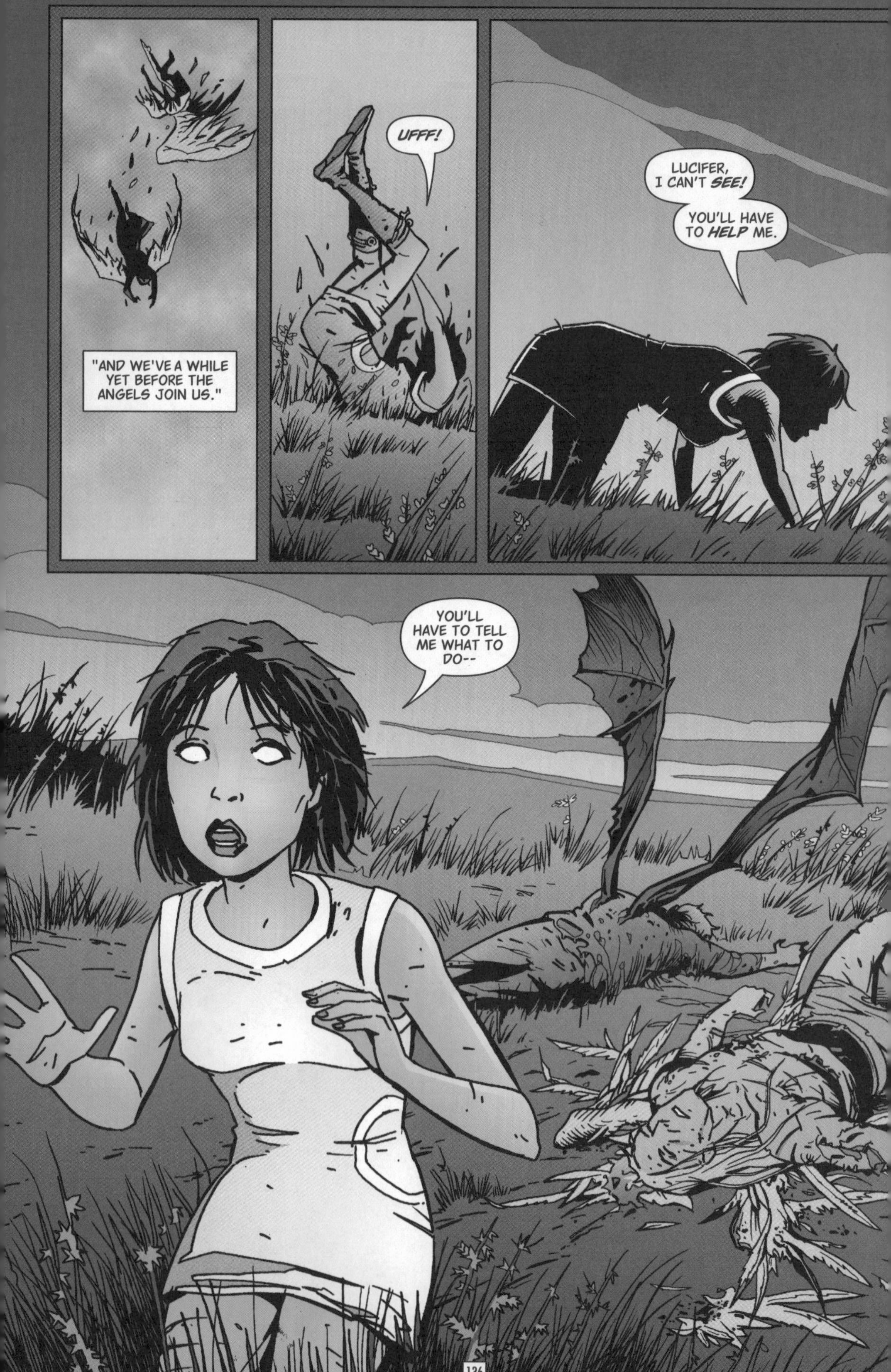
"AND WE'VE A WHILE YET BEFORE THE ANGELS JOIN US."
UFFF!
LUCIFER, I CAN'T SEE!
YOU'LL HAVE TO HELP ME.
YOU'LL HAVE TO TELL ME WHAT TO DO--

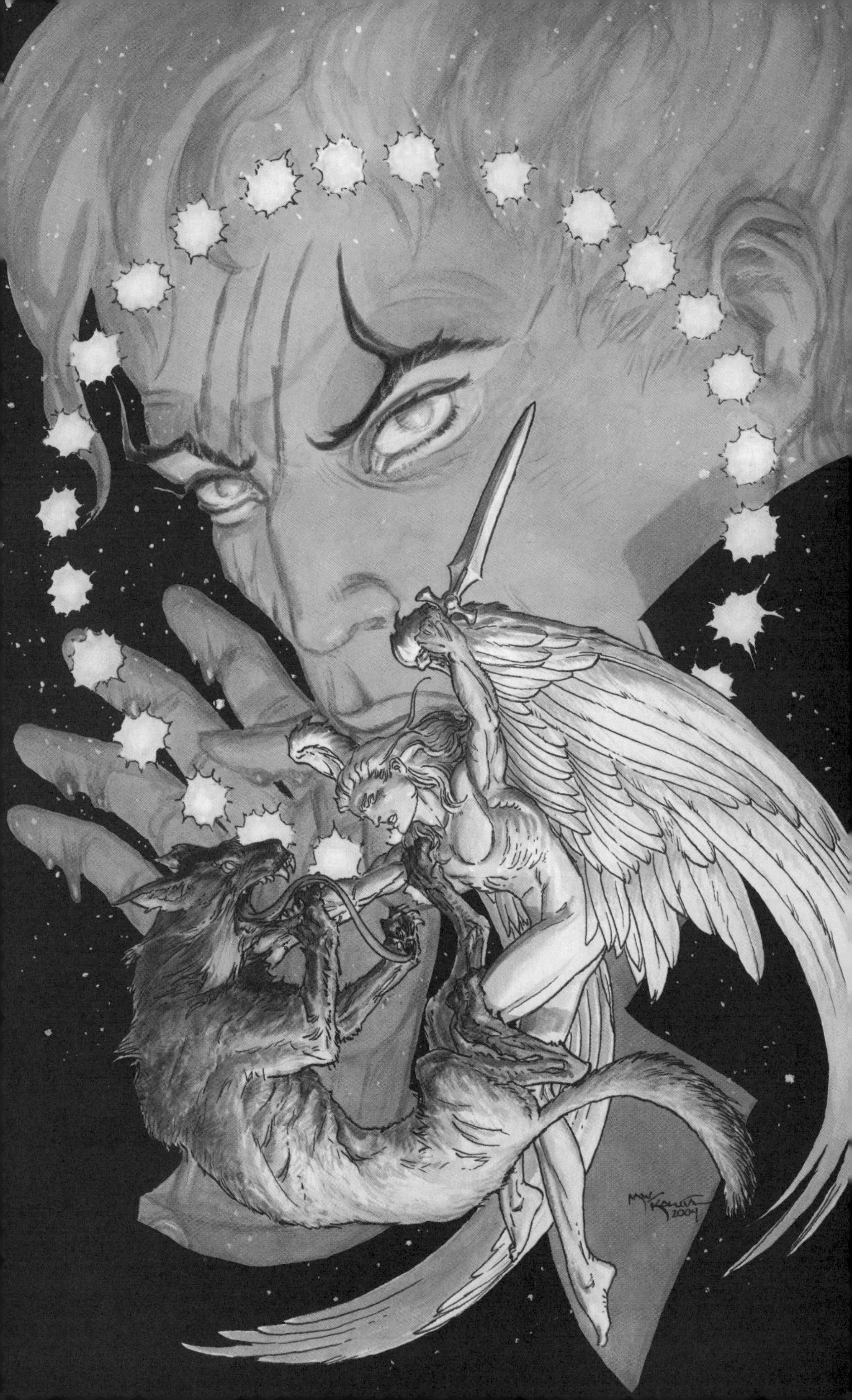

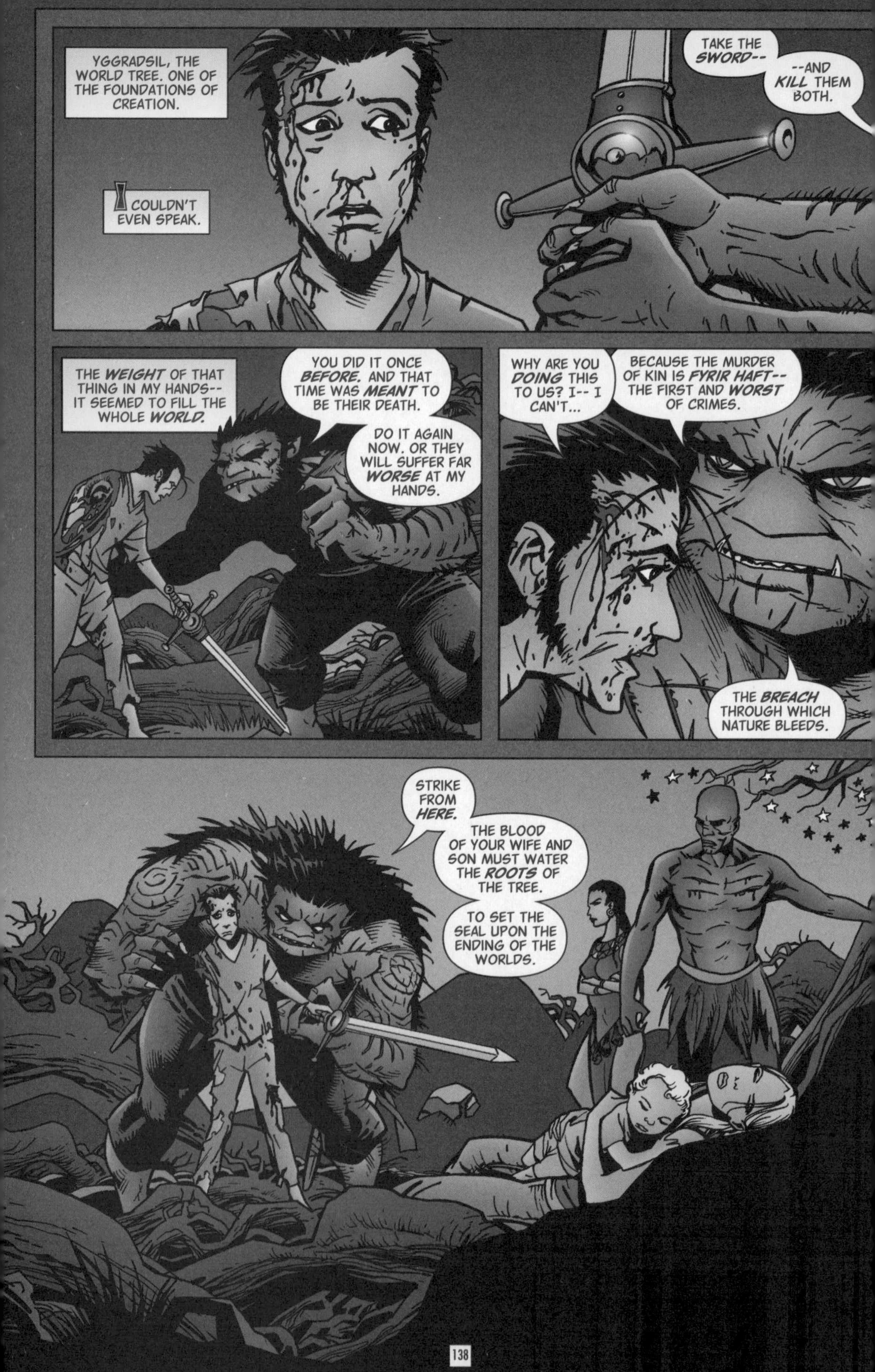
YGGRADSIL, THE WORLD TREE. ONE OF THE FOUNDATIONS OF CREATION.
I COULDN'T EVEN SPEAK.
TAKE THE SWORD--
--AND KILL THEM BOTH.
THE WEIGHT OF THAT THING IN MY HANDS-- IT SEEMED TO FILL THE WHOLE WORLD.
YOU DID IT ONCE BEFORE. AND THAT TIME WAS MEANT TO BE THEIR DEATH.
DO IT AGAIN NOW. OR THEY WILL SUFFER FAR WORSE AT MY HANDS.
WHY ARE YOU DOING THIS TO US? I-- I CAN'T...
BECAUSE THE MURDER OF KIN IS FYRIR HAFT-- THE FIRST AND WORST OF CRIMES.
THE BREACH THROUGH WHICH NATURE BLEEDS.
STRIKE FROM HERE.
THE BLOOD OF YOUR WIFE AND SON MUST WATER THE ROOTS OF THE TREE.
TO SET THE SEAL UPON THE ENDING OF THE WORLDS.

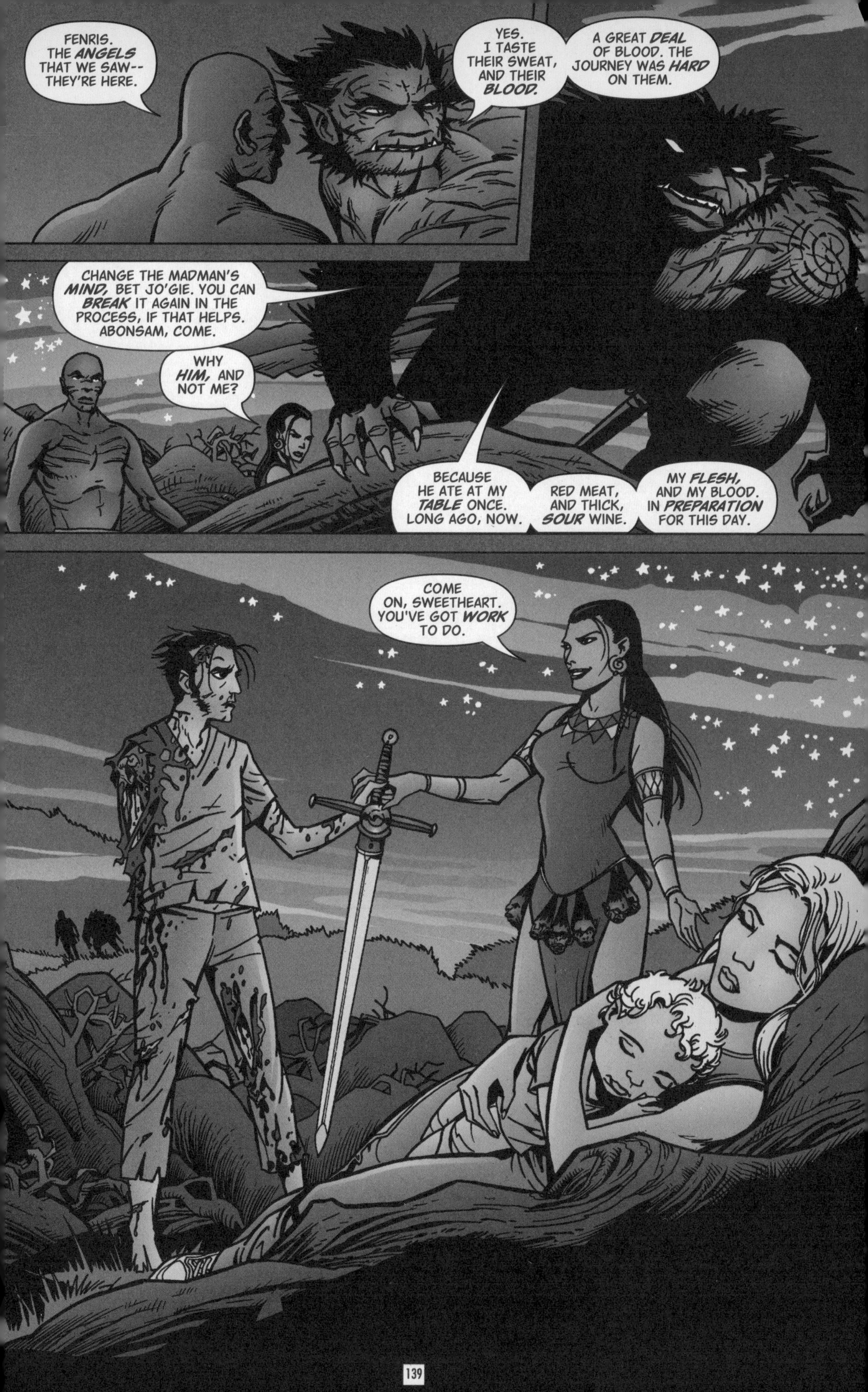
FENRIS. THE *ANGELS* THAT WE SAW-- THEY'RE HERE.
YES. I TASTE THEIR SWEAT, AND THEIR *BLOOD.*
A GREAT *DEAL* OF BLOOD. THE JOURNEY WAS *HARD* ON THEM.
CHANGE THE MADMAN'S *MIND,* BET JO'GIE. YOU CAN *BREAK* IT AGAIN IN THE PROCESS, IF THAT HELPS. ABONSAM, COME.
WHY *HIM,* AND NOT ME?
BECAUSE HE ATE AT MY *TABLE* ONCE. LONG AGO, NOW.
RED MEAT, AND THICK, *SOUR* WINE.
MY *FLESH,* AND MY BLOOD. IN *PREPARATION* FOR THIS DAY.
COME ON, SWEETHEART. YOU'VE GOT *WORK* TO DO.

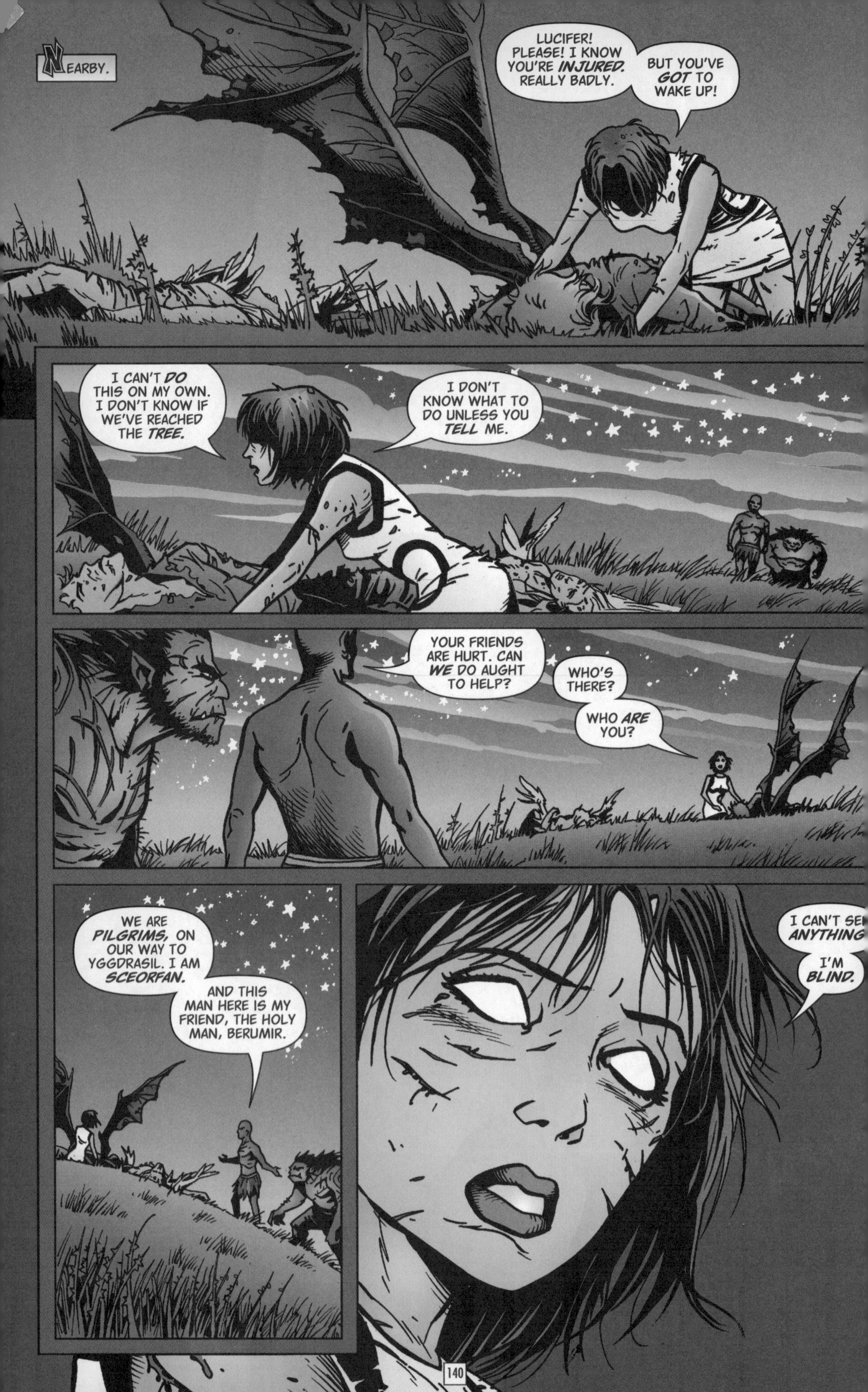
NEARBY.
LUCIFER! PLEASE! I KNOW YOU'RE INJURED. REALLY BADLY.
BUT YOU'VE GOT TO WAKE UP!
I CAN'T DO THIS ON MY OWN. I DON'T KNOW IF WE'VE REACHED THE TREE.
I DON'T KNOW WHAT TO DO UNLESS YOU TELL ME.
YOUR FRIENDS ARE HURT. CAN WE DO AUGHT TO HELP?
WHO'S THERE?
WHO ARE YOU?
WE ARE PILGRIMS, ON OUR WAY TO YGGDRASIL. I AM SCEORFAN.
AND THIS MAN HERE IS MY FRIEND, THE HOLY MAN, BERUMIR.
I CAN'T SE ANYTHING
I'M BLIND.

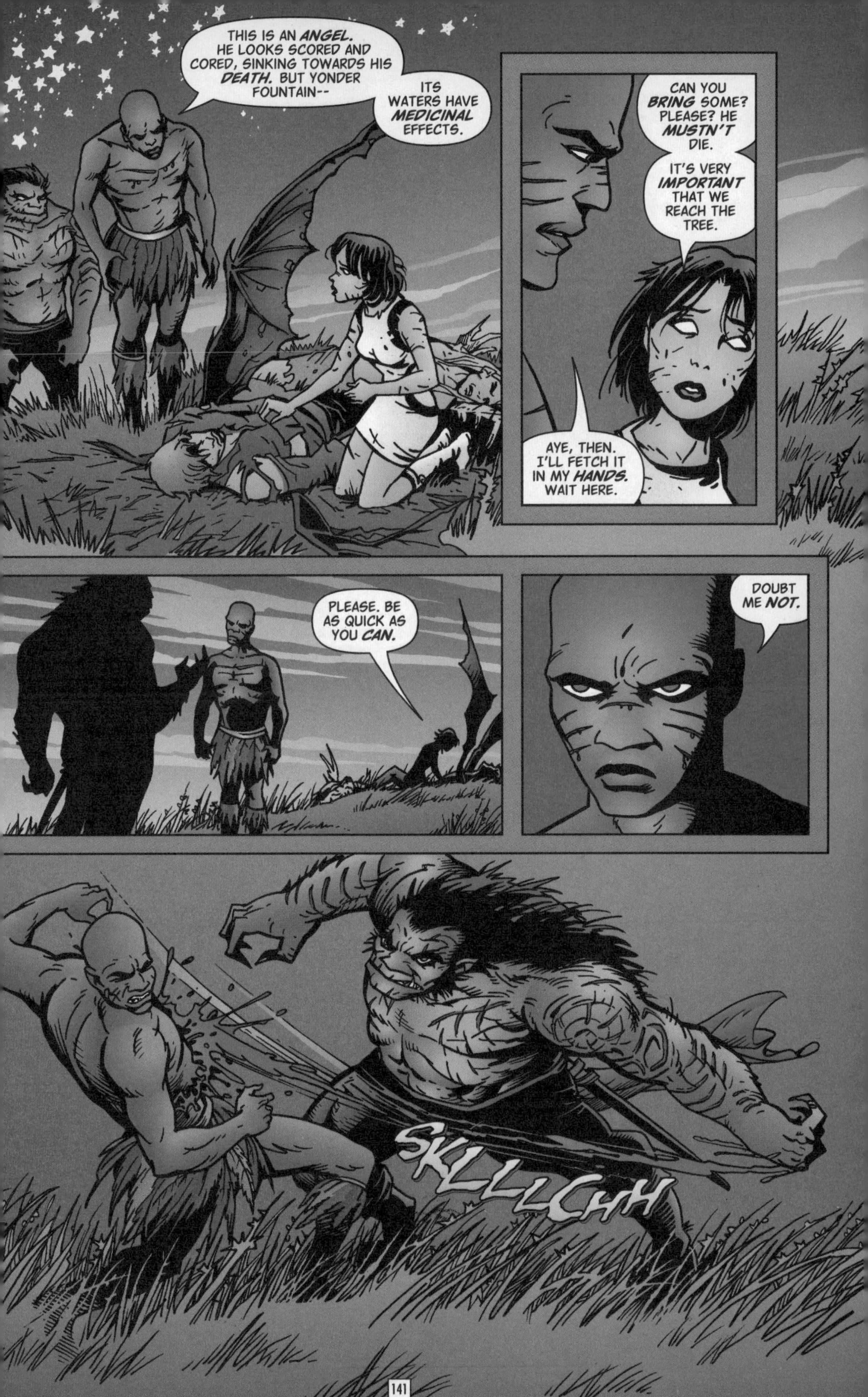

THIS IS AN *ANGEL.* HE LOOKS SCORED AND CORED, SINKING TOWARDS HIS *DEATH.* BUT YONDER FOUNTAIN--
ITS WATERS HAVE *MEDICINAL* EFFECTS.
CAN YOU *BRING* SOME? PLEASE? HE *MUSTN'T* DIE.
IT'S VERY *IMPORTANT* THAT WE REACH THE TREE.
AYE, THEN. I'LL FETCH IT IN MY *HANDS.* WAIT HERE.
PLEASE. BE AS QUICK AS YOU *CAN.*
DOUBT ME *NOT.*
SKLLLCHH

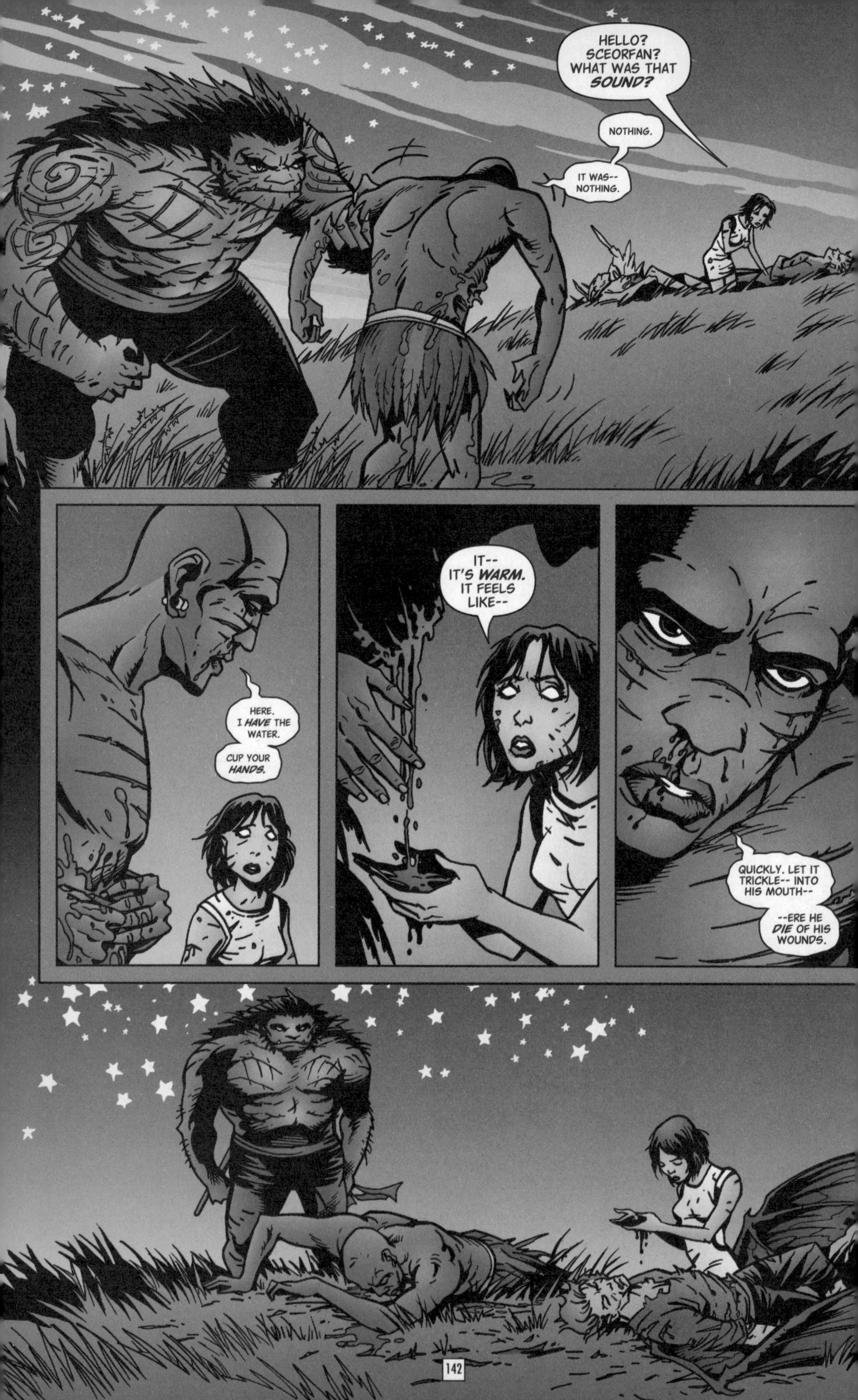
HELLO? SCEORFAN? WHAT WAS THAT SOUND?
NOTHING.
IT WAS-- NOTHING.
HERE. I HAVE THE WATER.
CUP YOUR HANDS.
IT-- IT'S WARM. IT FEELS LIKE--
QUICKLY. LET IT TRICKLE-- INTO HIS MOUTH--
--ERE HE DIE OF HIS WOUNDS.

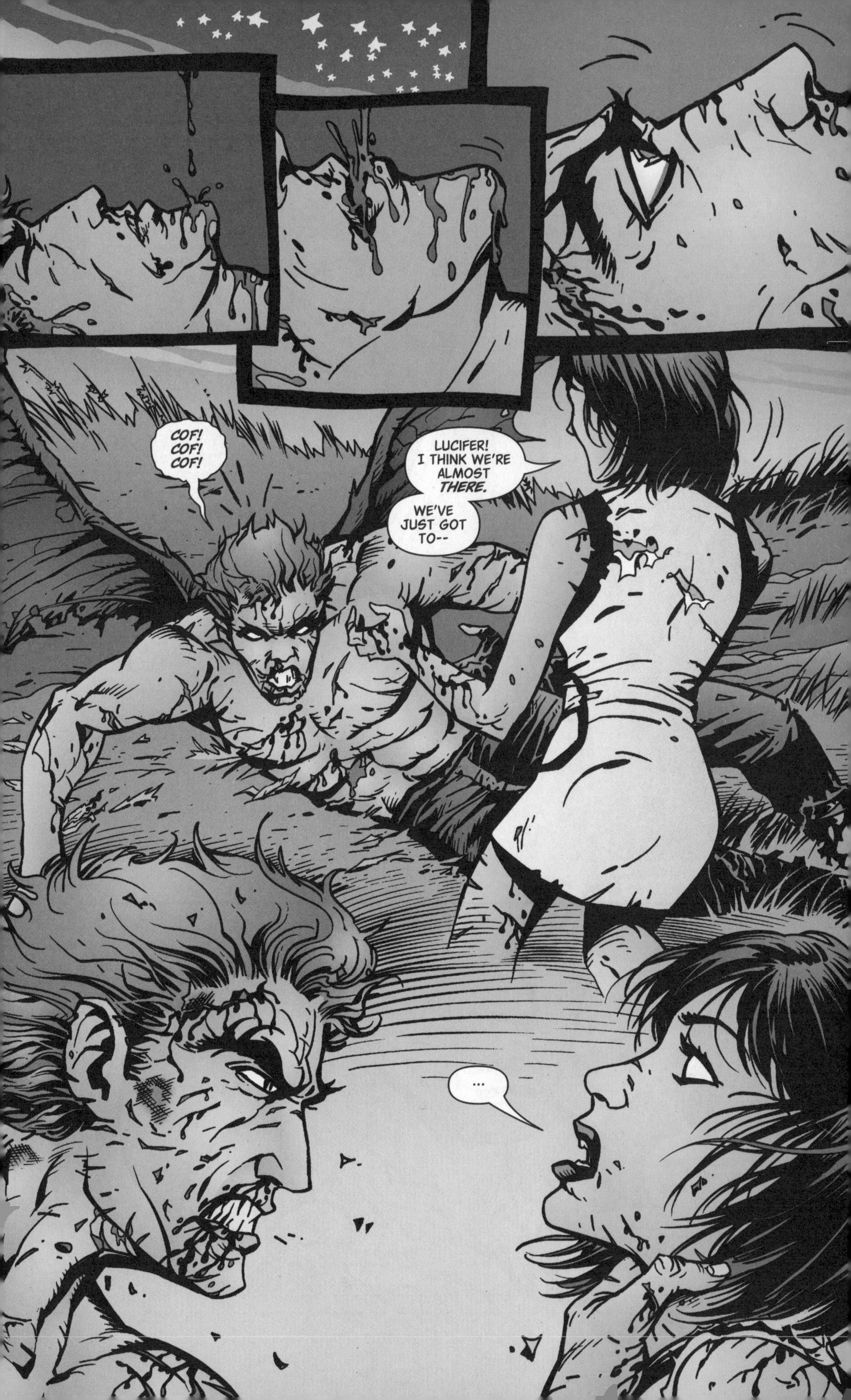
COF! COF! COF!
LUCIFER! I THINK WE'RE ALMOST *THERE.*
WE'VE JUST GOT TO--
...

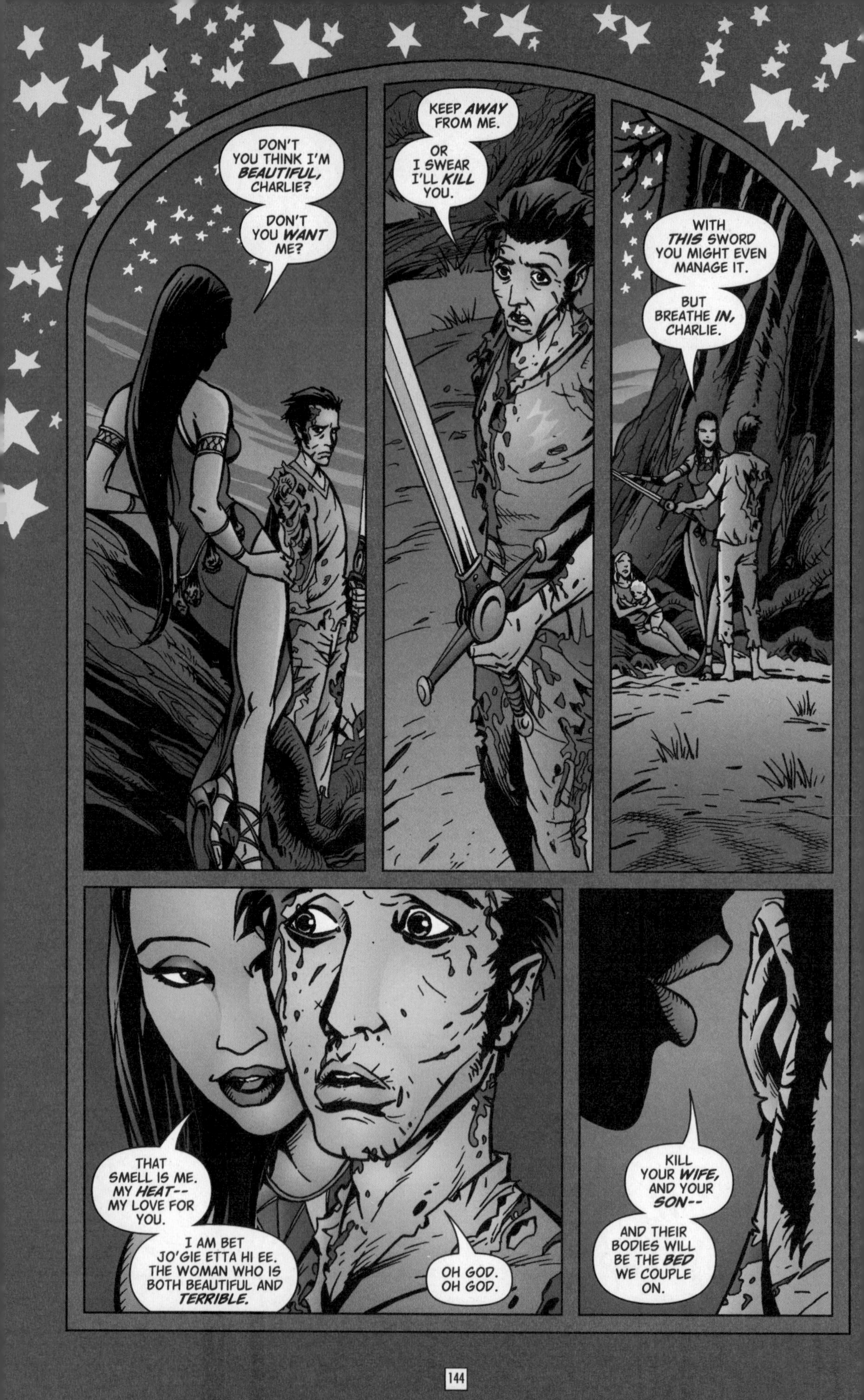
DON'T YOU THINK I'M BEAUTIFUL, CHARLIE?
DON'T YOU WANT ME?
KEEP AWAY FROM ME.
OR I SWEAR I'LL KILL YOU.
WITH THIS SWORD YOU MIGHT EVEN MANAGE IT.
BUT BREATHE IN, CHARLIE.
THAT SMELL IS ME. MY HEAT-- MY LOVE FOR YOU.
I AM BET JO'GIE ETTA HI EE. THE WOMAN WHO IS BOTH BEAUTIFUL AND TERRIBLE.
OH GOD. OH GOD.
KILL YOUR WIFE, AND YOUR SON--
AND THEIR BODIES WILL BE THE BED WE COUPLE ON.

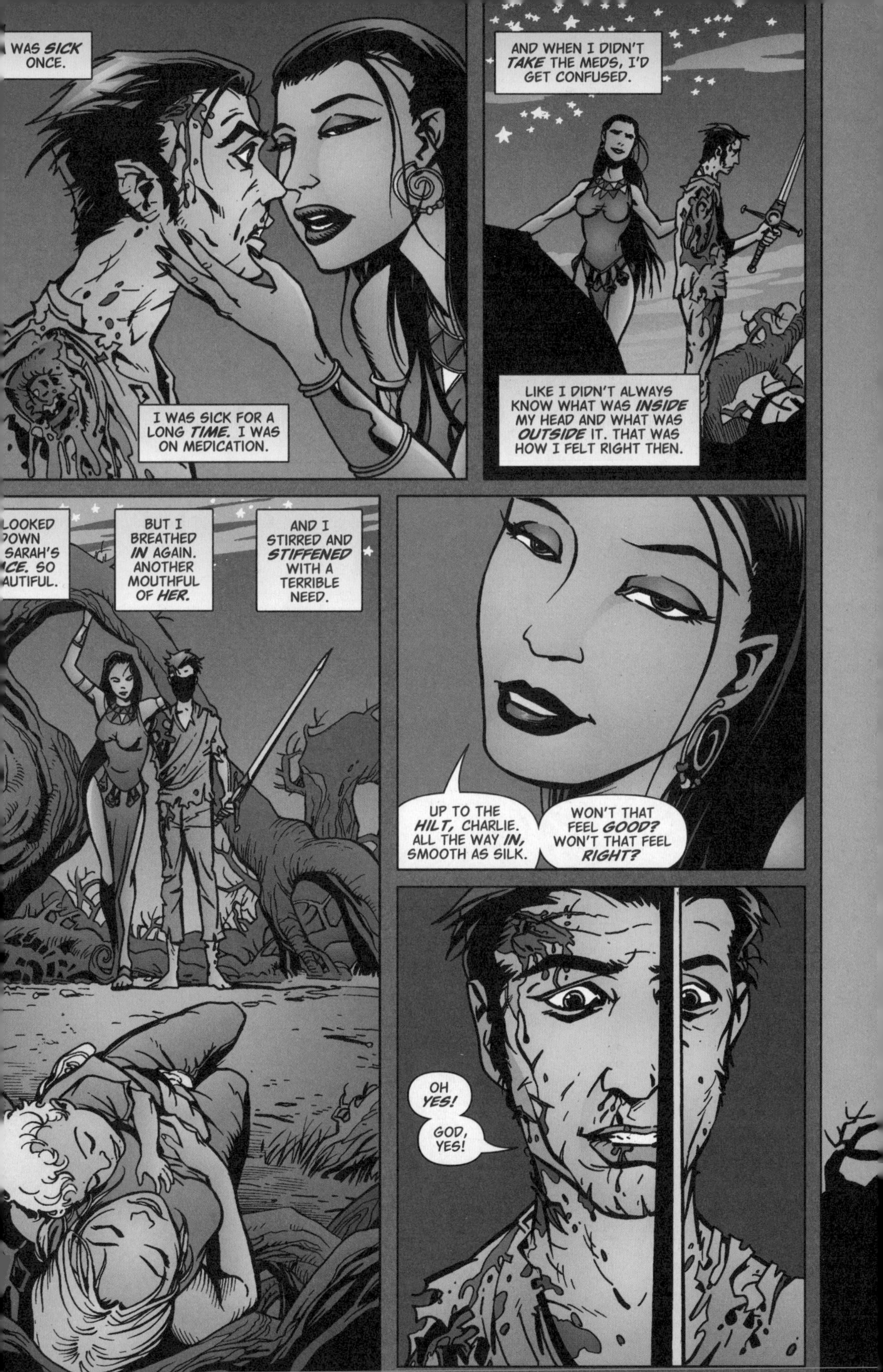
WAS SICK ONCE.
I WAS SICK FOR A LONG TIME. I WAS ON MEDICATION.
AND WHEN I DIDN'T TAKE THE MEDS, I'D GET CONFUSED.
LIKE I DIDN'T ALWAYS KNOW WHAT WAS INSIDE MY HEAD AND WHAT WAS OUTSIDE IT. THAT WAS HOW I FELT RIGHT THEN.
LOOKED DOWN SARAH'S CE. SO AUTIFUL.
BUT I BREATHED IN AGAIN. ANOTHER MOUTHFUL OF HER.
AND I STIRRED AND STIFFENED WITH A TERRIBLE NEED.
UP TO THE HILT, CHARLIE. ALL THE WAY IN, SMOOTH AS SILK.
WON'T THAT FEEL GOOD? WON'T THAT FEEL RIGHT?
OH YES!
GOD, YES!

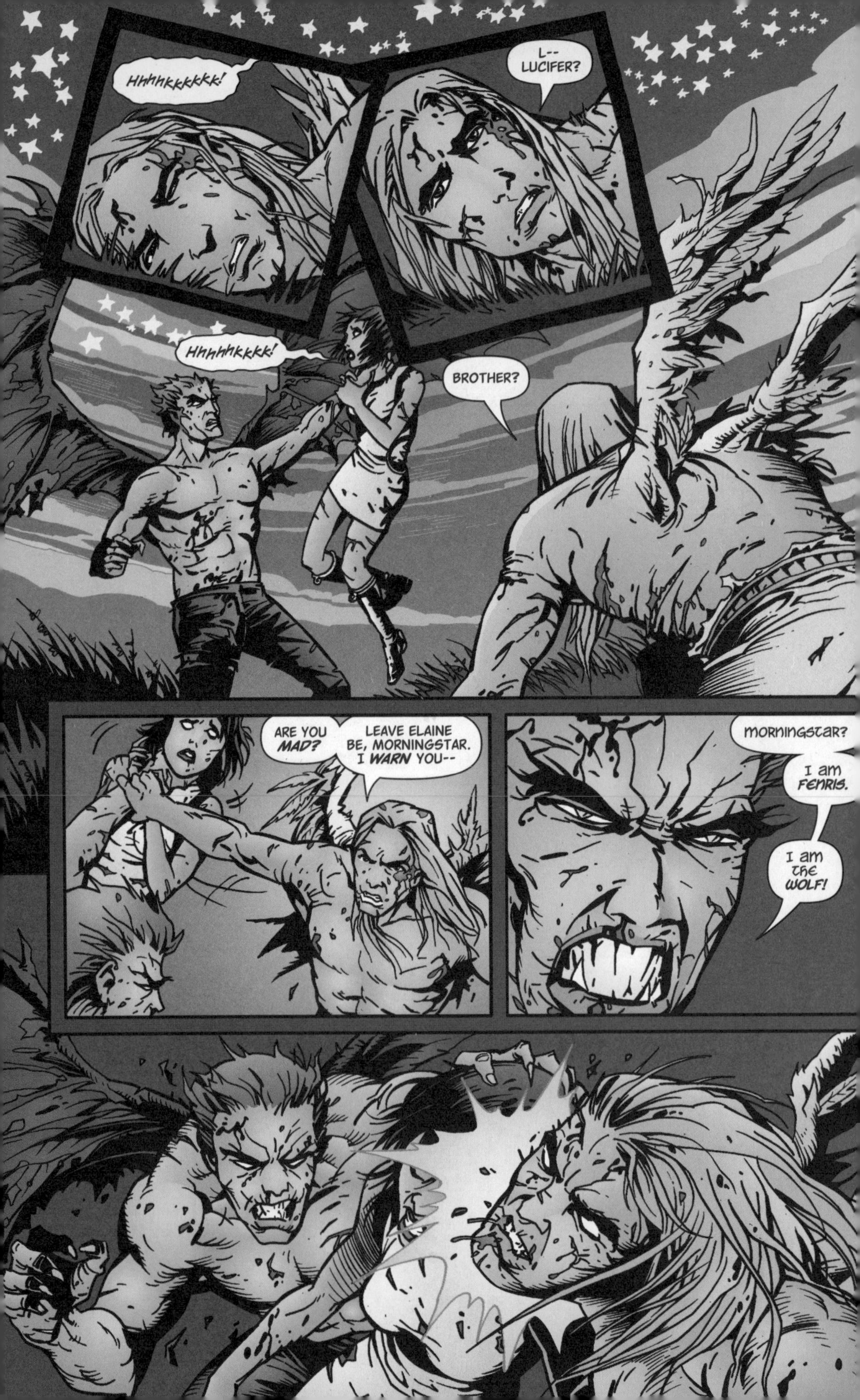
Hnnnkkkkkk!
L-- LUCIFER?
Hnnnhkkkk!
BROTHER?
ARE YOU MAD?
LEAVE ELAINE BE, MORNINGSTAR. I WARN YOU--
MORNINGSTAR?
I am FENRIS.
I am THE WOLF!

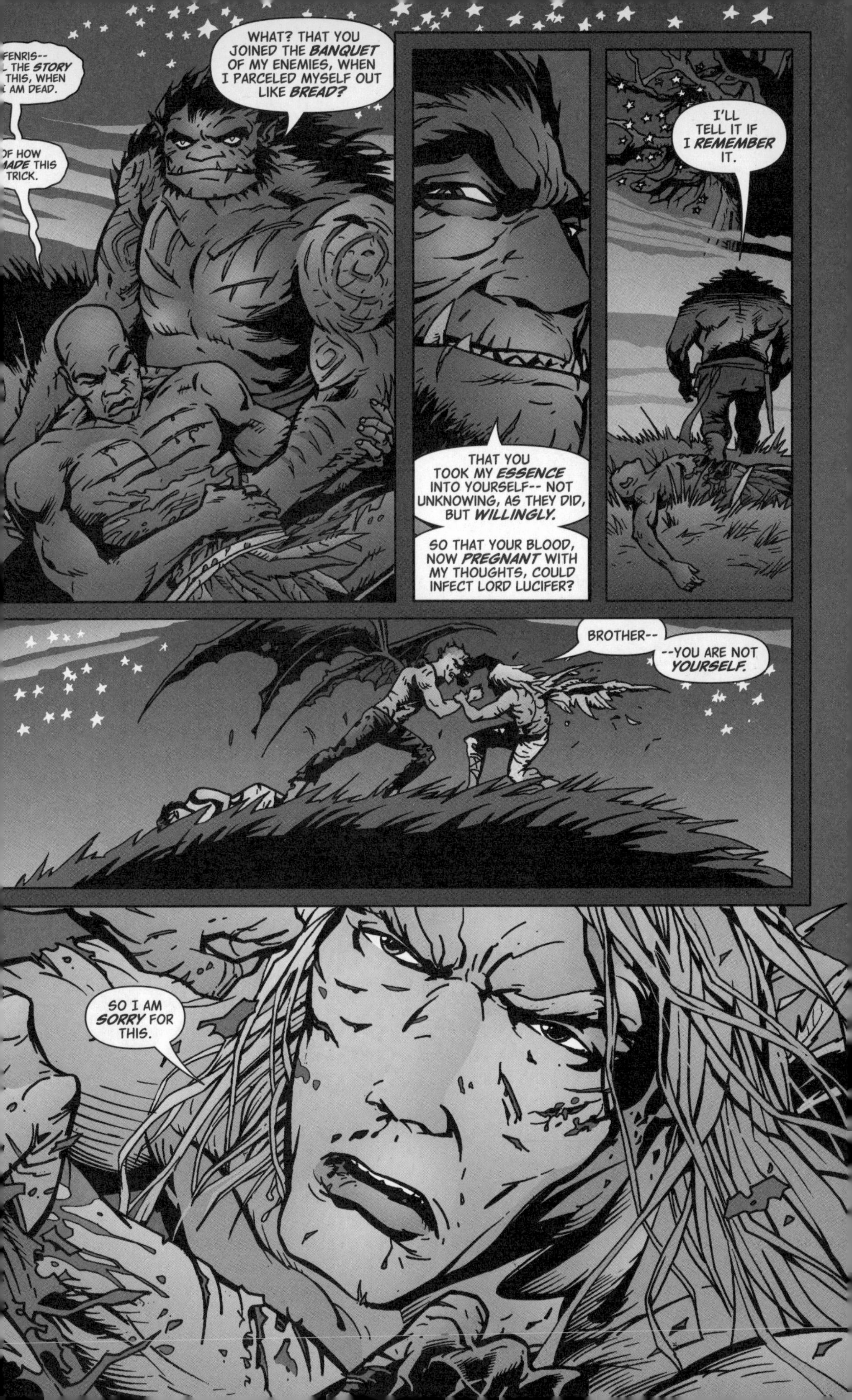

FENRIS-- L THE STORY THIS, WHEN I AM DEAD.
OF HOW MADE THIS TRICK.
WHAT? THAT YOU JOINED THE BANQUET OF MY ENEMIES, WHEN I PARCELED MYSELF OUT LIKE BREAD?
THAT YOU TOOK MY ESSENCE INTO YOURSELF-- NOT UNKNOWING, AS THEY DID, BUT WILLINGLY.
SO THAT YOUR BLOOD, NOW PREGNANT WITH MY THOUGHTS, COULD INFECT LORD LUCIFER?
I'LL TELL IT IF I REMEMBER IT.
BROTHER--
--YOU ARE NOT YOURSELF.
SO I AM SORRY FOR THIS.

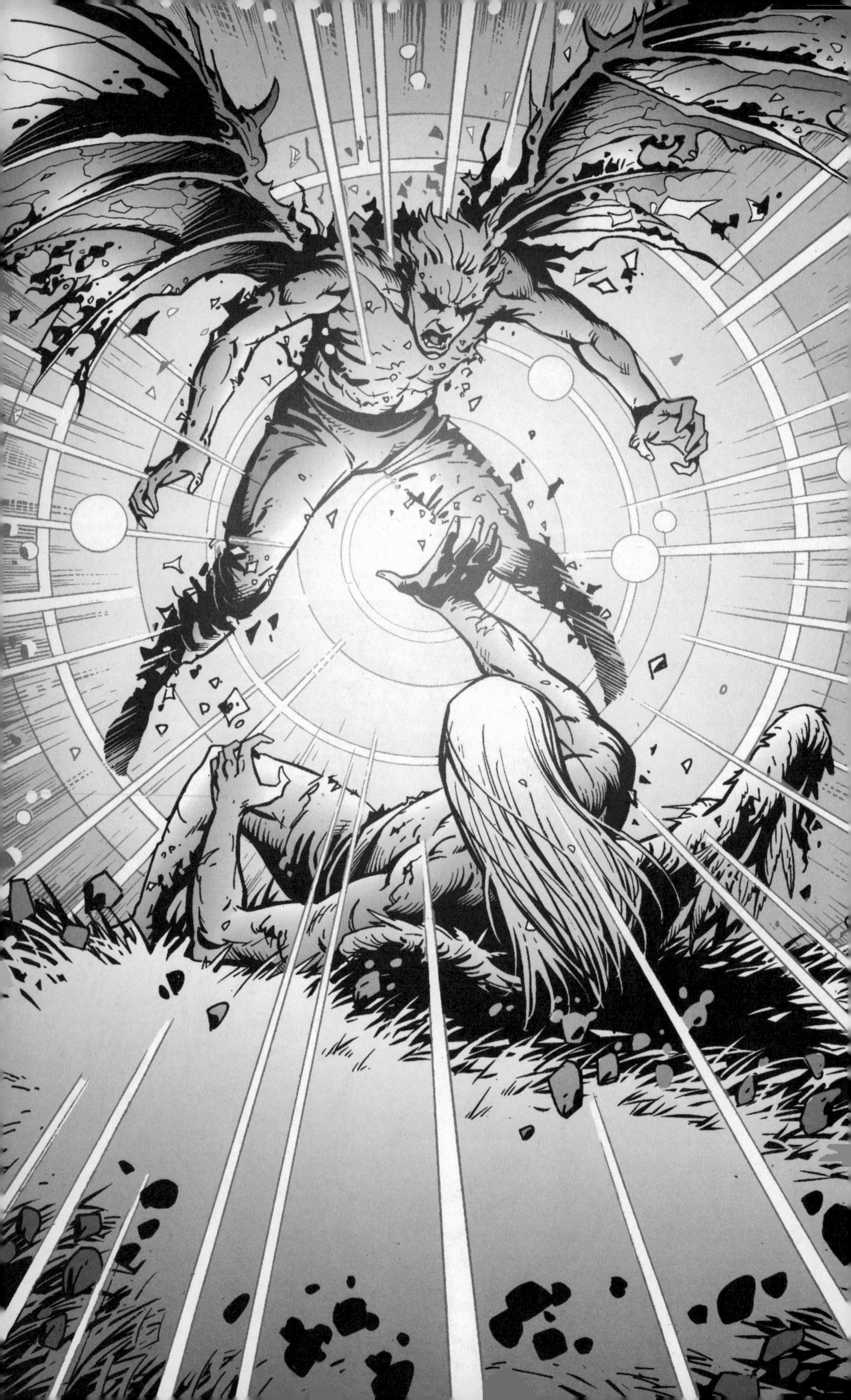

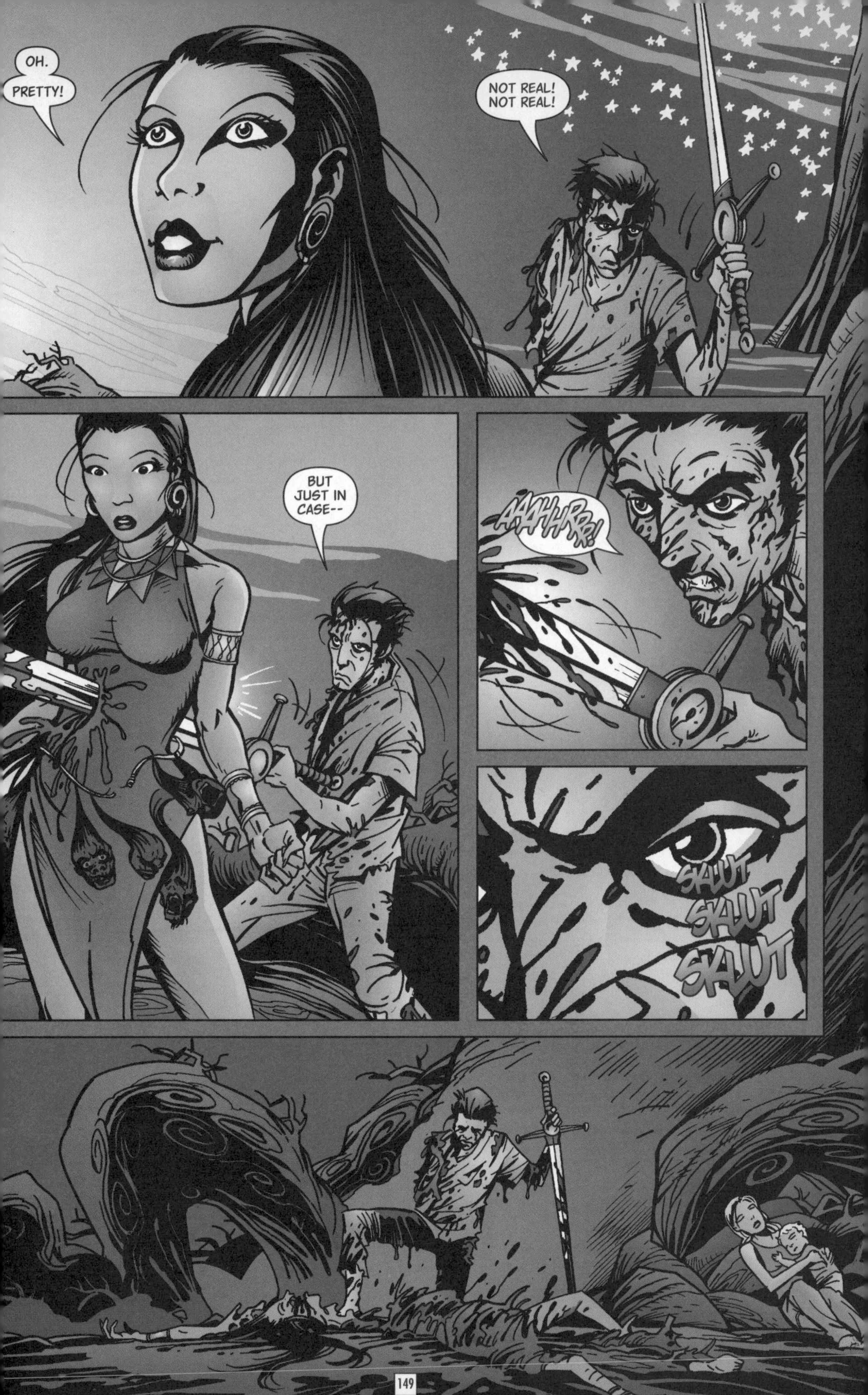
OH.
PRETTY!
NOT REAL! NOT REAL!
BUT JUST IN CASE--
AAAHHRR!
SKLUT
SKLUT
SKLUT

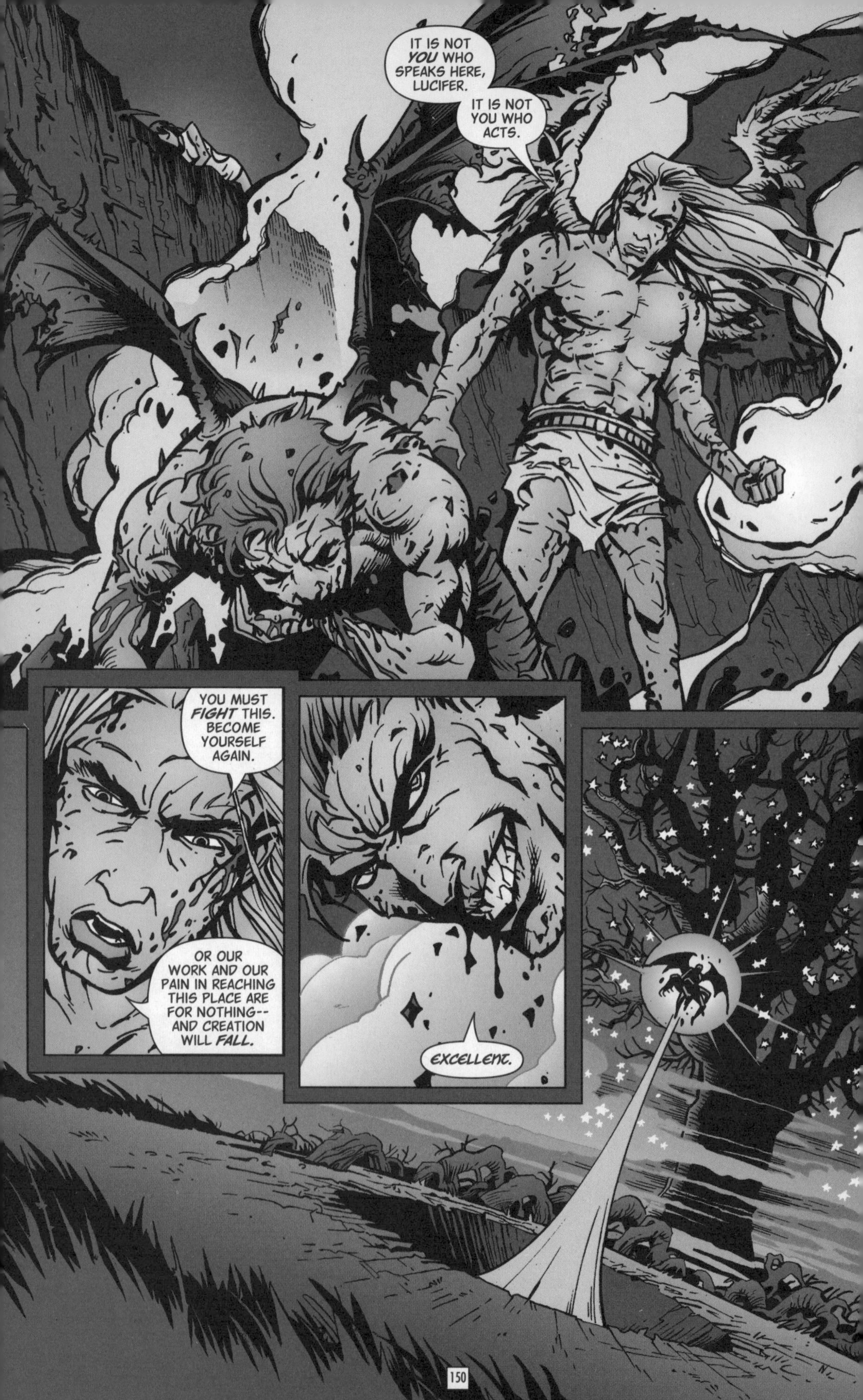
IT IS NOT *YOU* WHO SPEAKS HERE, LUCIFER.
IT IS NOT YOU WHO ACTS.
YOU MUST *FIGHT* THIS. BECOME YOURSELF AGAIN.
OR OUR WORK AND OUR PAIN IN REACHING THIS PLACE ARE FOR NOTHING-- AND CREATION WILL *FALL*.
EXCELLENT.

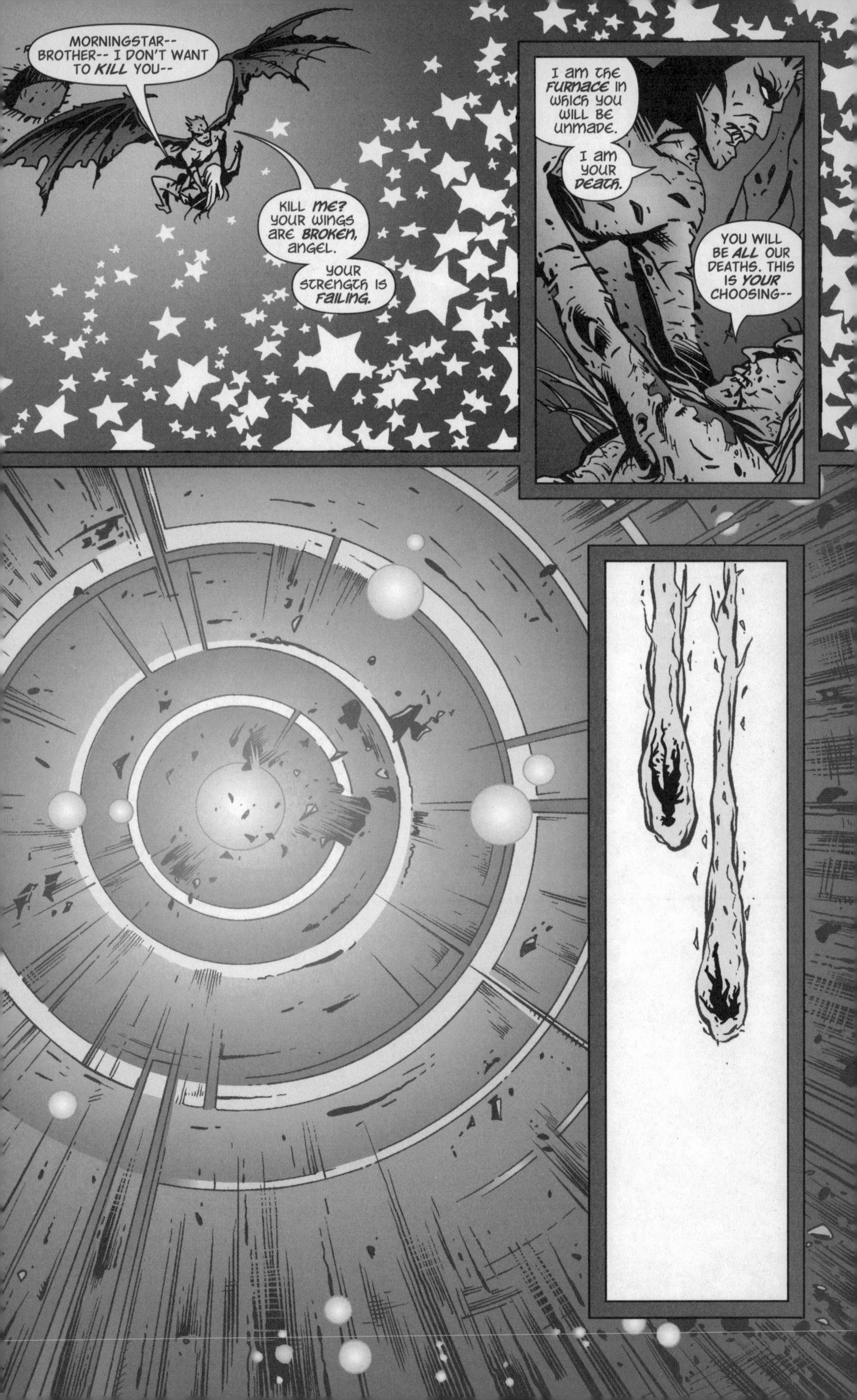

MORNINGSTAR-- BROTHER-- I DON'T WANT TO KILL YOU--
KILL ME? YOUR WINGS ARE BROKEN, ANGEL.
YOUR STRENGTH IS FAILING.
I AM THE FURNACE IN WHICH YOU WILL BE UNMADE.
I AM YOUR DEATH.
YOU WILL BE ALL OUR DEATHS. THIS IS YOUR CHOOSING--

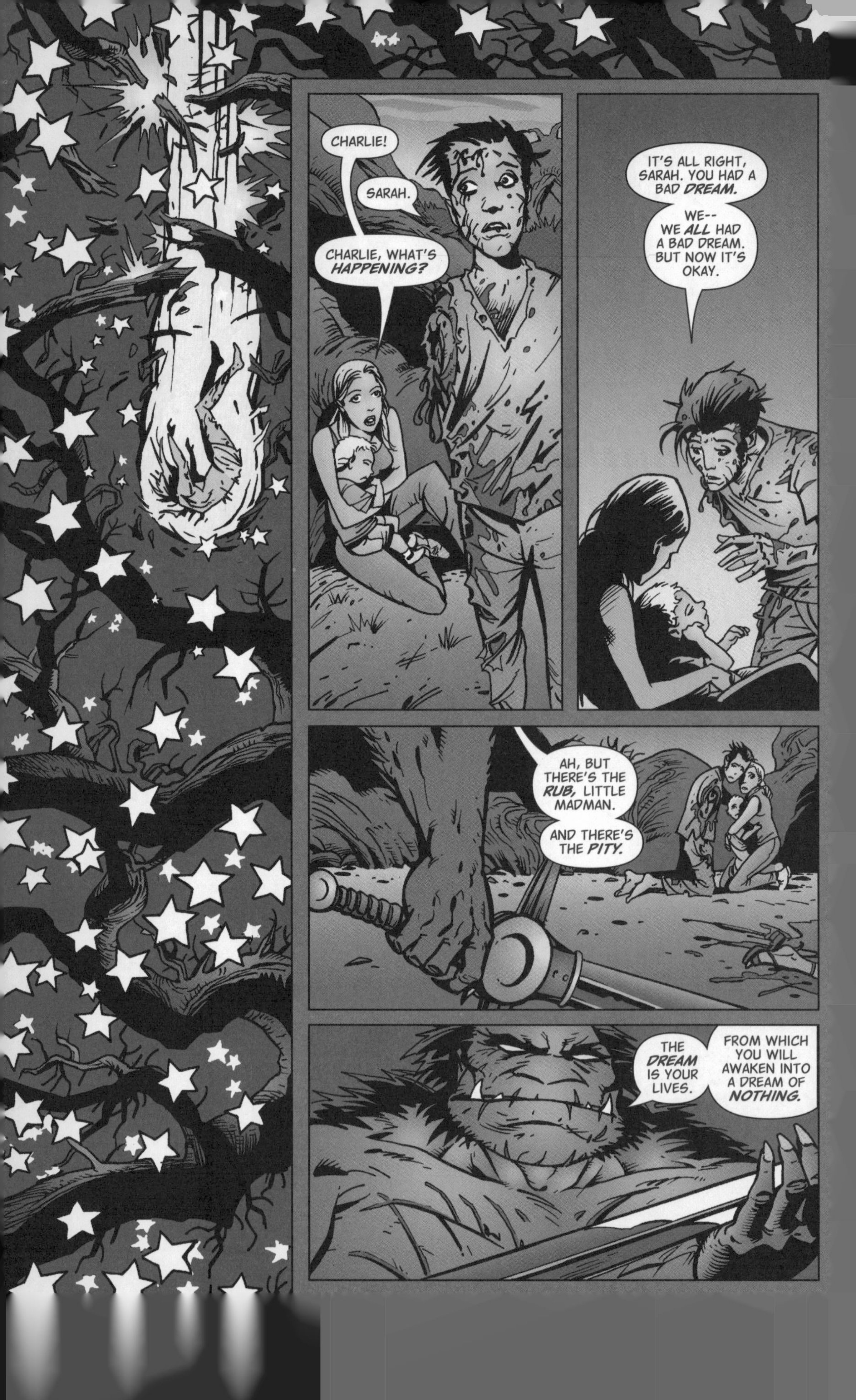
CHARLIE!
SARAH.
CHARLIE, WHAT'S *HAPPENING?*
IT'S ALL RIGHT, SARAH. YOU HAD A BAD *DREAM.*
WE-- WE *ALL* HAD A BAD DREAM. BUT NOW IT'S OKAY.
AH, BUT THERE'S THE *RUB,* LITTLE MADMAN.
AND THERE'S THE *PITY.*
THE *DREAM* IS YOUR LIVES.
FROM WHICH YOU WILL AWAKEN INTO A DREAM OF *NOTHING.*

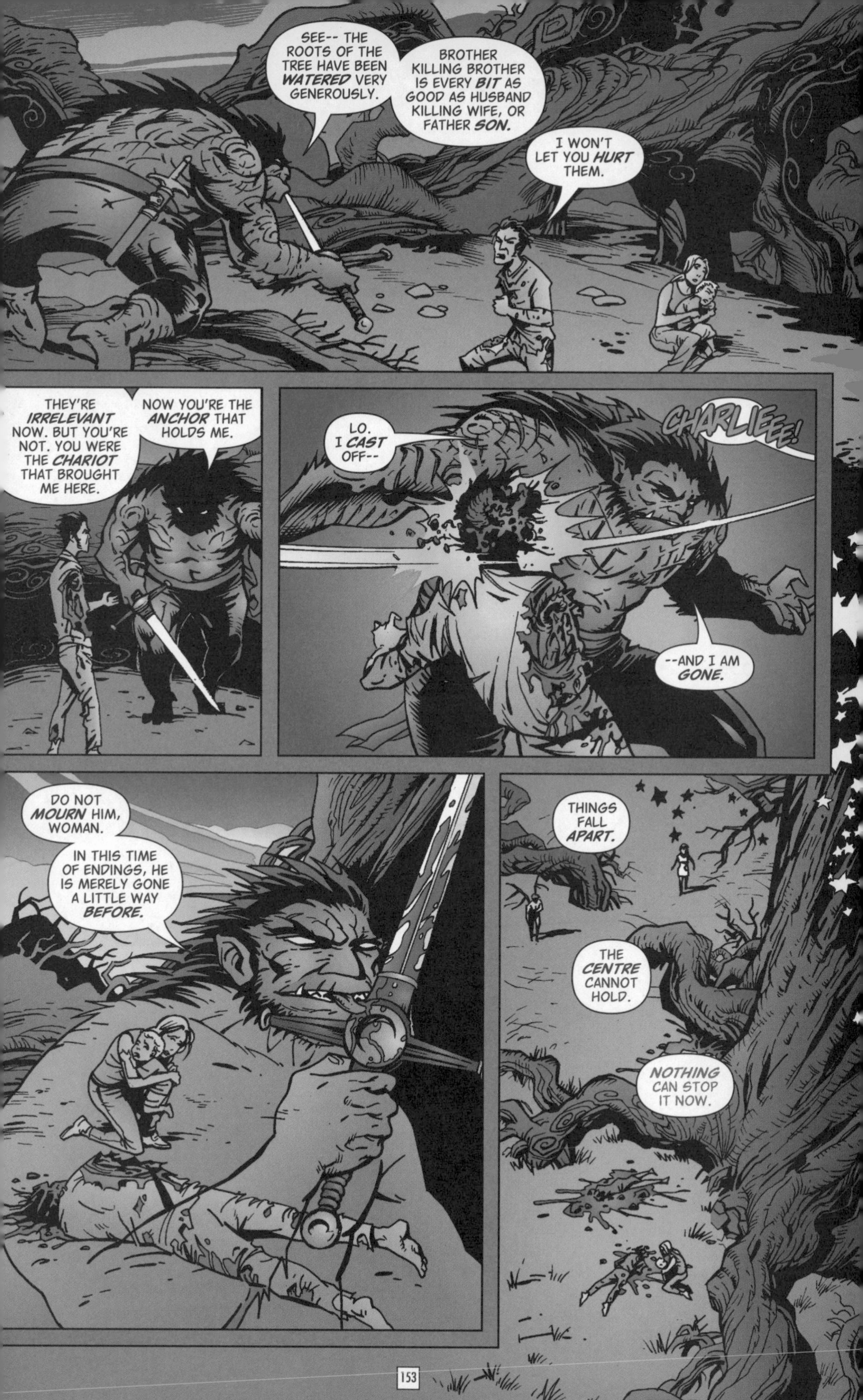
SEE-- THE ROOTS OF THE TREE HAVE BEEN WATERED VERY GENEROUSLY.
BROTHER KILLING BROTHER IS EVERY BIT AS GOOD AS HUSBAND KILLING WIFE, OR FATHER SON.
I WON'T LET YOU HURT THEM.
THEY'RE IRRELEVANT NOW. BUT YOU'RE NOT. YOU WERE THE CHARIOT THAT BROUGHT ME HERE.
NOW YOU'RE THE ANCHOR THAT HOLDS ME.
LO. I CAST OFF--
CHARLIEEE!
--AND I AM GONE.
DO NOT MOURN HIM, WOMAN.
IN THIS TIME OF ENDINGS, HE IS MERELY GONE A LITTLE WAY BEFORE.
THINGS FALL APART.
THE CENTRE CANNOT HOLD.
NOTHING CAN STOP IT NOW.

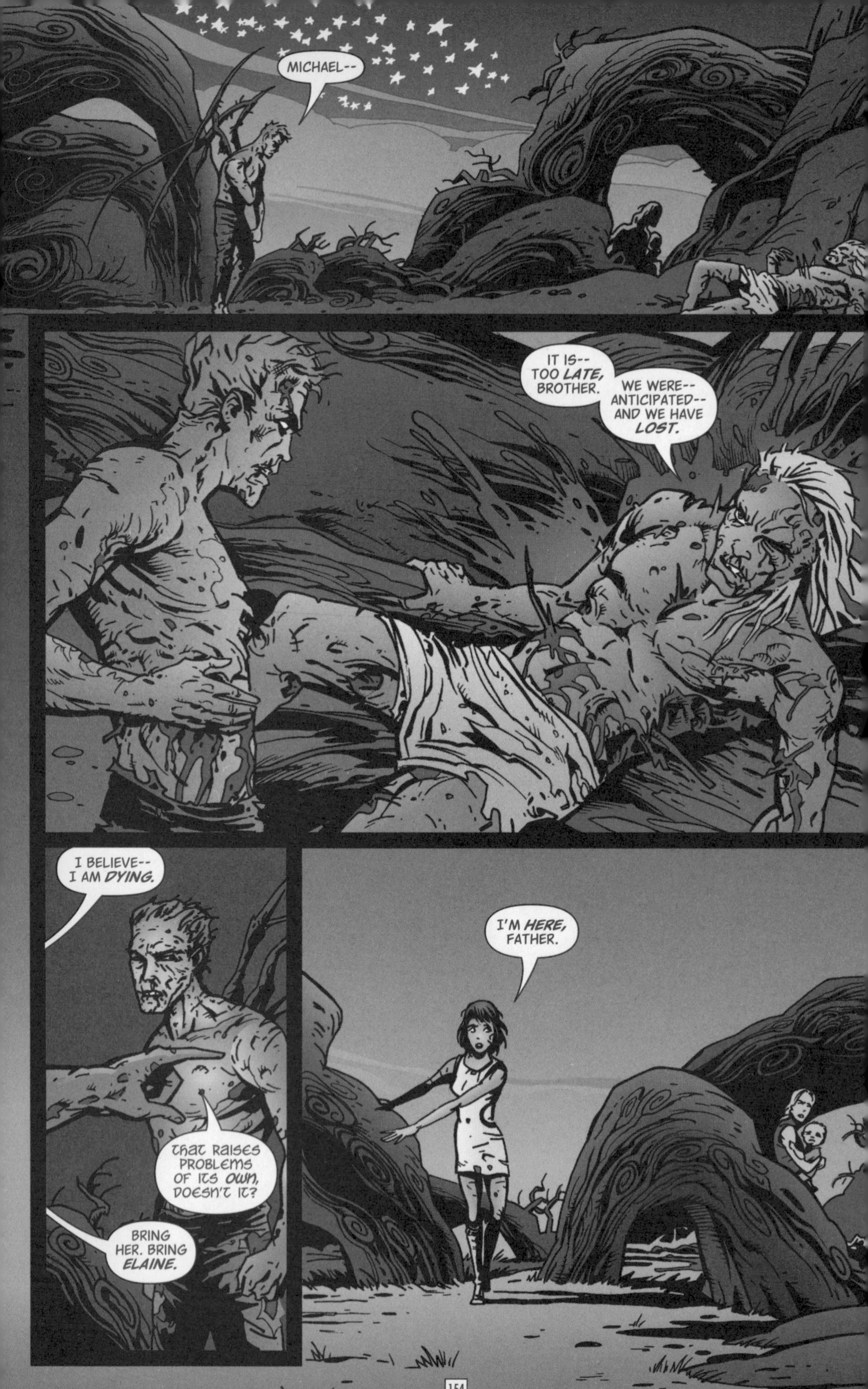
MICHAEL--
IT IS-- TOO LATE, BROTHER.
WE WERE-- ANTICIPATED-- AND WE HAVE LOST.
I BELIEVE-- I AM DYING.
THAT RAISES PROBLEMS OF ITS OWN, DOESN'T IT?
BRING HER. BRING ELAINE.
I'M HERE, FATHER.

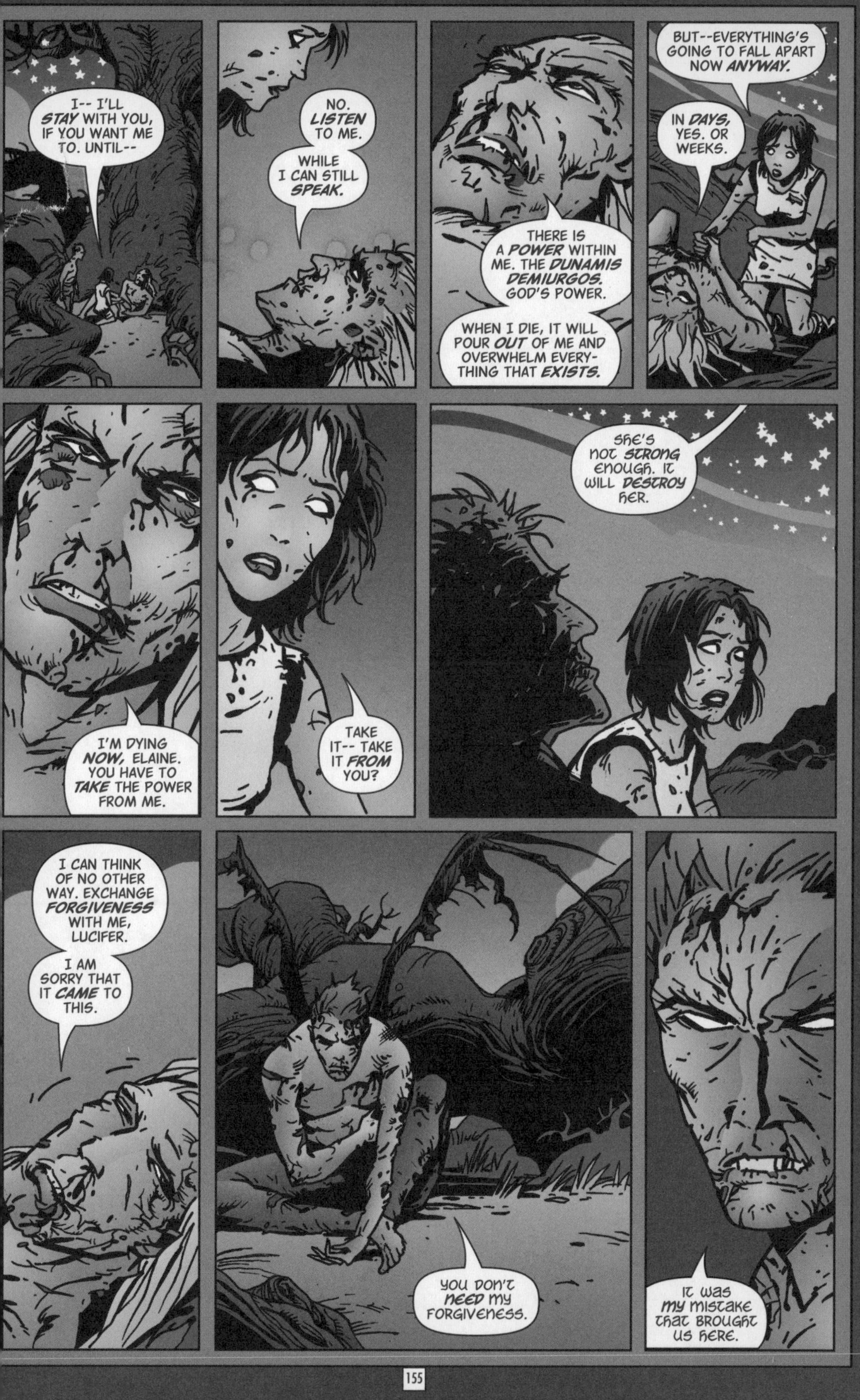
I-- I'LL STAY WITH YOU, IF YOU WANT ME TO. UNTIL--
NO. LISTEN TO ME.
WHILE I CAN STILL SPEAK.
THERE IS A POWER WITHIN ME. THE DUNAMIS DEMIURGOS. GOD'S POWER.
WHEN I DIE, IT WILL POUR OUT OF ME AND OVERWHELM EVERYTHING THAT EXISTS.
BUT--EVERYTHING'S GOING TO FALL APART NOW ANYWAY.
IN DAYS, YES. OR WEEKS.
I'M DYING NOW, ELAINE. YOU HAVE TO TAKE THE POWER FROM ME.
TAKE IT-- TAKE IT FROM YOU?
SHE'S NOT STRONG ENOUGH. IT WILL DESTROY HER.
I CAN THINK OF NO OTHER WAY. EXCHANGE FORGIVENESS WITH ME, LUCIFER.
I AM SORRY THAT IT CAME TO THIS.
YOU DON'T NEED MY FORGIVENESS.
IT WAS MY MISTAKE THAT BROUGHT US HERE.

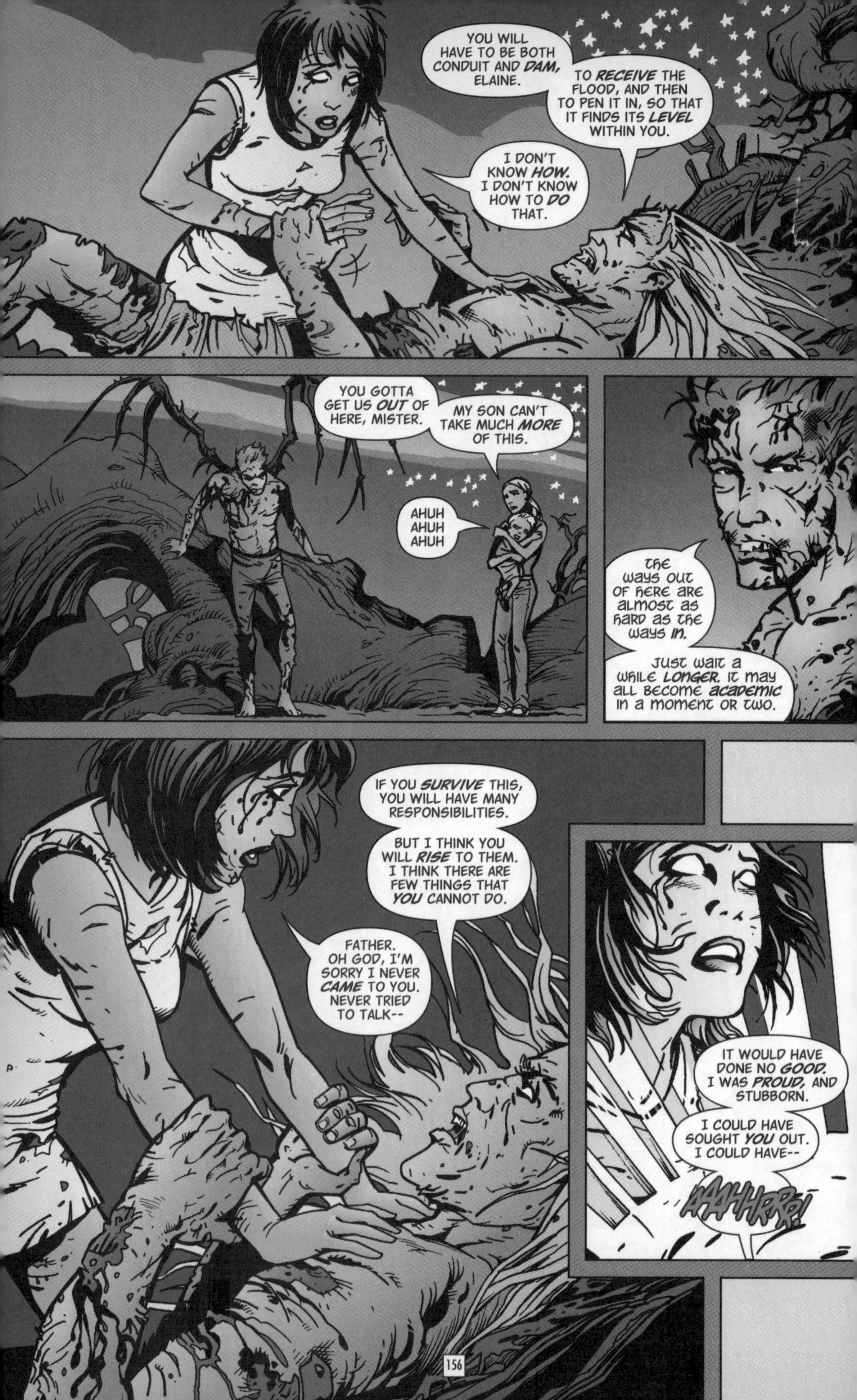
YOU WILL HAVE TO BE BOTH CONDUIT AND DAM, ELAINE.
TO RECEIVE THE FLOOD, AND THEN TO PEN IT IN, SO THAT IT FINDS ITS LEVEL WITHIN YOU.
I DON'T KNOW HOW. I DON'T KNOW HOW TO DO THAT.
YOU GOTTA GET US OUT OF HERE, MISTER.
MY SON CAN'T TAKE MUCH MORE OF THIS.
AHUH AHUH AHUH
THE WAYS OUT OF HERE ARE ALMOST AS HARD AS THE WAYS IN.
JUST WAIT A WHILE LONGER. IT MAY ALL BECOME ACADEMIC IN A MOMENT OR TWO.
IF YOU SURVIVE THIS, YOU WILL HAVE MANY RESPONSIBILITIES.
BUT I THINK YOU WILL RISE TO THEM. I THINK THERE ARE FEW THINGS THAT YOU CANNOT DO.
FATHER. OH GOD, I'M SORRY I NEVER CAME TO YOU. NEVER TRIED TO TALK--
IT WOULD HAVE DONE NO GOOD. I WAS PROUD, AND STUBBORN.
I COULD HAVE SOUGHT YOU OUT. I COULD HAVE--
AAAHHRRR!

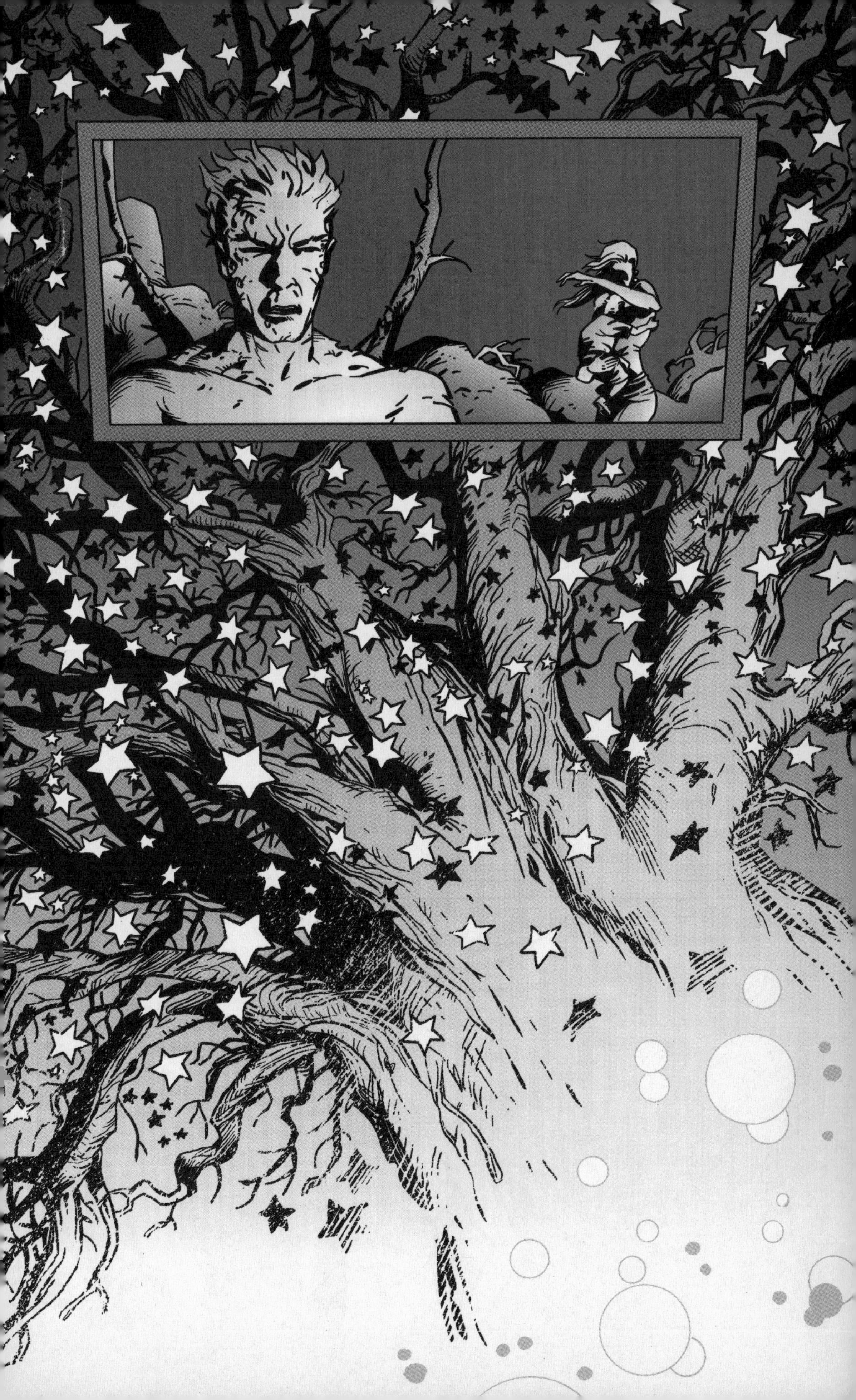

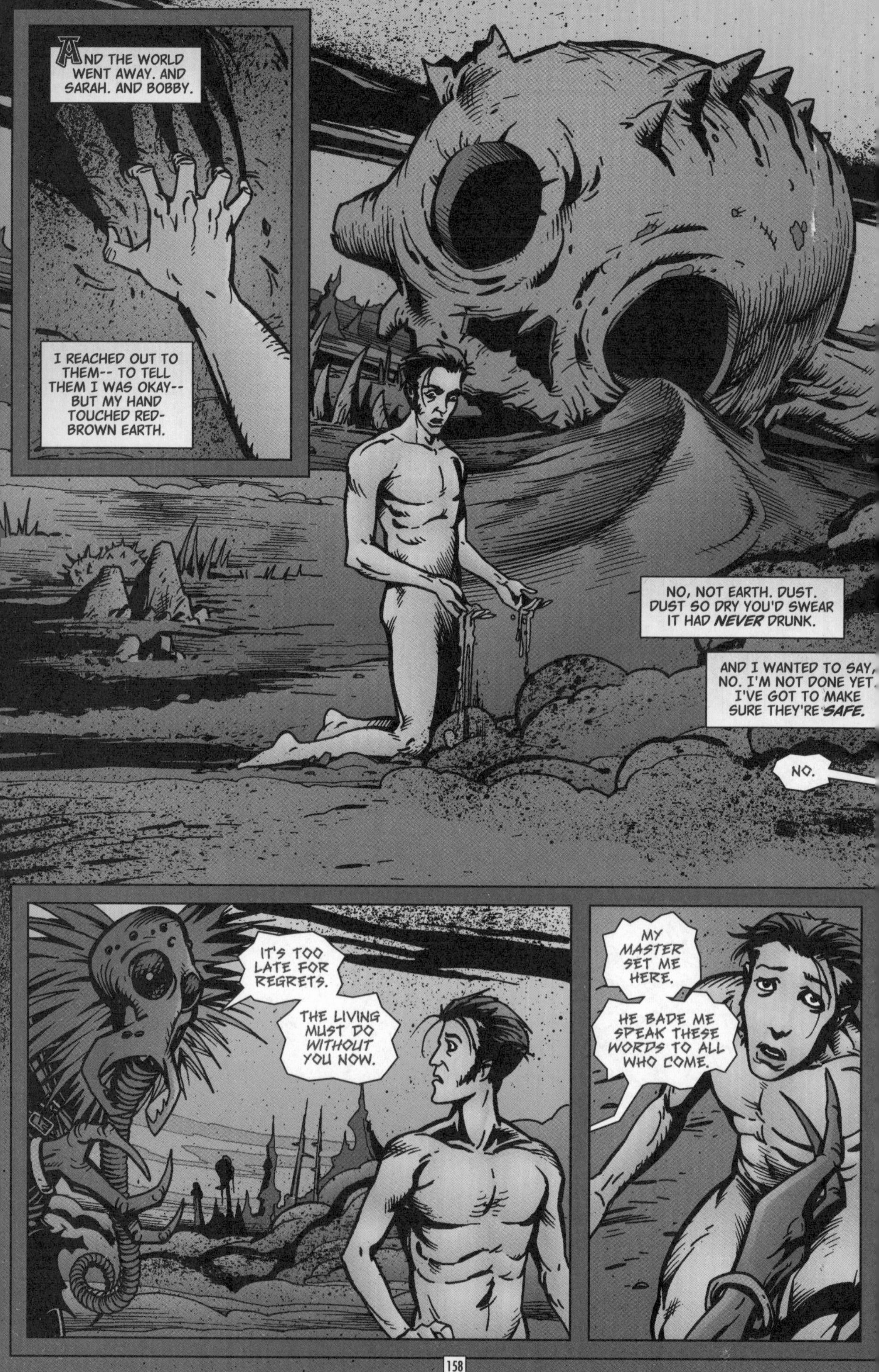
AND THE WORLD WENT AWAY. AND SARAH. AND BOBBY.
I REACHED OUT TO THEM-- TO TELL THEM I WAS OKAY-- BUT MY HAND TOUCHED RED-BROWN EARTH.
NO, NOT EARTH. DUST. DUST SO DRY YOU'D SWEAR IT HAD NEVER DRUNK.
AND I WANTED TO SAY, NO. I'M NOT DONE YET. I'VE GOT TO MAKE SURE THEY'RE SAFE.
NO.
IT'S TOO LATE FOR REGRETS.
THE LIVING MUST DO WITHOUT YOU NOW.
MY MASTER SET ME HERE.
HE BADE ME SPEAK THESE WORDS TO ALL WHO COME.

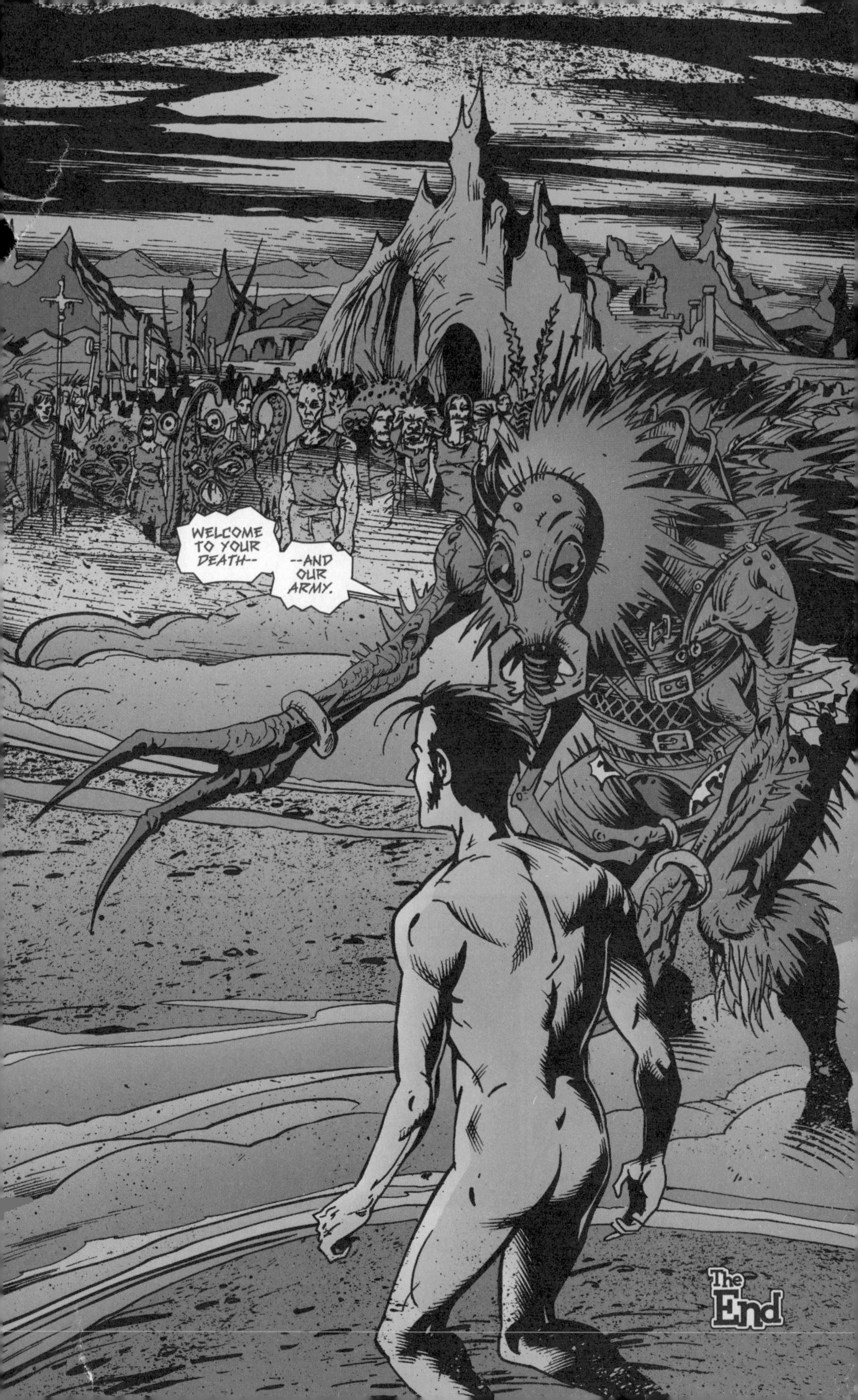
WELCOME TO YOUR DEATH--
--AND OUR ARMY.
The End

THE LUCIFER LIBRARY

BOOK ONE:
DEVIL IN THE GATEWAY

BOOK TWO:
CHILDREN AND MONSTERS

BOOK THREE:
A DALLIANCE WITH THE DAMNED

BOOK FOUR:
THE DIVINE COMEDY

BOOK FIVE:
INFERNO

BOOK SIX:
MANSIONS OF THE SILENCE

BOOK SEVEN:
EXODUS

BOOK EIGHT:
THE WOLF BENEATH THE TREE